Runaways of Colonial New Jersey

Indentured Servants, Slaves,
Deserters, and Prisoners

1720-1781

Richard B. Marrin

HERITAGE BOOKS
2007

HERITAGE BOOKS
AN IMPRINT OF HERITAGE BOOKS, INC.

Books, CDs, and more—Worldwide

For our listing of thousands of titles see our website
at
www.HeritageBooks.com

Published 2007 by
HERITAGE BOOKS, INC.
Publishing Division
65 East Main Street
Westminster, Maryland 21157-5026

Copyright © 2007 Richard B. Marrin

Other books by the author:

Abstracts from the Northern Standard *and* The Red River District *[Texas]:*
August 20, 1842-August 19, 1848
Richard B. Marrin and Lorna Geer Sheppard

*A Glance Back in Time: Life in Colonial New Jersey (1704-1770)
as Depicted in News Accounts of the Day*

Passage Point: An Amateur's Dig into New Jersey's Colonial Past

All rights reserved. No part of this book may be reproduced or transmitted in any form or by any means, electronic or mechanical, including photocopying, recording or by any information storage and retrieval system without written permission from the author, except for the inclusion of brief quotations in a review.

International Standard Book Number: 978-0-7884-4001-2

TABLE OF CONTENTS

Introduction v

Profile of a Runaway Servant Man. 1

Profile of a Runaway Servant Man. 21

Profile of Women Runaways. 37

Profile of Deserters and Escaped Prisoners. 41

Listing of Runaway Male Indentured Servants 45

Listing of Runaway Slaves 207

Listing of Women Runaways 253

Listing of Escaped Prisoners 267

Listing of Military Deserters 289

End Notes 317

Index to Personal Names 325

Introduction

A majority of white immigrants to the American Colonies south of New England - and nearly all the Africans - arrived in some form of servitude, either as indentured servants or slaves. They must be the ancestors of many Americans, yet theirs is a part of American history about which one learns little in school

The 19th century forty volume *Colonial History of the State of New Jersey* contains documents of all kinds, including extracts from Philadelphia, New York and Boston newspapers, relating to news in New Jersey. The papers, *The New York Gazette, The New York Post, The Pennsylvania Journal, The Pennsylvania Gazette, The New York Weekly Journal* and *The Boston Newsletter* often published notices seeking the return of runaway indentured servants or slaves, as well as deserters from the military and escapees from gaol - *i.e.*, jail. Thet were the "Wanted" posters we expect of the Old West.

If servitude were to be a source of reliable labor, runaways could not be permitted to flee. Thus, they were vigorously pursued.[1] · The notices of runaways published in the papers put everyone in every town on alert, suspicious of strangers passing through. Typically, the notice contained such information about the runaway as to give us a snapshot of him or her. For example

> *Run away from Dr Matthias Dehart, of Elizabeth -Town, an Irish servant man named William Davis, but, changes his name to Davidson a small fellow, lanthorn jawed, his left shoulder out of joint, pretends to be an Englishman and a sailor, red complexion, red hair and beard, about 24 years old, had on an old beaver hat cut across the crown, a light ratteen jacket, a striped under jacket, a new shirt, leather breeches & new shoes. It is likely he has tar*

spots on most of his clothes, as he worked on board a vessel for some time

Also run away with him, a servant Irish woman named Mary Kelley, belonging to Captain Jonathan Hampton, of the same Town, a likely girl, about 20 years old, t' is supposed they will pass for man and wife, she is short and well set, had on an old short red cloak, old brown callimanco gown, no bonnet, and otherwise but very poorly clothed

They are thought to travel by night and steal Fowl &c for Sustenance. Any Person that shall bring them back to their Masters shall have THREE POUND and all reasonable charges paid

There were nearly 1500 such advertisements among the documents preserved a century ago in *The Colonial History of the State of New Jersey*. They span a nearly seventy year period in New Jersey, from 1715 to 1781. They are doubly valuable, providing clues for genealogists as well as food for thought for those of us curious as to how the citizens of America's first century lived. Indeed, the advertisements can become encyclopedias of sorts, answer queries such as from where did they come? What names were in vogue among them? What were their occupations? Were they healthy? What did they look like? Were they tall short, thin or fat.? Age? Any personality quirks? Were they drinkers? Even the ratio of left handers to right handed?

And, of course, the ultimate line of inquiry - were you to be somehow magically transported back in time, say to the 1750s, could you pass as one of them? What was different? What was the same?

PROFILE OF THE RUNAWAY SERVANT MAN

Overview

Maybe as many as two thirds of all white immigrants to America's Middle Atlantic and Southland arrived as "indentured" servants. Recruited from England, Scotland, Wales, Ireland, the Netherlands, Germany and elsewhere in western Europe, they paid off the cost of their passage to the New World by agreeing – an indenture –to work for their sponsors for a period of years.

Make no mistake about it. While preferable to the involuntary lifelong servitude of the African slave, the life of an indentured servant was still harsh. It was a slave like labor system, not an apprenticeship. The origins of indentured class lay in the agricultural servitude of the serfs of England of the Middle Ages, from which they were not far removed.

These servants were among the first settlers n America. In the Virginia Colony, they were imported to cultivate the labor intensive tobacco crop as early as 1620.[1] Over the next century, the practice spread to the Middle Atlantic region. Then, by the end of the American Revolution, it had vanished, replaced solely with slavery at first, later supplemented and itself replaced with immigrant labor from Europe, then from all the world.

The early immigrants to New England and the Middle Atlantic regions came for religious freedom. The Puritan dissenters settled in New England, the Quakers in Pennsylvania and New Jersey, the French Huguenots in New York and the Roman Catholics in Maryland. However, that flow soon failed to sate the needs of a growing America. Many hands were needed. Among the workers imported were the indentured servants. Most came voluntarily, but not all. Some were fooled. Some were kidnaped and the British government on occasion transported convicts to America to be sold into servitude. America was also a handy place to get orphans, vagrants and paupers out of sight. But, by and large, the emigrants were poor people forced to leave home for a variety of reasons.

These indentured servants sold themselves to ship's captains for a period of up to a dozen years in exchange for passage to America. Upon arrival, the Captain would advertise and sell them in the countryside, to be used, alongside the African, as labor for the plantations and businesses. The indentured servant, quite literally, surrendered his liberty and, for a fixed period of time, was the chattel of his owner/master.

The New Jersey population had doubled in every generation since 1700. There had been only 15,000 inhabitants at the beginning of the century. By 1726, there were 32,000 Europeans and Africans living in the Royal Provinces of East and West New Jersey. Forty - seven per cent of them were female; eight per cent were Africans. By 1745, the population almost doubled to 61,000. Slightly fewer than forty-five per cent were female. Seven and a half per cent were African. By 1774, right before the Revolution, the population had more than doubled to 130,000 inhabitants out of the colonies total population of over three million. Many of these had come to America as indentured servants and are the forebears of millions of Americans today.

Information about the Runaways

From the approximate 1700 descriptions we have of these Jersey runaways, we can make some generalizations. They were twenty times more likely to be male, than female. They tended to be young and healthy, as we might expect. They were multi- tasked, with scores of skills and specialities as well as being agricultural laborers. Servants hoped for quick upward mobility, once they had done their time. Men became wage laborers, tenants, and sometimes landowners. Women looked toward marriage. Then, as now, there seemed to be no stigma as to how they came to the New World.

A fugitive's dress was a good way to identify him. The

notices almost always described what the runaway was wearing. Rarely, did a servant have a wardrobe from which to disguise himself. Basic garments have not changed: shoes, stockings, pants, shirts, jackets, coats and hats. The typical outfit for an indentured servant, for example, might include an old brown worsted greatcoat with a rent on one shoulder, a blue homespun jacket underneath, with a heavy linen shirt under that, a felt hat torn in the brim, old leather breeches, thick grey yarn stockings and half worn double "soald" calf skin shoes.

However, more important than dress to us are the people within those clothes. With the detail provided us in the preserved runaway notices, we can do more than just generalize. We can focus on composite individuals of the time and sketch a rough profile of the average servant on the run.

Places of Origin of the Runaways

For example, from where had these servants come? What were their nationalities? The advertisements of runaways help answer that. The birth places of more than half - some 763 - of the runaway servants, escaped prisoners and military deserters[2] were given.

Not all runaways were foreign born. One hundred and forty-five of the 763 runaways, or nearly twenty per cent, were stated to be "American born". They were from all different American colonies, the Provinces of Jersey included. They were the second generation children of earlier colonists, usually from the British Isles.

In fact, in the first decades, most of the runaways were from the British Isles, which. back then, was more a collection of different peoples, all of whom were governed in varying degrees by the British Monarch. One hundred and seven of them were from England, approximately fifteen per cent. Scotland provided another 22, nearly 3 per cent. This included the Roman Catholic Celtic Highlanders, defeated in rebellions in 1715 and 1745, as well as the Presbyterian Lowlanders, chased out by high rents and no jobs. Fifteen of the runaways had been born in Wales, another Celtic people. Another 11 were described as West Country men, from Somerset, Dorset, Devon and Cornwall in western Britain. They were reported to have markedly different accents than those from East England.

By far, the largest group to come from the British Isles or anywhere were the Irish. Nearly half of the runaways – 46 per cent - were from Ireland.

They were one of two "kinds" of Irish.

One was the so-called Scotch-Irish Presbyterians. A tough strain, it traced its lineage to lowland Scotland. Their ancestors, a mixture of the Viking, Norman, German tribes and the Scotti (a Celtic people from Ireland that had invaded Britain during the Dark Ages), thrived on frontiers, where independence was valued and authority challenged. They were perfect to populate Northern Ireland and buffer the Celtic Catholic Irish. But, squeezed in the vise of bad harvests and increased rents, strife with the native Irish and persecution by the Church of England for their Presbyterian belief, many opted to begin a new life in America[3].

> *Four ships, the Captains of which Montgomery, Pharis, M'Cutchen and Chevers, full of passengers, [have] lately sailed from [Newry, Ireland], for Philadelphia, where two of them have arrived. Another ship of 300 tons, Capt. Cunningham, for Philadelphia and the Brig Eliot, Capt. Waring, for South Carolina, both full of passengers, were expected to sail from Newry about the 25th of May. From the same place also, other vessels are going with settlers. We hear also that great numbers of vessels from Dublin, Londonderry, Belfast, Learn, Cork, and other ports have lately sailed or are soon expected to sail, full of passengers, for different parts of North America. These emigrations, it is thought, have already drained the northern parts of Ireland of near a third part of its most useful and industrious inhabitants. Nearly all of them being Protestants, those left behind begin to be greatly alarmed.*
>
> *Most of these people being well skilled in the linen manufactory, if proper encouragement is given to*

them, will be an important acquisition to the British colonies.
The Pennsylvania Chronicle, July 19, 1773

The other Irish emigrant was the native Catholic Celt. The runaway advertisements said they were from places like Enniskillen, Burrisakane, Tipperary, Limerick and Dublin. Some were said to speak good Irish –*i.e.*, Gaelic. Still others spoke English "with a brogue upon [their] tongues". One son of Erin was said to be "a short, thick man, sandy colored hair; with very short thick legs, such as the native Irish servants usually have." A pair of Irish born fugitives were described as "furnished with plenty of money and drink to excess. They carry a sword with them and are Roman Catholics". Another was spotted in Maryland at a funeral "at the Roman Church"[4].

There were a sprinkling of runaway servants from outside the British Isles: Spanish, Swedish, French and Portugese. Beginning in the 1750s, there was a flood of indentured servants arriving from Germany and the Netherlands. Totaling 92, 12 per cent of the runaway population, they were called Dutch (56), High Dutch (7), Low Dutch (2), Dutch Palatine (2), Holland born (1) and Germans (23). They included, a Joseph David, a German born Jew who, it was thought, would "likely will follow peddling as he has a great desire to follow that calling and has often talked about it; an artful fellow; kept a shop in Albany for the sale of goods."

Occupations of the Runaways

It appears that American "industry" recruited German workers. Advertised in *The Pennsylvania Journal*, June 12, 1766, were nine German born, "miners", who together fled the Ringwood Iron Furnaces[5]. None spoke much English and they all had three years and four months to go on their indentures.

The iron and brass foundries, like Ringwood, which employed iron masters, bloomers, finers and founders must have been difficult places to work. No fewer than 25 advertisements were for workers who ran away from the indentures to these forges.[6]

Often the runaway notice specified the occupations the runaways had performed before fleeing. Today's reader would be surprised at how few of these jobs have any relevance in today's labor market. The reason, of course, was the Industrial Revolution which began in the 1830s.[7] It introduced to America machines and manufacturing processes that yielded standard, uniform products and, in doing so, changed the country from a collection of more or less independent, rural, agricultural communities into a nation dominated by the cities and the manufacturers. [8]

The top professions in colonial America before the Industrial Revolution reflected how everything was hand made. Shoemakers, weavers, tailors, blacksmiths and carpenters headed the list. A number of professions worked with the tailors, weavers and shoe makers (including "cordwainers", another type of shoemaker).to dress America. They were curriers, tanners, fullers, hatters, breeches [trousers or "britches"] makers, buckle makers, flax dressers, potters, dyers, wool combers and those who "knitted caps for women and silk purses for men."

Runaway workers could also be classed by their industry. It also took a number of farmers – country or plantation work – and agricultural workers (plowers, sowers and ditchers) to feed themselves and the city people[9]. "Watermen" – sailors, fishermen and those who sailed on river craft like flat men, or shallop men. Many ran away to become "privateers". There were always ex-soldiers from both the British army and the state militias, who had tried their hands in the labor market and did not like it.

Early manufacturing facilities needed those "understanding the business of making pot ash, pearl ash and Boston Crown soap". The "metals" business employed many of the runaways: "tin plate workers","tin men","workers in brass, copper, and pewter"; braziers, tinkers, tin traders and "pedlars of tin products".

Other trades represented by the runaways included: coopers, miners or colliers, laborers, turners [carpenter], clock makers, saddle makers, butchers, bakers, stay makers, plasterers, brick makers, hostlers, nail makers, chimney sweeps, wood cutters, sawyers, carters, house painter, carriage and harness makers. There were also paper makers, masons, bookbinders, printers, pin makers, axe and scythe makers, ship wright, millwrights and wheel wrights. There were jockeys, riddle makers, and makers of wampum.

Some fugitives were "gentlemen's gentlemen", pedlars, "travelers" or had run shops, taverns or ferries before running away. Some "professions" were represented too: school masters, preachers, clerks and men "skilled in physics and surgery". One worked in a law office before being obliged to flee because of check forgery. Another was a barber, who could "shave, dress hair, bleed and draw teeth."

How does that compare with today? Progress has changed the job market, creating positions and skills never envisioned. One job, however, survived in the top ten from pre-Industrial Revolution days, where everything was handmade, to the 21st Century, the age of the computer and beyond – the humble carpenter.[10]

Given Names of the Runaways

There were nearly 5,000 names -- 4,820 -- in the runaway notices for servants, escaped prisoners and deserters. These included the masters, the ones giving notice, sheriffs, military officers, and jailers as well as the fugitives themselves.

While less a scholarly or genealogical inquiry than one motivated by curiosity, there was an irresistible temptation to determine which were the most popular given names in the seven decades of immigration. "John" was the hands down winner with 600. About 12 per cent of all runaways were named John.. It was followed by William (263 or approximately 4 per cent), Thomas (183 or approximately 2 and one quarter per cent) and James (159 or about 2 per cent). Garnering more than 1 per cent of the names were Samuel (126), Joseph (117), Daniel (66), Henry (57), George (56) with Edward, Francis, Richard and Robert at 1 per cent.

Old Testament names were frequent among the Quakers, Baptists and Presbyterians of New Jersey beginning with the first man, Adam: Samuel was the most popular, followed by Daniel, Jacob, Benjamin, Isaac and Abraham, although the Old Testament names ranged from Aaron to Zebulon. The New Testament was well represented too in the names given youngsters: Joseph, Peter, Paul and Philip as well as the first martyr Stephen. An Irish heritage was revealed by first names such as Hugh, Dennis, Terence, Owen and Patrick, Scotch by Alexander, Andrew and Archibald.

For two centuries, the preferences of parents in naming their sons did not differ much[11]. But, by 1960, there were larger changes afoot[12]. By the time of the New Millennium, almost all the old favorites were gone. Once mighty "John" (and William, James, Samuel and the rest of the popular given names of the 1700s) were no where to be seen, replaced by Michael, Jacob, Matthew, Christopher, Nicholas, Austin, Joshua, Andrew, Joseph, and Brandon. *Sic transit gloria mundi.*

Ages, Heights and Builds of the Runaways

The age of the runaway was given in nearly 800 of the notices, again a sampling large enough from which to make a few inferences. For example, running away was basically a young man's game. Ninety per cent were between the ages of 17 and 30 with the 18 to 22 year olds leading the pack. Yet, they ran away as young as 11 (there were twenty 16 years old or younger). On the other end of the spectrum, 140 were in their thirties, twenty-seven in their forties, a dozen in their fifties and several 60 year olders.[13]

America was indeed the Horn of Plenty. The colonists ate more food, loaded with more nutrition, than probably ever did any general population before them.[14] There is proof of it in a single statistic. American colonists and Europeans began the 1700s with men being of equal height - an average height of approximately 5 feet, 6 inches". However, three quarters of a century later, by the time of the American Revolution, the native born, male colonists had reached an average height of 5 feet, 8 inches, nearly comparable with that of late 20th century[15]. It would take the Europeans more than a full century to catch up.

Do the runaway notices back this up – i.e., confirm that the average height of the American born man in the second half of 1700s was two inches greater than the native Englishmen and only an inch shorter the modern American male?

We have two populations to consider. The ads are not all of American born. Many of the foreign born among the 1022 runaways in the population studied might have spent their growing years in poverty and hunger in Europe. Yet many were American born or came to the country young enough to make an analysis of their heights at least worth trying.

In the first decades, actual heights were not given. Descriptions were only "small", "middle" and " tall". By the mid 1750s, however, the heights were given in the vast majority of listings in feet and inches. Some were estimates as suggested by "5 feet 9 or 10 inches high". The heights of others, especially the military deserters, were exact –"5 feet, nine and one half inch". Thankfully, by those dozen or so occasions where a runaway's height was set forth both in feet and inches and by description, we have Rosetta Stones to help us determine what the colonists considered was short, middle sized or tall. Short was defined in some notices as someone who was 5 foot, 5 inches or shorter.[16] One percent of the runaways were said to be under five foot, the shortest being four foot high. Three percent were described as exactly five foot high. In total, whether described as short or by feet and inches, 30% of the runaway population was given as being short –5 feet 5 inches or below

The description "middle sized or "of middle stature" appears to have been given to those between five foot five and five foot nine inches. Fifty per cent of the runaways were described this way.

Anyone who was 5 foot, ten inches or higher was described as tall. This was about 20 per cent of the runaway population. The two tallest were 6 foot, six inches and six foot, seven inches high. About 6 per cent were exactly six foot tall.

The median height of all these runaway servants,

prisoners and deserters was right at the division line between 5 foot 7 and 5 foot 8 – above the European by an inch, but below the figures given for native born Americans of the period[17]. But, as mentioned, our first population under study was a combination of European emigrants, American born fugitives and others unidentified by national origin but who presumably fell into one of the those two categories.

However, we have a second, smaller population to consider. Some 116 of the 1022 advertisements were expressly identified as being American born, nearly 15 per cent. Were they taller than their European forebears?

They were. Were we to compare them to our earlier findings on the runaways generally, we would see that the native born Americans were taller than those in transition, who in turn, were taller than the average man in Britain. Thirty per cent of the total runaway population was described as being short – 5 feet 5 inches or less. Among those who were born in America, however, only 15 per cent, half the number, met the prevailing standard of being "short". From the larger group of runaways, middle sized was between five foot, five inches and five foot, nine inches. Fifty per cent of both general runaway population and the the American born group were reported to be "mid sized". The difference in the populations as to how many were described as "tall", five foot ten inches or higher, was noticeable but not dramatic. Among the general population about 20 per cent of the runaway population was a tall and 23 per cent for the American born group. Moreover, the mean height for the American born sub population was above 5 foot, 8 inches, while the mean for the general population had been on the borderline between it 5 foot, 7 inches and 5 foot, 8 inches tall.

The range of builds of the runaways are not different from today but the percentages of how many fell into whatever category has indeed changed over the last two centuries. For example, in the 1700s, 25 per cent of the runaways were described as "well set" or "shocky well set", and almost another 10 per cent as "thick set", "chunky", square set, bulky, strongly built, "squat", "able bodied", well shaped or "well proportioned". A sturdy physical build was depicted in the notices for more than a third of those in the 18th century.

Undoubtedly, manual labor, as well as genetics, helped form these builds. Approximately 12 per cent of the runaway population was described as "slim", "slim waisted", "slender", "thin", "spare", "light made", which again reflects genes and hard work. However, only 2 per cent of the runaways were described as "stout"or "portly". A weaver was said to "wear a leather apron to hide his being much bursten". In 2000, the prevalence of obesity among U.S. adults was 19.8 percent, which reflects a 61 percent increase since 1991."

Other descriptions of the runaways focused on their being "thick boned", "big boned", " raw boned", "square" "broad", "round " and "stoop shouldered", or "was clumsy made". Others were "large limbed ", "heavy limbed" or straight limbed. Many had "thick", "short" and "full" legs". Still others had "large feet", were "bandy legged", had a "nimble gait", "walked very upright" or walked "in slow motion".

Coloring of the Runaways: Complexions and Hair

A person's genes determines the hair coloring as well as those of skin and eyes. Scientists tell us there are six distinct types: Celtic, Northern, European, Mediterranean, South Asian and Negro. The Celtic type has red-blonde or sandy hair, pale, sensitive skin and very often freckles. Today, about 2 per cent of the U.S. population are natural redheads. The Scotch and Irish have the highest percentages of natural redheads, 13 and 10 per cent respectively. The Northern type has blonde to dark blonde hair and pale skin. The European type has middle blonde to brown hair and slightly tanned skin.

Since almost all of the first colonizers were of Western European background, in the beginning principally English, Scotch and Irish, later German and Dutch , we would expect to see their coloring to cover a same rainbow of hues of the European continent. Do they?

Americans support a multi- billion dollar business growing, cutting, coloring, styling , washing, conditioning, straightening, strengthening etc. their hair. And for good reason. We are known and remembered by our hair. So it is quite understandable that nearly half the advertisements for runaways - almost 550 - describe the color of the runaway's hair and how he wore it.

Colonial hair came in all hues from light, white, yellow, flaxen, sandy and red, all the way to brown and black, with shades of light and dark of each. Hardly remarkable, but there might be some information to extract from this.

Today, our population is from every nation of the world, but, as said, in the mid 1700s, the white population was exclusively from Western Europe, from England, Germany, Holland, Ireland, Scotland and Wales. What should the percentage of, say, red heads in New Jersey been then back then? Surprisingly – or maybe not so – about ten per cent of the white population had red or sandy hair, revealing the higher percentage of Irish and Scotch blood . Eighty- five per cent had brown or black hair, as did the Europeans, and about five per cent yellow or flaxen, what we would call blonde today, reflective of the Northern types.

Some grew gray, of course with "grizzled hair and gray beard". Some graying was premature ["gray haired notwithstanding his youth] but others looked like the natural result of aging [black hair with gray hairs mixed amongst his hair, but mostly grey hair on top of his head".]

For some runaways, their hair was described as "thinning". There were bald runaways, some intentionally, others not. Wigs were not uncommon. They ranged from one "pinned to the ears with a fashionable, high top powdered" to something unattractively called "a piss-burnt wig". Caps too were available for those "bald on the fore part of [their] heads".

What hair styles were popular?" The runaway's hair was four times as likely to be short than long. In the first few decades, up until the 1750s, it was common that runaways had their hair "newly cut off" and sometimes their heads shaved. Maybe, this was to disguise themselves in flight. Or maybe, it was style. However, in the next three decades of runaways, only one fugitive in each decade had "his hair cut off". Conversely, wearing one's hair " tied behind," rose from a single description in the early 1700s to forty, beginning at the end of the 1750s. Sometimes it was tied by a colored ribbon. Other times it was clubbed. A fad?

Many were described as having curled hair "much like a mulatto". Others had straight hair and half as many with "bushy" hair. Others were said to have thick hair, lank or frized, scragging or worn "Indian style".

What about their skin colorings – their complexions? We have slightly over 1000 descriptions to study. The complexions of the runaway white males fell, rather unremarkably, into one of three types. There were the "light" "fair", "fresh", "pale", sandy, yellow or sanguine complexions – about 53 per cent of the population. At the other end of the color spectrum, 40 per cent of the complexions noted were "dark", "black" "brown" "swarthy" and "tawny". In between, were the remaining 7 per cent, whose coloring was described as either red or ruddy. Of course, with the African and Native American slaves, including the mulattos, there were as many different colors around as there are today.

Facial Features of the Runaways

What else, besides his hair and complexion, might be so noticeable in a runaway as to give him away to an inquisitive sheriff? Noses, for example. There were "large noses" and "long noses", "Roman noses" and "large hooked noses". Some noses were "sharp", others "drooped". There were also "short and stumpy" noses, cock noses and "flat" noses, the last "occasioned by the gristle of its being broke, so that a fellow placing his finger slightly on the tip of it, lays it flat to his face." On some of the noses were hair moles, warts, black patches and "scars or bumps" from " a fall or blow."

Another identifying facial feature among runaways were their eyes. Their coloring was varied: blue, hazel, brown, gray, black and even whitish. On the happy side, some fugitives were described as "full eyed" or it was said "their eyes disappear when they laugh." The eyes of others were imperfect: " to be a little inclined before, " sunk in his head, and very small". Some had blemishes like styes; others were blind or "purblind", a word of the time meaning completely blind. Some "cannot well look a man in the face." There was even the familiar "he has been fighting and has a black eye."

Some, but by far a minority, wore beards. If so, their color was duly noted in the advertisement. So were eyebrows: "remarkable large broad black eye brows." Faces were described as freckled, smooth, square, long, short, broad, thin, full, round bluff, bold and flat. The man who "carries his head something on one side" was pointed out. Jaws were described as "lanthorn", "the under jaw projecting a little" or "apt to snap when eating". Chins were long and lips thick, sore, hanging or with "a seam down" them. Mouths in some instances were reported to be noticeably wide or full or even that the runaway "keeps his mouth much open". While missing front teeth was common, it did not stop smiling: "glissens much when he smiles" and "shows his teeth very much in talking and very apt to laugh".

Less common descriptions were losing one's ear "by the bite of a horse", "very remarkable for often sucking his tongue", "being pretty hairy on his breast", "having two brown marks, one on each side below his breast, the bigness of a penny, one rather smaller than the other", "having a long neck" or with a "remarkable spot on his forehead resembling a pear."

Maladies and Disabilities of the Runaways

In Colonial times, America was a healthy place to live, with many births and few deaths. The population had doubled every 25 years, *"a rapidity of population not to be paralleled in the annals of Europe. It has never been equaled since the patriarchal ages"*, according to a press item of the time. Newspapers reported feats of fertility such as the woman from Morris County, New Jersey, who had borne 18 sons and two daughters in 17 years of marriage. It also offered as "a specimen to the longevity of its inhabitants, reported by the Elizabeth correspondent, that the last three deaths in that place were to "Mrs. Crane. aged 74; Mr. Price, 97; and Mrs. Garthwait, 73"[18] or the obituary of Elizabeth Thatcher of Kingwood in West Jersey, who died at the age of 87, having had 17 children, 118 grandchildren, 133 great grandchildren and one great, great grandchild.

But, while nearly Eden, America was far from free from illness, injury and aging. The hundreds of advertisements for runaways, escapees and deserters, describing in detail abnormalities about the person sought, are sources for learning the maladies and deformities of the colonists.

One conclusion quickly emerges. The strides that have been made in medical knowledge and health care since colonial times are huge. What we take for granted today was either unknown or just being probed back then. A trip to the doctor's office today would get rid of many a condition that plagued a colonist for life.

Perhaps, the most notable change between "then" and "now" was smallpox and its ravages. A contagious, sometimes fatal infectious disease for which there is no specific treatment, its only prevention was a crude vaccination.[19] The name pox refers to the raised bumps that appear on the face and body of an infected person. After the illness, they became pits in the skin, scars to forever let others know he had been vaccinated the hard way.

In nearly 15 per cent of the notices seeking their return, runaways were described as "pock marked", "poxed" or "pox fretten", reflecting how many suffered from the disease and were permanently marked by it. An outbreak of small pox was to be feared and efforts, even primitive inoculations, were taken to avoid its spread through the population.[20]

Runaway notices also described another skin condition of the period, also now a memory only:" "he is much scarified under one of his cheek bones caused by the King's Evil." The disease, with the ominous name, is better known in medical circles as *cervical lymphadenitis* or *scrofula*. Tubercular in nature, it is characterized chiefly by swelling and degeneration of the lymphatic glands, especially around the neck area.[21]

Scars, not from natural causes, scalds from spilled boiling water and burns were commonplace - plastic surgery still far in the future. They evidenced the accidents, misadventures and violence of the Colonial era. Several runaways had their ears bitten off by horses; were crippled from ill set broken bones; had missing fingers, limbs and eyes; or suffered permanent damage from gunshot wounds. Others were described as having one leg, arm, thumb or "an ankle larger than the other".

Remember the runaway notice which described the fugitive barber who could "shave, dress hair, bleed and draw teeth." That was about the extent of the dental profession. Scores and scores of runaways are described as missing their front teeth. Orthodontists with their braces would have rectified conditions such as "three of his upper teeth stick out farther than the rest", "she is snaggle toothed" or "his eye tooth on the same side sticks over his lower teeth in a very remarkable manner;" and "remarkable for having his teeth all double".

The same might be said for ear and eye doctors. Many of the ailments could be corrected today. " hard" or a "little dull in hearing", "sore" or "weak eyes"," or those nearsighted or who squinted. Eyes were inflicted with "cast", " pearls" and "styes". Some had vision problems such as "when he looks into a fellow's face he is apt to wink and close one of his eyes" or he "mostly shuts one of his eyes when he speaks". Others were missing eyes, one poor man had "lost one eye which is entirely sunk".

Leg disabilities and walking problems, often due to birth defects, were frequent and varied: "splaw footed"; "bowlegged"; "knock need"[22]; "bandy legged"; "walks with his leg turned outward"; "his right foot twisting and the toe of the same inclining to turn outward as he walks and his right knee bending inwards towards the left"; "wangles in his walk" and "turns out his feet pretty much as he walks". Others were said to be "hunched back", "round" and "stoop shouldered" . One "stoops and rocks much in his walk" and another displayed "a clumsy heavy gate in walking." Speech defects of lisping, stammering, stuttering, slow in speech or "speak[ing] by clusters","hard to understand" "impediments"; "stoppages in speech;" and "speaks hoarse as if he had a cold". One child was said to be "dumb". Even the sturdy skull could have a difficulty. "On examining his head close, you will find a soft spot on top, occasioned by a blow."

Dermatologists would have had no end of business back then. Among the skin conditions listed were "great ringworms on her breast and arms"; "ring worm on his face"; "all around his neck and above his shirt collar and all over his body his skin is greyish like a fish scale"; and "face somewhat bumped".

Other ailments are not so easy to diagnose, at least to a layman, but sound either serious or potentially so: "is a little swelled with the dropsy"; "much afflicted with a dry cough"; "yellow complexion"; " has a great lump on his throat"; "troubled with a phthisick"; "goes crooked and often groans in his sleep"; or "he halts as he walks seemingly rocking". Mental illness was also present, but, based on the notices, rare: "he ran away from the master he formerly lived with and was discovered by his barking like a dog and crowing like a cock."

Social and Personality Traits of the Runaways

Usually, the masters, who understandably did not think highly of the fugitives, wrote their identifying personality traits. Surprisingly, on occasion, they actually described them charitably such as being "well discoursed", "a strong, hearty good humored fellow", having "an easy, soft, smooth manner of speaking", "or as having "lively pert", "pleasant", "proper looking", "subtle", or "complaisant" countenances. More likely, however, the descriptions of the runaways given by the masters were less kind. Their dislike of them is apparent in the descriptions of the runaway as being: "cross", "crafty", "cunning", "homely", "straggling", "fractious", "grim", "hard favored", "ill-looking", "mean", "sliving", "sneaking", "sour", "surly", "shame faced", "stern" or "rough looking". More than fifty of the runaways, about 5 per cent of the population, had a "down [or downcast] look when speaking to strangers". Others were said to look "bashful when in company", "indifferent", "lusty", "likely", "active" or "have a very effeminate look". Eccentricities were duly pointed out: "apt to laugh at his own expressions" or "very apt to use the word 'really'".

Some of the runaways demonstrated an aptitude or fondness for music in its various forms, but there were not many of them, less than two per cent as compared to the African slave (see *infra*) where more than 5 per cent of the runaway population appeared musically inclined. The runaway white indentured servants played the fiddle, flute, fife, bag pipes and violin. Some were said to "sing a good song by note", and others "very fond of dancing and company". Some were adept at entertainment of the non musical variety: magic shows ("sleight of hand"), ventriloquy ("can counterfeit his voice to cats and dogs") and something called "walking upon ropes", presumably a balancing act of some sort.

One fellow was described as "not talkative", while twenty four were said to be very talkative especially with a glass of spirits on hand: "slow of speech except when in drink and then very talkative"; "very silent when sober and talkative when drunk;" and "slow in speech if not in liquor".

Speaking of drinking, only one of the 1,200 runaways was an abstainer –" drinks no rum". On the other hand, 114 of them, nearly a tenth of the runaway population were, said to be "addicted to drink". This percentage is close to the 7.4 per cent addiction rate in the United States today.[23] If some of the descriptions are accurate, many were prodigious drinkers, even in a time when alcohol was more prevalent than now. For example: one fellow was said to be "apt to take a LARGE DRINK and often uses those words". Another was "very apt to get drunk when he can come by liquor". A third "drank hard when he had the opportunity". As true today, overuse of alcohol can cause singing, swearing, quarreling, being impudent, gaming, dancing, boasting and acting "saucy". Some descriptions are humorous, the makings for stories the next day: "he is very apt to crow when in liquor" and "loves to be at Frolics and Taverns and apt to get into liquor and, when so, is subject to fits". Some drinking was destructive. It does not take much to imagine the tragedies that strong drink could do to an otherwise promising life, such as with the doctor who,"given to liquor and when in liquor talks much of his skill in Physic and Surgery" or the school master who "fond of strong liquor and, when drunk, which will be as often as he can get rum, is fond of speaking much in his own praise, particularly his great abilities in school keeping."

Many of the runaways were what is today called, "cross addicted". They were devoted to more than one "vice". For example "much addicted to card playing and horse racing"; "chews tobacco very much" and is "a great taker of snuff". Others had psychological addictions. More than a few were reported to have run off with other mens' wives and one fellow was said to be "remarkably fond of exercising with a musket".

Neither humility nor honesty was universal. Bragging was noted on more than a few occasions in runaways who, like one, was "apt to tell of what he has done and what he has seen" and another who was "subject to live high and boast much of his former circumstances". Not unexpectedly, a number were called dishonest by those from whom they fled on their indenture, their bail or their enlistment agreement. Some comments were short and to the point, the runaway being "a great liar", "a grand villain" or "a notorious rogue." Other comments rely more on inference: "his honesty is far from being unquestionable"; "even though he has lived in Newport and Philadelphia for 18 months, he has no acquaintance at either place who can testify that he is either a free or an honest man; he has been detected in many gross untruths"; or "he is not too honest, nor quite honest enough, if he has but the opportunity to be a rogue".

A man is sometimes judged by how he speaks. So were the runaways. Some descriptions perhaps illustrate an underlying personalty as well. For example, runaways were said to "speak bold", "plainly", or with "a smooth tongue" or a "coarse" one, or was "very fawning in his speech". Even the cadence and tone of his speech might be reported: "speaks short"; "talks thick and fast"; "speaks very low"; "talks quick"; "drawling"; "slow spoken"; or even " speaks little". What exactly does it mean to "talk very broken and backward"? Or what was the Master really intending when he described his runaway servant as a man who "can talk quite enough for one of his station"?

Since so many of the runaways had been emigrants to America,. they often were described to speak "little", "bad", "broken" or "no English". Others spoke "tolerable good English", although with Irish brogues, Welch or Scotch accents and West Country dialects: "on the Scotch Irish order" or "in the broad West Country way". Emigrants being bi-lingual were not unusual. Many spoke a language in addition to English, including Irish (Gaelic), Welsh, Scotch, French, Dutch, Low Dutch, High Dutch, German. A few were multi-lingual: "can speak all languages" and "talks very poor English but says he could speak German, French, Spanish and the Portugese languages". There was even a fellow, with an obvious knack for language, "who can speak Indian, even though he had just come over from Ireland".

There were schools in colonial America but few and basic in their offerings. While a few of the runaways were described as not being able to read or write, fifteen times as many were said to be able to do both. In two instances, the literacy of the runaway was begrudgingly described by the owner: "appears to be half witted, but is a sharp fellow, good scholar and can write and cypher [reason] very well". Another was "a good scholar" despite his being also "a great rogue and much given to strong drink".

We left handers –known for our creativity –constitute about 13 per cent of the world's population. What it always so? Probably, because it is genetic, but no one knew it back then. The well known bias until the mid 20th century against left handed people was principally for sanitary reasons. Children were forced to become righthanders. That things have changed is strikingly shown by a comparison between then and now. In the more than 1200 notices only one white male was said to be left handed – 1/12 of 1 per cent as compared to today's 13 per cent rate! As shortly shall be seen, about 1 ½ per cent of the runaway slaves were said to be left handed in playing the fiddle, which we can assume is a sign of his true handedness.

PROFILE OF THE RUNAWAY SLAVE MAN

The concept of slavery is repugnant to us today. How can one person, morally or legally, own even for even a moment, much less a lifetime, the liberty, labor and offspring of another fellow human? Yet, the practice has existed as long as recorded history – from the ancient civilizations of Babylonia, Egypt, Greece, and Rome, through the serfdom of medieval Europe, to the plantations of the American South in the 1800s and even into the 1960s in places like Saudi Arabia and Angola. Historians suggest, however, that it was not so much a moral issue then as it was just the fate - one's lot in life- that some unlucky captured people suffered. [24]

The ugly institution of slavery in the United States can be traced to the arrival of twenty Africans in Virginia in the latter part of August, 1619, a year before the Pilgrims landed on the *Mayflower*. They were booty taken by Dutch pirates from a South America bound Spanish vessel and sold to the recently arrived English planters at Jamestown. Their names included Antoney,[25] Isabella and Pedro. In the first years, the English would treat the blacks colorlessly as indentured servants, freeing them, after they had worked off their purchase price. However, so necessary proved to be their labor on the plantation, Africans soon were enslaved, rather than indentured. Now, they were permanent servants. Not only did these unpaid workers not have to be replaced periodically, but they replenished themselves with offspring who belonged to the owner.

The slave trade had begun from the Ivory Coast of West Africa, (modern day Nigeria, Ghana and the Sierra Leone) or from Gambia or Madagascar. Chieftains sold the captured members of enemy tribes to Arab traders who, in turn, delivered them to waiting Spanish, Portugese, Dutch and English vessels. Chained in the bowels of the slave ships, the bewildered victims-- some 11 million of them -- were sent across the Atlantic, the vast majority, 95 per cent, bound for the Carribean

For most of the 17th century, the flow of slaves to the

British colonies in North America had been monopolized, with the approval of the Crown, by the Royal African Company. However, competition appeared in 1697 and, soon, with more slaves for sale, the prices fell, making slaves now more affordable. This, of course, increased the demand for them, which spurred on the race among the slave traders to bring more of the unfortunates from Africa, until, by the turn of the new century, there were about 25,000 of them, approximately 10 per cent of the population, a percentage not unlike today's of 12 per cent. By 1760, the number of African slaves in America would increase tenfold to 250,000. The increase would come less from African imports or from the sugar plantations in the Carribean colonies than from American born slaves.

From its earliest days, the plantations of New Jersey had slaves. In 1680, there were about 120 black slaves in New Jersey, about 60 to 70 of those at a the properties of Lewis Morris, at his plantation in Shrewsbury, Monmouth County and an iron mill in Tinton Falls, Monmouth County.

It is estimated that, by 1726, there were 32,000 Europeans and Africans living in the Royal Province of New Jersey. Forty seven per cent were female; eight per cent were Africans. By 1745, the population almost doubled to 61,000. Slightly less than 45 per cent were female. Seven and a half per cent were African.

Not all in America approved of slavery. The Quakers had opposed the slave trade as early as 1696, and by 1776 refused membership to their yearly "Meeting of Friends" to any slave owner. A few newspaper items also revealed that the anti-slavery sentiment extended beyond the Quakers. The degrees of opposition differed. For example, some appreciation of the dignity of his slaves might be gleaned from this owner's advertisement. Nonetheless, he sold, not freed, them:

TO BE SOLD

Sundry Negroes, consisting of two men and two women, two boys and two girls. The oldest of the men is a miller, a carter and a farmer and is about 50 years old. The other is a stout likely fellow, a farmer, and about 35 years

old; he is father to three of the children viz. one girl nine years old, one six years and a boy ten months old by the oldest wench who is a good cook and dairy woman. The youngest wench, about twenty seven years old, is an excellent house servant and, besides washing and ironing, can spin wool and flax, knit &c., understands the management of a dairy and making butter and cheese; she is the mother of the other boy, about eleven years old and as fine a boy of his age as any in America. The man and wife and three children must not be parted, nor the mother and son, as they have lived long in one family together; it would be most agreeable if they could be fixed near each other. They are sold for no fault, the owner only intending to change his plan of life. Whoever the above may suit will please to inquire of Mr. Henry Worly, Inn Keeper at the North Branch of Raritan, Somerset County, East New Jersey.
The Pennsylvania Packet, March 18, 1778

On another occasion, neighbors and the Law combined to protect the rights of a former slave boy, whom some wanted to enslave again and sell:

> Whereas Isaac Johnson, formerly of the City of New-York, Shop-Keeper, but late of the Navesinks, deceased, did, by his Will, set at Liberty a Mulatto Slave, called Thomas Jackson, and provided Security to render his Manumission effectual, but the Bond given for that purpose hath been destroyed and an unjust attempt lately made to sell him at vendue, which induced certain persons from motives of humanity, to indemnify the city or place he may reside in, whereby his freedom is perfected. These are therefore to caution all persons against purchasing the said Thomas, if he should again be offered to Sale. And threats having been thrown out by persons claiming the Estate of Isaac Johnson that

they would dispose of the said Thomas beyond the Sea, all Masters of Vessels are prohibited from carrying him off, as they will answer it at their peril, the persons who have taken him into their protection being resolved to procure him Justice. He is about 14 Years of Age, five Feet high, of slender Make, born in this Country and can read and write.
The New York Gazette, July 18, 1763

As the Revolution approached, one citizen, calling himself *"Benevolus"* (literally one who wishes good) was bold enough to raise the subject of freedom for slaves before the New Jersey General Assembly. Echoing a view which was to become the cornerstone of our Constitution in 1789 and the 13th amendment in 1865, he wrote in the January 12, 1775 issue of *The New York Journal*:

> *"The true foundation of American liberty is in human nature and the salus populi suprema est lex ought to be written on the hearts as well as on the foreheads of every civil magistrate, while the good of society remains to be the end of civil government.*
> *[But] is not the voice of slavery heard in our land? Does not the cry of oppression from half a million of wretched beings daily enter into the ears of the Lord of Sabbath? Is the slavery of the unhappy African of a disputable or doubtful nature? Is it not a professed, avowed absolute slavery in the highest degree, whereby our fellow men, made in the image of God -- rational creatures -- capable subjects of the same divine grace, become (horrible to be told) the subjects of personal property and are sold as the beasts of the field, not only without the pretensions of even a supposed or virtual consent, but directly contrary thereto. . .*
> *I do, therefore, in the name of a very large majority of your constituents, in the name of every true and real lover of his country, in the name of those wretched beings groaning beneath an iron yoke, in the name of our common humanity and in the awful name of*

God whose divine protections we are entreated so devoutly to implore, beseech you seriously and feelingly to consider this, which to many appears to be one of the procuring causes of our present unhappy contest [with Britain]. [Forget] the idea that these poor creatures are treated with more humanity in this colony than in some parts of North America, for, however you may think they are favored, they are still slaves, and every Negro in our colony is a living unanswerable argument against your claim to freedom. And, as long as this precept stands in full force 'that with the same measure you mete to others, it shall be measured to you' again in vain are your resolutions, associations and non-importations, in vain will be all your attempts to enjoy yourselves what you so unjustly and oppressively refuse to others."

The American Revolution, while it brought liberty to the European descended settlers, did not free the slaves of New Jersey, except those who had fled to New York City in response to Sir Henry Clinton's promise in his Philipsburg Proclamation of 1779 that "every Negro who shall desert the rebel standard. . . full security to follow [within the British] lines any occupation which he shall think proper." At war's end, the British, before leaving New York, kept Sir Henry's pledge. From May, 1782 to November, 1783, on every Wednesday morning, Negroes came to the Queens Head Tavern. The building, by then, already a half century old, was owned by Samuel Fraunces.[26] Maintained there by a joint commission of Americans and British was the *Book Of Negroes*. It determined which Negroes, at war's end, were eligible to be evacuated and which had to be returned to slavery with their American masters. In it was logged details of each black's enslavement, escape and military service. If their stories checked out, the former slave would be given a pass.[27]

Former slaves were given the choice of relocating in Florida, the West Indies or Nova Scotia. Fearing re-enslavement if they ventured near the plantations of the south or the Caribbean, they elected to sail north to Canada and Nova Scotia, a region that Britain had obtained from France in 1749.

It was the northernmost frontier of European settlement in the New World and among the least desirable because of the cold and thin rocky soil. Their descendants can be found there today.[28]

But what of those slaves who remained, willingly or unwillingly, with the Rebels? Sadly, they had to wait longer to be freed.

Through the steady pressure of Quakers and other *Benevoli,* the laws of New Jersey joined those of the other Northeastern states towards more humane treatments. In 1804, New Jersey, last in the region, passed its gradual emancipation act, essentially freeing any child born of slaves. Females born of slave parents after July 4, 1804, would be free upon reaching 21 years of age and males upon reaching 25. The abolition law of 1804 freed 12,460 slaves in New Jersey by 1820. The number of blacks still held as slaves was 7,557 at that time[29].

However, the 1804 law held a hidden subsidy for slave owners. A provision allowed them to free their slave children, who would then be turned over to the care of the then equivalent of the state's social welfare agency, the local Overseers of the Poor. The law provided $3 a month for the support of such children. A slave owner could then agree to have the children "placed" in his household and collect the $3 monthly subsidy on them. The evidence suggests this practice was widespread. The costs for "abandoned blacks" rose to be 40 percent of the New Jersey budget by 1809. Moreover, Black voters were disenfranchised by an 1807 state law that limited the franchise to "free, white male" citizens.

In 1846, New Jersey passed a second emancipation law. It formally outlawed slavery, but again had a loophole. Under the act, all black children born after the act's passage were free, but those blacks were to be "apprentices" for life. The act did offer former slaves greater legal protection. They could sue for their freedom if abused or mistreated and they could not be sold without written consent.[30] This act was eventually superceded in 1865 by the 13th Amendment to the U.S. Constitution, which abolished slavery nationally.

What do we know of this tragic population? The advertisements sought the return of runaways of all descriptions

-- indentured servants, escaped felons and deserters -- and preserved for us in this collection of notices were some 325 slaves, mostly males. It constituted approximately 20 per cent of the runaway population. While a modest statistical base, it does tease us to speculate on the characteristics – physical and sociological – of the larger slave population of New Jersey before the Revolution.

Places of Origin of Runaway Slave Men

For example, from where did they come? The runaway slave advertisements reveal that there were sub groups within the term "slave". While rarely associated with slavery, there was a sizeable population of Indian --Native American -- slaves, especially through the 1740s.

Captured by other tribes in raids, they were sold by their captors into slavery. The victims were from South Carolina and Georgia (referred to as "Carolina slaves"), from Florida ("Spanish Indian slaves") and from the west, as far as Texas. Alan Gallay in his *The Indian Slave Trade: the Rise of the British Empire in the American South (1670 -1717)* suggests that by 1715, somewhere between 24,000 and 51,000 unfortunate Native Americans had ended up as slaves in the colonies.[31] The Chickasaw were major dealers in the trade, assisted by the British. In the first 25 years of our study, more than a third of the runaway slaves in New Jersey were of Indian blood.

They had a wide range of names. Some, as Nim or Wan, might still have carried a remnant of their given native names. Others had been renamed by their new masters, which explains North American Indians with incongruous names from the Biblical (Moses) and Classical Ages (Pompey and Caesar). Others had single word names – Stoeffels or Jack, and other quite proper, English like names, such as Isaac Gunnit.

Compared to the other runaway slaves and their cousin runaway servants, deserters and escapees, there was nothing remarkable in the heights, ages and builds of the Indian slaves. Most seemed to be on their way to be blended in the melting pot and becoming "Americanized". They were said to speak "good English" and worked as carpenters, wheel wrights, coopers and butchers. One could even play on the fiddle. However, there is always an exception. One slave who resisted civilization was Jacob *(aka* James Smart and James Pratt), of mixed African and Native American blood, who seems to have thrown away the new life to return to the old one. When last seen he had "left from his work at the plough, without shoes or stocking", heading home.

Aside from the Indians, the remainder of the slaves were at first almost all directly from Africa. For example, during the 1720s, of the five runaway slaves noted in New Jersey, three of them were recent arrivals in America. Called "New Negroes", two, named Jersey and Popaw, were described as speaking no English, and, as further proof that the latter was recently brought to America, probably directly from Africa, it was noted that "his teeth seem to be filed or whet sharp". The third runaway slave, Fransh Manuel, was described as "speaking indifferent English", and could have been imported from the Caribbean. Later descriptions indicated that the imports from Africa continued: "he had nothing on but a crocus shirt [and] can speak no English"; a "Madagascar Negro man" and another "African from Guinea". A Negro "wench" by the name of Nell, was pictured as sporting "three diamonds on her face, one on each side and the other on her forehead."

The newspapers also confirmed the African origins

> *Just imported from the River Gambia, in the Schooner Sally, Barnard Badger, Master and to be sold at the Upper Ferry (called Benjamin Cooper's Ferry), opposite to this City, a Parcel of Likely Men and Women*
>
> *SLAVES*
>
> *with some Boys and Girls of different Ages. Attendance will be given from the hours of nine to twelve o' clock in the Morning and from three to six in the Afternoon, by W. Coxe, S. Oldman & Company*

N.B. It is generally allowed that the Gambia Slaves are much more robust and tractable than any other Slaves from the Coast of Guinea and more capable of undergoing the Severity of the Winter Seasons in the North American Colonies, which occasions their being vastly more esteemed and coveted in this Province and those to the northward than any other Slave whatsoever. The Pennsylvania Journal, No. 1016, May 27, 1762

A number of the runaways were born outside the colonies but were already a generation or more removed from Africa. They were from Havana, Bermuda, Jamaica. Guadeloupe and Barbados. A few others, listed as "Spanish", presumably were from the Spanish colonies in South America or the Carribean.

After some years, most slaves were born here. A sign that the slave population was growing more by its internal birth rate than by imports was the increasing number of New Jersey runaway slaves being described as mulattos -- that is racially mixed Caucasian/African or African/Indian. Unlike Spanish America, where persons of mixed blood ranked ahead of the African or Indian, no such elevation was recognized in the British colonies. White fathers must have watched their children -- the fruits of assaults or loving relations with slave women -- sold or raised in peonage. Many runaway slaves wore the label of "mulatto". Most likely, these runaways had been conceived in America, not Africa.

Names of Runaway African American Slave Men

What were the slaves called? What were their names? In everyday life, when a person wants to get to know another better, the first thing he or she learns is the other's name. Why should that not be true as well in our study of the slave in America?

Unlike citizens of today, most of the slaves only had a single name. Study of advertisements for runaway slaves reveals several distinct sources for these names. For example, names from the New and especially the Old Testaments of the Bible were popular. In order of popularity, they included: Ishmael, Jacob, Peter, Moses, Sampson, Dan, Simon, Isaac, Lot, Abraham, Benjamin and Ezekiel.

The colonial aristocracy had a fascination for ancient times, the Republics of Greece and Rome. Indeed, classical Athens and Rome had no small impact on us today. We are, after all, like they, the *Republic* of the United States. Interest in this period also provided the slave owner with a number of famous names with which to identify his slaves. Again in the order of popularity, they included Cato, Caesar, Primus, Pompey, Nero, Hannibal, Esop, Syron, Scipio, and Titus.

Africa and its languages must have been a source of names for the slaves. Or perhaps, they were of Spanish or Indian origin or simply made up. These unique names include Mando, Traso, Swacarnockum, Eben, Briss, Cudge, Chels, Quash, Hack, Nean, Lun, Pero or Cip.

Most slaves, however, had every day names and nick names, some of which remain common today. Again in their order of popularity in the runaway notices, they included : Jack, Joe, Tony, Bristol, Harry, Tom, Robin, Will, Charles, Frank, Ben, Sambo, Cuff, Claus, Bill, Prince, Sam, Toby, Jim, Grig, Mark, Peet, James, Forde, Fortune, Lewis, Ash, Sandy, Jemmy, Glascow, Linden, Richard, York, John, Dick, Annie's Joe, Ned, Joseph, Phil, Sim, Ames, George, Constant, Osborn, Kent, Brit, Silas and Pen.

However, while most of the slaves in New Jersey, judging by the profiles of those who tried to flee, had single names a surprising number -- almost 10 per cent -- had surnames as well: James Smith, Lazarus Kenny, Peter Waldren, James Bell, William Colson, James Rouse, Lonen Genens, Jupiter Hazard, John Juster, Benjamin Kipp; James Wilson, James More, Jack Johnson, Daniel Rogers, John Johnson, James Smart, James Pratt, Charles Quite, Garret Harbour, Cornelius Gallaghan, Jack Sharpe, Samuel Wright, James Pemberton, Anthony Welsh, John Solomon, Daniel Kent and Enos Patterson.

Ages, Heights and Builds of Runaway Slave Men

The notices seeking the return of the runaway slave, often described the fugitive in some detail, what they were wearing when they left, their occupations and personality, builds, hair colors and styles, scars, deformities etc. Some of what can be extracted from several hundred of these notices can be interesting.

The runaway slave's age was given in about two third of the instances. They ranged from as young as 11 years old to as old as 60. The average age was 27. In the earlier decades, the fugitives tended to be older, but during the American Revolution, with Great Britain promising freedom to any slave that crossed over to its lines in New York City, the average dropped to about 23 and 1/2 years.

Heights were given for 205 of the fugitive slaves from New Jersey, approximately two-thirds of the population of runaways. Some sixty, were described generally as being "short", "of middle stature" or "tall. Almost 15 per cent were described as tall, but three time that number was described as short[32]. With respect to those for whom actual heights in feet and inches were given, the average height of the runaway was over 5 feet, 8 inches and a surprising 26 of the 209 (12 ½ per cent) were 6 foot or taller[33]. The shortest slave runaway was five foot even and the tallest, six foot, four inches.

Slaves like the rest of us come in all different shapes. A full 20 per cent of them were described as being either well built or well set. Others were described as being thick or strong fellows. "Squat", "chunky" "sturdy" and "straight" were also frequent descriptions. A fair number were pictured as "thin", "slim" or "slender", but almost as many were called fat. Sometimes, the fugitives were described as being "well limbed" or as having large feet -- one 12 inches long.

Facial and other Identifying Features of Runaway Slave Men

As far as their facial features were concerned, the slaves again seemed to include all types. Some were round, full or even fat faced", while others were of "thin visage", "flat faced", "long faced" or "smooth faced". Noses did not seem to draw much attention with a few described as having a straight nose and one who had a nose "remarkably large and sharp". Eyes too were rarely detailed. Indeed, except for a few large eyes or bloodshot eyes, only one runaway slave out of more than 300 were described by the color of his eyes, that is, gray. "Thick lips",on the other hand, was a relatively frequent adjective.

The descriptions of the fugitive's hair styles were often provided. They ranged from long wooly, very black hair, to bushy, to curled. to black straight hair, "which he generally wears tied back". Surprisingly, only a few were bald and only one was gray.

More than 15 per cent of the runaway slaves had scars or other readily noticeable features like a wart, moles or sores. One "lost a piece of one of his ears bit off by a horse"; another had "a scar in the forehead from the kick of another steed." Burns and cuts also left identifying features for a conscientious citizen to note and report. Another was described as "walks straight and swings his arms partly behind him."

Occupations of Runaway Slave Men

Most slaves worked on plantations, the name for farms in the North as well as the South in colonial times. Frequently, the notice on a runaway would include such descriptions as: "understands plantation work"; "understands all parts of farmer's work"; "understands farming and milking"; "talks a great deal about his abilities as a farmer"; "has been bred to plantation work."

In the beginning, this was not surprising. Slaves recently transported from Africa or the Carribean were not trained for trades. However, by the 1740's, that had changed. Slaves began to develop talents for specialized labor – even what today we would consider to be learned professions. For example, occupations listed for the fugitives included one who could "bleed and draw teeth, pretending to be a great doctor" and the other "as very religious and says he is a churchman". These were probably their avocations rather than their occupations.

The runaway notices reflect a variety of occupations, such as working at sawmills, forges and mills. One slave was recognized as "understanding very well how to manufacture flour and can invoice the same". Another was said to "understand the pot ash business". Some were in the clothing business of the time being "skinners", "tanners", "tailors" and some one who "spins well on the foot wheel." Slaves proved handy as carpenters and mill wrights, coopers and blacksmiths, butchers and bakers, brick makers and shoemakers, even chimney sweeps. Others were house servants, cooks or coach drivers. One was even known as a fortune teller.

Again the colonial press indicates jobs the slaves did

TO BE SOLD

TWO likely Negro Men, one of them a Ship-Carpenter by Trade and the other understands a Team or Plantation Work; Also a Negro Wench with two small children; the Wench understands House Work. Any Person inclining to purchase may apply to Susannah Marsh, Widow, at Perth-Amboy, who will dispose of them on reasonable Terms.
The New York Weekly Post Boy, March 9, 1747

Two Negro men, both under thirty, healthy and strong, one of them a valuable and complete farmer in all its branches, to which he has been bred since a child and is very stout. The other a genteel footman and waiter, who understands the care of horses well, the management of a carriage, drives either on the box or as a postilion and, in every respect, suitable for a genteel family or single gentleman and is fond of farming. Both have had the smallpox. Enquire of Mr. Coxe at Trenton or of Doctor Redman at Philadelphia.
The Pennsylvania Journal, February 28, 1776

Maladies and Disabilities of Runaway Slave Men

As was the case with the male indentured servants, the state of health care in the 1700's was minimal. The descriptions of the runaway slaves provide us many reminders of that. For example, more than five per cent of them had been victims of small pox. Phrases, like "pock mark'd" or "pox fretten", reflect how many of the survivors of this disease were permanently scarred by it. An outbreak of small pox was to be feared. By 1770, however, progress had been made, both in determining the cause of small pox and preventing it. Canceling public functions, such as county fairs, when there was an outbreak was one method to prevent the spread of small pox through the population. Primitive inoculations attempted to block its occurrence. It was not unusual to see in an advertisement for the sale of a slave the representation that he already had had the pox or had been inoculated against it.[34] It was not fool proof, however: "he has just been inoculated with the small pox, not yet cleaned up, his arm still sore and is very liable to spread that infection."

A number of slaves were somewhat disabled from birth. Sometimes, it was of an orthopedic nature. For example, one fugitive was described as having his "right foot twisting and the toe of the same inclining to turn outward as he walks and his right knee bending inwards toward the left." Others were called "lame" or were said to "walk stooping" or with a "hitch". Still others were termed "something knock kneed", "splaw footed", "bandy legged" or as "walking loose in the knees". Accidents or other misadventures accounted for lameness as well. One fellow was "lame in the right leg by the bite of a boar" or walked "somewhat crippled his feet having been frozen".

Speech defects were not uncommon either as fugitives were described as lisping or being apt to stutter or stammer if they speak in haste. Vision difficulties also existed ranging from having an eye out, to near sightedness, squinting, having "a blemish" in one eye" to having a " lively eye". Teeth were often missing or broken.

Personality and Social Traits of Runaway Slave Men

The longer they were in America, the more the slaves began to fall to addictions which they had been spared in Africa, especially alcohol or, in the words of a typical notice being someone "much given to strong drink". There were none out of a population of 50 in the first 3 decades of the 1720s, 1730s or 1740s. In the 1750s, there was a single fugitive whose use of alcohol was mentioned -- about 2+ per cent of the population of slave fugitives from New Jersey. By the 1760s the percentage of the runaways who "love[d] grog" had increased to 6+ per cent. From 1770-1782, 7.5 per cent of the fugitive population was described as having a problem with alcohol, approaching the rate of alcoholism of indentured servants, deserters and escapees and not far from the estimate of the alcoholism rate in the United State today.

Not surprisingly, some of the familiar aspects of drinking as well as cross addictions and other baggage associated today with problem drinkers, were evident back then too, as is evident in the following handful of descriptions: "very talkative fellow in liquor and apt to swear"; "much addicted to smoking and drinking"; "much addicted to liquor and troublesome when drunk"; "chews tobacco and loves strong liquor"; "fond of strong liquor, and, when drunk, very saucy"; "good tempered fellow, when sober, but sulky or quarrelsome in liquor"; "much given to strong drink and then playing on the fiddle".

Somewhat surprisingly, according to an analysis of the runaway notices, many slaves were educated. This had not necessarily been the case with the white population, even the native born, non servant residents of the time. Approximately, 6 per cent of the runaway slaves at least could "read, write and cypher". Many were said to speak English well and a number were bi-lingual. In Northern New Jersey, there were many Dutch descended settlers therefore the slaves spoke "Low Dutch" as well. Spanish, Danish and German were also spoken by some of the runaways.

The notices seeking the runaways often made attempts at describing the personality of the fugitive. Some of the traits pointed out in the notice were positive ones such as "he laughs much"; "likely black fellow"; "has a pert look and when talking, is always either laughing or smiling"; "talkative"; "is a very handy fellow"; "a smart, active, lively Negro". Others are called "sensible", "serious" and "civil". Some were said to have a "down look", an inability to look into the eyes of the master. The most often used description of the runaway slave was that "he was a cunning artful fellow".

However, there were derogatory descriptions given to the runaways as had been the case with their white counterparts. Masters were not pleased with their property running away: "so prodigious a liar that if observed he may be discovered by it"; "the person who takes him up is desired to be careful lest he deceive them"; "has a sly look"; "crafty fellow"; "oily tongued chap"; "is very plausible in his talk and crafty in his behavior"; "has been caught in several lies"; "is a very great liar"; and ;"is very plausible in his talk and crafty in his behavior; whoever takes him must use great care or he will give them the slip.".

Out of about 1,200 notices for runaway servants, deserters and escapees, only 2 per cent were described as having a musical talent or playing an instrument. On the other hand, of 300 runaway slaves, seventeen – more than 5 per cent - were described as playing a fiddle, violin or fife "tolerably well". Ishmael was said to be "a great fiddler and often showed sleight of hand tricks". Perro Smith, an American born Mulatto slave, "could play on the violin and sing at the same time". He was also described as "playing with his left hand and much addicted to liquor". Surprisingly, several others runaway slaves, with musical talents were described also as being left handed, a great rarity then, and being addicted to drink.

Finally, on a dozen and a half occasions, the slaves ran away in groups of two or three from the same master at the same time. Either they encouraged each other to flee or the Master must have been a horror. Some runaways were caught, and ran away again and again. Slave women often fled with young offspring.

PROFILES OF WOMEN RUNAWAYS

Only about 5 per cent of the runaways of the slave and servant population combined were women. Although hardly a statistical base from which to draw any conclusions, the listing does offer some opportunity for speculation and amusement.

Twenty per cent of the women runaways were African and about 40 per cent were Irish. Dutch women were 12 ½ per cent. Welsh, Scotch and English women combined to form another 5 per cent. The origins of the balance of the runaways of the fairer sex were not given. Some were home grown.

Among the runaway female servants, the most popular name was Mary, just as John had been among the men. Elizabeth and Sarah followed with Catherine, Ann, Eleanor, Margaret, Anna, and Betty forming the top nine names. Some of the slave women had western English names like Susan, Nell, Molly, Betty, Lucy, Phoebe. Others had exotic ones like Hecatissa, Savina, and Amoritta.

The ages of the runaways curiously showed that most of runaway woman servants were under the age of 30, while it was the opposite for the slaves. Among the white servants, about 13 per cent were younger than 18. The bulk of the runaways --(67 per cent) --were between the ages of 18 and 29. Twenty per cent were 30 years of age or older. The youngest was a nine year old apprentice and, for the oldest, it is a Hobson's choice between "about 40 years of age but looks much older" and "between 40 and 50 years of age". With the slaves, however, 70 per cent of the runaways were 30 or older. Why did one group runaway later in life?

There was an apparent difference between the heights of the servants and slaves, as well. Half of the white servants were said to be "short", about 45 per cent of them were called "mid sized" and only 5 per cent were "tall". Among the slave women, however, while 40 per cent were short, 40 per cent were also "tall" (six feet, the highest) and only 20 percent middle sized. That women slaves were taller is consistent with the result for the male slaves.

The runaway women were of all complexions, from fair

to dark. Their faces were equally varied . They were described as being "round faced", "flat faced", "full faced", "with a long or a thin visage", and "freckled". Eyes were of the usual shades from gray to blue to black. One runaway was said to be "hollow eyed", others with "dull countenance", "a full mouth", "thick lips", "rosy cheeks"and "large teeth". Their noses were said to be "flat", "large","humped" or "high". Some had moles on their faces, others scars and more than a few had "sour" or "downcast" looks. One woman had "three diamonds on her face, one on each side and the other on her forehead." Some were said to "squint, eyes wider apart than usual". Another had full eyes and another had a small cast in one eye. One was said to have a "lively eye" which perhaps meant a wandering eye.

    We saw that men wore their hair in a number of different styles, from shaved, to short, to long, to tied behind with colored ribbons , to under a wig. While one would think by today's standards, women would be at least as equally *chic,* the small sampling we have indicates the contrary. Their hair was unremarkable. It was light, dark, brown, black but rarely more detail was given. In fact, the only hair style found was "short black curled hair, much like a mulatto". Beards were not in vogue among women – except in one instance, with a woman in her late thirties, who had "a swarthy complexion with black hair and a black beard on her upper lip." Do not despair for her. She was reported "to have run off with Henry Ustick, nailer".

    Hair was not the only thing about runaway servant and slave women which would be a disappointment to today's male admirer. Certainly, in their body shapes, few resembled the super models of today. They were probably more like today's population, than different. A full 20 per cent were described as "well set", "thick", "stout", "fat", "strong" or "broad shouldered", while 5 per cent were called "thin","slender" or "slim". Some of the runaways were not described in very attractive terms. Witness the 26 year old Dutch woman who was said to be "thick and fat [with] a hobbling walk [who] stoops pretty much, has one [front] tooth out and great ringworms on her breast and arms." Another Dutch servant woman was described as "aged about 23 years; 5 feet high; short chunky body; one shoulder higher than the other and a large humped nose". A third one had "a little body with a hump back; high nosed and marked with the small pox."

Again, while not Hollywood perfect, a number of the runaways were said to be "lusty" (meaning healthy), "well made in proportion", "well looking" and "very likely to look upon."

Some of them sound as if they would make interesting dates. There was the mid sized thirty year old "with large breasts and [who] can sing well and dance the ropes [tight rope walker] with many other tricks". And what about the 22 year old "very likely, round favored woman, her cheeks very rosy, talkative and very fond of singing?" She did have some flaws, however minor in the final analysis: "a little flat nose and her eyes stand[ing] at a greater distance from one another than women's eyes commonly do; has a small scar under her right nostril, something resembling a cross and has lost two of her fore teeth."

As with the men runaways, women were not spared the scars of life, missing teeth, scalds and burns and "troubled with cholic" or marked for life with small pox. Indeed, a full 20 per cent of the population was "pockfretten". They were hunchbacked too, stoop shouldered or with "one shoulder higher than the other".

The wanted ads give us glimpses of the personalities and eccentricities of some of the women runaways: "smart", "handy", "active", "talkative" and "fond of singing". One had a "hardy bold look" and another "looks remarkably innocent". People were warned "not to believe" what one gal said "because she certainly will tell many lies". Another was said to be apt to be light fingered" and a third "smooth tongued and very artful". One girl not to bring home to meet mother, "had a cross on her right arm, put in with gun powder and the first two letters of her name and the date of the year". A shade over 6 per cent were described as "fond of liquor", less than the men folk but still substantial.

Some fled by themselves, some with men. Nearly ten per cent ran away with young children in tow. One had a four year old, named Jane, described as "well made, fat, round faced and lively". Another, a mulatto herself, left with her 6 year old son Bob, "who has amazingly fair complexion and flaxen hair."

Another had a "child of 14 months, which she calls Billy; with black eyes". One runaway abandoned "her 2 year old son with the Overseers of the Poor". Another left with a "brindle dog with her, known by the name of Bellanamony".

In our search through the runaway notices, we stumble upon a nearly three century old drama that remains both poignant and relevant today.

In May, 1735, the Sheriff and Undersheriff of Monmouth County put out "wanted" notices for two women who had escaped from the jail in Freehold, about 50 miles south west of New York City. One, whose name was Eleanor White, appeared especially attractive: "tall and slender, round faced, freckled with black hair and black eyes." She was awaiting execution, being " under sentence of death for the murder of her bastard child.". The other woman, Mary Bowman, English born, was a servant in the home of the Gaol Keeper. She was – or more likely had become - Eleanor's friend. While she was not as attractive: "thick, short and fat; pockfretten and of brown complexion", her inner beauty must have been stunning. She risked her life for Eleanor's. Her crime? "Assisting in the escape of Eleanor White from the Gaol of Monmouth".

How did Eleanor come to be jailed, convicted and sentenced? How did her friendship with Mary develop? What about their escape? Where did they go? Were they caught? What was their future? We shall never know.

PROFILES OF DESERTERS AND ESCAPED PRISONERS

The details about deserters and escapees – their physical characteristics, personalities, occupations and the like – are included with the fugitive servants above. However, there are few additional comments peculiar to their status as either deserters or prisoners.

The Colonies fought in three major wars during the 1700s. The first was from 1744 to 1748 -- King George's War -- when Great Britain and her American colonies fought France and her colonies. It was a repeat bout from 1756-1763. This one, however, The French and Indian War, also called the Seven Years War, was won by Britain and France was expelled from Canada. The victory gave the Crown control over much of North America. Ironically, it was prelude to a third war. Freed from fighting with France, Britain turned its attention to the American colonies, forcing them to shoulder some of the cost of defeating France. In hindsight, that was unfortunate for the Crown. Disciplining a people grown independent led to a third war, the American Revolution (1775 through 1783). Now it was Britain and her American colonies who were at war with each other.

The deserters in the first two wars were all from the British ranks, although they included many nationalities. A third were Irish. However, during the Revolution, the deserters were from the American army. That is not to say that many British soldiers did not desert. Many did, especially the Hessian mercenaries. However, the British, holed up in New York City and Philadelphia, had no one to whom to give notice. The Patriots in the Jersey countryside were not about to return deserters to their enemy. On the other hand, they would be quick to return deserters from their own American cause so American deserters were pursued.

There were nearly 225 deserters who were posted. They seemed to be older than the average age of runaways generally.

There were several 17 year olds, yet eight fold more 30 years and older. There was a 50 year old deserter. One suspects that things had to be really bad – or the grass so much greener on the other side --for a soldier to desert and risk the punishment for it, which was hanging.

We have a population of approximately 130 escaped prisoners. Their nationality was Irish; 32 per cent, followed by Americans at 12 per cent and about 20 per cent other western Europeans: The remainder were not identified.

The average age of the escaped prisoners, however, was even higher than among the deserters, even though, if they were apprehended, death was rarely the punishment. Perhaps, their advanced age illustrated the recidivism of criminal conduct. Thirty six of the escaped prisoners were under 30, but forty six were over 40 years, of which four were in their mid fifties. Several others were called "mid aged".

Twenty-two of them were said to be addicted to alcohol -- 17 per cent - which is double the rate among the general runaway population. Perhaps, it was these alcohol problems that led to the prisoners' criminal problems in the first instance.

The descriptions of the escaped prisoners give a glimpse of the penal system of the time. For example, many of the fugitives were shackled. Some had iron collars around their necks, were handcuffed or had horse locks on one of their legs. As whipping was a frequent punishment for transgressions, many wore the proof of past punishment: "whipped for theft which his back now shows sufficient proof of"; "is well acquainted with the whipping post in Philadelphia"; or "his back, if examined, will appear to have been lately under the discipline of the cat o' nine tails" Being caught stealing could result in as many as 30 lashes.

Branding was also a common punishment and could not be hidden. One fellow, who married the delightfully named Merica Bourn "being his third wife, if so she may be called, was branded in the hand for marrying the second."

Their crimes in Colonial America ran the gamut – from blasphemy to homicide with all sorts of offenses in between. Some were for wrongs no longer recognized. No longer are people jailed for debt or for not appearing in court on a civil matter. There are no more runaways to be jailed until claimed by their masters or owners. In a real sense, that was what the American Revolution was all about.

Others were not hardened criminals but were jailed merely for having a good time or proving a point: " a person of infamous character and a disturber of the peace in general" or "committed for a riot and a breach of the King's peace".

There were two types of crime –those against another's property and those against his person. Of the first type, horse theft – and sheep theft – were common examples. One fellow was reported "to be the greatest horse stealer and most accomplished villain that has been in the country". It was feared that another convicted of horse stealing "will join a gang on the frontiers". House burglary, counterfeiting, forgery and "stealing" in its various forms were also reported: "this fellow makes a practice of defrauding the continent by enlisting in several different companies"or "entrusted with goods to a considerable value [which] he sold and made off with the money". One man was "confined for embezzlement and high treason" and another, presumably disgruntled, "lately burnt his master's house".

There were also crimes of violence against people: assault and battery, infanticide, "abusing a servant and was found guilty of homicide by the coroner's inquisition for the same" and outright murder.

LISTING OF RUNAWAY MALE SERVANTS

EDWARD JONES, a servant man; runaway from BENJAMIN DAVIS of Indian town in Salem county, near Cohansie; aged about 35 years; of short stature, having a scar under one of his eyes, short hair, a sandy colored beard; advertised in *The American Weekly Mercury*, December 22, 1724

WILLIAM HIDE, an English born servant man; runaway from GEORGE RESCARRICK of Middlesex county; middle stature, with light colored hair, "which curls very much"; advertised in *The American Weekly Mercury*, February 16, 1725

JOHN MILLER, a servant man; runaway from GEORGE RESCARRICK of Middlesex county; small stature, hair cut off, black complexion; advertised in *The American Weekly Mercury*, February 16, 1725

THOMAS SCHOWTHRIP, an English servant man; runaway from GEORGE RESCARRICK of Middlesex county; described as of middle stature, thick well set, with very short red hair; a Yorkshire man who talks "broad"; a carpenter by trade; advertised in *The American Weekly Mercury*, February 16, 1725

ROBERT HARRIS, a servant man; runaway from JOSEPH GOULDING of Middletown, in Monmouth county; aged about 30 years; pretty tall and slender with a thin face and black eyes; he has five blue spots on his left hand; advertised in *The American Weekly Mercury*, June 26, 1725

PHILIP DAWSIT, a servant lad; runaway from SAMUEL SMITH of Burlington; thick well set fellow of black complexion and beard; advertised in *The American Weekly Mercury*, October 28, 1725

DANIEL REYNES, a servant lad; runaway from

ENNION WILLIAMS of Bristol in Bucks county, Pennsylvania; advertised in *The American Weekly Mercury*, October 28, 1725

JOHN LEWIS, a servant man; runaway from RICHARD WRIGHT of Burlington; aged about 25 years; middle stature, with short brown hair; can speak some Welch; notice to be directed to OWEN OWEN, Esq., High Sheriff of Philadelphia; advertised in *The American Weekly Mercury*, August 25, 1726

JOHN EDWARDS, a Welch servant man; runaway from RICHARD WRIGHT of Burlington; aged about 21 years; middle stature, short black hair; can speak good English; direct notice to OWEN OWEN, Esq., High Sheriff of Philadelphia; advertised in *The American Weekly Mercury*, August 25, 1726

JOHN PRITCHARD, a servant man; runaway from JOHN THROCKMORTON of Shrewsbury; about 24 years of age; short thick man, with "a round bluff face, dark skin, short black hair, very much curled"; he has some impediments in his speech; direct notice to NATHANIEL LEONARD, at Trent Town; advertised in *The American Weekly Mercury*, September 8, 1726

Unnamed Irish servant lad; runaway from THOMAS SPICER, of Glouster; about 18 years of age; "pretty shocky well set Irish lad; not tall; pock broken; lightish thin hair; large nose"; advertised in *The American Weekly Mercury*, November 17, 1726

Unnamed servant man; runaway from ISAAC PEARSON of Burlington; short, well set fellow and "purblind", about 30 years of age; "round visage, his hair cut off"; advertised in *The American Weekly Mercury*, March 30, 1727

THOMAS GRIFFE, a Welch servant man; runaway from ALEXANDER LOCKHART of Trenton, Hunterdon county; aged about 40 years; low stature; "black beard and hair with grey hairs mixed amongst his hair, but mostly grey hair on top of his head"; advertised in *The American Weekly Mercury*,

August 24, 1727

WILLIAM FERRY, a servant man; runaway from LAWRENCE SMYTH of Monmouth County; "a lusty, well set, round faced fellow; about 19 years of age; has short black hair"; advertised in *The American Weekly Mercury*, September 14, 1727

WILLIAM CONALLY, an Irish servant man; runaway from JOSEPH FORMAN of the Township of Freehold, County of Monmouth; "a weaver by trade; of middle stature; about 25 years of age; thin face, long nose, something pockfretten, dark brown hair, something curling; his eyes a little inclined before"; advertised in *The American Weekly Mercury*, April 4, 1728

JOHN HENRY, a servant man; runaway from JOSEPH BRITTAIN of the township of Crosswicks, lately belonging to ISAAC WATSON, near Trenton; "a lusty man, fresh complexion; 'I. H.' pricked with gunpowder on one of his hands, has three long scars on his head, supposed to be cut with a sword"; give notice JOSEPH PEACE in Bristol; advertised in *The American Weekly Mercury*, April 18, 1728

JOSHUA NICHOLS, an English servant man; runaway from ARCHIBALD CRAIGE of the township of Freehold, County of Monmouth; "is of middle stature, fair complexion, with his hair off; it is of a light color; says he was born in London; speaks very plain; a stocking weaver by trade"; advertised in *The American Weekly Mercury*, June 6, 1728

DARBY BRODRICK, an Irish servant man; runaway from SAMUEL WRIGHT of the township of New Hanover, Burlington County; "well set fellow, with short hair, somewhat curled, of a fresh complexion"; advertised in *The American Weekly Mercury*, June 27, 1728; also advertised in *The American Weekly*, February, 18, 1729

LAWRENCE CONOR, an Irish servant man; runaway from WILLIAM REED of the township of Great Egg Harbor;

"of short stature; aged about 26 years; of a homely complexion and down look; his hair cut off"; advertised in *The American Weekly Mercury*, July 18, 1728

WILLIAM MORFFEE, a servant man; runaway from WILLIAM HARRISON of the township of New Hanover, County of Burlington; "pretends to be a stay maker by trade; of a short stature; of a pale complexion; he goes a little limping on one side"; advertised in *The American Weekly Mercury*, August 1, 1728

MORGAN JONES, a Welch servant man; runaway from THOMAS BOELS of the Township of Freehold, County of Monmouth; "aged about 30 years; of middle stature, his hair cut off or shaved; he is but indifferent, fresh colored face; his nose something flat by a knock he got on it; lisps or stutters when he speaks in earnest, especially when he is in liquor, as he is very apt to be; on one of his feet, next to his great toe, he has two toes grown together; he has a cut on his chin by occasion of a fall on the edge of a board; has sort of a proud hambling gate; pretends to be a mighty plower, sower and ditcher; one JOHN JAMES is expected to be with him; give notice to ROBERT ELLIS or ANDREW BRADFORD of Philadelphia or WILLIAM BRADFORD of New York"; advertised in *The American Weekly Mercury*, September 19, 1728

JOHN HARRIS, a servant man; runaway from HUMPHREY DAY of Glouster County; "aged about 19 years; well set fellow; five feet and a half high; much pockfretten; a bluff face, short hair"; advertised in *The American Weekly Mercury*, February, 18, 1729

EDWARD GREEN, an Irish servant man; runaway from RICHARD KIRBY of the Township of New Hanover, County of Burlington; "of middle stature"; advertised in *The American Weekly Mercury*, February 18, 1729

THOMAS LOWRY, an Irish servant man; runaway from SAMUEL WARNE of the township of Middletown, County of

Monmouth; "a shoe maker by trade; of short stature, with black hair, dark complexion; aged 23 years"; advertised in *The American Weekly Mercury*, March 20, 1729

JAMES DAVIS, a servant man; runaway from THOMAS WILLSON and WILLIAM WILLSON, his son, of the Township of New Hanover, Burlington County; "of middle stature; about 30 years of age; a fresh color, with curled hair, of a light sandy color; somewhat pockfretten"; advertised in *The American Weekly Mercury*, April 10, 1729

NEAL McNEAL, an Irish servant man; runaway from JOHN MATLACK, farmer of Waterford Township, Glouster county; "aged about 20; of a pale complexion, very freckled"; advertised by BENJAMIN PASCAL in *The Pennsylvania Gazette*, March 22, 1729

JOHN FINLEY, a servant man; runaway from MARY STOCKDALE of Evesham, Burlington county; "aged about 20, a farmer; he has a brown swarthy complexion and thick legs; his hair lately cut off"; give notice to JOHN BREINTNAL in Chestnut Street; advertised in *The Pennsylvania Gazette*, April 5, 1729

JAMES ROBERTS, a West Countryman servant man; runaway from WILLIAM BRADFORD's paper mill at Elizabeth Town; "about twenty years of age; a middle sized, well set fellow with dark brown hair, somewhat curled; a round visage; gray eyes; about one year in this country; is a paper maker by trade"; ran away with JOHN HILL, "a strong, well set fellow who says he came from Boston and in a poor Habit"; give notice to WILLIAM BRADFORD in New York, or ANDREW BRADFORD in Philadelphia or to JOHN BARCLAY in Perth Amboy; advertised *The American Weekly Mercury*, July 3, 1729.

JOHN COPE, a servant man; runaway from EDWARD KEMBLE of the Township of Springfield, County of Burlington; "of a small stature, brown complexion and short black hair"; advertised in *The Pennsylvania Gazette*, June 7, 1729.

HENRY STACK, a servant man; runaway from BENJAMIN AETON of Salem; "short of stature and has scar on face; his hair, newly cutoff and of a tawny complexion"; advertised in *The American Weekly Mercury*, September 4, 1729

THOMAS BRYAN, a servant man; runaway from SIMON WARNER of Alloways Creek in the County of Salem; "a short, slender man with black hair"; direct notice to ANDREW BRADFORD of Philadelphia; advertised in *The American Weekly Mercury*, September 28, 1729.

JOHN SPARROW, a servant man; runaway from SIMON WARNER of Alloways Creek in the County of Salem; "being a little man with black hair, having a sore leg and hard of hearing;" give notice to ANDREW BRADFORD of Philadelphia; advertised in *The American Weekly Mercury*, September 28, 1729.

JAMES WILLSON, a servant man; runaway from the Widow EARLINGTON of Rocky Hill in East New Jersey; "of a middle stature, dark brown hair, fair complexion, blue eyes; a weaver by trade and has taken with him some weaver's tools"; advertised in *The American Weekly Mercury*, October 16, 1729.

THOMAS BROADLEY, an Irish servant man; runaway from the Widow EARLINGTON of Rocky Hill in East New Jersey; "has dark brown hair, of a fair complexion, a little taller than [companion in flight, James Willson] and speaks much upon the brogue"; advertised in *The American Weekly Mercury*, October 16, 1729

DAVID WILLINGS, an Irish servant man; runaway from JOSEPH BRITAIN of the Township of Nottingham, Burlington county; tall, lusty fellow, with short black hair and "two warts on his nose"; advertised in *The American Weekly Mercury*, June 11, 1730

CONSTANTINE MACKMANNERS, an Irish servant man; runaway from JOSEPH BRITAIN of the Township of Nottingham, Burlington county; short fellow; no hair; a tailor by trade; has a scar between his eyebrows; advertised in *The American Weekly Mercury*, June 11, 1730

EDWARD HOLLAND, a servant man; runaway from SAMUEL THRAGMORTON of Freehold in Monmouth county; of a middle stature; sandy straight hair; lived formerly with JOHN MALTSBURY at High Street Ferry; advertised in *The American Weekly Mercury*, April 16, 1730.

MICHAEL HAMBLETON, [aka JOHN HUES] a servant man; runaway from ROBERT CHAPMAN of Chesterfield in the county of Burlington; "a short, thick man, full faced and fresh colored; with short bushy hair, with some gray hairs; walks crimplin as thought he was lame of his feet or toes; pocked"; butcher by trade; advertised in *The American Weekly Mercury*, October 1, 1730; later advertised as having runaway from JOSEPH LEIGH of Perth Amboy, in *The New York Gazette*, March 22, 1731

JOHN SMITH, a servant man; runaway from PETER ROSE, a brewer, of Burlington; aged about 21 years; a weaver by trade, and "understands country work; pretty full faced; of middle stature and bushy hair and with a large scar down his fore head"; advertised in *The American Weekly Mercury*, October 1, 1730

THOMAS DEALE, an Irish servant man; runaway from PETER WREN of Woodbridge Town, Middlesex county; about 22 years of age; of small stature, hair cut off; has initials "T.D." on left hand with gunpowder; there is with him a likely little woman he calls his wife; advertised in *The American Weekly Mercury*, March 2, 1731

ALEXANDER MACLANE, an Irish servant man; runaway from JAMES ENGLISH of Freehold Town, Monmouth county; about 20 years of age; of short stature; well set; dark brown bushy hair; advertised by ISAAC STELLE in *The Pennsylvania Gazette*, April 29, 1731

GEORGE TOMPSON, an Irish servant man; runaway from JOHN GORDON of Freehold town, Monmouth county; about 21 years of age; of stature tall and slender; short lightish hair; pale complexion; by trade a shoemaker; he writes well and is much inclined to reading and smoking; he has lately runaway from Boston and has served his time there or in Rhode Island; advertised in *The American Weekly Mercury*, July 22, 1731

WILLIAM LAUGHLIN GWIN, a servant man; runaway from JOHN REDFORD of Shrewsbury in Monmouth county; aged about 24 years; of a middle stature; short black hair; black eyes; swarthy complexion; "he is used to any sort of husbandry work"; give notice to GABRIEL STILL, Esq. [GABRIELLE STELLE] in Amboy or to ANDREW BRADFORD; advertised in *The American Weekly Mercury*, August 19, 1731

DUKE TINTSON, a West Country servant man; runaway from ANDREW JOHNSTON, Merchant, of Perth Amboy; about 35 years of age; of low stature; pale, sandy complexion; speaks the West Country English; "seems sickly and dejected having had the ague and fever"; he arrived lately from Nevis, notice to ROBERT KING, Esq. Of Amboy; advertised in *The American Weekly Mercury*, August 26, 1731

WILLIAM WILLIS, a servant man; runaway from DANIEL BACON, of Chesterfield Town, Burlington County; about 24 years of age; of middle stature; thick and well set; black curled hair; swarthy brown complexion, advertised in *The Pennsylvania Gazette*, January 11, 1732; re advertised, as a runaway from JOHN BLACK, of Springfield Town, Burlington County; in *The American Weekly Mercury*, April 18, 1734

SAMUEL FREEMAN, a servant man; runaway from DANIEL BACON, of Chesterfield Town, Burlington County; about 23 years of age; of small stature and thin, with his hair off; pale complexion, advertised in *The Pennsylvania Gazette*,

January 11, 1732

GRIFFIE JONES, a Welch servant man; runaway from JOHN REED of Trenton; of slender middle stature; short black hair; speaks tolerable good English, notice to WILLIAM BRADFORD in New York; advertised in *The New York Gazette*, January 18, 1732

PHILIP WELCH, a servant man; runaway from JAMES WARD of Monington Township in Salem County; about 19 years of age; of small stature; lean visage; "neither hair nor roots of hair on his head except a small lock in the nape of his neck"; advertised in *The American Weekly Mercury,* March 7, 1732

JOHN GOWEN, goes by the name WILLIAM TAYLOR, a servant man; runaway from JAMES DUNCAN of Hackensack, Bergen County; well set, middle sized fellow with short brown curled hair, notice to ANDREW BRADFORD in Philadelphia; advertised in *The American Weekly Mercury,* April 27, 1732

WILLIAM DORRINGTON, a servant man; runaway from WILLIAM OVERTHROW, sawyer of Waterford Township, Glouster County; "about 25 years of age; a thick, short, well set fellow; lightish colored hair; pale complexion; he has a little blemish in his eye and is near sighted; advertised in *The American Weekly Mercury,* June 29, 1732;

STEPHEN PARSLOW, an English servant man; runaway from WILLIAM COX of New Brunswick; "about 21 years of age; of middle stature; black curled short hair; swarthy complexion; advertised in *The Pennsylvania Gazette,* July 10, 1732; re advertised by the same master in *The New York Gazette,* August 5, 1734 with the added description " wears a light natural wig, has down look, and his right hand is marked 'SP' with gunpowder, because of his earlier running away;

WILLIAM DENIM, a servant man; runaway from a plantation in Hopewell belonging to JOSEPH REED, of

Trenton; "lusty, well made; speaks good English and is a tailor by trade"; advertised in *The Pennsylvania Gazette*, July 10, 1732

JAMES DUNN, an Irish servant man; runaway from HENRY DOUGHTY of Town of Crosswicks, Monmouth County; about 30 - 40 years of age; "pretty well set; stoop shouldered; pockfretten; he is marked on one of his hands J.D."; advertised in *The American Weekly Mercury*, July 13, 1732

JAMES MACKBRIDE, a servant man; runaway from ELIACOM ANDERSON at Trent Town Ferry; about 21 years of age; of tall stature; has little or no beard; no hair; pockfretten; advertised in *The American Weekly Mercury*, August 31, 1732

JAMES CROSWEL, a servant man; runaway from JACOB JOHNSON, near Mount Holly; "about 30 years of age; tall of stature; light sandy hair with a long nose and a wild look"; by trade a shoemaker; last seen in Philadelphia; notice to WILLIAM PYWELL, Tanner in Philadelphia; advertised in *The Pennsylvania Gazette*, October 26, 1732

AARON MIDDLETON, a servant man; runaway from ISAAC PEARSON of Town of Burlington; about 26 years of age; of short stature; square shouldered; his hair cut off; advertised in *The American Weekly Mercury*, November 2, 1732

JAMES SMITH, a servant man; runaway from RICHARD HATNES of Salem Town, county; "about 24 years of age; tall of stature; well built; short red hair; fair complexion; his teeth decayed"; advertised in *The American Weekly Mercury*, December 2, 1732

JOHN MEDLEY, a servant man; runaway from RICHARD FLOYD of Glouster County; about 24 years of age; of short stature; well set; black hair and full faced; by trade a buckle maker; advertised in *The American Weekly Mercury*, May 17, 1733

WILLIAM WOOD, a servant boy; runaway from THOMAS POSTGATE, of Township of Manington, Salem County; about 18 years of age; short hair; "has lost some of his fore teeth and stammers much in his speech when he speaks hastily"; has a large mole in one of his eye brows; advertised in *The Pennsylvania Gazette*, July 19, 1733

WILLIAM HASSEY, a servant man; runaway from ABEL PRESTON, baker, of Cooper's Ferry; about 22 years of age; of short stature; black hair but cut off and wears a wig; advertised in *The American Weekly Mercury*, August 16, 1733

WILLIAM DORRINGTON, a servant man; runaway from JACOB MEDCALF, Esq. of Cooper's Ferry; about 30 years of age; of middle stature; lightish hair; advertised in *The American Weekly Mercury*, August 16, 1733

BENJAMIN GREENSTREET, a servant man; runaway from JACOB MEDCALF, Esq. of Cooper's Ferry; about 24 years of age; of short stature; thick; bushy sandy colored hair; fresh colored; advertised in *The American Weekly Mercury*, August 16, 1733

JOHN CLARK, an Irish servant man; runaway from BENJAMIN VINING, near Salem Town, Salem County; about 50 years of age; "grizzled hair and gray beard; lusty and stout; by trade a gardener and a good workman at that or any kind of country work; he is apt to drink and then has the brogue upon his tongue; he has about three years to serve"; advertised in *The American Weekly Mercury*, August 30, 1733

GEORGE SMITH, an Irish servant man; runaway from JACOBUS HEGEMAN of Somerset County; "about 18 years of age; of middle stature; he is not very thick but raw bone; he has no trade but understands farming very well"; advertised in *The American Weekly Mercury*, September 27, 1733

CHARLES CHRISTY, an Irish servant man; runaway from SAMUEL BOGGS of Mannington, Salem County; about

35 years of age; of short stature; short black hair; pale faced with a large nose"; advertised in *The American Weekly Mercury*, November 1, 1733

MICHAEL MC'DERMOT, a servant man; runaway from DANIEL QUIGLEY of Burlington; about 25 years of age; of short stature; black hair; dark complexion and down look; advertised in *The Pennsylvania Gazette*, March 21, 1734

THOMAS ROBARDS, a Welch servant man; runaway from WILLIAM ELLIS of Waterford Town, Glouster County; "about 22-23 years of age; pretty tall of stature; slim; full faced and fresh colored with short brown curled hair; his knees bending somewhat inward; speaks good English and Welch and some Irish"; advertised in *The American Weekly Mercury*, May 16, 1734

SIMON GUILMAN, a servant man; runaway from ROBERT LAWRENCE of Monmouth County; "about 40 years of age; of middle stature; sandy complexion; well set; has often been in Pennsylvania and the Lower Counties and had liberty from his master to work about the county for full wages to pay his debt"; advertised in *The American Weekly Mercury*, June 6, 1734

JOHN HAVERSACH, a Palatine servant man; runaway from FRANCIS SMITH of Evesham Town, Burlington County; "about 40 years of age; of middle stature; brown hair with whitish beard; ruddy complexion; has traveled with the armies by land in Spain, France, Germany, Italy, Turkey, England and Scotland and can speak their languages; speaks English indifferently well"; advertised in *The Pennsylvania Gazette*, June 13, 1734

DAVID JONES, a Welch servant man; runaway from JOHN MICKEL near Town of Glouster, Glouster County; of middle stature; fair complexion; round shouldered; advertised in *The Pennsylvania Gazette*, September 5, 1734

JOHN M'DOWEL, a servant man; runaway from JOHN FENTON of Freehold, Monmouth County; about 35 years of age; of low stature; is a tailor by trade; "lame in one leg; has a scar on his forehead"; wears a wig; notice to JOHN PAINTER, merchant in New York; advertised in *The New York Gazette*, October 7, 1734

LAWRENCE STAKEPOLE, an Irish servant man; runaway from ANN COOPER, widow, of Deptford Township in Glouster County; aged about 20 years; tall and thin; of a pale complexion and pitted with small pox; with short black hair; advertised in *The American Weekly Mercury*, October 17, 1734

JOHN PEARCE, a servant man; runaway from NATHAN BEAKES of Chester Township; in Burlington; small stature; aged about 25 years; advertised in *The American Weekly Mercury*, December 24, 1734

OWEN WARD, an Irish servant man; runaway from THOMAS USTICK of Second River in Newark; about 23 years of age; "a slender grown man; with a large scar on the left side of his face under his eye and the forefinger of one of his hands has lost its first joint; professes to be a husbandman and miner; had been taken up at Burlington but made his escape"; give notice to THOMAS DUNNING at the George Inn in Philadelphia; advertised in *The Pennsylvania Gazette,* June 19, 1735

MATTHEW BURROWS, an English servant man; runaway from JOSEPH YARD of Burlington County; short, thick, well set fellow with black hair and "talks very thick"; direct notice to JOHN APPLETON; advertised in *The American Weekly Mercury*, June 19, 1735, advertised again *The American Weekly Mercury* for March 16, 1736 which also referred to him as being of "middling stature, ruddy complexion".

WILLIAM FINN, an Irish servant man; runaway from PHILIP DOYL of Glouster town, Glouster county; middle stature; aged about 23 years; "dark swarthy complexion; speaks on the brogue; short brown dark hair and sometimes wears a piss-burnt wig; he goes crooked and groans very much in his sleep"; by profession a flax dresser; advertised in *The American Weekly Mercury*, July 17, 1735

EBENEZER EDEY, an American born servant man; runaway from THOMAS CROASDALE of Burlington; born in New England; a thin, spare man of a swarthy complexion; short brown hair; by trade a ship carpenter; advertised in *The Pennsylvania Gazette*, August 7, 1735

JOSEPH MORRIS, a servant man; runaway from SILAS CRISPIN of Burlington, aged about 22 years; of a middle stature; swarthy complexion; light grey eyes; his hair clipped off; marked with a large pit of the small pox on one cheek under the eye."

ABRAHAM HENDRICKS, an apprentice lad; runaway from JOHN ROSS of Elizabeth Town; about 19 years of age; of a small stature; took a set of shoemaker tools with him, being a shoemaker by trade; advertised in *The New York Gazette*, August 25, 1735

NELL BRINAN, an Irish servant man; runaway from JOHN BREACH of Glouster County; about 25 or 26 years of age; short of stature and well set; of a sandy complexion; short dark brown hair and is a very talkative fellow; advertised *The American Weekly Mercury*, November 20, 1735

WILLIAM BUSH, a servant man; runaway from JACOB LIPPINCOTT of Burlington; "about 18 or 19 years of age; short stature; well set; brownish hair curling a little; whitish complexion; smooth face; three of his finger nails shriveled up in a remarkable manner"; advertised in *The Pennsylvania Gazette*, April 1, 1736

THOMAS MACHON, a servant man; runaway from WILLIAM HARRISON of the township of New Hanover, county of Burlington; about 24 years of age; "middle stature;

black curled hair; red complexion; has been scalded on left leg; he is a weaver by trade and has been in the business of flax and is an indifferent hand at farming"; advertised in *The Pennsylvania Gazette*, June 17, 1736

ANIEL SULIVAN, a servant man; runaway from MAHLON STACY of the town of Mount Holly, county of Burlington; about 25 years of age; tall, spare man; hair lately cut off; ruddy complexion; black eyes; he took a scythe with him on the pretense of looking for work; advertised in *The Pennsylvania Gazette*, August 7, 1736

THADYMACK DONOYL, a servant man; runaway from WILLIAM SNOWDEN of Trenton; of middle stature; short hair; very much pitted with the small pox; advertised in *The New York Gazette*, November 15, 1736

HENRY MOODY, a servant man; runaway from EZEKIEL SMITH of the Town of Windsor, county of Middlesex; about 20 years of age; of middle stature; "short brown hair about an inch long; pretends to be a shoemaker by trade; is very confident in his talk"; advertised in *The New York Gazette*, November 15, 1736

CORNELIUS HANNIGAN, an Irish servant man; runaway from CORNELIUS JOHNSON of Amwell, Hunterdon County; about 35 years of age; "of short stature and a round visage"; advertised in *The American Weekly Mercury*, February 28, 1737

THOMAS DUNPHY, an Irish servant man; runaway from WILLIAM MONTGOMERIE of Burlington county; about 21 years of age; of middling stature; has short black hair; he can play on the flute; advertised in *The American Weekly Mercury*, January 13, 1737

CHRISTOPER SLADES, an English servant man; runaway from GEORGE EYRES of Burlington county; about 20 years of age; "short, slim man that has no beard and is freckled in the face; has been brought up in the plantation business in this country for eight years and pretends to be a brick maker"; advertised in *The American Weekly Mercury*, March 24, 1737

JOHN MACNEIL, an Irish servant man; runaway from HENRY WYNKOOP Salem County; about 21 years of age; of middling stature; smooth face and a fresh color; advertised in *The American Weekly Mercury*, April 7,1737

WILLIAM FORBUSH, a servant man; runaway from MICAJAH HOW of Burlington county; about 20 years of age, of middle stature, hair lately cut off, sandy complexion, by trade a shoemaker; advertised in *The Pennsylvania Gazette*, May 12, 1737

SAMUEL MACBON, a servant man; runaway from WILLIAM HARRISON of the Town of New Hanover, county of Burlington; about 24 years of age; of middling stature; "very black curled hair; red complexion; by trade a weaver, but understands plantation work; scald on one of his legs"; advertised in *The American Weekly Mercury*, July 28, 1737

WILLIAM CATON, an Irish servant man; runaway from THOMAS WOODWARD, of the town of Upper Freehold, county of Monmouth; of middling stature; dark short hair and black eyes; advertised in *The American Weekly Mercury*, July 28,1737

JOSEPH BALFORD, an Irish servant man; runaway from AMOS AUSTIN of the town of Evesham, county of Burlington; about 19 years of age; of short stature; red hair; a little freckled; advertised in *The Pennsylvania Gazette*, August 11, 1737

JOHN WILLIAMS, a West Country servant man; runaway from ISAAC PEARSON of Burlington county; about 37 years of age; very short; square set; by trade a clock maker;

speaks by clusters, hard to understand; advertised in *The Pennsylvania Gazette*, August 25,1737

JOSEPH KENT, a servant man; runaway from JOHN EMLEY of the town of Bethlehem, county of Hunterdon; about 20 years of age; much pitted with small pox; hair cut off; formerly belonged to CORNELIUS LOW, Merchant at Raritan Landing in Piscataqua[Piscattaway]; advertised in *The American Weekly Mercury*, August 25, 1737

EVAN JONES, a servant man; runaway from JOHN EMLEY of the Town of Bethlehem, county of Hunterdon; about 20 years of age; swarthy complexion; hair cut off; advertised in *The American Weekly Mercury*, August 25 ,1737

WILLIAM PATRICK, a West Country servant man; runaway from JOHN HENDERSON of the Town of Freehold, county of Monmouth; about 19 years of age; of middle stature; short hair; fair complexion; something marked with the small pox; second time he has run away; "came as a convict from Bristol, speaks after the West Country manner"; advertised in *The American Weekly Mercury*, September 15, 1737

WILLIAM DAVIES, an English servant man; runaway from BENJAMIN SMITH from Trenton; about 25 years of age; of short stature; well set; no hair; swarthy complexion; much pock broken; advertised in *The Pennsylvania Gazette*, September 29,1737

ARTHUR HOLLAND, an Irish servant man; runaway from RICHARD NOLAND of Trenton; about 30 years of age; tall and slender; no hair; fair complexion; has the brogue on his tongue; advertised in *The Pennsylvania Gazette*, September 29,1737

JAMES HAGEN, an Irish servant man; runaway from PETER ROSE of Burlington county; "about 35 years of age; tall and lusty; red complexion; is in company with a short young woman that has a hump back"; advertised in *The Pennsylvania*

Gazette, November 17, 1737

DAVID FINLY, an Irish servant man; runaway from JOHN SHANKLAND of Sussex County on the Delaware; of middling stature; short dark hair; with a scar on the right side of his upper lip, about an inch long; by trade a blacksmith; advertised in *The American Weekly Mercury*, November 24, 1737

ARCHIBALD KIER, a Scotch servant man; runaway from Mr. WARRELL at Trenton; about 24 years of age; of middle stature; slender but well limbed; brown hair but wears a wig; pitted with small pox; speaks pretty broad Scotch and writes a tolerable good hand; advertised in *The Pennsylvania Gazette*, December 1, 1737

HEZEKIAH KINNICUT, a servant man; runaway from THOMAS STEVENSON of Princetown; about 24 years of age; "smooth faced; of middle stature; fresh colored; his hair cut off and wears a brown wig; by trade a joiner"; advertised in *The Pennsylvania Gazette*, January 10, 1738

Went away from Salem county, a PETER CREELY, an Irishman, of a middle size; "black lank hair; does not speak plain and is a laborer"; advertised by JOHN KING of the Salem gaol, said John King being suspected of having made away with or murdered the said Peter Creely; advertised in *The Pennsylvania Gazette*, January 31, 1738

SAMUEL WOODSEN, an American born servant man; runaway from CHARLES OAKFORD of Alloways Creek in Salem County; aged about 20 years; born in or near Salem; middle stature; fresh complexion; "full cheeks and dark brown hair"; took a boat belonging to JOSEPH WARE; advertised in *The American Weekly Mercury*, April 13, 1738

WILLIAM TAYLOR, an American born servant man; runaway from CHARLES OAKFORD of Alloways Creek in Salem county; aged about 17 years; "tall, slender lad; light colored; short, straight hair; pale complexion"; took a boat belonging to JOSEPH WARE; advertised in *The American Weekly Mercury*, April 13, 1738

JAMES YATES, an English servant man; runaway from CORNELIUS VAN HORNE and others in Upper Freehold, Monmouth County; "short, round shouldered fellow, stoops forward as he walks; of a dark complexion and pox broken; speaks short and quick; by trade a schoolmaster; pretends to be a great scholar and to have met with his great losses in his travels and trading"; advertised in *The American Weekly Mercury*, April 20, 1738

JOHN DOYLING, an Irish servant man; runaway from WILLIAM TATEHAM of Woodberry Creek, Glouster County; aged about 17 or 18 years; "middle stature; short bushy hair; pock broken; two of his fingers lately cut"; advertised in *The Pennsylvania Gazette*, February 28, 1738

Unnamed English servant man; runaway from MOSES WARD of Woodberry Creek, Glouster county; of middle stature; very much pox marked; light colored bushy hair; advertised in *The Pennsylvania Gazette*, February 28, 1738

JAMES MORDOX, an Irish servant man; runaway from HENRY SPARKS of Glouster Township; aged about 60 years; grey hair but cut off; well set; dark complexion; by profession a smith; advertised in *The American Weekly Mercury*, June 29, 1738

CORNELIUS DELANEY, servant man; runaway from DAVID BRAY of Freehold, Monmouth county; "middle stature; full faced; fresh colored; long black curled hair; much given to drink"; advertised in *The American Weekly Mercury*, July 13, 1738

ABRAHAM BILLIN, an English servant man; runaway from ABRAHAM PERKINS of Wellingborough in Burlington County; aged about 27 years; middle stature; "dark hair; well set; brown complexion; hazel eyes; long nose and thin face"; advertised in *The American Weekly Mercury,* July 20, 1738

WILLIAM DOWELL, a servant man; runaway from SAMUEL HOLMES of Middletown, Monmouth County; "aged about 23 years; short, thick man; short hair; full faced; limps a little when he walks as if one leg was shorter than the other"; advertised in *The New York Gazette,* July 31, 1738

ROGER MURREY, a servant man; runaway from PATRICK REYNOLDS of Edge Pillick, Burlington county; aged about 28 years; middle stature; "dark brown hair but lately cut off; well set; fair complexion; branded with the letter "R" on the palm of his left hand"; advertised in *The Pennsylvania Gazette,* August 3, 1738

CORNELIUS KELLY, a servant man; runaway from Mount Holly iron works; aged about 21 years; "tall and slim; thin faced; short brown hair; a blemish in one eye"; advertised by MAHLON STACY in *The Pennsylvania Gazette,* August 17, 1738

JOHN CROOK, a servant man; runaway from JOHN HOLCOMBE of Amwell, Hunterdon County; middle stature; thin faced, much freckled; short reddish hair; turns in his feet much as he walks and his knees incline to strike together; talks West Country; advertised in *The American Weekly Mercury,* August 17, 1738

WILLIAM SUNDERLAND, an English servant man; runaway from JOHN BUNTING of Chesterfield in Burlington County; aged about 20 years; middle stature; born in London; brown hair lately cut off; fresh complexion; round shouldered holding his head forward; advertised in *The Pennsylvania Gazette,* August 31, 1738

THOMAS POWELL, a servant man; runaway from ALEXANDER MORGAN of Waterford township in Glouster county; "tall and slender stature; dark complexion and dark curled hair"; advertised in *The Pennsylvania Gazette* October 12, 1738

HENRY WATKINS, a servant man; runaway from ALEXANDER MORGAN of Waterford Township in Glouster County; short stature; advertised in *The Pennsylvania Gazette* October 12, 1738

HENRY WINGATE, a servant man; runaway from WILLIAM DRAPER of Sussex County; aged about 22 years; tall stature; "remarkable scar on left ankle"; advertised in *The American Weekly Mercury*, November 16, 1738

JOHN BOWLS, a servant man; runaway from JOSEPH DECOW of Trenton, Hunterdon County; middle stature; "black complexion; black eyes; by trade a shoemaker"; advertised in *The Pennsylvania Gazette*, December 14, 1738

STEPHEN PARSTOW, an English servant man; runaway from WILLIAM COX of New Brunswick; aged about 22 years, "short, black curled hair; swarthy complexion; down look; wears a light natural wig; has the letters "S.P." marked on his right hand with gunpowder; by trade a blacksmith"; advertised in *The American Weekly Mercury*, March 1, 1739

ISAAC TAILER, an English servant man; runaway from JOHN BURR of Burlington County; "lusty, young red headed, red faced fellow, with a crooked finger on his left hand; small white specks in his upper fore teeth; his right shin very sore; speaks West Country; was imported two years ago to Virginia and was sold to RICHARD MANWARRING"; advertised in *The Pennsylvania Gazette*, March 1, 1739

SAMUEL GUIN, an Irish servant man; runaway from JOHN EMLEY of Bethlehem, Hunterdon County; middle stature; "brown hair cut off; a bold flat face; speaks good English; by trade a weaver"; advertised in *The American Weekly Mercury*, May 17, 1739

JACOB LASANT, a Dutch Palatine servant man; runaway from HARMON RICHMAN of Piles Grove, Salem County; aged about 20 years, middle stature, "black straight hair, swarthy complexion, speaks very good French, by trade a butcher, well set"; advertised in *The American Weekly Mercury*, May 31, 1739

EDWARD CURRY, an Irish servant man; runaway from ABRAHAM BRYAN of Burlington County; aged about 26 years; "short stature; thin visaged; brown complexion; has the brogue upon his tongue"; belonged to JOHN MACKINTOSH; advertised in *The Pennsylvania Gazette,* June 7, 1739

JOHN DOLIN, an Irish servant man; runaway from WILLIAM TETEHAM, of Glouster County; aged about 18 years; short and well set; round faced; fresh colored; black curled hair; has the brogue on his tongue; went off with DENNIS M'GLAUGH, also a runaway, in a wherry stolen from JOHN LADD, Jr.; advertised in *The Pennsylvania Gazette,* June 7, 1739

JOHN WOOD, a West Country servant man;, runaway from FRANCIS SMITH of Burlington; aged about 40; "has been in this country about 10 or 12 years and had been in London before that; says he came in free but, falling into bad company, was brought into trouble and became a servant"; middle stature; fresh colored with black curled hair; "has a hurt on the middle finger of his right hand, the end of which is broad and lumpy"; advertised in *The Pennsylvania Gazette*, July 19, 1739

BRYAN MCDONNEL, an Irish servant man; runaway from ROBERT CARR of Hopewell; about 20 years of age; middle stature; "brown complexion; black curled hair; pock broken; lisps when he speaks"; advertised in *The Pennsylvania Gazette*, August 2, 1739

JAMES GRANT, an Irish servant man; runaway from JOHN COWARD of Upper Freehold in Monmouth county;

aged about 21 years; advertised in *The Pennsylvania Gazette*, August 14, 1740.

JOHN CUFFEY, an English servant man; runaway from MICHAEL BRANIN of Evesham Township, Burlington County; aged about 30-40 years; "short stature; dark complexion; his hair cut off with shears; a scar upon one of his cheeks and his legs bowed forward"; advertised in *The Pennsylvania Gazette*, August 21, 1740.

EDWARD TOWNSHEND, an English servant man; runaway from WILLIAM and SAMUEL PANCOOST of Mansfield Township in Burlington Township; aged about 30 years; "lusty big boned fellow; stooping forward in his shoulders; brown complexion and brown hair, cut very short; talks broad West Country and has been in this country but about 8 weeks"; advertised in *The Pennsylvania Gazette*, September 11, 1740.

JOHN LEONARD, an English Servant Boy; runaway from WILLIAM and SAMUEL PANCOOST of Mansfield Township in Burlington Township; aged about 18 years; "short of stature; fair complexioned; no hair; by trade a weaver; talks broad West Country and has been in this country but about 8 weeks"; advertised in *The Pennsylvania Gazette*, September 11, 1740.

JOSEPH MATHAS, an American born (in East New Jersey) indentured servant; runaway from JOSEPH KELLEY of Upper Freeehold, Monmouth County; "about 24 years of age; of a middle stature; has some scars under his right jaw; is a weaver by trade"; advertised in *The Pennsylvania Gazette*, March 6, 1740.

MATTHEW M'DANIEL, an Irish servant; runaway from MARGARET JACKSON of Burlington; "aged about 21 years; of a middle stature; well set; dark complexioned and short black hair"; had served before in Arundel County, Maryland; advertised in *The Pennsylvania Gazette*, March 6, 1740

WILLIAM JONES, a Welch servant man; runaway from SAMUEL DOVE, from Freehold, Monmouth County; "of middle stature; dark brown hair, pretty straight; well set fellow"; advertised in *The New York Gazette*, March 19, 1740

JOHN ABBERNATHY, a servant man; runaway from JAMES JOHNSTON of Allenstown, Monmouth County; "entrusted with goods to a considerable value [which] he sold and made off with the money; about 20 years of age; low of stature; full faced; black hair; has lost some of his fore teeth and lisps when he talks"; advertised in *The Pennsylvania Gazette*, April2 1741

ANDREW DAILY, an Irish servant man; runaway from JOSHUA BRICK of Salem County; "tall lusty fellow; of red complexion; red beard; curled sandy hair"; advertised in *The Pennsylvania Gazette*, May 14, 1741

WILLIAM HAINS, a young servant man; runaway from MARTEN RYERSON of Readingtown, Hunterdon County; "small stature; ruddy complexion; big nose; big blue eyes; pock broken; had no hair; branded on the brawn of his thumb of the left hand; has already passed by the name Robinson or Thomson; advertised in *The New York Weekly Journal*, June 15, 1741

ALEXANDER SCROGGS, a Scotch servant man; runaway from WILLLIAM MONTGOMERIE of Hunterdon County; "of middle stature and well set; red hair but cut off and wears a cap"; advertised in *The American Weekly Mercury*, October 1, 1741

JAMES REILLY, an Irish servant man; runaway from WILLIAM SELTHRIDGE of Cedar Creek in Sussex county; "aged about 30 years; a weaver; pretty lusty fellow; somewhat long visaged; a mole on one of his cheeks; some freckles on his face and hands; straight bodied; dark hair, but lately cut, and wears a cap; sore legs; can sing well; he can play on the violin; can read and write tolerably well; stolen his indenture, sworn to before Magistrates KOLLOCK and HOLT of Lewestown"; advertised in *The Pennsylvania Gazette*, October 8, 1741

PATRICK M'CLANE [aka PATRICK M'CLONE], an Irish servant man; runaway from WILLIAM SELTHRIDGE of Cedar Creek in Sussex County; "a well set fellow;, stole JOHN WALTON'S canoe; advertised in *The Pennsylvania Gazette*, October 8, 1741

WILLIAM PAYTON, an English servant man; runaway from THOMAS LIPPINCOT, near Pensawkin Creek in Burlington County; "aged about 23 years; of short stature and pretty well set; of a fresh complexion and short brown hair; advertised in *The American Weekly Mercury*, November 12, 1741

THOMAS SMITH, a servant man; runaway from JOSEPH DECOW of Trenton, at the Falls of Delaware; "of middle stature; fresh complexion; goes somewhat stooping; by trade a currier and tanner; short flaxen hair"; advertised in *The Pennsylvania Gazette*, December 17, 1741

JAMES MARTIN, an Irish servant man; runaway from FOLKART DERICKSON, of Reding Township in Hunterdon; "he was lately taken up and made his second escape, from Frankford and calls himself PATRICK BRUPSTES; he is about 22 years of age, of middle stature and pretty well set; of a sandy complexion; very talkative and nimble; he went away with handcuffs on; pretends to be a weaver and some other trades, but understands none of them"; advertised in *The American Weekly Mercury*, January 28, 1742

GEORGE GARDINER, a servant man; runaway from ABRAHAM MERRIOTT of Springfield Township, Burlington County; "aged about 40; of middle stature"; advertised in *The Pennsylvania Gazette*, March 10, 1742.

JOHN CORTNEY, an English servant man; runaway from JEORY TILLDINE of Trenton, Hunterdon County; "about

28 years of age; well built; of a middle size; by trade a shoemaker and tanner; a middling good workman; has also absconded himself from his bail in a civil action and has been a great traveler on the continent"; advertised in *The Pennsylvania Gazette,* April 8, 1742

WILLIAM WAHUP, an Irish man; alleged to have stolen horse from HUGH BLACKWOOD, a fuller, and JOHN BLACKWOOD from Cohansie of Salem County; "a fellow of middle stature; of a sandy complexion; very much marked with small pox; left a horse in place of the stolen one"; advertised in *The Pennsylvania Gazette,* June 16, 1742

JOHN MAHANY, an Irish servant man; runaway from DANIEL WILLS of Northhampton, in Burlington County; aged about 22 years; "of middle stature; black curled hair; much pox broken and has lost the sight blind in one eye"; advertised in *The American Weekly Mercury,* July 1, 1742

RICHARD WHITE, an Irish servant man; runaway from JOHN SCOTT and JACOB FORD of Hanover Town, Morris County; about 30 years of age; "of short stature; brownish complexion; he is a ditcher; carries his spades with him and worked lately in the Great Meadows of Mr. GEORGE GREEN; is very impertinent in his talk"; travels with MICHAEL COLLINS, "are furnished with plenty of money and drink to excess; they carry a sword with them and are Roman Catholics"; notice may be given to MANUEL CREEL at Well's Ferry or to JAMES JOHNSON at Trenton; advertised in *The Pennsylvania Gazette,* July 8, 1742.

MICHAEL COLLINGS, an Irish servant man; runaway from JOHN SCOTT and JACOB FORD of Hanover Town, Morris County; about 24 years of age; "of middle stature and well set; has the brogue on his tongue; much pock-broken; a weaver by trade"; travels with RICHARD WHITE, "are furnished with plenty of money and drink to excess; they carry a sword with them and are Roman Catholics"; notice may be given to MANUEL CREEL at Well's Ferry or to JAMES

JOHNSON at Trenton; advertised in *The Pennsylvania Gazette*, July 8, 1742.

THOMAS MORAN, an Irish Servant man; runaway from RICHARD PORTER and ARCHIBALD MORRISON, both of Readings Town, Hunterdon County; about 30 years of age; 5 foot 10 inches high; "a likely fellow, fresh complexion, black eyebrows; cock nosed; square shouldered; thick legged and one leg thicker than the other; speaks but very indifferent English"; advertised in *The American Weekly Mercury,* July 29, 1742

WILLIAM KEASEY, an Irish Servant man; runaway from RICHARD PORTER and ARCHIBALD MORRISON, both of Readings Town, Hunterdon County; about 30 years of age; 5 foot high or thereabouts; "a middling well set fellow, short visaged, black hair, fresh colored in the face; speaks pretty good English"; advertised in *The American Weekly Mercury,* July 29, 1742

JOHN MARSHALL, an English servant man; runaway from ISAAC FORMAN of Crosswicks; "a lusty, well set fellow and has ring worm on his face"; advertised in *The Pennsylvania Gazette*, July 29, 1742.

WILLIAM WRIGHT, a servant man; runaway from OBADIAH HIRETON of Springfield Township, County of Burlington; about 24 years of age; "of middle stature, his hair lately cut off, but not shaven"; advertised in *The Pennsylvania Gazette*, July 29, 1742.

RICHARD DOUD, an Irish servant man; runaway from SAMUEL BLAIR of Bethlehem Township, Hunterdon County; aged about 20 years; five foot high; "of a sandy complexion with short sandy hair, well set, a little marked with the small pox and pretty full faced; believed he has an indenture belonging to one JOHN BATH, who served his time in Lancaster County and it is believed he will use his name"; advertised in *The Pennsylvania Gazette*, September 16, 1742.

JOHN TOOL, an Irish Servant man; runaway from GEORGE MUNROW of Evesham Township, Burlington County; "a short well set fellow with short dark brown hair and gray eyes"; advertised in *The American Weekly Mercury, October 14, 1742*

JOHN GREEN, an Irish Servant man; runaway from JOHN GILL and SAMUEL BOGGS of Hattonfield in Glouster County; about 25 years of age; of middle stature; sandy complexion; brown bushy hair; thin visaged; man is a weaver; "will suppose that he and KATHERINE M'KEW will attempt to pass for man and wife, which they are not"; advertised in *The Pennsylvania Gazette*, September 16, 1742.

EPHRAIM COLAM, an American born (on Long Island, New York) servant man; runaway from RICHARD CHEW, of Timber Creek in West Jersey; about 35 years of age; "tall and slim; no hair; stoops a little and is troubled with a phthisick"; advertised in *The Pennsylvania Gazette*, December 2, 1742.

WILLIAM SIMSON, a servant man; runaway from ARCHIBALD HOME of Trenton; aged about 30; "of a low stature and nimble gait; has a fresh complexion and is a little pitted with the small pox"; advertised in *The Pennsylvania Gazette*, January 6, 1743.

PATRICK KELLY, an Irish indentured servant; runaway from DAVID WHEELER of Hanover Town, Morris County; "has the brogue on his tongue; middle stature; dark complexioned; black hair; thick beard; and wore a wig; about 26 years of age"; notice to BENJAMIN FRANKLIN, Postmaster, Philadelphia or MANUEL CRELL at Well's Ferry or to JAMES JOHNSON of Trenton; advertised in *The Pennsylvania Gazette*, March 24, 1743

JOHN GREEN, an Irish servant man; runaway from GEORGE WARD Jr. from Deptford Township in Glouster county; "about 23 years old and stammers much in his speech"; advertised in *The Pennsylvania Gazette*, May 26, 1743

THOMAS REDMON, an Irish servant man; runaway from JOHN EDWARDS of Salem; "a little of the brogue upon his tongue; about 25 years of age; of middle stature; round shouldered; somewhat marked with the small pox; dark complexioned; short black hair"; advertised in *The Pennsylvania Gazette*, May 26, 1743

EDWARD BANBURY, a servant man; runaway from STEPHEN or EVAN BURROWS of Amwell Township, Hunterdon County; "about 40 years of age; a stout, portly man; of black complexion; smooth tongued; blacksmith by trade"; advertised in *The Pennsylvania Gazette*, June 16, 1743.

WILLIAM COOPER, an English servant man; runaway from STEPHEN or EVAN BURROWS of Amwell Township, Hunterdon County; "of low stature; well set; fresh complexion and is a collier; had one of his thighs broke and there is a lump on the bone"; advertised in *The Pennsylvania Gazette*, June 16, 1743.

THOMAS BURROUGHTS, an Irish servant man; runaway from ELIHU LONG of Penns Neck in Salem County; "of small stature, down look, with a broad face, much pock broken"; advertised in *The Pennsylvania Journal*, June 16, 1743

EDWARD REDIKEN, an Irish servant man; runaway from THOMAS MERSHON of Maidenhead, Hunterdon County; "about 22 years of age; of middle stature; a weaver by trade; somewhat pale faced; supposed that one GEORGE DUCKWORTH is in company with him"; advertised in *The Pennsylvania Gazette*, September 8, 1743

JOHN ROACH, an Irish servant man; runaway from the Iron Works near Bordenstown; "about 20 years of age; was used to the sadler's trade; give notice to JOSEPH PEACE or ANDREW READ at Trenton or FRANCES BOWES at Christina Bridge; advertised in *The Pennsylvania Gazette*, September 8, 1743

DANIEL NORRIS, servant man; runaway from the Iron Works near Burdenstown; "tall lusty well set fellow; very hard favored and thick legs"; give notice to JOSEPH PEACE or ANDREW READ at Trenton or FRANCES BOWES at Christina Bridge; advertised in *The Pennsylvania Gazette*, September 8, 1743

JOHN HACKET, American born servant man; runaway from BENJAMIN THOMSON of Cohansie; "short and thick and aged about 28 years; took with him guns and dog by name of Gunner and, when they are traveling, paces"; advertised in *The Pennsylvania Gazette*, September 8, 1743

RICHARD LANE, American born servant man; runaway from BENJAMIN THOMSON of Cohansie; "of middle stature; brown hair and about 28 years of age; took with him guns and dog by name of Gunner and when they are traveling, paces"; advertised in *The Pennsylvania Gazette*, September 8, 1743;

RICHARD POORE, an Irish servant man; runaway from JOHN BLACKWOOD, Fuller, of Glouster County, upon Timber Creek; "low stature; well set; of a fractious countenance"; advertised in *The Pennsylvania Gazette*, September 15, 1743

JOHN MARSHAL, an English servant man; runaway from ISAAC FORMAN of New Hanover in Burlington County; "tall of stature and portly; warts on hands; brown hair; yellowish on the ends; lately cut his left arm, near the elbow, with a scythe and it is hardly well"; advertised in *The Pennsylvania Gazette*, September 15, 1743

DANIEL BRIEN, an Irish servant lad; runaway from FRANCIS COSTIGIN of New Brunswick; "about 18 years of age; middle sized and well set; face very much freckled; short brown hair and wears a cap; lost one of his ears by the bite of a horse"; advertised in *The Pennsylvania Gazette*, September 29, 1743

THOMAS KING, a Welch servant man; runaway from RICHARD SINGLETON, Cordwainer, of Burlington; "aged about 24 years; short and well set; full faced and full complexioned; black hair; shoemaker by trade"; advertised in *The Pennsylvania Journal*, October 6, 1743

Unnamed servant lad, runaway from ZACHARIAH ROBBINGS of Upper Freehold, Monmouth County; "about 17 years of age; by trade a shoemaker; lame in his left leg and mostly puts his hand on his thigh when he walks"; has a pass signed RICHARD STEVENS; advertised in *The Pennsylvania Gazette*, October 27, 1743

JAMES FITZGERALD, an Irish servant man; runaway from JOHN CROSS of Baskenridge of Somerset County; "of a low stature; well set; but has but one eye; much marked with the small pox; short hair having cut it off last spring; appears to be half witted, but is a sharp fellow; good scholar and can write and cypher very well"; advertised in *The Pennsylvania Gazette*, December 6, 1743

HENRY ROCK, a servant man; runaway from JOHN HENDERSON of Freehold, Monmouth County; "a lusty tall man; a weaver by trade; full faced, somewhat marked by small pox; slow of speech but a great boaster of what he can do either at his trade or at farming work"; advertised in *The Pennsylvania Gazette*, December 15, 1743

MAURICE WHEELER, an Irish servant man; runaway from PAUL KOUL, of the Township of Amwell in Hunterdon County; about 21 years of age; "he is a short, thick man; sandy colored hair; with very short thick legs, such as the native Irish servants usually have; he is marked ion the right hand with five spots of gunpowder, like a star; marked with the small pox in his face; speaks Irish very well;" used to be a fisherman; advertised in *The Pennsylvania Gazette*, January 19, 1744

PHILIP CANADA, a Irish servant man; runaway from WILLIAM COX of New Brunswick; "aged about 25 years; a lusty well set fellow; a little pock fretten; full face; his head newly shaved and speaks good English and Irish; advertised in *The New York Weekly Post Boy*, June 25, 1744

Unnamed Welch servant man; runaway from JOHN COX of Upper Freehold, Monmouth County; "short stature and well set; short black hair; potter by trade; speaks good English; walks with his knees much bending inwards"; advertised in *The Pennsylvania Gazette*, April 5, 1744.

VALENTINE NEAL; Irish servant lad; runaway from WILLIAM BULLOCK of New Hanover Township, Burlington County; "fair complexion with brown hair; his thumb on his left hand has been cut off by the root of the nail"; advertised in *The American Weekly Mercury,* May 17, 1744. He was advertised again, in *The Pennsylvania Gazette* of June 27,1745, as having runaway from JACOB WARRICK of Upper Freehold, Monmouth County.

JAMES DOWNEY, Servant Man; runaway from ZEBULON COOK of Upper Freehold, Monmouth County; 35 years of age; middle stature; "round shouldered and stoops a little; black curled hair and black eyes; part of one blacker than the other; can neither read nor write; has the brogue"; advertised in *The Pennsylvania Gazette,* May 17, 1744.

JOHN HAMILTON, an Irish servant boy; runaway from JOSEPH KAIGHIN of Glouster County; 15 years of age; short black hair; swarthy complexion; advertised in *The Pennsylvania Gazette,* May 17, 1744.

MICHAEL DOWDLE, an Irish servant man; runaway from JOHN SCHOLEY of New Hanover, Burlington County; 20 years of age; "short, thick well set fellow; fresh complexion; pretty much pockfretten; has had his hair cut off; formerly belonged to WILLIAM COOK"; advertised in *The Pennsylvania Gazette,* May 31, 1744.

MICHAEL WELCH, an Irish servant lad; runaway from

CHRISTOPHER BEEKMAN of New Brunswick; "lusty, full face, thick nose; aged about 19; his hair lately cut off; and speaks pretty good English and Irish"; advertised in *The New York Weekly Post Boy*, June 25, 1744

HENRY CARTY, an Irish Servant Man; runaway from BENJAMIN FIELD of Chesterfield, Burlington County; about 19 years of age; of middle stature; "thin visage and slim body; straight yellowish hair; had no shoes nor stockings"; advertised in *The Pennsylvania Gazette*, July 5, 1744

JOHN MILL, an Irish servant man; runaway from JOB SHEPPARD of Cohansie in Salem County; about 21 years of age; "wears his own hair, brown colored"; advertised in *The Pennsylvania Gazette*, July 5, 1744.

ANDREW GOODSON, an English servant man; runaway from TIMOTHY MATLOCK of Hadonsfield, Glouster County; "looks pale, having had the Fever and Ague"; advertised in *The Pennsylvania Journal*, July 11, 1744

THOMAS GORDON, a servant man; runaway from SAMUEL COX of South River; aged about 26 years; "of a middle stature; fresh color; pretty much pock-fritten; much given to drink and is very quarrelsome when in liquor"; advertised in *The New York Weekly Post Boy*, July 25, 1744

MORRIS AHIERN; an Irish servant man; runaway from JOHN ROLSE of Salem; "tall, well set man; fair complexion; thick legs and wore his own hair"; advertised in *The Pennsylvania Gazette*, November 1, 1744

JOHN BURNS, an Irish servant man; runaway from JAMES WELSH of New Brunswick; aged about 16 years; "of a middle stature; dark complexion and pretty much pock-fretten"; peddler; advertised in *The New York Weekly Post Boy*, December 17, 1744

DANIEL MOORE; a servant man; "likely proper man of

a fresh complexion and black hair who pretends to be a pedlar"; advertised in *The New York Weekly Post Boy,* December 17, 1744

JEREMIAH HINDS, an Irish servant man; runaway from JAMES ANDERSON of Lebanon in Hunterdon County; aged about 22 years; about 5 foot, 8 inches high; "thin bodied, well made; has black curled hair about 3 inches long; has a scar on his right cheek occasioned by a hurt"; advertised in *The New York Weekly Post* Boy, December 31, 1744

DENNIS ----, an Irish Servant Man; runaway from EBENEZER BROWN of Glouster; aged about 25 years; pale complexion; middle stature; advertised in *The Pennsylvania Gazette,* January 1, 1745

JOHN PARRA; about 24 years of age; well set fellow and pretends to know something of the hatter's trade; advertised in *The Pennsylvania Gazette,* April 4, 1745.

JOHN KING, an English Servant Man; runaway from PETER COCRAN of New Brunswick; aged about 23 years; of a middle stature; "he halts as he walks, seemingly rocking, and is what is called splaw-footed"; advertised in *The New York Weekly Post* Boy, May 27, 1745.

JAMES FITZ RANDEL, an apprentice lad; runaway from WILLIAM FOORD of Woodbridge, shoemaker; about 20 years of age; "light complexioned; his hair cut off and well set"; *The New York Weekly Post* Boy, June 17, 1745.

TIMOTHY MALONEY, an Irish servant man; runaway from FRETWELL WRIGHT of Burlington; about 20 years of age; "short and well set with short black hair"; advertised in *The Pennsylvania Gazette,* August 1, 1745.

RICHARD HOLLAND, an English servant; runaway from Zachariah Robins of Upper Freehold in Monmouth County; about 20 years of age and is a shoemaker; "he is exceedingly lame in his left knee and cannot walk without keeping his hand on it"; advertised in *The Pennsylvania Gazette*, August 8, 1745.

HAMBLETON CASTEN, an Irish servant man; runaway from THOMAS FORSTER of Springfield of Burlington County; "aged about 25 years; of middle stature and pretty well set; of a fresh complexion, with yellowish short hair and strait; had been but two days out of prison in Philadelphia from an escape he made three months ago from his master"; advertised in *The Pennsylvania Journal*, September 19, 1745

JOHN SWAN, a servant man; runaway from JOSEPH FORMAN of Freehold in Monmouth County; "of short stature; good features; appears a weildly young man; prodigal in his walk and much so in his speech; speaks English and can talk Dutch; much addicted to drinking"; advertised in *The Pennsylvania Gazette*, September 26, 1745

DANIEL NEALL, an Irish servant man; runaway from DANIEL ONELL of Timber Creek, Glouster County; "aged about 28 years; well set; pock pitted; long visage and has a scar on his forehead"; advertised in *The Pennsylvania Gazette*, March 15, 1746

WILLIAM MACKINNEY, an American born servant man; runaway from DANIEL ONELL of Timber Creek, Glouster County; middle stature; "black curled hair; long visage"; advertised in *The Pennsylvania Gazette*, March 15, 1746

BRYAN CONNER, a servant man; runaway from WILLIAM OAKFORD of Alloways Creek; "aged about 35 years; 6 feet high; lame in his right arm having been shot in the elbow; talks English, Irish and French"; advertised in *The Pennsylvania Gazette*, July 31, 1746

FRANCIS ATTERBURY, an English servant man; runaway from THOMAS SHEPPERD of Cohansey; aged about

27 years; middle stature; advertised in *The Pennsylvania Gazette*, August 28, 1746

ROGER MEDDIN, an Irish servant lad; runaway from JOHN PASS of Mount Holly, Burlington County; "thick, middle sized fellow; full faced and wears his own hair"; advertised in *The Pennsylvania Gazette*, September 4, 1746

MICHAEL CLARK, a servant man; runaway from SAMUEL ATKINSON of Chester Town, Burlington County; "aged about 40 years, middle stature, pale complexion, black eye brows, has a cut on the forepart of one of his legs, a little above the shoe"; advertised in *The Pennsylvania Gazette*, November 27, 1746

BARTHOLOMEW MILES, an Irish servant man; runaway from HENRY COOPER of New Hanover Township, Burlington County; aged about 26 years; "fair complexion; speaks pretty good English; pitted with small pox"; advertised in *The Pennsylvania Gazette*, June 25, 1747

PATRICK MITCHELL, an Irish servant man; runaway from JAMES LESTRANGE of Piles Grove, Salem County; aged about 22 years; low stature; "thick set and black curled hair; talks bad English"; advertised in *The Pennsylvania Gazette*, August 20, 1747

JOHN CANADA, an Irish servant man; runaway from JOSEPH BURR of Burlington; aged about 23 years; "well set; likely fellow; has short brown hair"; advertised in *The Pennsylvania Gazette*, October 1, 1747

SAMUEL ROYALS, an English servant man; runaway from ROBERT NEWELL of Freehold, Monmouth county; aged about 24 years; "pretty slim; 6 feet high; long visaged; drooped nose and a scar on each of his wrists; one on the inside of his right knee and another across his knee; somewhat pock marked; has been several years in the army and speak all languages"; advertised in *The New York Gazette revived in the Weekly Post*

Boy, November 9, 1747

MARTIN DUNN, an Irish servant man; runaway from JAMES ENGLISH of Freehold, Monmouth county; aged about 20 years; "pretty lusty, red faced; no hair; scar pretty high on his forehead"; advertised in *The New York Gazette revived in the Weekly Post Boy*, November 9, 1747

HUGH BRADFORD, an Irish servant man; runaway from JOHN INSKAPE of Evesham Township, Burlington county; "pretty well set; middle stature; fresh complexion; has two moles on his left cheek"; advertised in *The Pennsylvania Gazette*, March 8, 1748

CORNELIUS SULLIVAN, an Irish servant lad; runaway from JOHN ROBERTS of Chester Town; aged about 20 years, middle stature, "very freckled, speaks pretty good English and can read and write pretty well, wears his own brownish colored hair but may have had it cut off, has a down look; is round shouldered and goes about very heavy"; advertised in *The Pennsylvania Gazette*, April 21, 1748

ANTHONY HAINES, an apprentice lad; runaway from JONATHAN ELLIS of Waterford Township, Glouster County; "short stature; well set; dark complexion; down look; scar on his under lip; suppose to have gone with his brother HUGH HAINES towards Opekon"; advertised in *The Pennsylvania Gazette*, June 3, 1748

JAMES MOORE, an Irish servant man; runaway from THOMAS HARRIS of Reden's Town, Hunterdon County; aged about 22 years; "middle stature; fresh complexion; short hair turning to red; pretty much pock broken and lame in one of his heels which causes him to limp"; advertised in *The Pennsylvania Gazette*, June 9, 1748

JAMES GREENWOOD, an English servant man; runaway from JAMES VAHAN of Upper Freehold, Monmouth County; middle stature; "red complexion; red hair; freckled; can write"; advertised in *The New York Gazette*, June, 9 1748

 MORGAN GROCK, an Irish servant man; runaway from JACOB GASKELL of Burlington County; aged about 19 years; short stature; well set; fresh complexion; "dark brown hair; large mole on his cheek"; advertised in *The Pennsylvania Journal*, June 9, 1748

 PATRICK MITCHEL, an Irish servant man; runaway from ANDREW BALL of Mannington, Salem County; aged about 24 or 25 years; "black curled hair; black complexion; speaks a little of the brogue"; advertised in *The Pennsylvania Gazette*, June 23, 1748

 DAVID DUNDAS, a Scotch servant man; runaway from JONATHAN HOUGH of Springfield Township, Burlington County; aged about 35 years; "a very coarse spoken man; pitted very much with the small pox"; advertised in *The Pennsylvania Gazette*, June, 23, 1748

 MICHAEL COLLINS, an Irish servant man; runaway from JOHN GRANT of Basking Ridge; "aged about 21 years; short stature; reddish complexion; well set; bald on the fore part of his head and has a coarse voice; speaks good English"; advertised in *The New York Gazette revived in the Weekly Post Boy*, July 4, 1748; re advertised in *The Pennsylvania Gazette*, October 20, 1748 as "about 22 years of age; a little well set fellow; reddish complexion; full faced and full eyed and pretty much freckled; bald headed; speaks pretty good English and has a coarse voice."

 EDWARD HENDRICK, an Irish servant man; runaway from BENJAMIN HERITAGE of Chester Township, Burlington County; aged about 25 years; "down look; speaks good English; walks very clumsy; has a cut on the middle joint of his little finger of his left hand"; advertised in *The Pennsylvania Gazette*, August 4, 1748

 DANIEL MCDANNOLD, an Irish servant man;

runaway from WILLIAM LOGAN of Reddings Town, Hunterdon County; aged about 18-19 years; "about 5 feet high; of a fair complexion; down look; a little pock fretten"; advertised in *The New York Evening Post*, September 19, 1748; also advertised in *The Pennsylvania Gazette*, June 8, 1749 as being "an Irish or Highland servant man and having runaway from PATRICK BROWN of Lebanon Township, Hunterdon County; "about 18 to 20 years of age, of short stature [described as 5 feet in prior advertisement], middling well set; short thick brown hair; down look; bashful countenance"

EDWARD OLIVE, an Irish servant man; runaway from ALEXANDER MORGAN of Waterford Township, Glouster County; "aged about 18 years, thick, chunky fellow, light eyes, light hair"; advertised in *The Pennsylvania Gazette*, October 20, 1748

WILLIAM PRICE, an English servant man; runaway from SAMUEL COLES of Glouster County; "about 19 years of age; of middle stature; has a down look; is pitted with small pox;" advertised in *The Pennsylvania Journal*, November 10, 1748

JOHN GAMBLE, an Irish servant lad; runaway from JAMES ANDREW of the North Branch of the Raritan; "of a fair complexion; and a scar under his right eye"; advertised in *The New York Gazette, revived in the Weekly Post Boy,* February 6, 1749

NICHOLAS COWALT, a Holland born servant man; runaway from ALEXANDER MURRAY, of the Union Iron Works of Hunterdon County; "about 25 years of age; wears his own hair; brown complexion; ill-looking fellow; much addicted to swearing when in liquor; he can talk High Dutch;" advertised in *The Pennsylvania Gazette*, June 8, 1749

WILLIAM THOMPSON, American born [Duck Creek, Newcastle County] servant man ; runaway from JOHN SPARLING of New Brunswick; "short and thick"; advertised in

The Pennsylvania Gazette, July 6, 1749

ELISHA BULLINGHAM, an apprentice lad; runaway from MATTHEW FORSYTH of Chesterfield Township, Burlington County; "about 16 years of age; by trade a house carpenter; supposed to be gone off to New England"; advertised in *The Pennsylvania Gazette*, July, 13, 1749

JOHN HAINS, an English servant man; runaway from JOSEPH ELLIS of Newtown Township, Glouster County; "about 30 years of age; of small stature; fair complexion; red beard"; advertised in *The Pennsylvania Journal*, July 20, 1749

THOMAS WELCH, an Irish servant man; runaway from JOSEPH ELLIS of Newtown Township, Glouster County; "about 18 years of age; well set; round visaged; black short hair; has a large cut resembling a "C" on the top of his head"; advertised in *The Pennsylvania Journal*, July 20, 1749

CORNELIUS SULLIVAN, an Irish servant man; runaway from JOSEPH BIDDLE of Burlington; "about 21 years of age; middle sized; brown hair cut off; a little freckled; speaks pretty good English and can read and write pretty well; has a down look; is round shouldered and stoops and goes very heavy; worked in the iron works in New York"; advertised in *The New York Gazette, revived in Weekly Post Boy*, August 14, 1746 and again in the same paper on August 31, 1749

JOHN CUNNINGHAM, a servant man; runaway from RICHARD MOSS of Salem; "about 21 years of age, of middle stature"; advertised in *The Pennsylvania Journal*, September 7, 1749

DANIEL M'DANIEL, a Irish servant man; runaway from JOHN HORNER of Princeton; "about 20 years of age; five feet, six inches high; speaks tolerable good English but a little of the Scotch; is something pitted with the small pox; of a down look and an mean and bashful countenance"; advertised in *The Pennsylvania Gazette*, November 2, 1749

HENRY TIBB, a West Country servant man; runaway from JOHN HORNER of Princeton; "about 30 years of age; a well set low fellow; professes to be a seaman; speaks very thick and in the West Country way"; advertised in *The Pennsylvania Gazette*, November 2, 1749

THOMAS BENNET, an English a servant man; runaway from JAMES CLARK of Windsor Township, Middlesex County; "about 40 years of age; of middle stature; black curled hair; dark complexion; something pock marked"; advertised in *The Pennsylvania Gazette*, November 23, 1749

JOHN M'COY, an Irish servant lad; runaway from THOMAS CARNEY of Penn's Neck Township, Salem County; "about 17 years of age; of short stature; smooth faced; very bold countenance; he could read and write; went away by canoe and took a gun with him as far as Bohemia, where he left it with Mr. TRUEAXE and was seen later at the head of the Bohemia at the Roman Church at a funeral and afterward at WILLIAM ELLIS' plantation at Cecil County, Maryland with WILLIAM DRESSNER and his wife, shipmates of the said servant"; advertised in *The Pennsylvania Gazette*, November 30, 1749

PETER GARRAGAN, an Irish servant man; runaway from GEORGE MIDDLETON of Nottingham Township, Burlington County; "about 20 years of age; of short stature; middling well set; has a grim look and is pretty much pock broken; his hair cut off"; advertised in *The Pennsylvania Gazette*, February 6, 1750; repeated in *The Pennsylvania Gazette*, August 2, 1750 but listed there as having runaway from BENNET BARD of Burlington; subsequently, having changed his name to PETER CONLIN; he was advertised again in *The New York Gazette revived in the Weekly Post Boy*, August 20, 1750

HONOS YERACK GRUMBLE, a Dutch servant man; runaway from WILLIAM ALBERTSON of Newtown Township, Glouster County; "about 28-30 years of age; well set; of middle stature; long black hair; dark complexion"; advertised in *The Pennsylvania Gazette*, February 6, 1750

EDWARD ORLIFF, an Irish servant man; runaway from ALEXANDER MORGAN, of Waterford Township, Glouster County; "about 19 years of age; thick, chunky fellow; light eyes and lightish hair"; advertised in *The Pennsylvania Gazette*, February 6, 1750

JOSEH FREEMILLER, a Dutch servant man; runaway from SAMUEL BURROWS; "17 or 18 years of age; a short well set fellow; black complexion"; advertised in *The Pennsylvania Gazette*, March 6, 1750

CHARLES HUNT, a servant man; from ALEXANDER PARKER of Philadelphia; "about 25 years of age; of short stature; brown; ruddy complexion; wide mouth; very talkative and shows his teeth very much in talking and very apt to laugh"; advertised in *The Pennsylvania Gazette*, March 20, 1750.

ARTHUR HARVEY, an Irish servant man; runaway from JAMES BANKS, Newark, County of Essex and formerly servant of SOLOMON COMES of Staten Island; is about 20 years of age; "of short stature; has a down look with short dark hair"; advertised in *The New York Gazette revived in the Weekly Post Boy*, April 9, 1750

NATHANIEL PARKER, Jr.; runaway from NATHANIEL WARD, Newark, County of Essex; in company with two runaway servants; "16 years of age; is of tall stature and has white hair"; advertised in *The New York Gazette revived in the Weekly Post Boy*, April 9, 1750

JAMES RAY, an Irish servant man; runaway from JOHN STOKES, of the township of Willingborough of Burlington county; "23 years of age; with short brown curled bushy hair"; advertised in *The Pennsylvania Journal*, June 21, 1750.

MALACHIAH [MELCHOR] COLPEN [CALVIN] a

High Dutch servant man; runaway from JACOB OVEM of Pepeck, Somerset County; "about 21 years of age; speaks tolerable good English; short well set fellow with black curled hair; of a brownish complexion"; advertised in *The Pennsylvania Gazette*, August 9, 1750.

JOHN CONLIN, an Irish servant; runaway from RICHARD JORDAN in Bucks County, Pennsylvania; "aged about 23 years of age; a short, slender fellow, with black beard and black bushy hair; pale, smooth complexion; tailor; struts much in his walk and takes abundance of snuff"; advertised in *The New York Gazette revived in the Weekly Post Boy*, August 20, 1750.

ABRAHAM MAGEE, an Irish servant man; runaway from PHILIP MAROT of Bordentown; "about 25 years of age; of middle stature; a pale complexion; a tailor by trade and a good workman; has black hair and a red beard, but has his hair off"; advertised in *The Pennsylvania Gazette*, November 1, 1750

JOHN CLARKE, a New England born man; runaway from PHILIP MAROT of Bordentown; "about 25 years of age; of middle stature; a fresh complexion; a carpenter and joiner by trade"; advertised in *The Pennsylvania Gazette*, November 1, 1750

DANIEL TOY, an Irish servant man; runaway from ABRAHAM LORD of Pilesgrove, Salem County; "about 26 years of age; of middle stature; pale complexion; well set; speaks but middling English and had been on the Expedition [to Canada]"; advertised in *The Pennsylvania Gazette*, December 25, 1750

BENJAMIN HINGHAM, an English servant man; runaway from JACOB READOR of Amwell in Hunterdon County; about 5 feet, 6 inches high; aged about 32 years; "straight limbed and slender; dark complexion"; advertised in *The Pennsylvania Journal*, March 28, 1751

BENJAMIN ALBURTIS, an apprentice lad; runaway from JOHN EVANS of Trenton; about 5 feet, 7 inches high; aged about 20 years; "had a very sore shin; by trade a cooper"; advertised in *The Pennsylvania Gazette*, April 4, 1751

REUBEN JONES, American born servant man; runaway from JOHN FRENCH of Mount Holly; "about 6 feet high; fresh complexion"; advertised in *The Pennsylvania Gazette*, April 18, 1751

PETER CLEARWATER, an American born servant man; runaway from EPHRAIM OLIPHANT of Amwell, Hunterdon County; "about 6 feet high; aged about 34 years; thin face; light colored thin hair; blue eyes; down look; impediment in his speech"; advertised in *The Pennsylvania Gazette*, August 8, 1751

DANIEL MILLER, an Irish servant man; runaway from SAMUEL STONE, Brewer, of Millstone, in the County of Somerset; "aged about 36 years; round faced; black hair; brown complexion; was a soldier upon the expedition against Canada"; advertised in *The New York Gazette revived in the Weekly Post Boy*, August 12, 1751

JOHN WELCH, a servant man; runaway from ARTHUR M'LLVEEN, near Woodberry in Deptford Township, Glouster County; "about 5 feet, 6 inches high; aged about 25 years; well set fellow"; advertised in *The Pennsylvania Gazette*, January 7, 1752

JOHN NEWCOMB, an Irish servant man; runaway from THOMAS BLAIR of Bethlehem Township, Hunterdon county; "about 5 feet, 9 inches high; aged about 22 years; well set; full faced"; advertised in *The Pennsylvania Gazette*, January 7, 1752

MOSES WITTEN, an American born servant man; runaway from CORNELIUS QUICK, living in the Great Swamp, in Hunterdon County; aged about 22 years; middle stature; dark complexion; black eyes; somewhat a stoop in his shoulders; advertised in *The Pennsylvania Gazette*, April 16, 1752

WILLIAM DAVIS, an Irish servant man; runaway from JOSEPH FRAZIER, living at Timber Creek, Glouster County; aged about 21 years; "low stature; slim with sandy colored hair; has a sore shin"; advertised in *The Pennsylvania Gazette*, June 1, 1752

JAMES KILLSEY, an Irish servant man; runaway from JOSEPH SHEPERD of Middletown; aged about 22 years; advertised in *The New York Gazette revived in the Weekly Post Boy*, June 15, 1752

THOMAS KILLING, a servant man; runaway from JOSEPH SHEPERD of Middletown; "spare man; very much pock broken"; advertised in *The New York Gazette revived in the Weekly Post Boy*, June 15, 1752

THOMAS BUNN, an Irish servant man; runaway from WILLIAM WILKINS of Woodberry Creek; thick well set fellow; of middle stature; full faced; hair lately cut off; little pock marked; speaks pretty good English and pretends to be by trade a shoemaker; has a scar on his belly and is marked on the upper side of his right thumb with TB"; advertised in *The Pennsylvania Gazette,* June 18, 1752

GEORGE MONROW, a Scotch servant man; runaway from JOHN BROWN of Glouster County; "about 5 feet, 9 inches high; aged about 30 years; thick; well set fellow; down look; fresh complexion; talks broad Scotch and can talk Dutch and Irish; has brown hair"; advertised in *The Pennsylvania Journal*, June 25, 1752

JAMES HAMILTON, an Irishman; runaway from his bail; "a likely well limbed fellow; pitted with the small pox; fresh colored; about 27 years of age; by trade a shoemaker; gray haired notwithstanding his youth; very ignorant and apt to laugh at his own expressions"; thought to have gone off to Albany;

notice to M. JOHN DURHAM, at the *Sign of the Boat*, near the Old Slip in New York or to J. THOMPSOM in New Brunswick or F. HALINSHEAD, Esq. at the Court House in Somerset; advertised by FRANCIS HALL in *The New York Gazette, revived in the Weekly Post Boy*, July 20, 1752

JOHN M'CLAUGHLIN, an Irish servant man; runaway from PETER BARDS and Company, owners of the Mount Holly Iron Works; about 35 years of age; of a middle stature; notice to JOHN ABRAHAM DENORMANDIE, Esq. at Bristol or MORRIS MORGAN in Philadelphia; advertised in *The Pennsylvania Gazette*, August 20, 1752

NICHOLAS MAGAHEY, an Irish servant man; runaway from WILLIAM WOODWARD of Crosswicks; "short, about 5 feet, 5 inches high; well set; swarthy complexion; black eyes; his hair lately cut off; speaks with a brogue; he understands all sorts of plantation work but lately has been used to cut wood at Messrs ALLEN and TURNER's Works;" notice to JOHN ALLEN of Trenton; advertised in *The Pennsylvania Gazette*, August 13, 1752

JAMES M'CUNY, a servant lad; runaway from PHILIP DAVIS of Peter's Township in Cumberland County; aged about 18 years; ruddy complexion; fair and smooth faced; is well set for his age; advertised in *The New York Gazette*, September 28, 1752

JOHN BURK, an Irish servant lad; runaway from JOSEPH LUDLAM of Cape May County; short and well made; aged about 19 years; has short brown hair and brown eyes; came from Dublin and can neither read nor write; advertised in *The Pennsylvania Gazette*, September 28, 1752

WILLIAM KITCHEN, an English servant man; runaway from ALEXANDER MILLER of Conagogee, in Cumberland county; about 5 feet, 5 or 6 inches high; aged about 35 years; well set; much marked with the small pox; has short brown hair and a little bald before; advertised in *The Pennsylvania Gazette*,

October 19, 1752

WILLIAM BLAKE, a servant man; runaway from JACOB CHANDLER of Kingwood, Hunterdon County; by trade a tailor and a stay maker; tells various stories concerning his place of birth; advertised in *The Pennsylvania Gazette*, October 19, 1752

WILLIAM TAYLOR, an English servant man; runaway from JOHN CARMAN of Northampton in Burlington County; about 5 feet, 6 inches high; thin man; brown complexion; hair cut off and stutters much when he talks fast"; advertised in *The Pennsylvania Gazette*, November 9, 1752

RICHARD MALONE, an Irish servant man; runaway from JOSEPH WOOD of Piscataway; near 6 foot high; took with him his wife, aged about 24 years; well set; ruddy and pockfretten; suppose to have gone to Rockaway or Barnegat"; advertised in *The New York Gazette Revived in the Weekly Post Boy*, November 20, 1752

WILLIAM DAVIS [DAVIDSON], an Irish servant man; runaway from DR. MATHIAS DEHART, of Elizabeth town; small; lanthorn jawed; his left shoulder out of joint; pretends to be an Englishman and a sailor; red complexion; red hair and beard; aged about 24 years; advertised in *The New York Gazette revived in the Weekly Post Boy*, November 29, 1752

JOHN CHALANER, American born servant man; runaway from NATHANIEL HAINES in Evesham, Burlington County; a very assuming fellow; has gray eyes; 5 feet, 6 inches high; by trade pretends to be a turner"; advertised in *The Pennsylvania Gazette*, December 20, 1752

SAMUEL COOPER, an English servant man; runaway from ROBERT MILBURN of Elizabeth Town; "about 30 years of age; middle stature [5 feet, 7 inches]; black complexion; full face and very talkative; by trade a blacksmith; addicted to drinking; accompanied by a journeyman blacksmith DANIEL

EATTON, also addicted to drinking and very much given to swearing"; advertised in *The New York Gazette revived in the Weekly Post Boy*, December 25, 1752

RICHARD BROWN, an Irish servant man; runaway from ROBERT MILBURN of Elizabeth Town; "5 feet, 8 inches; a strong made fellow with a remarkable brown spot on his right cheek; by trade a blacksmith"; advertised in *The New York Gazette revived in the Weekly Post Boy*, December 25, 1752

THOMAS WOOD, an Englishman; "aged about 19 years; a short set man; about 5 feet, 5 inches high; swarthy complexion; pretends to be a sailor; had an iron collar around his neck, says his master's name is JOHN SMITH and lives in Maryland, within four miles of Patapsco"; advertised in *The Pennsylvania Journal*, December 26, 1752

JOHN SIMMONDS, an Englishman in the city of Norwich, runaway from JOHN BOHAM, brick maker, of Lancaster county; aged about 20 years; sandy complexion; advertised in *The Pennsylvania Journal*, December 26, 1752

DAVID GREENWOOD, an Englishman; aged about 60 years; lusty big boned man; speaks broad English; a weaver by trade; has been in country for 11 years but will not give any account as to where he lived or where he came from; advertised in *The Pennsylvania Journal*, December 26, 1752

Now in custody of WILLIAM HAY, gaolkeeper of Chester County, ANDREW DUN, an Irishman, says he was brought in by one JOSHUA ROBERTS in West New Jersey and sold to one WILLIAM WALKER in Northampton, Burlington Township; "aged about 22 years; 5 feet, 8 inches high; a brown complexion; has a down look; very much pitted with small pox; wears his own black hair and has a white lock of his hair on the back part of his head about the bigness of a penny"; advertised in *The Pennsylvania Journal*, December 26, 1752

CORNELIUS COLLINS, an Irish servant man; runaway from ABEL HARRIS of Mannington Township, Salem County; "aged about 22 years; of low stature; short hair; thin; pale faced"; advertised in *The Pennsylvania Gazette*, January 2, 1753

WILLIAM PROSSER, an apprentice lad; runaway from THOMAS WITHERILL, Jr. of Burlington; "about 5 feet, 8 inches high; aged about 18 years; middling slender; down look; wears his own hair; dark complexion"; advertised in *The Pennsylvania Gazette*, January 16, 1753

WILLIAM RICHARDSON, an American born servant man; runaway from JAMES BALDWIN of Watertown Township in the Jerseys; aged about 24 years; "pock marked; short black, curled hair; pale complexion; born in Amwell in New Jersey"; advertised in *The Pennsylvania Gazette*, January 23, 1753

JOHN MACWIER, a servant man; runaway from SAMUEL COLE of Glouster; "aged about 18 years; short stature; sandy hair; fair complexion; one of his legs is larger than the other and has a large scar on the inside of the small one"; advertised in *The Pennsylvania Journal*, January 23, 1753

ROBERT STEWART, a servant man; runaway from GEORGE MARPLE of Evesham in the County of Burlington; a short, well set fellow about 27 years of age; square faced and light complexion"; advertised in *The Pennsylvania Journal*, April 19, 1753

PHILIP CANTLOW, an Irish servant man; runaway from THOMAS RAMBO of Mantua Creek, Glouster County; aged about 30 years; "thin faced; pitted with small pox and has a down look"; advertised in *The Pennsylvania Gazette*, April 26, 1753

THOMAS BROWN an American born servant man; runaway from ISAAC CONROE of Burlington; aged about 25-26 years; "short stature; by trade a weaver; bold spoken; red faced man with short black bushy hair; very much addicted to drink; talkative and very quarrelsome; has been a traveler through most of the neighboring provinces; born in Lancaster, Pennsylvania; advertised in *The Pennsylvania Gazette*, April 26, 1753

ROBERT WHITEHEAD, an English servant man; runaway from JOHN BURROUGHS of Trenton, Hunterdon County; "5 feet high; notorious thief; branded and whipped at Trenton"; advertised in *The Pennsylvania Gazette*, April 26, 1753

THOMAS JAMES, an American born servant man; runaway from PATRICK REYNOLDS of Mount Holly; "aged about 19 years; born in Philadelphia or thereabouts; has a large scar on his right cheek; has been used to driving a team for BENNET BARD in the County of Burlington"; advertised in *The Pennsylvania Journal*, May 3, 1753

THOMAS WEEBLEY; 5 feet and a half high; light colored short hair; well set; freckled and pock fretten; ran away in a small sloop named the *Charity*, JOHN HAVENS, owner, of Manasquan and taking parcel of goods belonging to CATHERINE GRIFFITH, wife of SAMUEL GRIFFITH"; advertised in *The New York Gazette or Weekly Post Boy*, May 14, 1753

BENJAMIN PELTON, a servant man; "short, well set fellow with a surly countenance ran away in a small sloop, named the *Charity,* JOHN HAVENS, owner, of Manasquan and taking parcel of goods belonging to CATHERINE GRIFFITH, wife of SAMUEL GRIFFITH"; advertised in *The New York Gazette or Weekly Post Boy*, May 14, 1753

ISAAC GARRISON, American born servant man; runaway from his bail, living at Cohansy bridge in Cumberland County; "aged about 32 years, 5 feet, 9 inches high; one of his thumbs short and has no bone the length of it from the hand to the knuckle joint; brown straight hair; has his wife him but no children as he never had any, ran away with him one JOHN LANGLEY"; notice to J. JAMES, Jr. or JOHN LASEY; advertised in *The Pennsylvania Gazette*, June 14, 1753

JAMES DUN [aka JAMES DUNNEBO], a native Irish servant man; runaway from JONAS SCOGGIN of Alloways Creek, Salem County; "aged about 35 years; 5 feet, 10 inches high; pretty lusty; has a scar on his left cheek; wears his own straight black hair; also took a young woman, who he will probably pass as his wife; speaks much of the brogue"; advertised in *The Pennsylvania Gazette*, June 14, 1753

JACOB RUBB, a High Dutch Servant man; runaway from PHILIP TITUS of Hopewell in Hunterdon County; "aged about 28 years; 5 feet, 3 inches high; straight black hair; a swarthy complexion"; advertised in *The New York Gazette or Weekly Post Boy*, June 18, 1753

RICHARD MORGAN, a Welch servant man; runaway from FRANCIS BATTEN, of Glouster County; small; pale complexion; has a blemish in one eye and speaks with a Welch accent"; advertised in *The Pennsylvania Gazette*, August 30, 1753

TIMOTHY LINCH, an Irish servant man; runaway from THOMAS HOOTON living near Trenton in Burlington County; "aged about 25 years; 5 feet, 6 inches high; a ruddy complexion; inclined to be freckled; has a down look; talks very thick with the brogue upon his tongue and has several scars on his left leg"; advertised in *The Pennsylvania Gazette*, September 6, 1753

MICHAEL M'LAUGHLIN, a servant man, runaway from ALEXANDER HILL of Piles Grove; about 5 feet, 6 inches; "full faced and well set"; advertised in *The Pennsylvania Gazette*, July 19, 1753

HENRY CLARK, an English man; runaway from JOSEPH ARNEY, living in Burlington; "aged about 30 years; of middle stature; a smooth spoken man; by trade a stocking weaver, but it is said that he keeps school now in the Lower counties; has a wife with him who is tall, slender, of a pale complexion and dull countenance with a lusty boy of about 18 months; went down the river to Philadelphia in ANDREW DOZ's"; advertised in *The Pennsylvania Gazette*, August 9, 1753

MORGAN EVANS, a Welsh servant man; runaway from LAWRENCE DEBOW of Upper Freehold, Monmouth County; about 5 feet 8 inches; brown complexion; advertised in *The Pennsylvania Gazette*, August 9, 1753

WILLIAM PRIEST, an Englishman; runaway from JOHN KINGSLAND of Bergen County; "aged about 20 years; 5 feet, 6 inches; thin visaged and of a swarthy complexion"; advertised in *The New York Gazette or the Weekly Post Boy*, August 13, 1753

WILLIAM MOORE, an Irish Servant man; runaway from PHILIP WELSH of Nottingham Township in Burlington County; "about 5 feet, 6 inches high; black hair; by trade a butcher; stoops much in his walk; thin visage; inclines to sore eyes and talks middling good English"; advertised in *The Pennsylvania Gazette*, September 13, 1753

JONATHAN SMITH, a servant man; runaway from THOMAS CANBY in Wilmington; "about 6 feet inches high; aged about 40 years; dark complexion; by trade a carpenter"; advertised in *The Pennsylvania Gazette*, September 27, 1753

JOHN HAGLIN, an Irish servant man; runaway from PATRICK PORTER living in Chester Township in Burlington County; "aged about 26 years; middle stature; pock marked; speaks good English; wears his own black hair; served his time with ENOCH ROBERTS of Chester and has since been a servant to THOMAS JARRAD at Greenwich in Glouster County; advertised in *The Pennsylvania Gazette*, October 11, 1753

HENRY HRUBB, a Dutch servant man; runaway from WILLIAM CARNAGIE of Bedminister Township, Somerset county; "about 5 feet, 6 inches high; aged betwixt 30 and 40 years; has a large scar on one of his middle fingers; thin; black colored hair; can talk but very little English; by trade a stocking weaver"; advertised in *The Pennsylvania Gazette*, October 25, 1753

JOHN M'CABE, an Irish servant man; runaway from ARCHIBALD HAMILTON in Mannington Township, Salem County; about 5 feet, 8 inches high; "aged about 23 years; has a pretty large mouth, large eyes, and stoops as he walks; lost one of his middle toes; by trade a tailor and can work well at plantation work"; advertised in *The Pennsylvania Gazette*, November 1, 1753

JAMES MURPHY a servant man; runaway from JOHN SCOT of Hanover Township, Morris County; "5 feet, 8 inches high; long yellowish hair tied behind; much pitted with small pox; had been a soldier in the French service and talks good French; has been a school master"; advertised in *The New York Gazette and Weekly Post Boy*, January 14, 1754; also listed as JAMES MURPHEY, an Irish servant man; runaway from JOHN SCOTT, living in Hanover Township, Morris County; "middle stature; somewhat long visaged; sharp nose; much pitted with the small pox; grey or light colored eyes; flaxen hair; reddish beard; about 28 years of age; was a school master, sometimes ties his hair behind with a string; a very proud fellow; loves drink and, when drunk, is very impudent and talkative, pretends much and knows little; was sometime in the French service and can talk French"; advertised in *The New York Gazette or Weekly Post Boy*, April 3, 1754

JOHN ERMUS [JOHN HUCKABACK] an American born servant man; runaway from JOHN LADD of Glouster County; "aged about 28 years; middle size; pale complexion; blind in one eye it being sunk in his head; can speak Dutch"; lived for several years, about two miles eastward of Germantown with THOMAS ROBERTS Jr.; advertised in *The*

Pennsylvania Gazette, January 22, 1754

  NICHOLAS GODDARD, an English servant man; runaway from SAMUEL KEMPTON, living in Amwell, Hunterdon county; "aged about 28 years; short stature; born in London; walks somewhat stooping; dark complexion; full mouthed; black straight hair; much scarified under one of his cheek bones caused by the King's Evil and very much given to drink; by trade a tin plate worker"; advertised in *The Pennsylvania Gazette*, March 26, 1754

  JOSEPH HEDAY, American born servant man; runaway from GEORGE MUMFORD of Fisher's Island; native of Newark, "short, well set fellow; ruddy complexion"; ran away with three Negroes; advertised in *The New York Gazette or the Weekly Post Boy*, April 1, 1754

  THOMAS DEAL [THOMAS DEAN], an Irish servant man; runaway from PETER JONES at the Lake in Glouster County; "aged about 36 years; 5 feet, 6 inches high; has a scar over his right eye and a cut in his belly, a little bit above the waistband of his breeches which was sewn up; wears his own straight hair"; advertised in *The Pennsylvania Gazette*, April 4, 1754

  GEORGE TATE, an Irish servant man; runaway from JAMES GROVER of Middletown, Monmouth county; "has lately been a servant to THOMAS RATTOON of Amboy Ferry; middle stature; brown hair; well set; scar on one cheek, believed to be the left"; advertised in *The New York Gazette and Weekly Post Boy*, April 8, 1754

  WILLIAM FURR, an English servant man; runaway from JAMES GROVER of Middletown, Monmouth County; "well set"; advertised in *The New York Gazette and Weekly Post Boy*, April 8, 1754

  PHILIP CLAVE, an Irish servant man; runaway from JACOB FORD of Morris County; "about 19 or 20 years of age;

5 feet, 6 inches high; thick set; square shouldered, with a down look; has much of the brogue upon his tongue"; formerly belonged to HUGH M'CLEAN of Chester County; advertised in *The New York Gazette or Weekly Post Boy*, May 6, 1754

THOMAS FILER, an English born servant man; runaway from THOMAS ANDREWS, living in Evesham township, Burlington County; "about 33 years of age; 5 feet, 6 inches tall; black complexion; talks West Country; black hair and beard; pretty hairy on his breast"; advertised in *The Pennsylvania Gazette*, May 9, 1754

WILLIAM DARBEY, a servant man; runaway from THOMAS TALMAN, of the Township of Evesham, Burlington County; "about 19 years of age, 5 feet, 8 inches high; has a scar under one of his eyes; he is of a dark complexion and had his hair cut off lately"; notice to WILLIAM FISHBOURNE of Philadelphia; advertised in *The Pennsylvania Gazette*, June 6, 1754

ANDREW LANIN, an Irish servant man; runaway from PHILIP FITZGERALD, of Edinburg, Salem County; "aged about 23 years; near 6 feet high; pock marked; large nose and round shouldered with a large scar on his forehead; a pretty good scholar"; advertised in *The Pennsylvania Gazette*, July 25, 1754

THOMAS LEITCH, a Scotch servant man; runaway from JOSHUA BISPHAN (executor to the estate of BENJAMIN BISPHAN, deceased) of Chester Township, Burlington County; "aged about 40 years; 5 feet, 9 inches high; fresh complexion; thin visage; black hair; weak grey eyes; is a carpenter and joiner by trade; speaks good English and has been in the country many years"; advertised in *The New York Gazette*, July 29, 1754

BALTUS SPACKHOLTZ, a High Dutch servant man; runaway from WILLIAM MCKNIGHT, of Upper Freehold, Monmouth County; "aged about 25 years; middle stature;

speaks bad English; pretends to be a miller; has short black hair; advertised in *The Pennsylvania Gazette*, August 8, 1754

CHRISTIAN FRITS, a Dutch servant man; runaway from JOHN CORYELL at his ferry in Amwell, 15 miles above Trenton; "about 5 feet, 4 inches high; aged about 20 years; swarthy complexion; brown eyes and eyebrows and wears his own hair"; advertised in *The Pennsylvania Gazette*, July 18, 1754

GEORGE HAMILTON, a Scotch servant man; runaway from GEORGE MAY of Egg Harbor, Glouster County; middle stature; well set; advertised in *The Pennsylvania Gazette*, August 29, 1754

JOHN ENGLE, a Dutch hired servant man; runaway from PETER TEN EICK, living upon Raritan River; "middle stature; well set; red faced; speaks bad English; pretends to be a miller; brown complexion with brown bushy hair; has a flat nose, occasioned by the gristle of its being broke, so that a fellow placing his finger slightly on the tip of it, lays it flat to his face; notice to JAMES HAMBRICHT at the White Horse in Chester County or to HENRY PAWLING; advertised in *The Pennsylvania Gazette*, August 22, 1754

JOHN DWYER, an Irish servant man; runaway from JOHN HANCE, mariner of Shrewsbury; "aged about 20 years; fair complexion; dark brown hair, pretty long; he has had the small pox, though not much pitted; writes a good hand"; advertised in *The New York Mercury*, September 30, 1754

WILLIAM THOMPSON, an Irish servant man; runaway from ROBERT ALLAN, of Roxbury in Morris County; aged about 18 years; 5 feet, 7 inches tall; reddish complexion"; advertised in *The New York Gazette or the Weekly Post Boy*, October 14, 1754

THOMAS LEAN, an American born servant man; runaway from CORNELIUS VAN CAMPIN, of Kingwood; by trade a shoemaker; "took with him a fiddle and plays very well thereon; loves to be at Frolicks and Taverns and apt to get into liquor and, when so, is subject to fits; served his time in Chester county; he is very antic, he crows like a cock and barks like a dog and is very apt to do so"; notice to ROBERT AINSWORTH of Amwell; advertised in *The New York Gazette or The Weekly Post Boy*, November 11, 1754; he ran away again and was advertised six months later in *The Pennsylvania Gazette*, May 22, 1755 as THOMAS LANE, a servant man; runaway from JOHN WOOD of Amwell Township in Hunterdon County; "5 feet high; by trade a shoemaker; can play on the fiddle and dance and loves liquor; he ran away from the master he formerly lived with and was discovered by his barking like a dog and crowing like a cock; last seen at the Forks of Delaware and when he is in liquor, he is subject to fits"

JAMES SIMS, an American born servant man; runaway from MATHIAS VAN HORNE of Castle Saw Mill in Burlington County; "aged about 40 years; tall, slim man; red faced; has a big nose and pretends to be a cooper"; notice to THOMAS SHREVE, opposite WILLIAM WALTON's, Esq. in New York; advertised in *The New York Mercury*, January 5, 1755

THOMAS KING, a servant man; runaway from GEORGE NORRIS, tin man, of Prince Town [Princeton]; "aged about 40 years; 6 feet high; has a very effeminate look; hunch shouldered; long neck and short legs; has sore eyes; works in brass, copper and tin and speaks very good English;" notice to PAUL RICHARD, Esq., merchant in City of New York; advertised in *The New York Mercury*, January 6, 1755

PAULUS SMITH, a High Dutch servant man; runaway from JOHN ZABRISKI, at Hackinsack; aged about 30 years; "middle stature; brown bushy hair; speaks very short; by trade a miller"; advertised in *The New York Gazette or Weekly Post Boy*, January 27, 1755

TURRENCE MAGWIGIN, an Irish servant man;

runaway from WILLIAM ALLEN of Chester Township, Burlington County; aged about 27 years; 5 feet 6 inches high; palish complexion; dark brown hair; very thin and scragging; advertised in *The Pennsylvania Gazette*, February 4, 1755

THOMAS SMITH, an English servant man; runaway from RICHARD STILLWELL of Middletown, Monmouth County; "aged about 30 years; short stature; short hair; broad faced; down look; by trade a dyer"; advertised in *The New York Gazette or Weekly Post Boy*, April 14, 1755

JOSEPH REINE, an English servant man; runaway from FRANCIS DUDLEY of Evesham in Burlington County; "aged about 19 years; 5 feet, 7 inches high; lightish hair; fair complexion"; advertised in *The Pennsylvania Gazette*, May 8, 1755

JOHN MILLER, a Dutch servant man; runaway from FRANCIS DUDLEY of Evesham in Burlington County; "aged about 19 years; 5 feet, 7 inches high; dark hair; dark complexion; scar on his right jaw bone which it is thought came by the King's Evil"; advertised in *The Pennsylvania Gazette*, May 8, 1755

WILLIAM STRINGER, a servant man; runaway from THOMAS BLAIR of Bethlehem in Hunterdon County; "aged about 22 years; 5 feet, 7 inches high; short lightish colored hair; and the scar of a burn on his right cheek"; advertised in *The Pennsylvania Gazette*, May 15, 1755

JOHN CLODE MESHA, a French servant man; runaway from JAMES HANKINSON of Freehold in Monmouth County; "5 feet, 6 inches high; black hair; brown complexion; dark eyes;and speaks very broken English"; advertised in *The Pennsylvania Gazette Journal*, May 22, 1755

GEORGE BYRN, an Irish servant man; runaway from BENJAMIN COOPER, living at the Ferry [Cooper's Ferry] opposite Philadelphia; "aged about 20 years; full faced and freckled; middle stature; by trade a baker"; advertised in *The Pennsylvania Journal*, May 22, 1755

GEORGE FREDERICK MASTER, a Dutch servant man; runaway from BENJAMIN COOPER, living at the Ferry [Cooper's Ferry] opposite Philadelphia; "aged about 23 years; short black hair; dark complexion; middle stature; by trade a carpenter; speaks very bad English; has a great lump on his throat"; advertised in *The Pennsylvania Journal*, May 22, 1755

JOHN WALLACE, an Irish servant lad; runaway from GEORGE NORRIS, at Prince-Town; "aged about 16 years but small for his years; short fair hair; little pock-marked"; advertised in *The Pennsylvania Gazette*, May 29, 1755

AARON ALLEN, an American born servant man; runaway from ANDREW SINNICKSON living in Penn's Neck, Salem County; "hair newly cut off, except for a lock at his nape; dark complexion with black eyes; middle stature; has a mother and brother living at or near Princeton; his brother's name is MOSES ALLEN; he may have gone to Lancaster, Pennsylvania"; advertised in *The Pennsylvania Gazette*, June 26, 1755

TOBIAS MEEK, a Dutch servant man; runaway from JOHN GILL living near Haddonfield, in Glouster County; "aged about 22 years; his own light colored hair; a seam down his upper lip; middle stature"; advertised in *The Pennsylvania Gazette*, July 10, 1755

PETER BARRA, a French servant man; runaway from SAMUEL LEONARD in Shrewsbury, Monmouth County; "5 feet 6 inches high, short brown hair, pale complexion, speaks broken English"; advertised in *The Pennsylvania Gazette*, July 24, 1755

HACKETT, a servant man; runaway from PATRICK O'HANLON; "aged about 24 years, about 5 feet inches high, sandy complexion, short curled hair a great stoppage in his speech and pretends to be a shoemaker"; advertised in *The Pennsylvania Gazette*, August 7, 1755

EDWARD RUBIE; runaway from his bail; "about 5 feet 6 inches high; pock marked, professes to be a school master, and writes a very fair hand, plays well upon the flute and had one in his pocket when he went away"; had passes signed by ELISHA BASSET, Esq. and CHARLES CLINTON; give notice to GABRIEL COPNER and JOHN RICHMAN in Salem County; advertised in *The Pennsylvania Gazette*, August 14, 1755; he was re-advertised two years later in *The Pennsylvania Gazette*, September 8, 1757 as a runaway from GABRIEL COPPNER, living in Salem Town, Salem County; "says he was raised in the City of Cork and that he served his time in Philadelphia to a ship carpenter; pretends to know something about sawing with a whip saw; he has been privateering and in the army; has a brother living in the Highlands of New York, where he taught school some time; came to Piles Grove in Salem where he also taught school for some time, then ran from his bail and took a horse with him; became an indented servant for three years in February, 1757; a middle aged man and about five feet five inches tall; has short curled hair, much pox marked and can play on the flute."

CHRISTIAN LUDERMAN, a Dutch servant man; runaway from NATHANIEL FITZRANDOLPH of Princeton; "about 6 feet high; out mouthed; of a sandy complexion; large grey eyes; sandy beard; thick bushy sandy hair; large scar across one of his legs occasioned by the cut of an axe"; advertised in *The Pennsylvania Gazette*, August 14, 1755

THOMAS RUTHERFORD, an English servant man; runaway from ROBERT SHERWOOD of Bedminister Township in Somerset County; aged about 30 years; "5 feet, 4 inches high; pale complexion; red beard and scar across his nose"; advertised in *The New York Gazette or the Mercury Post Boy*, August 18, 1755

EDWARD MAYBE, an English servant man; runaway from JACOB HUGG of Glouster County; "a short fellow; dark complexion; wears own black hair; has a hair mold on his left cheek"; advertised in *The Pennsylvania Gazette*, September 4, 1755

JOHN SKINNER, an English servant man; runaway from JONATHAN STOUT of Middletown, Monmouth County; "about 6 feet high; cordwainer by trade; has the letters 'I.S.' with the date of the year on one of his hands"; advertised in *The New York Gazette or Weekly Post Boy*, September 8, 1755

JOSEPH HINSON, an American born servant man; runaway from Dr. STEPHEN TALMAN of Shrewsbury in Monmouth County; "aged about 30 years; about 5 feet, 11 inches high; swarthy complexion; thin visage; has black hair and dark eyes; is very talkative and stammers much in his speech;" born in Maryland; advertised in *The Pennsylvania Gazette*, September 11, 1755

GEORGE LEONARD HAMELS, a Dutch servant man; runaway from CLEMENT HALL of Elsinborough in Salem County; "near 6 feet high; lusty, broad faced fellow; has short brown hair and a sore on his under lip"; advertised in *The Pennsylvania Gazette*, September 18, 1755

RICHARD KINNERSLY, an English servant man; runaway from ARCHIBALD MICKLE of New Town, Glouster County; "aged about 30 years; about 5 feet, 9 inches high; pretty long visage; of a lightish complexion; has thin flaxed hair; has a mole on his left cheek but keeps it shaved; his eye tooth on the same side sticks over his lower teeth in a very remarkable manner"; advertised in *The Pennsylvania Gazette*, November 27, 1755

THOMAS MORRAH, an Irish servant man; runaway from ARCHIBALD MICKLE of New Town, Glouster County; "aged about 20 years; about 5 feet, 6 inches high; pretty much pock marked; has a down look; short brown hair; walks very stooping; has a clumsy heavy gate in walking and throws his feet very much out and bends his knees as he goes"; advertised in *The Pennsylvania Gazette*, November 27, 1755

TIMOTHY LINCH, an Irish servant man; runaway from THOMAS HOOTEN in Trenton; "aged about 30 years; about 5 feet, 7 inches; has short brown hair with a down look; a little freckled and often has sore lips; speaks thick and has much of the brogue"; advertised in *The Pennsylvania Gazette*, December 18, 1755

DAVID KEIGHN, an Irish servant man; runaway from THOMAS ANTRAM of Springfield in Burlington County; aged about 20 years; "a short well set man; black curled hair and a fresh complexion; is a likely man"; advertised in *The Pennsylvania Gazette*, December 18, 1755

Taken up as a runaway and now in Chester gaol, JOHN PETER OVERTON, "says he is a freeman and served his time to one WILLIAM FOSTER of Evesham township, Burlington county"; advertised by SAMUEL SMITH, Gaoler in *The Pennsylvania Gazette*, February 5, 1756

Taken up as a runaway and now in Chester gaol, JOHN BRYAN, an Irish servant, says he was born in County Cork in Ireland and has been almost two years in the country; brought in by JAMES WHITE; advertised by SAMUEL SMITH, Gaoler, in *The Pennsylvania Gazette*, February 5, 1756

JOHAN JEREMIAH MYAH, a German servant man; runaway from JOSIAH HALSTEAD of Shrewsbury, Monmouth County; "about 5 feet, 4 inches high; well set; a little pitted with pox; speaks very broken English; pretends to know something of the blacksmith's trade; is about 21 years of age"; advertised in *The Pennsylvania Gazette*, February 26, 1756

PATRCIK WELDON, an Irish servant man; runaway from EDWARD PANCOAST, living in Bordentown, Burlington County; "about 19 years of age; likely fellow with brogue and fair complexion; somewhat down looking; pretends to be a sailor and will go to sea"; advertised in *The Pennsylvania Gazette*, March 4, 1756

JOHN CHRISTIAN MILLER, A Dutch servant boy; runaway from STEPHEN VAN CORTLANDT of Second River; "tall, about 5 feet 10 inches; slim; aged about 18 years; ruddy complexion and turns out his feet pretty much as he walks; speaks good English and reads it indifferently well"; came from Hamburg; by profession a baker and miller; give notice to HENRY SCHLEYDORN in Philadelphia; advertised in *The Pennsylvania Gazette*, April 15, 1756

PATRICK HINES, Irish servant man; runaway from LAWRENCE HOWARD, Springfield Township, Chester County; "5 feet, 7 inches tall; well set; aged about 20 years; fresh complexion; short black curled hair; marked with small pox; very talkative and speaks very much with the brogue; pretends that he made his escape from the soldiers because they enlisted him fraudulently when he was intoxicated;" may have gone to Egg Harbor Cape May; advertised in *The Pennsylvania Gazette*, April 22, 1756

EDWARD HARVEY, an English servant man; runaway from MICHAEL BRANIN of Evesham, Burlington County; "5 feet 4 inches, dark brown curled hair, scar on upper lip and is pretty full mouthed"; advertised in *The Pennsylvania Gazette*, April 29, 1756

THOMAS FREEMAN, an English servant man; runaway from SAMUEL SHIVERS of Greenwich Town in Glouster County; "well set; middle stature; aged about 24 or 25; much given to drinking and very talkative"; was a servant of SAMUEL FLOWER, from whom he ran away and was advertised about two years ago; advertised in *The Pennsylvania Gazette*, May 13, 1756

LAWRENCE TENSLE, a Dutch servant man; runaway from ARTHUR VANKIRK; "5 feet 3 or 4 inches tall; of a very black complexion; with small black eyes and short black hair; by profession a carpenter"; advertised in *The Pennsylvania Gazette*, August 5, 1756

PETER RUFF, a servant man; runaway from ELIZABETH FORMAN of Upper Freehold, Monmouth County; "short, well set fellow with a bushy head of hair; with an iron collar around his neck; he has runaway several times before"; advertised in *The Pennsylvania Journal*, September 9, 1756

JOHN PATTISON, a servant man; runaway from WILLIAM KELLY; "about 32 years old; 5 foot, 6 inches high; short hair and an impediment in his speech; of a slender make"; advertised in *The New York Mercury*, October 11, 1756

EDWARD BREWER, an Irish servant man; runaway from WILLIAM KELLY; "about 5 foot, four inches high; well set; pockfretten; has black eyes; house carpenter by trade"; advertised in *The New York Mercury*, October 11, 1756

WALTER COOK, a servant man; runaway from WILLIAM KELLY; "about 35 years of age; six foot high; wears his own light colored hair; long thin visage"; advertised in *The New York Mercury* October 11, 1756

DAVID CLARK, an apprentice lad, runaway from SAMUEL CLIZBE. of Lyons Farms New Jersey; "about 19 years of age; brown hair and round shouldered; intends to go aprivateering"; advertised in *The New York Mercury*, October 11, 1756

NATHANIEL JEWELL, an apprentice lad; runaway from ICHABUD GROMMON of Lyons Farms New Jersey; "about 17 years of age, well made, sturdy lad with light brown hair; intends to go aprivateering"; advertised in *The New York Mercury*, October 11, 1756

PINEYL, a high Dutch servant; runaway from DANIEL

WALDRON of Reding Town West New Jersey; "he had a mark under the cheek of the King's Evil; the toes on his right foot are swollen by a weight's falling on it; he has light straight brown hair; advertised in *The Pennsylvania Journal*, October 14, 1756

JOHN NOWLAND, an Irish indentured servant; runaway from RENSELEAR WILLIAMS, in New Brunswick; "a laborer who came from Ireland three years before, and was under the Command of Sir WILLIAM JOHNSON last year at Lake George; tall; well made man; about 5 foot, 10 inches high; of a sandy complexion; with a large down hanging lip and 23 years of age"; apply to JACOB VAN WAGGENON in New York; advertised in *The New York Mercury*, October 18, 1756

BENJAMIN FITZ RANDOLF, an apprentice lad; runaway from WILLIAM STEWART, blacksmith, of Somerset County; "of a fair complexion and about 5 foot 10 inches high"; advertised in *The New York Mercury*, November 1, 1756

JACOB TAYLOR, an apprentice; runaway from THOMAS LONGWORTH in Newark; "supposed to have to New York to go a privateering on the privateer *Prince George*"; advertised in *The New York Mercury*, December 6, 1756

JOHN ANDERSON; runaway from a pilot boat meeting Sloop *Patty*, Captain HOUSE; "went ashore at Glouster Point with stolen money; is a shoemaker by trade; 5 foot, six inches high; has dark brown hair, well made and about 30 years of age"; apply to Captain HOUSE in Water Street, Philadelphia; advertised in *The Pennsylvania Journal*, December 9, 1756

PAULTUS FLATT, a Dutch servant lad; runaway from JOSEPH MICKLE in Newtown in Glouster county; "about 19 years of age; near 5 foot, 5 inches high; pretty much pock marked on the face; has dark flaxen bushey hair; supposed to be going to his father, CHRISTAIN FLATT, living near Conestogue"; advertised in *The Pennsylvania Gazette*, December 9, 1756

MATTHIAS YARNOD, a Dutch servant man; runaway from JOHN SHURTS in Amwell, about nine miles from Bordentown; "about 50 years of age; about 5 foot 3 inches high; can speak but little English"; advertised by THOMAS JAMES, Gaoler in Philadelphia, in *The Pennsylvania Gazette*, December 9,1756

SAMUEL WILLIS, runaway from RICHARD ARREL of Deptford Township, Glouster; "of little stature; schoolmaster; thin face and pale complexion"; advertised in *The Pennsylvania Gazette*, December 16, 1756

JOHN HINSON, a servant man; runaway from STEPHEN TOLLMAN of Shrewsbury, Monmouth county; "aged 29 years; a tall fellow; thin visaged; wears his own black hair, tied behind; has a small impediment in his speech and is a prodigal like fellow"; notice to JOSEPH FURMAN in New York; advertised in *The New York Mercury*, January 3 1757

Unnamed, an apprentice lad; runaway from JOHN DENNIS, hatter, of the Borough of Elizabeth; "about 20 years old; of a fresh complexion; and of a middling stature; is suspected of going aprivateering"; advertised in *The New York Mercury*, July, 18, 1757

JOHN ASHTON, an Irish servant man; runaway from WILLIAM NEWBOLD of Chesterfield Township, Burlington County; "aged 35 years; 5 feet, 5 inches high; says he has been a privateering with Capt. King"; advertised in *The New York Mercury*, August, 22 1757

WILLIAM ROSS, an apprentice lad; "supposed to be secreted by his mother CATHERINE MONTGOMERY, living in the Town of Bound Brook; about 14 years old; is pretty tall for his age, but slender and much freckled"; advertised by H. GAINE (editor) in *The New York Mercury*, August 22, 1757

JOHN BOUDENHAGEN, a Dutch servant man; runaway from MATTHIA KIGER of the town of Piles Grove,

Salem County; "a short, thick set fellow; has a red beard and light colored hair; is lame on his left leg and ham; between 30 and forty years of age; speaks neither good English or good Dutch"; advertised in *The Pennsylvania Gazette*, October 6, 1757

Taken up and confined in Glouster Gaol under suspicion of being a runaway servant, THOMAS HEADEN, English born; "a short thick fellow of a swarthy complexion; much pitted with small pox"; advertised by ROBERT FRIEND PRICE, Sheriff in *The New York Gazette*, October 27, 1757

JOSEPH DEALY, an English servant man; runaway from CHARLES READ, Esq. at Beesey Ridge in Burlington County; "about 45 years of age; about 5 feet 6 inches high; born in Buckinghamshire; has been a soldier; is a quiet still fellow when sober, but apt to get into liquor and, then, very talkative"; advertised by HUGH DUNN in *The Pennsylvania Journal*, August 17, 1758

EDWARD MAYBE, an English servant man; aged about 22 years; 5 feet tall; well set; darkish complexion; wears his own black hair; hair mole on his left cheek"

GEORGE LEONARD GEIST, a German servant man; runaway from ADAM LEGERGER of Pilesgrove in Salem county; "aged about 20 years; of middle stature; full faced; yellow hair"; advertised in *The Pennsylvania Gazette*, June 1, 1758

WILLIAN GARNET, a servant man; runaway from KENDAL COLE, living in Glouster County; aged about 40 years; yellow, thin hair; a hump on his right shoulder; had lived in Pennsylvania"; advertised in *The Pennsylvania Journal*, June 22, 1758

EDWARD HICKS, an American born servant lad; runaway from THOMAS BAKER of Glouster; "short, 5 feet tall; well set; fair complexion; short curled brown hair";

JOSEPH SIMMONDS, an Irish servant lad; runaway from JOSEPH HACKNEY of Chester Township, Burlington County; "aged about 18 years; 5 feet, 6 inches high; sandy complexion; formerly belonged to JOHN OGBURN, carter, in Kensington"; advertised in *The Pennsylvania Gazette*, April 2, 1759

WILLIAM BURNS, an Irish servant man; runaway from JOHN COX, from Upper Freehold, Monmouth County; "about 45 years of age; about 5 feet, 6 inches high; wore his own hair, Indian style; his face much shaped like an Indian; a very impertinent, talkative fellow; very apt to get drunk when he can come by liquor; speaks good English; is acquainted with most places in America, especially the Jerseys and Pennsylvania"; advertised in *The Pennsylvania Gazette*, April 19, 1759

SAMUEL M'NEAL, an apprentice lad; runaway from WILLIAM RIDDLE living in Bound Brook, Somerset County; "about 20 years of age; well set; somewhat pitted with small pox; is supposed to be in or about New York"; advertised in *The New York Mercury*, May 14, 1759

ELIJAH ROWLAND, an apprentice lad; runaway from SAMUEL BOWNE of Somerset County; "about 18 years of age; about 5 feet, 11 inches high; has been one cruise aprivateering"; advertised in *The New York Mercury*, May 28, 1759

ADAM COONS, a German servant man; runaway from AARON LOUZADA, of Bridgewater in the County of Somerset; "about 35 or 40 years of age; brown complexion; long thin visage; speaks good English; wears his own hair; was out last cruise in the Brig *Earl* of London, JOHN WALLACE, late commander; advertised in *The New York Mercury*, June 4, 1759

JOHN CHRISTOPHER SCHUTTS, a Dutch servant man; runaway from CALEB EVANS; "of a thin visage; 5 feet, 6 or 7 inches high; pale hair almost white; has had a cut on his right instep which makes him drop his toe as he walks; bought about five weeks ago from JOHN STOKES"; advertised in *The Pennsylvania Gazette*, August 16, 1759

JOHN DAVIS, an Irish servant man; runaway from JOSIAH CRANE at Pissipiny [Parsippany], Morris County; "5 feet, 6 inches high; black complexion; well set; short black hair"; notice to Capt. LEMUEL BOWERS in Parsipiny; advertised in *The New York Mercury*, October 1, 1759

FRANCIS CLOWSON, an apprentice boy; runaway from MATTHIAS BOATMAN, near Mount Holly in Burlington County; "aged about 18 years; 5 feet high; fair complexion; short brown hair"; advertised in *The Pennsylvania Gazette*, November 22, 1759

JOHN STILLWELL, an English servant man; runaway from the farm of JOHN LAWRENCE in Mansfield, Burlington County; advertised in *The Pennsylvania Gazette*, November 29, 1759

WILLIAM CRAWFORD, a servant man; runaway from the Andover Iron Works in the County of Sussex;, "about 30 years of age; about 6 feet; wears his own hair; fair complexion"; advertised by JOHN HACKETT at the Union Iron Works and BENJAMIN COOPER at Andover Furnace in *The Pennsylvania Gazette*, March 19, 1761

JOHN NORMAND, a servant man; runaway from the Andover Iron works in the County of Sussex; "about 25 years of age; about 5 feet, 10 inches high; wears his own hair; pale complexion; has been sick of late"; advertised by JOHN HACKETT at the Union Iron Works and BENJAMIN COOPER at Andover Furnace in *The Pennsylvania Gazette*, March 19, 1761

JOHN PINTER, a High Dutch servant man, runaway from VALENTINE BRYANT of Hopewell Township, Hunterdon County; "aged about 27 years; about 5 feet, 7 inches high; is a short, well set fellow; short black hair; dark complexion"; advertised in *The Pennsylvania Gazettte*, April 2, 1761

WILLIAM BUTTERWORTH, an American born servant man, runaway from JOSEPH GIBSON, living in the Township of Deptford, Glouster County; "about 5 feet high; long, straight, yellowish hair; yellowish complexion"; advertised in *The Pennsylvania Gazette*, January 7, 1762

JOSEPH MACMEIN, a servant man, runaway from JONATHAN FOX and JAMES GINIS of Springfield in Burlington County; "a short, thick set fellow; dark eyes; short grey hair; pale faced; pockmarked; speaks hoarse; wears a leather apron to hide his being much bursten and appears to be aged about 50 years; a weaver by trade"; advertised in *The Pennsylvania Gazette*, January, 7 1762

PETER HUNTER, a servant man, runaway from WILLIAM FOX in Springfield, Burlington County; "aged about 22 years; brought up in Egg Harbor; of middle stature, but slim; of a light complexion; has grey eyes; light colored, short hair and is slow of speech"; advertised in *The Pennsylvania Gazette*, February 11, 1762

JAMES LAPSLEY, an Irish servant man, runaway from JACOB STERN of Grenwich in the County of Sussex; "aged about 28 years; about 6 feet high; well made; has formerly followed peddling in these provinces; sometimes pretends to be a mill wright by trade, sometimes an iron master; he is subject to live high and boast much of his former circumstances, but is a notorious rogue having been whipped in Philadelphia for horse stealing"; advertised in *The Pennsylvania Gazette*, March 4, 1762

WILLIAM COOPER, a servant man, runaway from MATTHIAS WILLIAMSON of Elizabeth Town; "aged about 28 years; about 5 feet, 8 inches high; slim built; by trade a coach harness maker and trimmer"; advertised in *The Pennsylvania Journal*, April 15, 1762

JOHN MARTIN, a servant man, runaway from Sterling iron works in Bergen County; "aged about 27 years; about 5 feet, 6 inches high; a laborer under contract; grey eyes; light complexion; long hair, which he commonly wears tied and much marked with small pox"; advertised by WILLIAM HAWXHURST in *The New York Mercury*, April 19, 1762

JOHN CANNON, an American born servant man, runaway from JOHN RAMBO of Mantua Creek, Glouster County; "aged about 18 years; straight black hair; very talkative"; advertised in *The Pennsylvania Gazette*, May 6, 1762

DENNIS M'MAHAN, an Irish servant man, runaway from GEORGE JOHNSON of Perth Amboy; "aged about 28 years;, about 5 feet, 6 inches high; brown complexion; full faced; much pitted with small pox"; advertised in *The New York Mercury*, June 21, 1762

RICHARD MULLHARRON [M'CARRON], an Irish servant boy, runaway from JAMES WALLACE in Philadelphia; "about 5 feet, 4 inches high; wears his own hair which is long and reddish and lately cut short on the crown of his head; his left eye is black and scratched in the face, which is freckled; he has been working on a boat so that his hands and clothes are tarry"; advertised in *The Pennsylvania Journal*, June 24, 1762

THOMAS ADAMS, an apprentice, runaway from SAMUEL ADAMS of Pluckamin Town, Somerset county; "aged about 19 years; about 5 feet, 7 or 8 inches high; brown hair; dark complexion"; advertised in *The Pennsylvania Gazette*, July 1, 1762

JOHN STEDHAM, a servant man, runaway from SOLOMON SMITH in Salem County; "about 5 feet, 6 inches high; short black curled hair; red complexion; very much given to drink"; advertised in *The Pennsylvania Gazette,* July 8, 1762

WILLIAM KOSADY, a servant man, runaway from BURBAGE BROCK and SAMUEL ESTILL, living in New

Hanover, Burlington County; "aged about 22 years; about 6 feet high; brown hair tied behind; fresh complexion; is commonly pretty talkative"; advertised in *The Pennsylvania Journal*, August 5, 1762

JOSEPH JONES, an apprentice lad, runaway from BURBAGE BROCK and SAMUEL ESTILL, living in New Hanover, Burlington Ccunty; "aged about 19 or 20 years; about 5 feet, 6 inches high; wears his own hair which is lightish in color; pale complexion"; advertised in *The Pennsylvania Journal*, August 5, 1762

WILLIAM KELLY, an apprentice lad, runaway from ELIAS VAN COURT, living at Bound Brook in the County of Somerset; "aged about 18 years; tailor; about 5 feet, 6 inches high; long brown hair; a well set, likely boy"; advertised in *The New York Mercury*, August 9, 1762

JACOB HARRIS, an apprentice lad, runaway from ELIAS VAN COURT, living at Bound Brook in the County of Somerset; "aged about 18 years; tailor; light colored hair and pretty short"; advertised in *The New York Mercury*, August 9, 1762

THOMAS BROWN,, a servant man, runaway from DARBY DURELL, living in Chester Town, Burlington County; "aged about 25 years; about 5 feet, 8 inches high; black, bushy hair; brown complexion; a scar on the side of his head, a little above his forehead, whereon lightish colored hair grows; has a sore leg"; advertised in *The Pennsylvania Journal*, August 5, 1762

WILLIAM CURRY, an Irish servant man, runaway from GEORGE TRENCHARD of Penn's Neck in Salem County; "aged about 35 years; about 5 feet, 2 inches high; light, brown curled hair; sandy complexion; much freckled on his face and hands; is a great taker of snuff; his legs are pretty thick and short; steps very short in walking; says he is a butcher by trade but has been used to plantation work for several years past";

advertised in *The Pennsylvania Gazette*, August 26, 1762

CHARLES DUGRAY, an Irish servant man, runaway from JACOB STARN and JOHN HUGHES of Greenwich Forge, West New Jersey; "about 30 years of age; wears his own hair and speaks hoarse as if he had a cold"; advertised in *The Pennsylvania Gazette*, October 7, 1762

JOHN HOWELL, an Irish servant man, runaway from JACOB STARN and JOHN HUGHES of Greenwich Forge, West New Jersey; "aged about 30 years; wears his own hair; has lost the forefingers of one of his hands"; advertised in *The Pennsylvania Gazette*, October 7, 1762

JAMES ANDERSON, an apprentice lad, runaway from SACHEVERALL WOOD, living in Philadelphia; "aged about 18 or 19 years; about 5 feet, 8 inches high; a tailor by trade with better than two years to serve; he has a smooth face and fair complexion; wears his own hair pretty long; is pretty likely and is pretty shame faced"; has a mother and brother living in East Town in New Jersey; advertised in *The Pennsylvania Journal*, November 11, 1762

UZAL WOODRUFF, an apprentice lad, runaway from MOSES OGDEN; "aged about 18 years; about 5 feet, 6 inches high; cordwainer and shoemaker"; advertised in *The New York Mercury*, November 15, 1762

EPENETUS BEACH, an apprentice lad, runaway from MOSES OGDEN; "about 5 feet 5 inches high, cord wainer and shoe maker"; advertised in *The New York Mercury*, November 15, 1762

JOHN KELLY, a servant man, runaway from THOMAS FORMAN of Hanover Township in Burlington County; "aged about 18 years; about 5 feet, 4 inches high; straight yellowish hair; fair complexion; somewhat marked with the small pox; very remarkable for often sucking his tongue"; advertised in *The Pennsylvania Gazette*, September 23, 1762

JOHN WHITE, a servant man, runaway from JIERARD SAXTON, living in Pennington, West New Jersey; "aged about 21 years; about 5 feet, 6 inches high; well set and wears his own hair; pale complexion; shoe maker by trade; of a light color; much given to card playing"; advertised in *The New York Mercury,* January 3, 1763

JOSEPH SMITH, an apprentice, runaway from JOSEPH DONELSON of Maidenhead; "aged about 18 or 19 years; about 5 feet, 2 inches high; short brown hair; thin long face; speaks English only; advertised in *The Pennsylvania Gazette,* January 23, 1763

PETER BURIS, an American born servant man; runaway from WILLIAM KILLE in Greenwich Township between Rackoon and Oldman's Creek; "aged about 25 years; 5 feet, 8 inches tall; of Dutch descent; fresh colored complexion; great swearer and wrestler; apt to drink hard; gray eyes and black short hair; had driven a team on an expedition to Ohio"; stole from BENJAMIN HOWELL; advertised in *The Pennsylvania Gazette,* March 24, 1763

JAMES SMITH, an American born servant man; runaway from WILLIAM KILLE in Greenwich Township between Rackoon and Oldman's Creek; "aged about 22 years; 5 feet, 10 inches tall; born in Queen Ann's County, Maryland; gray eyes; a little freckled; slender built; brown hair; walks stooping"; stole from BENJAMIN HOWELL; advertised in *The Pennsylvania Gazette,* March 24, 1763

THOMAS JONES, a servant man; runaway from EDMUND BEAKES, near Allen Town; "middle sized man; brown complexion; long black hair, which he commonly wears tied behind; by profession a shoemaker"; advertised in *The Pennsylvania Gazette,* March 31, 1763

RICHARD CLARK, an English servant boy; runaway from JOHN KAIGHIN, in Haddonfield, Glouster; "a chunky thick fellow; 4 feet tall; has a full face; sandy hair; much marked with small pox"; advertised in *The Pennsylvania Gazette*, April 7, 1763

WILLIAM MCKABE [MCKAPE] a servant man; runaway from NATHANIEL PARKER, at Trenton Ferry; "aged about 20 years; 5 feet, 10 inches tall; fresh complexion; has three hair molds on his face; one on each cheek and the other one on a side of his chin"; advertised in *The New York Gazette*, April 11, 1763

EDWARD MAY, an English servant man; runaway from JOSIAH HALSTEAD of Shrewsbury; "aged about 24 years; 5 feet, 4 inches tall; can neither read nor write; dark hair; by trade a brick maker; a very swift workman; somewhat marked with the small pox; has a particular roll in his gait"; advertised in *The New York Gazette*, April 18, 1763

JOSEPH DAVID, a German born Jew servant man; runaway from THOMAS MAYHEW, of Salem; "aged about 30 years; 5 feet, 3 inches tall; dark complexion; well set; three scars on his head; likely he will follow peddling as he has a great desire to follow that calling and has often talked about it; an artful fellow; kept a shop in Albany for the sale of goods"; advertised in *The Pennsylvania Gazette*, May 5, 1763

CHRISTIAN LEER, a Dutch servant man; runaway from WILLIAM FLENTHAM; "aged about 19 years; dark complexion; black curled hair; a sliving down look"; advertised in *The Pennsylvania Gazette*, May 19, 1763

JOHN RICHMAN, a servant man; runaway from JOHN VOORHEES; "aged about 20 years; 5 feet 10 inches tall; well set, and active"; advertised in *The Pennsylvania Gazette*, July 7, 1763

CORNELIUS CAMPBELL, a servant man; runaway from JOSEPH STONE BANKS of Pile's Grove, Salem County; "aged about 25 years; 5 feet, 2 inches tall; brown complexion; long black hair tied behind; by trade a weaver; something marked with the small pox; sings a very good song; something inclined to liquor; pretends to know about riding and race horses"; advertised in *The New York Gazette*, August 1, 1763

JAMES MARTIN, an Irish servant man; runaway from JOHN ESTAUGH HOPKINS, living in Glouster County; "aged about 27 years; 5 feet, 6 inches tall; sprightly countenance; short brown hair; has been used to country business"; advertised in *The Pennsylvania Gazette*, August 18, 1763

JOHN MORRISON, a servant man; runaway from THOMAS GRAVES of Piles Grove, Salem County; "5 feet 5 inches tall; well set; brown complexion; short, black hair"; advertised in *The Pennsylvania Gazette*, September 1, 1763

HUGH BARKLEY, a servant lad; runaway from SAMUEL RODGERS, living in Hanover Township, Burlington County, near Iven's Mill; "aged about 18 years; short, black curled hair"; advertised in *The Pennsylvania Journal*, September 15, 1763

HENRY COLE, a servant man; runaway from ROBERT EMLEY and PETER ROBESON, living in Kingwood, Hunterdon County; "aged about 18 years; 5 feet, 10 inches tall; slim built; raw boned; has large feet; brown hair tied behind; very talkative"; advertised in *The Pennsylvania Gazette*, September 15, 1763

WILLIAM FRAZIER, a Scotch servant man; runaway from SAMUEL HENRY of Trenton; "aged about 25 years; 5 feet, 7 inches tall; dark complexion; down look; bushy, dark brown hair; lately taken out of Amboy gaol by one HILL; had been in the country for some time, but because of some misdemeanor he was put in Amboy gaol and became a servant"; advertised in *The New York Gazette*, September 19, 1763

DAVID BROWN, an Irish servant man; runaway from NATHAN FOLWELL in Springfield, Burlington County; "came in about 8 weeks ago; middle stature; very much freckled about the face; by trade a weaver"; advertised in *The New York Gazette*, September 26, 1763

Committed to the Hunterdon gaol on suspicion of being a runaway, ZACHARIAH RIGTON, belongs to CONRAD SMITH, Mason, in Baltimore; advertised by SAMUEL TUCKER, Sheriff, in *The Pennsylvania Gazette,* September 29, 1763

Was committed to Cumberland County gaol, for want of a pass, WILLIAM LLOYD; says he was born in Queen Ann's county in Maryland; aged about 26 years; advertised by HOWELL POWELL, Sheriff, in *The Pennsylvania Gazette*, October 20, 1763

JOHN WILLIAMS, an apprentice lad; runaway from ADAM PARKER in Burlington County; "aged about 15 years; 5 feet, 5 inches tall; brown complexion; short curled hair; six months ago, he escaped from the Indians where he had been a captive for two years"; notice to THOMAS STORY at the Crooked Billet Wharf in Philadelphia; advertised in *The Pennsylvania Journal*, October 27, 1763

TERRY M'VERMIK, an Irish servant lad; runaway from ROBERT TAYLOR, of Greenwich Township, Glouster County; "aged about 18 or 19 years; middle stature; freckled and talks good English; brown hair"; advertised in *The Pennsylvania Journal*, November 3, 1763

JOHN MCKAY, a servant man; runaway from a shallop between Glouster Point and Chester on the New Jersey side of the Delaware; "aged about 19 years; 5 feet, 6 inches tall; black complexion; wears a black wig"; been at sea; lately imported from Leith in the Ship *Boyd*, Capt. DUNLOP; advertised by ROBERT RITCHIE in *The Pennsylvania Journal*, November 3, 1763

WILLIAM MCQUEEN, a servant man; runaway from a shallop between Glouster Point and Chester on the New Jersey side of the Delaware; aged about 21 years; 5 feet, 9 inches tall; ruddy complexion; black wig; been at sea; lately imported from Leith in the Ship *Boyd*, Capt. DUNLOP; advertised by ROBERT RITCHIE in *The Pennsylvania Journal*, November 3, 1763

CHRISTOPHER WEIGNER, Swedish or Danish servant man; runaway from a shallop between Glouster Point and Chester on the New Jersey side of the Delaware; "aged about 26 years; 5 feet, 6 inches tall; strong made; fair complexion; wears his own hair; speaks bad English"; been at sea, lately imported from Leith in the Ship Boyd, Capt. DUNLOP; advertised by ROBERT RITCHIE in *The Pennsylvania Journal*, November 3, 1763

J. DAWSON, a servant man; runaway from a shallop between Glouster Point and Chester on the New Jersey side of the Delaware; "aged about 22 years; 5 feet, 9 inches tall; fair complexion; well made; wears a black wig or cap;" been at sea, lately imported from Leith in the Ship *Boyd*, Capt. DUNLOP; advertised by ROBERT RITCHIE in *The Pennsylvania Journal*, November 3, 1763

ALEXANDER MCDONALD, a servant man; runaway from a shallop between Glouster Point and Chester on the New Jersey side of the Delaware; "aged about 26 years; 5 feet, 6 inches tall; brown complexion; wears his own hair; marked with the small pox; a tin man or pewterer;" lately imported from Leith in the Ship *Boyd*, Capt. DUNLOP; advertised by ROBERT RITCHIE in *The Pennsylvania Journal*, November 3, 1763

DAVID GRAHAM, a servant man; runaway from a shallop between Glouster Point and Chester on the New Jersey side of the Delaware; "aged about 28 years; 5 feet, 6 inches tall; swarthy complexion; short red hair; a tin man or pewterer;" lately imported from Leith in the Ship *Boyd*, Capt. DUNLOP; advertised by ROBERT RITCHIE in *The Pennsylvania Journal*, November 3, 1763

JAMES DOBSON, an English servant man; runaway from SAMUEL HEWES, of Greenwich Township in Glouster County; "5 feet, 4 inches tall; fair complexion; a cast in his eyes"; advertised in *The Pennsylvania Journal*, November 17, 1763

ABRAHAM WILLIAMS, servant man; runaway from JAMES GRAY, living at Little Falls on the Passaic River; "thick set man; sandy complexion; red hair"; advertised in *The Pennsylvania Gazette*, November 17, 1763

DAVID FOSTER, an apprentice lad; runaway from HENRY TUDER, Pilot of Reedy Island, New Castle County; "aged about 21 years; well set; down look; swarthy complexion; long straight black hair; talkative fellow"; advertised in *The Pennsylvania Journal*, November 24, 1763

HENRY GORMAN, an Irish servant man; runaway from GEORGE DAVIS, Merchant in Philadelphia; lately come in Brig *Boscowan*; advertised in *The Pennsylvania Journal*, December 1, 1763

ABRAHAM LORD, an American born servant man; runaway from JOHN DUEL in Piles Grove, Salem County; "5 feet, 10 inches tall; pock marked"; advertised in *The Pennsylvania Gazette*, December 15, 1763

JOSEPH BYARD, a Dutch servant man, runaway from JOB LIPPINCOTT, living in Springfield, Burlington county; "aged about 21 years; about 5 feet, 5 or 6 inches high"; advertised in *The Pennsylvania Gazette*, February 2, 1764

THOMAS OSBURN [THOMAS HARDBURN], a servant man; runaway from WILLIAM NALLS, near Princeton; "about 21 or 22 years of age; thick build; smooth face; wears his own hair; talks very thick; brown complexion"; advertised by GEORGE CAMPBELL at Princeton in *The Pennsylvania Journal*, March 15, 1764

JOHN REEKER, a Dutch servant man; runaway from JOHN GIBBON living in Cohansey, West Jersey; "5 feet high; wore his own hair of a dark brown color; talks broken English and has lost some of his fore teeth; by trade a stocking weaver"; advertised in *The Pennsylvania Journal*, March 22, 1764

BERNARD M'CINDRED, an Irish servant lad; runaway from DANIEL LIPPINCOTT, Jr. of Evesham, Burlington county; "about 16 -17 years of age; a large well set fellow for his age; very much freckled; red complexion; somewhat pitted with small pox; talks pretty good English for the time he has been in the county, which is about 6 or 7 months; a lively pert countenance; very talkative"; advertised in *The Pennsylvania Journal*, March 22, 1764

Committed to the Gaol of York County on suspicion of being a runaway, ELIJAH DAVIS, born in West Jersey and brought up in Cumberland County; "about 26 years of age; of a ruddy complexion; about 5 feet, 11 inches high"; advertised by JACOB GRAYBILL, Gaoler in *The Pennsylvania Gazette*, March 29, 1764

Committed to the Gaol of York County on suspicion of being a runaway, JOHN M'PETERS, born in Kent County on the Delaware; advertised by JACOB GRAYBILL, Gaoler in *The Pennsylvania Gazette*, March 29, 1764

Committed to the Gaol of York County on suspicion of being a runaway, JOSEPH THOMAS, born in Philadelphia; advertised by JACOB GRAYBILL, Gaoler in *The Pennsylvania Gazette*, March 29, 1764

WILLIAM BOWEN, a servant man; runaway from MICHAEL LEE of Cumberland County; "about 35 or 40 years of age; red faced; lost one of his thumbs and some of his fore teeth; about 5 feet 6 or 7 inches high"; advertised in *The Pennsylvania Gazette*, March 29, 1764

WILLIAM COOPER, an English born servant man;

runaway from JOSIAH WINANTS and JONATHAN HAMPTON; "about 32 years of age; 5 feet, 8 inches high; born in London; slim; lanthorn jawed; is very apt to drink and, when drunk, is much inclined to singing; wears his own short brown hair, with a thin sandy beard; marked with small pox; by trade a coach harness maker and trimmer"; advertised in *The New York Mercury,* April 2, 1764

Committed to the Gaol of Salem County on suspicion of being a runaway, DANIEL MURFEY, who says he was a servant to one NIEL GAULEHER in Warwick; "about 20 years of age; says he is a tailor"; advertised by JOHN BUDD, Sheriff in *The Pennsylvania Gazette,* April 5, 1764

MICHAEL BARRAT, a servant man; runaway from JOHN NICHOLSON of Salem County; "about 27 years of age; 5 feet, 8 or 9 inches high; wears bushy, curled hair; sandy complexion; has been a soldier"; advertised in *The Pennsylvania Gazette,* April 5, 1764

PETER MARSH, an English born servant man; runaway from RALPH NORTON; "about 30 years of age; middle sized; slender built; brown eyes; wears his own short brown hair; pretty likely fellow; has a few marks from small pox; says he came from Lancashire in England but last from Ireland and arrived here last fall; is a remarkably complaisant, fair spoken fellow and has been used to waiting on a gentleman"; advertised in *The Pennsylvania Journal,* April 12, 1764

JAMES CRAZE [JAMES BAGLY], an apprentice boy; runaway from JAMES CAMPBELL in Springfield, Borough of Elizabeth Town; "about 17 years of age; middling size; wears his own straight black hair; marked with small pox"; advertised in *The Pennsylvania Journal,* April 12, 1764

RICHARD THETFORD, an Irish servant lad; runaway from JOSHUA LORD, living in Deptford Township, Glouster county; "about 15 years of age; 5 feet, 4 inches high; well set; fair complexion; marked a little with small pox"; has been in this country 5 months; advertised in *The Pennsylvania Journal*, April 12, 1764; re advertised two years later on June 12, 1766 as having run away again from the same master, now "aged about 17 years; 5 feet 5 or 6 inches tall; fair complexion; brown hair; cut close upon the top and short behind; is a smart looking fellow and very talkative; has been in this country about 2 and a half years; marked a little with small pox"

BERNARD ---, an Irish servant man; runaway from WILLIAM FOSTER living in Burlington county; "about 19 years of age; 5 feet, 2 inches high; well built; dark hair"; advertised in *The Pennsylvania Gazette*, April 26, 1764

JOHN SMITH [PHILIP KENTLING], an Irish servant man; runaway from ANDREW BOZORTH, living in Evesham, Burlington county; "middle aged; 5 feet, 10 inches high; wears his own hair; thin faced; brown complexion"; advertised in *The Pennsylvania Gazette*, April 26, 1764

PATRICK BREASTLAND, an Irish servant man; runaway from JAMES COOPER, living in Glouster County; "about 18 or 19 years of age; 5 feet 7 inches high; black hair; slim; pitted with small pox"; advertised in *The Pennsylvania Gazette*, May 3, 1764

ALEXANDER M'DONNAUGH [ALEXANDER M'DONNELL], an Irish servant man; runaway from ABRAHAM MATLACK living in Evesham, Burlington County; "about 24 years of age; 5 feet 7 inches high; slim; thin face; down look; subject to drink; wears his own dark hair; a little curled with a sandy beard; supposed to have gone to Lancaster, Pennsylvania as he has a brother there"; advertised in *The Pennsylvania Gazette*, May 10, 1764

JACOB FIZELER, a Dutch servant lad; runaway from JUDAH CLEMANS, living near Haddonfield, West Jersey; "about 16 years of age; 5 feet high; fair complexion"; advertised in *The Pennsylvania Journal*, May 24, 1764

CHRISTOPHER BURNS, an Irish servant man; runaway from RICHARD TOWNSHEND'S shallop; about 18 years of age; 5 feet, 5 inches high; smooth face; speaks pretty good English; pretty fair complexion; just arrived from Ireland"; advertised by AARON LEAMING of Cape May and ROBERT BOYD, Hatter, in Front Street, Philadelphia in *The Pennsylvania Gazette*, May 24, 1764

EBENEZER HAULBEET, a servant man; runaway from JOSEPH KING of Morris Town; "about 25 years of age; 5 feet, 8 or 9 inches high; flax colored straight hair; light complexion with small pox; by trade a carpenter"; thought to be going near Sharon Connecticut where he has some relations by the same name; advertised in *The New York Mercury*, June 18, 1764

JAMES BAIN, a Scotch servant man; runaway from JOHN ESTAUGH HOPKINS living in Deptford Township, Glouster County; "about 23 years of age; 5 feet, 6 or 7 inches high; wears his own long brown hair cut short before; has a smooth face with a small dimple in his left cheek and speaks pretty much in the Scotch dialect"; advertised in *The Pennsylvania Journal*, June 28, 1764

PHILIP JACOB BARGOLT [JOHN BACKMAN], a high Dutch servant man; runaway from DAVID WILLIAMSON, living near Cranberry, Middlesex County; "middle stature; knock kneed; brown complexion"; advertised in *The Pennsylvania Gazette*, July 5, 1764

JAMES HODGES, an English born servant man; runaway from the Sterling Iron Works; "aged about 13 years; 5 feet, 7 inches high; brown complexion; long hair; born in Bristol, Old England; by trade a groom or ostler"; advertised by WILLIAM HAWXHURST of New York in *The New York Mercury*, July 9, 1764

BENJAMIN DARBY, an apprentice lad; runaway from MOSES OGDEN at Elizabeth Town; "aged about 20 years; 4 feet, 7 inches high; fresh complexion; dark hair; broad faced and bulky; gray eyes and when he laughs you can hardly see them; his countenance looks very guilty, much like a thief; a down look; carries his head something on one side; cannot well look a man in the face; loves strong liquor; by trade a cordwainer and tanner"; advertised in *The New York Mercury*, July 9, 1764

MARK M'CLOUGHLAND, an Irish servant man; runaway from LAWRENCE SALTER of Lambarton fishery; "aged about 18 years; low in stature with thick legs; fair complexion; slightly marked with small pox; his hair is brown and curls; his under jaw projects a little; he speaks quick and has the brogue upon his tongue"; advertised in *The Pennsylvania Journal*, August 9, 1764

THOMAS FENTON, an American born apprentice lad; runaway from FREDERICK HAGENER and CHRISTOPHER HANSMAN living in Freehold, Monmouth County; "aged about 18 years; middle stature; dark straight hair; slim; by trade a tailor; born in Freehold"; advertised in *The Pennsylvania Gazette*, August 23, 1764

JOSEPH HUGHES, an American born apprentice lad; runaway from FREDERICK HAGENER and CHRISTOPHER HANSMAN living in Freehold, Monmouth County; "aged about 17 years; fair faced lad; short curled hair; and is well set; by trade a tailor; born in Freehold"; advertised in *The Pennsylvania Gazette*, August 23, 1764

DANIEL M'AFEE, a servant man; runaway from EDWARD MURPHEY, living on Derham Road in Bedminster Township, Bucks County, near Teheken Creek; "5 feet, 9 inches high; brown complexion; black hair; has followed weaving for some time at one CHRSITIAN SHARP's house, near Mr. JOHNSON's Iron Works in Hunterdon County; is much addicted to drinking and swearing and is of a fractious, quarrelsome disposition; by trade a weaver, but has followed privateering"; advertised in *The Pennsylvania Gazette*, August 30, 1764

Was committed in the Cumberland county gaol on the suspicion of being a runaway, JOHN BACK; aged about 25; says he has served his time to JOSEPH BANTLENT in Talbot County, Maryland; advertised by HOWELL POWELL, Sheriff in *The Pennsylvania Journal*, September 6, 1764

THOMAS ADLEY, an Irish servant man; runaway from the ship *Newry Assistance*, Capt. WILLIAM CHEVERS, Master; "aged about 23 years; 5 feet, 6 inches high; dark complexion; slow in speech if not in liquor; by trade a brazier or brass founder but has worked a little at the business of barber; notice to JOHN PRINGLE, Merchant in Philadelphia; advertised in *The Pennsylvania Journal,* October 13, 1764

Was committed on suspicion of being a runaway, JOHN GALLAHA, [JOHN READ, JOHN M'DANIEL] says he belongs to one DANIEL GLASS, tanner, who lives on the Forks of the Brandywine; 18 or 19 years of age; advertised in *The Pennsylvania Gazette*, March 13, 1766

FRANCIS FLOOD, an Irish servant man; runaway from MOSES IVINS and WILLIAM SHREVE, living in Mansfield, Burlington county; "5 feet, 7 inches high; well made; fresh complexion; remarkable red hair, tied behind; dark eyes"; advertised in *The Pennsylvania Gazette*, April 10, 1766

JAMES NAYLAND [JAMES NALLON], an Irish servant man; runaway from MOSES IVINS and WILLIAM SHREVE, living in Mansfield, Burlington county; "5 feet, 7 inches high; pale complexion; smooth faced and has a very flat nose, wide mouth; no beard; light long hair tied behind and very knock kneed"; advertised in *The Pennsylvania Gazette*, April 10, 1766

JAMES M'GRADY, an Irish servant man; runaway from BENJAMIN HEGEMAN of Somerset county; "short stature; fair complexion; has brown curled hair"; had been a servant before near Lancaster, Pennsylvania; advertised in *The Pennsylvania Gazette*, April 10, 1766

WILLIAM SERELS, a servant man; runaway from WILLIAM SPARLING and DAVID WILLIAMSON living in New Brunswick, Middlesex County; "of short stature; black curled hair; has taught at school and has formerly been in His Majesty's Service"; advertised in *The New York Gazette or Weekly Post Boy*, May 1, 1766

MATTHEW MORRISON, an Irish servant man; runaway from JOHN RAMBO, living in Glouster County; "5 feet, 5 inches high; is very talkative and forward in company; on examining his head close, you will find a soft spot on top, occasioned by a blow; he can counterfeit his voice to cats and dogs and served his time in Chester County, Pennsylvania"; advertised in *The Pennsylvania Gazette*, May 8, 1766

GEORGE DAILEY, an English servant man; runaway from JOSEPH HEIGHT, living in Burlington; "aged about 30 years; 5 feet, 6 or 7 inches high; swarthy complexion; long straight black hair; marked with small pox; remarkable large mouth and crooked shins"; advertised in *The Pennsylvania Gazette*, Journal, May 29, 1766

CARL BRUDERLIN, a German indentured servant, runaway from Ringwood Iron Works; "aged about 38 years; 6 feet high; pitted with pock; sandy haired; dark complexion; miner; talks very little English; has 3 years 4 months remaining on his contract"; notice to JOHN ROSS, merchant in Philadelphia; advertised in *The Pennsylvania Journal*, June 12, 1766; also advertised by PETER HASENECLEVER in *The New York Gazette or Weekly Post Boy*, June, 1766

JOSEPH LANGEIDER, a German indentured servant, runaway from Ringwood Iron Works; "aged about 36 years; 5 feet, 7 inches high; bandy legged; miner; talks very little English; has 3 years 4 months remaining on his contract"; notice to JOHN ROSS, merchant in Philadelphia; advertised in *The Pennsylvania Journal*, June 12, 1766; also advertised by PETER HASENECLEVER in *The New York Gazette or Weekly Post Boy*, June, 1766

MATTHIAS ORTMAN, a German indentured servant, runaway from Ringwood Iron Works; "aged about 24 years; 5 feet, 6 inches high; yellowish hair, miner; talks very little English; has 3 years 4 months remaining on his contract"; notice to JOHN ROSS, merchant in Philadelphia; advertised in *The Pennsylvania Journal*, June 12, 1766; also advertised by PETER HASENECLEVER in *The New York Gazette or Weekly Post Boy*, June, 1766

BARTOLEMEW BAUM, a German indentured servant, runaway from Ringwood Iron Works; "5 feet 6 inches high; black hair; miner; talks very little English; has 3 years 4 months remaining on his contract"; notice to JOHN ROSS, merchant in Philadelphia; advertised in *The Pennsylvania Journal*, June 12, 1766; also advertised by PETER HASENECLEVER in *The New York Gazette or Weekly Post Boy*, June, 1766

SIMON DENCK, a German indentured servant, runaway from Ringwood Iron Works; "aged about 25 years; one eye; short hair; miner; talks very little English; has 3 years, 4 months remaining on his contract"; notice to JOHN ROSS, merchant in Philadelphia; advertised in *The Pennsylvania Journal*, June 12, 1766; also advertised by PETER HASENECLEVER in *The New York Gazette or Weekly Post Boy*, June, 1766

PETER HUTSCHLARA, a German indentured servant; runaway from Ringwood Iron Works; "5 feet, 6 inches high; thin and yellowish hair; miner; talks very little English; has 3 years 4 months remaining on his contract"; notice to JOHN ROSS, merchant in Philadelphia; advertised in *The Pennsylvania Journal*, June 12, 1766; also advertised by PETER HASENECLEVER in *The New York Gazette or Weekly Post Boy*, June, 1766

JOHN DURCK, a German indentured servant; runaway from Ringwood Iron Works; "short and pock marked; miner; talk very little English; has 3 years 4 months remaining on his contract"; notice to JOHN ROSS, merchant in Philadelphia; advertised in *The Pennsylvania Journal*, June 12, 1766; also advertised by PETER HASENECLEVER in *The New York Gazette or Weekly Post Boy*, June, 1766

HENRY SCHAEFFER, a German servant man; runaway from Ringwood Iron works, PETER HASENCLEVER; "aged about 38 years; 5 feet, 6 inches tall; dark complexion; black hair; has 3 years 4 months left on his contract; talks very little English"; notice to JOHN ROSS, merchant in Philadelphia; advertised in *The Pennsylvania Journal*, June 12, 1766

WILHOLM KONIG, a German servant man; runaway from Ringwood Iron works, PETER HASENCLEVER; 5 feet, 6 inches tall; whitish hair, has 3 years 4 months left on his contract; talks very little English; notice to JOHN ROSS, merchant in Philadelphia; advertised in *The Pennsylvania Journal*, June 12, 1766

EDWARD RICHARD, an English born servant man; runaway from ALEXANDER ADAMS, of Maiden Head, Hunterdon County; "aged about 26 years; 5 feet 4, inches; born in Chester, England"; advertised in *The New York Gazette and Weekly Post Boy*, July 24, 1766

JOHN JOHNSON, a servant man; runaway from Grubb's Forge in Lancaster County; "aged about 24 or 25 years; 5 feet, 7 or 8 inches; full faced; dark brown hair; marked with small pox"; stole goods from WILLIAM M'CORD in Lancaster; by trade a pedlar; worked at Union Iron works in Jersey; notice to Mr. GRUBB; advertised in *The Pennsylvania Journal*, July 24, 1766

CHARLES CRISMON, a Dutch servant man; runaway from THOMAS FRY of Glouster county; aged about 26 years, but looks older; 5 feet, 8 inches; dark complexion; short sandy curled hair; big and clumsy made; talks broken English; has a mother who lives with JOHN LETHERMON about 5 miles from Philadelphia on the Schuylkill and a brother who lives in Lancaster; notice to JOHN WEST at the Old Ferry house in Philadelphia; advertised in *The Pennsylvania Journal*, July 31,

1766

Committed to Glouster gaol on suspicion of being a runaway servant, WILLIAM FIRTH, belonging to Col. WILLIAM FITZHUGH of Rousby Hall on Patuxent River, Maryland; advertised in *The Pennsylvania Gazette*, July 31, 1766

JOSEPH HEWES, an American born servant man; runaway from CHRISTOPHER HANSMAN, living in Second street, near Vine Street, in Philadelphia; born in Freehold, Monmouth County; "5 feet, 6 inches; well set; smooth faced; brown, short hair; by trade a tailor; advertised in *The Pennsylvania Gazette*, July 31, 1766

BRIAN MAQUOD, an Irish servant lad; runaway from JOAB HILMAN, living in Newtown, Glouster County, about 7 miles from Cooper's Ferry; "aged about 20 years; 5 feet, 2 inches; has a defect in his left eye; black curled hair; with small pox"; advertised in *The Pennsylvania Gazette*, July 31, 1766

Committed to the workhouse of Philadelphia, JOHN QUIN, belonging to DAVID FERGUSON of Salem county; advertised by SAMUEL TUCKER, late Sheriff, in *The Pennsylvania Gazette*, July 31, 1766

Committed to the workhouse of Philadelphia, JAMES NORTON, belonging to SAMUEL NICKISON of Salem county; advertised by SAMUEL TUCKER, late Sheriff, in *The Pennsylvania Gazette*, July 31, 1766

EDWARD ASHTON, an Irish servant man; runaway from JOHN BREEDING in Salem; "5 feet, 6 inches; sandy complexion; served his time in Bristol Pennsylvania; by trade a tailor"; advertised in *The Pennsylvania Gazette*, August 7, 1766

CHARLES VILLANY, an Irish servant man; runaway from WILLIAM MURRAY, late of Haddonfield in Glouster County; "aged about 21 or 22 years; 5 feet, 8 inches; dark complexion; dark curled hair"; advertised in *The Pennsylvania Gazette*, August 14, 1766

Taken up on suspicion of being a runaway servant man, THOMAS COX; "says he was born in Jamaica; served his time at sea out of Liverpool; has been 2 years in ALEXANDER MILLAR's employ as a shallop man from Newport to Philadelphia; 5 feet, 8 inches; very straight; sandy countenance; short flaxen or sandy hair; red beard; long visaged; Roman nose; his middle finger nail on his left hand has been split and forms a ridge; even though he has lived in Newport and Philadelphia for 18 months, he has no acquaintance at either place who can testify that he is either a free or an honest man; he has been detected in many gross untruths"; advertised by JOHN DOWNEY in *The Pennsylvania Journal*, August 14, 1766

JOSEPH JONES, an apprentice lad; runaway from BURROUGHS ABIT, living in Glouster county; "aged about 17 years; 5 feet, 7 inches; lightish colored hair; complexion"; advertised in *Pennsylvania Gazette*, August 28, 1766

JAMES MORROW, an Irish servant man; runaway from THOMAS M'CAGHRY, collier, living in South Amboy township, Middlesex county; "5 feet, 4 inches; short black hair; cut off on top, mixed with grey and pretty long behind; down look; very much addicted to drink"; advertised in *Pennsylvania Gazette*, September 4, 1766

Taken up on suspicion of being a runaway, JOHN EDIMISTON; says he is a servant to THOMAS M'NEIL, late of Philadelphia; advertised by GEORGE BROWN, sheriff in Trenton in *Pennsylvania Gazette*, August 28, 1766

Taken up on suspicion of being a runaway, JOHN JOHNSON; says he is a servant to THOMAS M'NEIL, late of Philadelphia; advertised by GEORGE BROWN, Sheriff of Trenton in *Pennsylvania Gazette*, August 28, 1766

JOSEPH JONES, an apprentice lad; runaway from

BURROUGHS ABIT, living in Glouster County; "aged about years; lightish colored hair;" advertised in *The Pennsylvania Gazette*, August 28, 1766

Taken up on suspicion of being a runaway, JOHN GORDON, says he is a servant to SAMUEL SHARP in Cecil County, Maryland; about 18 years of age; 5 feet, 6 inches high; advertised by EPHRAIM PHILLIPS, Gaoler of Burlington in *Pennsylvania Gazette*, September 11, 1766

JOHN MOOR, an Irish servant man; runaway from SAMUEL HENRY of Trenton; aged about 22 years; about 5 feet, 9 inches high; with long brown dark hair tied behind; marked a little with the small pox; understands something of the carpenter's, wheelwright's and painter's business; much addicted to swearing and drinking"; ran off with a young woman, servant to JONATHAN HUTCHINSON; advertised in *The Pennsylvania Journal*, September 25, 1766

Taken up as runaway, PETER DEGNAR, who says he belongs to ANTHONY WOODCOCK of Philadelphia; advertised by EPHRAIM PHILLIPS, Gaoler in Burlington in *The Pennsylvania Journal*, October 9, 1766

Taken up as runaway, ABRAHAM COURLEY, son of RICHARD COURLEY, who lives in Philadelphia; advertised by EPHRAIM PHILLIPS, Gaoler in Burlington in *The Pennsylvania Journal*, October 9, 1766

PETER MILLER, a servant man; runaway from WILLIAM GOULD and ALEXANDER GOULD living in Westnantmil Township in Chester County, Pennsylvania; "about 6 feet high; wears his own long black hair tied with a black ribbon; is a well discoursed; well faced; blind of his left eye; a mason by trade, is very fond of liquor and to quarrel when drunk"; advertised in *The Pennsylvania Journal*, November 13, 1766

MATTHIAS WALKER, a servant lad; runaway from

PETER IMLAY of Imlay's Town in the Township of Upper Freehold in Monmouth County; "aged about 20 years; about 5 feet, 9 inches high; a likely slim fellow"; advertised in *The Pennsylvania Gazette*, November 27, 1766

JOHN WEIBEL, a Dutch servant man; runaway from JOHN WOLFF, living in Berks County about two miles from Reading; "aged about 24 years; a blacksmith by trade; well set and has black hair"; advertised in *The Pennsylvania Journal*, December 4, 1766

DANIEL EDWARDS, a servant man; runaway from JACOB TOWNSEND in Penn's Neck, Salem County; "about 20 years of age; about 5 feet, 3 or 4 inches tall; sandy complexion; pretty well set; wears his own lightish short hair; much given to jockeying"; advertised in *The Pennsylvania Gazette*, December 18, 1766

JOHN M'CULLOUGH, an Irish servant lad; runaway from HUGH NEWELL, living in Nottingham Township, Burlington County; "about 18 years of age; 5 feet, 6 inches high; fair complexion; scar on his left eyebrow and another on his nose; has lost one of his fore teeth"; advertised in *The Pennsylvania Gazette*, January 15, 1767

JOSHUA SHREAVE, an American born servant lad; runaway from GEORGE SPENCE, living in Northampton Township, Burlington County; "about 18 or 19 years of age; 5 feet, 8 or 10 inches high; fresh complexion; dark curled hair; speaks good Dutch;" notice to GARRET WINTER; advertised in *The Pennsylvania Gazette*, January 22, 1767

ISSAC BEATIE, an Irish servant lad; runaway from PHILIP J. LIVINGSTON; "about years of 14 age; 4 feet, 11 inches or 5 feet high; fair complexion"; advertised in *The Pennsylvania Journal*, January 22, 1767

JOHN LUPTON, an American born apprentice lad; runaway from ALEXANDER RUTHERFORD; "about years of

17 age; 5 feet, 3 or 4 inches high; fresh complexion; dark curled hair; well set; by trade a shoemaker; marked with small pox; born at Cape May; black eyes"; advertised in *The Pennsylvania Journal*, January 22, 1767

ANTHONY BOURN [BOURNS] servant man; runaway from his bail in Salem; 5 feet, 6 or 7 inches high; fair complexion; brown hair which he customarily wears tied with a ribbon; by trade a tailor; has been a soldier in the Royal Scots; advertised by SAMUEL DICK, JACOB HOLLINSHEAD, SAMUEL THOMPSON in *The Pennsylvania Chronicle*, March 16, 1767

WILLIAM DOLTON, an Irish servant man; runaway from WILLIAM BASSET, living in Pilesgrove, Salem County; "about 25 years of age; 5 feet, 5 inches high; pretty well set; dark hair; has a long red scar on the left side of his face; is a little swelled with the dropsy; has had a fit of fever and ague"; advertised in *The Pennsylvania Gazette*, April 9, 1767

JAMES MCDONAGH, a servant man; runaway from DARBY DOYLE, living at Canoe Brook, in Essex County; "about years of 19 age; black hair; full face; much given to trafficking"; advertised in *The New York Mercury*, May 4, 1767

EDWARD GODFREY, a servant man; runaway from JACOB MARTIN, living at Piscataqua; "about 19 years of age; dark complexion; dark brown hair; speaks good English"; advertised in *The New York Mercury*, May 11, 1767

WILLIAM WILLLIAMS, [WILLIAM SOUBRIAN] an English servant man; runaway from Change Water Forge in Sussex County; "about 45 years of age; 5 feet, 6 inches high; short black hair; by trade a clerk or school teacher; writes and speaks good English"; advertised by JACOB STARN in *The Pennsylvania Gazette*, May 21, 1767

THOMAS WILKINSON, a Irish servant man; runaway from ISAAC RETTINGHOUSE, living in Amwell; "about 19 years of age; small sized; fair complexion; straight hair; has two large scars on the insides of his thighs, near his private parts"; notice to JACOB BRIGHT in Front Street in Philadelphia; advertised in *The Pennsylvania Gazette*, May 21, 1767

JOHN ERHARD SCHLAGEL, a Dutch servant man; runaway from WILLIAM OAKFORD, living at the head of Alloway's Creek, Salem County; "about 30 years of age; 5 feet, 7 inches high; dark complexion; stoop shouldered; dark brown hair; middling long grey eyes; has a large scar on his face, near the corner of his eye to the corner of his mouth, occasioned by a cut; talks very poor English but says he could speak German, French, Spanish and the Portugese languages"; advertised in *The Pennsylvania Gazette*, May 28, 1767

Was committed to the gaol at Burlington on suspicion of being a runaway, THOMAS COYNE; says he was bound to ROBERT SETON of Dublin and came to Philadelphia with ANDREW SETON; advertised by EPHRAIM PHILLIPS, Gaoler in *The Pennsylvania Gazette*, May 28, 1767

PATRICK HUSSEY, an Irish servant man; runaway from JOHN ROBERTS and RICHARD HACKET of Mannington Township, Salem County; "aged about 21 years; 5 feet, 10 inches high; lusty; black hair; a little pock marked"; advertised in *The New York Journal or General Advertiser*, June 11, 1767

RICHARD HANNALY, an Irish servant man; runaway from JOHN ROBERTS and RICHARD HACKET of Mannington Township, Salem County; "aged about 20 years; long fair hair and a fair complexion; when he looks into a fellow's face he is apt to wink and close one of his eyes; a short chunky fellow"; advertised in *The New York Journal or General Advertiser*, June 11, 1767

ARTHUR SENNET, an Irish servant man; runaway from THOMAS READING of Amwell, Hunterdon County; "aged about 19 years; 5 feet, 4-5 inches high; marked with small pox; dark colored hair; fair complexion; apt to get into liquor and, when so, talks much in the sea faring way, as he has been on several vessels"; advertised in *The Pennsylvania Gazette*, June 11, 1767

EDWARD GODFREY, an Irish servant man; runaway from JACOB MARTIN of Piscataway; "aged about 20 years; about 5 feet high; slim fellow; thin visaged; wears his own brown hair; yellow complexion"; advertised in *The Pennsylvania Chronicle*, June 22, 1767

FRANCIS MATTHEWS, an Irish servant man; runaway from BENJAMIN CLARKE, of Princeton; "aged about 20 years; 5 feet, 8 inches high; thought he will change his name to RICHARD BROWN; short black hair; fair complexion; has a downcast look when he speaks to strangers; a weaver by trade"; advertised in The Pennsylvania Gazette, June 25, 1767

CHARLES GEISINGER, a Dutch servant man; runaway from MARTIN HALTER, living at the Glass House in Alloway's Creek, County of Salem ; "aged about 27 years; 5 feet, 4 inches high; marked with the small pox about his mouth; short brown hair and gray eyes; dark complexion; speaks little or no English, but can speak French and maybe Portugese as he came from Lisbon last fall where he was a soldier"; give notice to RICHARD WISTAR, in Market Steet; advertised in *The Pennsylvania Gazette*, July, 1767

WILLIAM RANKIN, an Irish servant man; runaway from JOHN HUTCHINSON of Windsor Township, Middlesex County; "about 20 years of age; short, well set man; sandy colored hair; fair skin; a whitish look out of his eyes; marked with the small pox; by trade a shoemaker"; advertised in *The New York Journal or General Advertiser*, July 23, 1767

Now in custody on suspicion of being a runaway, PATRICK MULLAN; says he belongs to SAMUEL SHARP in London Grove township; advertised by JOSEPH THOMAS , Goaler in *The New York Journal and General Advertiser*,

August 6,1767

Now in custody on suspicion of being a runaway, NICHOLAS HART, a lad of 14 years of age; says he belongs to MICHAEL STITES, at the head of North East; advertised by JOSEPH THOMAS , Gaoler in *The New York Journal and General Advertiser*, August 6,1767

SIMON ROGERS, an apprentice lad; runaway from JACOB TAYLOR, Shoemaker, of Princeton; "aged about 19 years; 5 feet, 3 inches high; dark complexion; short, straight, black hair and black eyes; speaks little and looks very grave"; advertised in *The New York Mercury*, August 10,1767

ISSIAH, an apprentice lad; runaway from JOHN DENTON of Princeton; "aged about 21 years; 5 feet, 8 inches high; dark complexion; short black hair"; advertised in *The New York Mercury*, August 10,1767

SIMON KEY, an American born apprentice lad; runaway from RICHARD COLLINGS of Newtown township, Glouster County; "aged about 14 or 15 years; well grown; fair complexion; flaxen curled hair"; advertised in *The Pennsylvania Gazette*, August 13,1767

DANIEL FAGAN, an Irish servant man; runaway from JACOB FORD, Jr. of Morrisitown; "aged about 38 or 40 years; 6 feet inches high; well built; looks like a strong, hearty good humored fellow; has a wen as large as a walnut over one eye; has lost one or more of his fore teeth; by trade a ditcher though sometimes used to cut wood for forges"; advertised in *The Pennsylvania Chronicle*, August 31, 1767

JOHN NEIL, an Irish servant man; runaway from JOHN HUGHES, living at Greenwich Forge, West Jersey; "5 feet, 10 inches high; dark hair; marked with pox"; notice to JOHN HUGHES in Philadelphia or JOHN HUGHES at Forge; advertised in *The Pennsylvania Chronicle*, October 5, 1767

JAMES MORRIS [MORRISON] a servant man; runaway from the Change Water Forge in Sussex County; "aged about 35 years; 5 feet, 6 inches high; brown complexion; short, black hair; thick and well made; has a pearl on one of his eyes and a remarkable long nose; speaks good English but seems always as if he had a cold"; advertised by JACOB STARN in *The Pennsylvania Gazette*, October 8, 1767

WILLIAM CRESSY, an apprentice lad; runaway from JOHN DENNIS living at New Brunswick; "aged about 19 years; well set; fresh countenance; smooth and full faced; a long hair mole on right cheek; a very down look and subject to drink hard at every opportunity; by trade a hatter"; advertised in *The Pennsylvania Chronicle*, November 2, 1767

WILLIAM WALSH, an Irish apprentice boy; runaway from JOHN TURNER living at the Barracks, Perth Amboy; "aged about 17 years; short reddish hair; freckled face and pale with pox"; advertised in *The New York Journal Weekly or General Advertiser*, October, 29 1767

PHILIP JACOBS, a Dutch servant man; runaway from RICHARD WISTAR from the Glass House in Salem County; "5 feet, 6 or 7 inches high; light gray eyes; thick lips; sandy hair; speaks but little English; took with him a fiddle upon which he is much addicted to play; both his legs are sore; by trade a stone mason; has served his time in Canawaka, Maryland"; advertised in *The Pennsylvania Chronicle*, November 9, 1767

Was committed to Monmouth County gaol on suspicion of being a runaway, JOHN CONGER, American born; "aged about 19 years; 5 feet, 8 inches high; light complexion; born in New Jersey"; advertised by WILLIAM COLE, Undersheriff in *The New York Journal and General Advertiser*, November 5, 1767

PETER BARKER, an apprentice; runaway from JOHN HOLLOWAY and ISAAC HOLLOWAY of Reckless Town, Burlington County; "a tall slim man; aged about 20 years; wears his own long hair tied behind; scar of a scald on his left arm under his wristband and another on the outside of his left knee; by trade a tailor; carried his tools so as to prevent being considered a runaway"; advertised in *The Pennsylvania Journal*, November 12, 1767

JOHN JONES, an apprentice; runaway from JOHN HOLLOWAY and ISAAC HOLLOWAY of Reckless Town, Burlington County; "aged about 17 or 18 years; pale complexion; short hair; by trade a shoemaker; carried his tools so as to prevent being considered a runaway"; advertised in *The Pennsylvania Journal*, November 12, 1767

JAMES FULLERTON, an Irish servant man; runaway from WILLIAM DEWEES, Jun. Potts Grove, Philadelphia County; "aged about 26 years; 5 feet, 4 inches high; thick set; stoops in his shoulders; dark, sandy colored hair; is very much given to strong drink; well built"; advertised in *The Pennsylvania Journal*, November 19, 1767

HENRY SIMMS, an Irish servant man; runaway from CONRAD KOTTS and RICHARD BORDEN of Trenton ; 5 feet, 6 inches high; yellow complexion; short curled hair, much like a mulatto; by trade a tailor; advertised in *The Pennsylvania Gazette*, December 3, 1767

JAMES GILLCREACE, an Irish servant man; runaway from CONRAD KOTTS and RICHARD BORDEN of Trenton; "5 feet, 4 inches high; short black hair; much marked with small pox; by trade a shoemaker; very talkative and stoops much in his walk"; advertised in *The Pennsylvania Gazette*, December 3, 1767

JACOB FOSTER, a servant lad; runaway from JOB RIDGWAY, of Burlington County; "aged about 18 years; middle sized; light hair; advertised in *The Pennsylvania Gazette*, December 24, 1767

HUGH WILSON, an Irish servant man; runaway from

HARMON YEATS of Newcastle county; "aged about 30 years; about five feet, 3 or 4 inches high; black hair; well set; marked with the small pox; a pleasant countenance; by trade a tanner"; lived some time in Haddonfield, New Jersey; advertised in *The Pennsylvania Gazette*, January 14, 1768

JAMES FLANNIGAN, an Irish servant man; runaway from JOSEPH HUGG of Glouster; "a slim fellow; a little knock kneed; has something of a brogue upon his tongue; inclinable to drink and very quarrelsome when in liquor; about five feet 11 inches high; short black or brown hair; fresh colored"; advertised in *The Pennsylvania Gazette,* January 14, 1768

FRANCIS NEVILL, an Irish servant man; runaway from SAMUEL SYKES of Chesterfield, Burlington County, "aged about 20 years; about five feet, 8 inches high; pretty talkative; has much of the brogue; yellowish brown hair; fresh complexion; by trade a wool comber"; advertised in *The New York Mercury*, February 1, 1768; re-advertised in *The Pennsylvania Chronicle*, March 14, 1768 as FRANCIS NEVIL, and stated he had a mole on his left cheek"; re advertised in *The Pennsylvania Gazette*, April 13, 1769 as FRANCIS NEVEL having runaway from SOLOMON RIDGWAY, living in Burlington County; as "5 feet, 10 inches high; light complexion; short thin straight hair; fresh colored with a mole on one cheek and a scar on the other".

WALTER LINDY, an English servant man; runaway from JOHN FIRTH of Elsenborough, Salem County; "aged about 24 years; 5 feet, 8 or 9 inches high; thick, well set; born in Wiltshire; straight black hair; fresh complexion; marked with the small pox; speaks somewhat in the West Country dialect; is a still, sly fellow"; came with Capt. JOHN SIMONS from Waterford; advertised in *The Pennsylvania Gazette*, February 11, 1768 ; advertised again in *The Pennsylvania Gazette*, August 9, 1770, two years later, where WALTER LINDY, was additionally described as "an ungrateful fellow"

JOSEPH MAYHALL, an English servant man; runaway

from JOB STOCKTON of Springfield Township, Burlington County; "aged about 22 years; light straight hair; fair complexion; white eyes"; advertised in *The Pennsylvania Chronicle*, February 22, 1768

SILAS PALMER, an American born (New England) servant man; runaway from MARY MOORE living in Morris town; "aged about 25 years; about 5 feet, 6 or 7 inches; light hair; blue eyes; addicted to drinking and, when in liquor, very talkative and impudent"; advertised in *The New York Gazette and Weekly Mercury*, February 29, 1768

AARON GIBBS, an American born servant man; runaway from CALEB NEWBOLD, of Springfield in Burlington County; "about 5 foot, seven or eight inches high; well set; much pitted with pox; dark hair; about 25 years old; understands how to do any farming business"; advertised in *The New York Gazette and Weekly Mercury*, April 4, 1768

JACOB NEWTON, an American born servant man; runaway from Change Water Forge in Sussex County; "aged about 37 years; about 6 feet high; born in New England; by trade a black smith and collier but lately employed as a wood cutter"; advertised by High Sheriff JACOB STARN in *The New York Journal or General Advertiser*, April 7, 1768

CORNELIUS [surname not known], a servant man; runaway from Change Water Forge in Sussex County; "full faced; broad shouldered; about 5 feet, 9 or 10 inches high"; advertised by High Sheriff JACOB STARN in *The New York Journal or General Advertiser*, April 7, 1768

WILLIAM MORRIS, a servant man; runaway from Change Water Forge in Sussex County; "aged about 35 years; about 5 feet, 5 inches high; speaks broad English"; advertised by High Sheriff JACOB STARN in *The New York Journal or General Advertiser*, April 7, 1768

THOMAS MURPHY, an Irish servant man; runaway

from Change Water Forge in Sussex County; "aged about 20 years; about 5 feet, 5 inches high; black hair; by trade a shoe maker"; advertised by High Sheriff JACOB STARN in *The New York Journal or General Advertiser*, April 7, 1768

JACOB HOLLER, a Dutch servant man; runaway from ROBERT TAYLOUR the Township of Woolrich in the county of Glouster; "aged about 30 years; about 5 feet, 6 inches high; forepart of head shaved"; had originally run away from EDWARD TONKIN; advertised in *The Pennsylvania Chronicle*, April 11, 1768

WILLIAM RYNAN, Scotch born servant man; runaway from JOHN L. JOHNSTON of South Amboy; "about 5 feet, 8 inches high; well set; round shouldered; came from Ireland about 20 months ago; good deal pitted with the small pox; speaks pretty broad"; advertised in *The Pennsylvania Chronicle*, April 18, 1768

CHARLES GEISINGER, a Dutch servant man; runaway from GEORGE MILLER of Salem County; "aged about 32 years; about 5feet, 2 inches high; black short hair; brown complexion"; advertised in *The Pennsylvania Chronicle*, May 2, 1768

PAULUS ABZICHER [PETER ABZICHER], a Dutch servant man; runaway from ISAAC CLARKE, living near Princeton; "aged about 40 years; about 6 feet or upwards; speaks very little English; is a well set lusty fellow; of a stern countenance; has a large nose; of a sandy complexion; very large beard"; advertised in *The Pennsylvania Chronicle*, May 23, 1768

JAMES HERRON, an Irish servant man; runaway from NICHOLAS FARMER of Alloways Creek; "ill looking fellow; by trade a black smith; black hair; stoops when he walks"; advertised in *The Pennsylvania Chronicle*, May 30, 1768

NATHAN COLLINS, a servant man; runaway from

WILLIAM DOWNS of township of Woodbury of Glouster County; "aged about 24 years; about 5 feet, 10 inches high; wore his own black straight hair; brown eyed and black eye brows; thin faced; fresh complexion; slender built; very talkative and boasts much about his valor when he was a provincial soldier"; advertised in *The Pennsylvania Chronicle,* May 30, 1768

JOSEPH SHARP, an apprentice boy; runaway from WILLIAM DOWNS of Township of Woodbury of Glouster County; "aged about 18 years; about 5 feet, 10 inches high; wears his own short brown hair; down look and well set"; advertised in *The Pennsylvania Chronicle*, May 30, 1768

MATTHEW KING, an Irish servant man; runaway from MARCUS KING, near Pluckemin; "aged about 17 years; about 5 feet, 9 inches high; short hair; speaks very much with the Irish accent or brogue"; advertised in *The New York Gazette and Weekly Mercury*, May 30, 1768

JOHN BURNS, an Irish servant man, runaway from WILSON HUNT, living at Maidenhead, Hunterdon County; "aged about 25 years; about 5 feet, 8 inches high; black hair but will probably cut it off; a little freckled; fresh complexion; advertised in *The Pennsylvania Chronicle*, June 13, 1768

THOMAS COLLAGEN, an English servant lad, runaway from HARMAN KNICKERBACKER of Shrewsbury, Monmouth County; "about 5 feet, 5 inches high; a brick layer by trade; square shouldered; black straight hair; black eyes; down cast countenance; boasts greatly about being born in London and is very fond of dancing and company"; advertised in *The Pennsylvania Chronicle*, June 13, 1768

JOHN RYAN, an Irish servant man, runaway from JACOB GOODING of Pitts Town Mills, formerly called Hoffs Town, in Hunterdon county; "about 5 feet, 9 inches high; wears his own short brown hair which curls well; a house carpenter by trade; has a remarkable strut in his gait; is neat in his dress; talks thick and fast, when he is in liquor"; advertised in *The Pennsylvania Chronicle*, June 13, 1768

JAMES QUIN, an Irish servant man, runaway from BENJAMIN NORTHRUP of Hardisto, Sussex county; "aged about 19 or 20 years; about 5 feet, 9 inches high; black straight hair; remarkable large broad black eye brows; clear complexion; somewhat pale; down look; having lived in a Dutch family he has but little Irish accent in his speech; can read and write very well"; advertised in *The Pennsylvania Journal*, June 16, 1768

JAMES M'DONNOUGH, an Irish servant man, runaway from DANIEL TAYLOR of Newark Mountains; "aged about 20 years; about 5 feet, 4 inches high; speaks the Irish brogue pretty strong; has dark brown hair which he wears tied; brown complexion"; advertised in *The New York Journal Mercury or General Advertiser*, June 23, 1768

Taken up and committed to Baltimore Town Gaol, on suspicion of being a runaway TIMOTHY MAHONY, an Irish man; advertised by Sheriff DANIEL CHAMIER in *The Pennsylvania Gazette*, June 20, 1768

Taken up and committed to Baltimore Town Gaol, on suspicion of being a runaway RICHARD WHITAKER [WHITACRE]; "aged about 22 or 23 years; a shoe maker by trade; short black hair; has a mole under his right eye and another on the left side of his neck; advertised by Sheriff DANIEL CHAMIER in *The Pennsylvania Gazette*, June 20, 1768

JONATHAN STOUT, a servant man, runaway from JOHN STYMETS of living in Penny Town [Pennington], Hunterdon county; "he is a lusty stout fellow and values himself much upon his fighting; formerly was an officer in the New Jersey Regiment"; advertised in *The Pennsylvania Chronicle*, July 4, 1768

RICHARD HANLEY, an Irish servant man, runaway

from JOHN ROBERTS of Mannington Township, Salem county; "aged about 19 years; short, chunky fellow; stoops as he walks; with fair hair; lately trimmed; of a fair complexion; speaks bad English; is left handed; and when he look's in a man's face, closes one of his eyes"; advertised in *The Pennsylvania Gazette*, July 7, 1768

ROBERT M'CORMACK [CARMACK], a servant man, runaway from ROBERT PEARSON in Hides Town [Hightstown]; "aged about 25 years; about 5 feet, 10 inches high; black hair and a down look"; notice to WILLIAM FISHBURN, Merchant in Philadelphia; advertised in *The Pennsylvania Gazette*, July, 14, 1768

THOMAS ROBINSON, an Irish servant man, runaway from WILLIAM CRAIG in Alloways Creek, Salem County; "aged about 23 years; about 5 feet, 3 inches high; brown hair; is well set and talks tolerable English; it has been about 3 years since he had left his native country"; advertised in *The Pennsylvania Chronicle*, July 18, 1768

THOMAS HARBER, an Irish servant man, runaway from MATHIAS BURNET and JAMES WILKINSON; "about 5 feet, 2 inches high; black curled hair; thin visage; sandy beard"; advertised in *The New York Gazette and Weekly Mercury*, August 22, 1768

ZEBULON HOGE, an American born servant man, runaway from Tanton Forge, Burlington county; "aged about 26 years; about 6 feet high; slim; black or brown hair; by trade a blacksmith; slow spoken"; thought to be about Augusta county, Virginia where his family lives; advertised by CHARLES READ in *The Pennsylvania Journal*, August 25, 1768

JOSEPH VANOTE, Amercan born servant man, runaway from Tanton Forge, Burlington county; aged about 30 years; born in Monmouth county; well known in his present walks, which are about Monahockin and Little Egg Harbor; advertised by CHARLES READ in *The Pennsylvania Journal*,

August 25, 1768

    RANDLE M'DONALD, an Irish servant man, runaway from Tanton Forge, Burlington county; "aged about 40 years; about 4 feet, 10 inches high; by trade a finer and has worked a little bit at blooming; black hair and a large black beard; slow spoken, if not in liquor; hard of hearing and smokes much"; advertised by CHARLES READ in *The Pennsylvania Journal*, August 25, 1768; advertised by CHARLES READ in *The New York Gazette or Weekly Post Boy*, November 21, 1768 as RANDAL MACDONALD, 5 feet, 2 inches high; very silent when sober and talkative when drunk; by trade a Bloomer and Finer; well known in Essex and Morris counties; round face; black eyes"

    Taken up on suspicion of being a runaway, by STEPHEN SKINNER, an Irish servant man, CHARLES CONNER; "a convict from Ireland who arrived in Maryland in 1765 and was sold to WILLIAM GILL, his present master, who lives in Baltimore county; aged about 39 years; about 5 feet, 7 inches high; brown hair; fair complexion; light gray eyes"; advertised by RICHARD CARNS, Jr. in *The Pennsylvania Journal*, September 1, 1768

    Taken up on suspicion of being a runaway, by STEPHEN SKINNER, an English servant man named, CHARLES LEE; "a convict from London, where he was born; arrived in Maryland in 1764; says he was consigned to STEVENSON and PLOWMAN and was sold to JOSEPH AUSBORN, who bought him for JOSEPH CRUMMEL, his present master; about 5 feet, 8 inches high; black curled hair; a remarkable brown complexion"; advertised by RICHARD CARNS, Jr. in *The Pennsylvania Journal*, September 1, 1768

    Taken up and committed to Amboy Gaol on the suspicion of being a runaway, WILLIAM DENNET [WILLIAM SMITH], an Englishman, belonging to JAMES RANKIN of Newbury Township, York County; advertised in *The Pennsylvania Chronicle*, September 5, 1768

JOSEPH COMPTON, a servant man, runaway from STEPHEN TALLMAN, Jr. of Shrewsbury; "of a small stature about 5 feet high; has a scar on his instep"; advertised in *The New York Journal or General Advertiser*, September 8, 1768

JOSEPH HANES, an English servant man, runaway from EDWARD TEST living in Salem; "aged about 25 years; about 5 feet, 7 or 8 inches high; black hair tied; he sings a good song and is much given to liquor; he can write"; advertised in *The Pennsylvania Gazette*, September 29, 1768

JOHN O'BRYAN, a, Irish servant man, runaway from JOHN MONROW, living in Mount Holly; "denies that the "O" belongs to his name; aged about 35 years; about 5 feet, 6 inches high; short dark curled hair; marked with the small pox; speaks pretty good English, but with a touch of the brogue; is a shoe maker by trade but can do plantation work"; advertised in *The Pennsylvania Gazette*, October 6, 1768; re advertised in *The New York Gazette and Weekly Mercury*, March 13, 1769 a shaving swapped a horse in Sussex with WILLIAM M'COY and called himself JOHN MOORE; can speak Indian, even though he had just come over from Ireland; had been sold by JOHN HARKINS of Philadelphia".

THOMAS MOREHEAD [THOMAS DOWEL], an Irish servant man, runaway from ARCHIBALD MAFFET, living in Greenwich Township in Glouster County; "aged about 19 years; black hair; has been four years in the country"; advertised in *The Pennsylvania Journal*, October 6, 1768

PATRICK LAMB, an Irish servant boy; runaway from ISAAC PEARSON, living near Trenton; "about 15 years of age; short, thick and clumsy; speaks very hoarse; has short brown hair; born in Dublin"; notice to GEORGE DOUGLASS; advertised in *The Pennsylvania Chronicle*, October 26, 1768

WILLIAM JENKINS, an English or Welsh servant man; runaway from ISAAC PEARSON; "about 20 years of age; 5 feet, 2 inches high; full faced and a fair complexion"; advertised in *The Pennsylvania Chronicle,* October 26, 1768

JOHN DAVIS, a servant man; runaway from AARON FITHIAN; "5 feet, 4 inches high; curled, lightish long hair; by trade a sadler"; advertised in *The Pennsylvania Gazette,* October 27, 1768

DANIEL DAYLEY, an Irish servant man; runaway from Etna Furnace, Burlington County; "about 22 years of age; 5 feet high; a squat thick fellow; round faced; thick lipped; black hair and very fawning in his speech"; advertised by CHARLES READ in *The New York Gazette or Weekly Post Boy,* October 31, 1768

JEREMIAH DRISCOL, a servant man; runaway from Etna Furnace, Burlington County; "about 22 years of age; 5 feet high; gray eyes with an uncommon look out of them; a wide mouth; black hair; slow of speech"; advertised by CHARLES READ in *The New York Gazette or Weekly Post Boy,* October 31, 1768

DANIEL STONE, an Irish servant man; runaway from JOHN CAREY; "about 20 years of age; 5 feet, 10 inches high; in country two years and has much of the brogue in his talk; fair complexion; black hair"; advertised in *The New York Journal or General Advertiser,* December 29, 1768

Taken up on suspicion of being a runaway, unnamed man, "about 30 to 35 years of age; 5 feet, 10 inches high; swarthy complexion; dark brown hair; a straggling person; has a stoop in his shoulders; appears to be a subtle person; writes in a good hand and has one ankle very much bigger than the other"; committed under authority of STEPHEN SKINNNER, Esq.; advertised by NATHANIEL HEARD, in *The Pennsylvania Gazette,* December 29, 1768

Was committed to the Gaol of Glouster county on suspicion of being a runaway, WILLIAM GOULD; "says he understands the business of making pot-ash, pearl-ash and

Boston Crown soap; lately lived in BENJAMIN KENDALL's Potash works"; advertised by JOSIAH CHATTIN, Gaoler, in *The Pennsylvania Gazette*, January 5, 1769

CHRISTOPHER ARCHIBOLD, a servant man; runaway from JOSEPH HAIGHT, living in the city of Burlington; "about 21 years of age; 5 feet, 4 inches high; short, well set fellow; wears his own hair, which is dark brown; advertised in *The Pennsylvania Chronicle*, January 16, 1769

JOHN JONES, a servant man; runaway from JOSEPH HAIGHT, living in the city of Burlington; "about 17 years of age; 5 feet, 4 inches high; thin faced; stoops in his walk and has a down look; short brown hair; marked with small pox"; advertised in *The Pennsylvania Chronicle*, January 16, 1769

ROBERT CAMPBEL, an Irish servant man; runaway from EVANT VAN ZILE, of Second River, Bergen county; "about 18 years of age; 5 feet high; slim bodied; fair complexion; pale face; one of his feet a little crooked, occasioned by a bruise; has a scaled head; is very fluent in speech; has much of an Irish accent; can speak English, Dutch and High Dutch"; advertised in *The New York Journal or General Advertiser*, January 19, 1769

Was committed to the Burlington county gaol on suspicion of being a runaway, JOSEPH BENNIN [BENNET], an Irish servant man; "about 29 or 30 years of age; born in Derry County, Ireland and came to this country seven years before with Capt. CORWELL; short black hair; very much marked with small pox; cooper by trade"; advertised by EPHRAIM PHILLIPS in *The Pennsylvania Gazette*, January 19, 1769

JOHN JENKINS, a Welsh servant man; runaway from ISAAC HAINS, living in Burlington County; "aged about 26 years; 5 feet, 4 inches tall; fresh looking man with black straight hair"; advertised in *The Pennsylvania Gazette*, January 26, 1769

SAMUEL THATCHER, a servant man; runaway from

ASHER CARTER, living in Oxford Township in Burlington County; "5 feet, 9 inches tall; wears his hair tied, although somewhat short and of a sandy color; a talkative fellow and often speaks of an estate he has near Newark, New Jersey where he says his friends live; by trade a carpenter"; advertised in *The Pennsylvania Chronicle*, February 6, 1769

MICHAEL BRADY, an Irish servant man; runaway from WILLIAM TUCKER, living in Trenton; "aged about 19 years; 5 feet, 4 inches high; well set; very thick legs and knock kneed; fair complexion; full gray eyes; lightish short hair; is a crafty person; by trade a shoemaker and pretends to the stuff work"; advertised in *The Pennsylvania Gazette*, March 23, 1769

TERENCE DOWNY, an Irish servant man; runaway from SAMUEL LEVIS, living in Springfield Township, Chester County; "aged about 25 years; 5 feet, 10 inches high; speaks good English; fresh complexion; light brown curled hair; broad shouldered and well shaped fellow"; advertised in *The Pennsylvania Chronicle*, March 27, 1769

MATTHEW KING, an Irish servant man; runaway from MARCUS KING, near Pluckimin; "6 feet high; marked with small pox"; advertised in *The New York Gazette and Weekly Post Boy*, March 27, 1769

Committed to Perth Amboy gaol on suspicion of being a runaway, TIMOTHY KEAFF, an Irishman; "says he broke out of Newtown gaol in Bucks county"; advertised by WILLIAM JOLLY, Gaoler in *The Pennsylvania Chronicle*, April 3, 1769

DENNIS SHEHAN [DENNIS STEVENS], American born servant man; runaway from Union Iron Works in Hunterdon County; "aged about 27 years; 5 feet, 8 inches high; fresh, healthy looking man; wears his own black hair tied; has a scar on one of his cheeks; remarkable white eyes and a down look when in conversation; his jaws are apt to snap when eating, and wants several of his fore teeth; appears to be a quiet simple fellow, but is artful and fond of strong liquor; very talkative when drunk; will say much of his knowledge in the mill wright trade; by trade a mill wright, but pretends to know something of the founders business at an iron furnace and many other things of which he is quite ignorant;" notice to JOSEPH TURNER of Philadelphia; advertised by ROBERT TAYLOR at Union Forge in *The Pennsylvania Gazette*, April 6, 1769

THOMAS MURPHY [THOMAS NEWMAN], an Irish servant man; runaway from JACOB STARN, living in Change Water Iron Works in Sussex county; "aged about 19 years; 5 feet, 8 inches high; well set; black curled hair; by trade a shoemaker; notice to DIRCK BRINCKERHOFF; advertised in *The New York Gazette and weekly Mercury*, April 10, 1769

PURMOT LEE, an American born servant man; runaway from JOHN JONES, living near Indian River; "aged about 25 years; 6 feet high; hard of hearing; born at Egg Harbor"; notice to JOHN MIFFLIN, Merchant in Philadelphia; advertised in *The Pennsylvania Gazette,* April 27, 1769

Dr. THOMAS OGLE, an Irish servant man; runaway from THOMAS HARTLEY, DANIEL LITHGOW, PETER AMBLER; "5 feet, 6 or 7 inches high; given to liquor and when in liquor talks much of his skill in Physic and Surgery; has had one of his legs broke"; advertised in *The Pennsylvania Gazette*, April 27, 1769; advertised later an escapee from gaol and "pitted from the pox" was added to the description.

CORNELIUS HURRY, an English born servant man; runaway from BROUGHTON REYNOLDS in Elizabeth Town; "aged about 19 years; 5 feet, 6 inches high; fair complexion; light colored hair; by trade a hostler and can trim a horse very well"; advertised in *The New York Gazette and Weekly Mercury*, May 8, 1769

THOMAS HOWEL, a servant man; runaway from STEPHEN TALLMAN, Jr. of Shrewsbury, Monmouth County; "aged about 30 years; 5 feet, 5 inches high; round faced; a very straight limbed fellow; left with MERICA BOURN, who is to marry him, being his third wife, if so she may be called; was branded in the hand for marrying the second"; advertised in *The New York Journal or General Advertiser,* May 11, 1769

JOSEPH COMPTON, a servant man; runaway from STEPHEN TALLMAN, Jr. of Shrewsbury, Monmouth county; "aged about 26 years; has a large scar on one of his insteps"; advertised in *The New York Journal or General Advertiser,* May 11, 1769

ABSALOM BARETT, an American born servant man; runaway from JOHN STEELMAN of Great Egg Harbor; "about 18 years of age; 5 feet, 6 inches high; blue eyes; mole on his left cheek and warts on his right hand; black hair; advertised in *The Pennsylvania Gazette,* August 3, 1769

JOHN MEAGHER, an Irish servant man; runaway from JOHN STEELMAN of Great Egg Harbor; "about 5 feet, 5 inches high; black hair which he wears clubbed"; advertised in *The Pennsylvania Gazette,* August 3, 1769

GEORGE GENGE, an English servant man; runaway from WILLIAM COOPER, living in Waterford Township, Glouster County; "about 18 years of age; 5 feet, 7 inches high; pale; swarthy complexion; wears his own black hair; talks very much with the West Country dialect"; advertised in *The Pennsylvania Journal,* August 3, 1769

MICHAEL BRADY, an Irish servant man; runaway from WILLIAM TUCKER, living in Trenton; "about 20 years of age; 5 feet, 3 inches high; well set; thick legs; knock kneed; speaks very quickly; fair complexion; full faced and large gray eyes; short light curled hair; born in Dublin; has some of the brogue and speaks very hoarse; advertised in *The New York Gazette and Weekly Mercury,* August 7, 1769

JACOB CARVEL, servant man; runaway from NATHAN HAINES, living in Evesham, Burlington County; "about 18 years of age; 5 feet, 5 or 6 inches high; well set;

yellowish complexion; coarse harsh hair, a kind of flax color and cut very close on the top; very much hump shinned"; father lives at Duck Creek; advertised in *The Pennsylvania Gazette,* August 10, 1769

NICHOLAS FITZGERALD, an Irish servant man; runaway from SAMUEL HENRY, living a Trenton; "6 feet high; black hair tied behind; marked with small pox"; advertised in *The New York Journal or General Advertiser,* August 17, 1769; also described as "aged about 24 years; 6 feet high; ruddy complexion; long, light brown hair tied behind; marked with small pox; speaks very much on the brogue"; in *The Pennsylvania Gazette,* August 24, 1769

GARRET MURPHY, an Irish servant man; runaway from SAMUEL HENRY, living a Trenton; "5 feet, 9 inches high; pale; black hair tied behind; marked with small pox; walks wide and lame"; advertised in *The New York Journal or General Advertiser,* August 17, 1769; also described as "aged about 24 years; 5 feet, 8 inches high; straight short black hair; marked with small pox; walks wide and speaks with a little of the brogue" in *The Pennsylvania Gazette,* August 24, 1769

JOHN JONES, an apprentice boy; runaway from ISAAC HOLLOWAY, living in Chesterfield Township, Burlington County; "a slim, thin visaged fellow; 5 feet, 8 inches high; dark brown hair; by trade a shoemaker"; advertised in *The Pennsylvania Chronicle,* August 28, 1769

JOHN WALKER, an English servant man; runaway from JOHN BESSONET; "aged about 23 years; 5 feet, 5 inches high; slender made; fair; much pitted with the small pox; is a great talker; by trade a brick maker; lately arrived in the *Duchess of Gordon*; advertised in *The New York Gazette and Weekly Mercury,* October 2, 1769

WILLIAM PITCHER, a servant man; runaway from JOHN BESSONET; "aged about 38 years; well set; has a wife in Shrewsbury"; advertised in *The New York Gazette and*

Weekly Mercury, October 2, 1769

 PETER MURPHY, a servant boy; runaway from JONATHAN BALDWIN of Princeton; "aged about 16 years; advertised in *The New York Gazette or General Advertiser,* November 27, 1769

 DAVID COX, an apprentice lad; runaway from JAMES TAYLOR of Hunterdon County; "aged about 20 years; 5 feet, 10 inches high; large boned; knock kneed; of a dark complexion; down look; black eyes; black hair worn tied; by trade a carpenter and joiner but may try to pass as a millwright as he has two brothers in that trade near Albany"; advertised in *The New York Gazette or Weekly Post Boy*, January 22, 1770

 WALTER CLARK, an American born servant man; runaway from BENJAMIN JACKSON of Shrewsbury Town, Monmouth county; "aged about 24 years; 6 feet high; black curled hair; keeps his mouth much open; by trade a blacksmith but understands farming business"; advertised in *The New York Journal or General Advertiser*, January 25, 1770

 THOMAS CLAY, a servant man; runaway from DANIEL GERARD, Jr., living near Morristown; "aged near 50 years; 5 feet, 10 inches high; brown curled hair; will drink to excess and then is noisy; likes to sing songs; by trade a cooper"; advertised in *The Pennsylvania Gazette*, February, 8, 1770

 JAMES GIPSON, a servant man; living in Piles Grove, Salem County; runaway from his bail; "small stature; thin visage; wears his own hair which is of a lightish color; by trade a weaver"; advertised by DANIEL HARKER, Constable in *The Pennsylvania Gazette*, February 15, 1770

 PETER MENNEL, a Dutch servant lad; runaway from DANIEL LIPPINCOTT, Jr., living in Evesham, Burlington County; "aged about 18 years; 5 feet, 2 inches high; swarthy complexion; black hair; had the first joint of the fourth finger of his left hand cut off"; advertised in *The Pennsylvania Gazette,*

August 9, 1770

WILLIAM KARRAGAN, an Irish servant man; runaway from ANDREW M'CULLAM of Lower Penn's Neck, Salem County; "aged about 21 years; 5 feet, 6 inches high; sandy complexion; red hair; well made; much marked with small pox; by trade a smith; stoop shouldered; speaks on the brogue"; advertised in *The Pennsylvania Gazette*, August 9, 1770

ADRIAN BRUST, a Dutch lad; runaway from RICHARD WISTAR'S Glass house in Salem County; "aged about 27 years; 5 feet, 7 or 8 inches tall; pale complexion; short light hair; two moles on his left cheek; a scar on his right temple and on his left foot near the ankle; has been a soldier in Portugal"; advertised in *The Pennsylvania Gazette*, April 26, 1770

JOHN WILLIAMS, an English servant man; runaway from SAMUEL BURROUGHS of Warerford Township, Glouster County; aged about 40 years; 5 feet, 5 inches tall; sandy hair; talks grave and artful"; advertised in *The Pennsylvania Gazette*, April 26, 1770

JOHN BLACK, an American born apprentice lad; runaway from WILLIAM DENNISTON of Elizabeth Township, Rahway, Essex County; "aged about 19 years; 5 feet, 6 inches tall; fair complexion; fair hair; large blue eyes; thick set; by trade a fuller; his father lives in Middletown; he is not too honest, nor quite honest enough, if he has but the opportunity to be a rogue"; advertised in *The New York Gazette or Weekly Post Boy*, May 14, 1770

EDWARD CLEMONS, an English servant man; runaway from JAMES HINCHMAN, living in Deptford Township, Glouster County; "aged about 23 years; 4 feet, 4 inches tall; sandy complexion; straight hair; good deal knock kneed; sour look; by trade a pin maker; has run away twice and had a horse lock on his leg"; advertised in *The Pennsylvania*

Gazette, August 30, 1770

    JOHN COLLINS, an English lad; runaway from Andover Iron Works, Sussex County; "aged about 19 or 20 years; 5 feet, 5 or 6 inches tall; round shouldered; full faced; a little freckled; has straight, short brown hair; slow in speech and a little dull in hearing; stoops and rocks much when he walks"; notice to JOSEPH TURNER, Esq. in Philadelphia; advertised by ARCHIBALD STEWART in *The Pennsylvania Gazette*, September 17, 1770

    JOHN HARTSHORN servant man; runaway from PHEBE BASSET, living in Pilesgrove, Salem County; "thin, spare looking man"; advertised in *The Pennsylvania Chronicle*, September 17, 1770

    EPHRAIM CASSAMOUR, an apprentice lad; runaway from JONATHAN FORD, living in Hanover, Morris County; "aged about 18 years; 5 feet, 9 inches high; speaks quick; short brown hair; by trade a bloomer; advertised in *The New York Gazette or Weekly Post Boy*, January 14, 1771

    JOHN PARKES, an apprentice lad; runaway from JONATHAN FORD, living in Hanover, Morris County; "aged about 18 years; 5 feet, 9 inches high; black eyes and hair; moves slow and speaks slow; by trade a bloomer"; advertised in *The New York Gazette or Weekly Post Boy*, January 14, 1771

    PETER HUGHES, an Irish servant man; runaway from ANDREW FRAZIER, living near the Head of the Elk, in Cecil County, Maryland; "5 feet, 6 or 7 inches high; straight black hair; was scalped before but is now growing back, with a small scar on his forehead; walks very smart and speaks tolerable English; very much addicted to steal; came last September with Captain MCCAUSLAND in the *Wallworth;* is apt to get drunk and, when drunk, very quarrelsome; by trade a weaver but knows very little about the trade"; advertised in *The Pennsylvania Gazette*, January 17, 1771

Taken up on suspicion of being a runaway, JOHN HARRIS [JOHN HARRISON], belongs to JOHN MOON of Kent County, Maryland; born in England; drinks hard and swears much; has been about Woodberry for 3 years"; advertised by RICHARD JOHNSTON, Gaoler in *The Pennsylvania Gazette*, January 17, 1771

WILLIAM WILSON [WILLIAM M'CULLEN], an Irish servant man; runaway from BENJAMIN INSPEEK, living near Cooper's Ferry, in Glouster County; "aged about 30 years; 5 feet, 4 or 6 inches high; well set; sandy complexion; very sandy yellow hair, tied behind and a very sandy beard; a very thick underlip; full face; a sour look; gray eyes"; advertised in *The Pennsylvania Journal*, January 17, 1771

JOHN HALL, an American born servant man; from Pilesgrove; "a blacksmith by trade; a rough looking fellow; thick set; born near Pennypack in Pennsylvania;"

WILLIAM POWELL, an American born servant man; runaway from THOMAS LUDLAM of Cape May; "aged about 30 years; 5 feet, 4 inches high; thin visage; tawny complexion; much given to strong drink; had been a soldier";

PETER JABIL, a Dutch servant man; runaway from ISRAEL WRIGHT of Chesterfield Township, Burlington; "aged about 40 years; 5 feet, 7 inches high; black hair; dark complexion; speaks bad English"

WILLIAM FANTON, a servant man; runaway from RYNIER PROBASCO, living in Shrewsbury, Monmouth County; "aged about 21 years, 5 feet, 6 or 7 inches high; dark eyes; straight, brown hair; can read a little but cannot write"; advertised in *The New York Gazette and the Weekly Mercury*, January 28, 1771

THOMAS COLLARD, an English servant man; runaway from JONAS REES, living in Lower Penn's Neck in Salem County; "aged about 21 years; 5 feet, 7 inches high";

advertised by in *The Pennsylvania Gazette,* February 28, 1771

WILLIAM M'CABE, an Irish servant man; runaway from WILLIAM SMITH living in Baltimore Town; aged about 21 years; fair hair; a little sandy and fresh complexioned"; advertised in *The Pennsylvania Journal,* March 21, 1771

GEORGE WILLIAM, a Dutch servant man; runaway from WILLIAM SMITH living in Baltimore Town; "short set fellow who lived for sometime in the Jerseys; is a freeman who can write"; advertised in *The Pennsylvania Journal,* March 21, 1771

AMOS REED, an apprentice boy; runaway from BENJAMIN RUNYAN, living in Amwell, Hunterdon County; "aged about 20 years; 5 feet, 7 inches high; thick set; brown complexion; black hair, generally tied behind; lively spirited; somewhat given to drink; by trade a shoe maker"; advertised in *The Pennsylvania Gazette,* March 28, 1771

ROBERT SMITH, an English servant lad; runaway from JOSHUA BUNTING, living in Burlington County; "aged about 18 years; 5 feet, 7 or 8 inches high; fair complexion; light brown hair; gray eyes; thin visage; writes a good hand; by trade a tailor"; advertised in *The Pennsylvania Gazette,* April 4, 1771

THOMAS WELLS, a servant man; runaway from ABRAHAM BRITTAIN, living in Upper Freehold, Monmouth County; "aged about 23 years; 5 feet, 8 inches high; well built; stout strong fellow; fresh complexion; curled black hair; black eyes; is apt to get in a frolic and drinks freely"; advertised in *The Pennsylvania Journal,* April 11, 1771

DAVID SANFORD, an apprentice boy; runaway from WILLIAM LAWSON, shoe maker at *The Sign of the Boot and Star,* near Peck's Slip in New York; "aged about 16 years; 5 feet, 6 inches high; brown complexion; advertised in *The New York Journal or The General Advertiser,* April 25, 1771

WILLIAM DOWDEN, an apprentice boy; runaway from DAVID GOSLING, living in South Amboy; "aged about 20 years; 5 feet, 5 inches high; pale complexion; round shouldered; short straight hair; went off in a boat belonging to JOHN ROSSA of Bonham's Town"; advertised in *The New York Journal or The General Advertiser*, April 25, 1771

JOHN ALCUT, a servant man; runaway from RUEL ELTON, living in Northampton County, between Mount Holly and Burlington; "5 feet, 10 inches high; a very likely portly looking fellow; sandy complexion with gray eyes; has a down look; a large hooked nose; wears his hair tied; supposed to be gone to Baltimore; he is by trade a flatman"; advertised in *The Pennsylvania Chronicle*, April 15, 1771

WILLIAM POWELL, American born servant man; runaway from THOMAS LUDLAM of Cape May; "aged about 30 years; 5 feet, 4 inches high; thin visaged; tawny complexion; much given to strong drink; was a soldier in the last war with New Jersey regiment"; advertised in *The Pennsylvania Gazette*, May 9, 1771

JOHN MERK, a Dutch servant man; "aged about 19 years, 5 feet, 5 inches high; dark straight hair; speaks bad English; remarkably bow legged; his father lives by Lancaster or Berks and he is expected to go there"; notice to MARY BLACK, JONATHAN BARTON or BENJAMIN DAVIDS at *The Sign of the George*, in Philadelphia; advertised in *The Pennsylvania Gazette*, May 9, 1771

GEORGE GARNER, an American born servant man; runaway from BENJAMIN LODGE, living at Billingsport in Greenwich County; "aged about 21 years; 5 feet, 7 inches high; well set fellow; dark brown hair; went off with an ordinary woman, RACHEL SCOTT, American born; she is a lusty, strong hussy and is apt to be light fingered"; advertised in *The Pennsylvania Gazette*, May 9, 1771

HENRY, an English servant man; runaway from

WILLIAM M. BARNET living in Elizabeth Town; "aged about 18 or 20 years; fair complexion; light long hair; can shave, dress hair, bleed and draw teeth"; advertised in *The New York Gazette and Weekly Mercury*, May 20, 1771

ROBERT SMITH, an Irish servant man; runaway from SAMUEL GARRISON, living at Pittsgrove, Salem County; "aged about 18 years; short, well set fellow; long black hair tied behind; has a mark on the left side of his head about two inches long and half an inch wide, without any hair, occasioned by a scald when he was a child; he has blue eyes; a very thick upper lip; is an impudent looking fellow; thought to have runaway with ELEANOR BUTLER, wife of JOHN BUTLER of Pittsgrove; advertised in *The Pennsylvania Gazette*, August 8, 1771

CORNELIUS HURRY, an English servant man; runaway from BROUGHTON REYNOLDS, living at Elizabeth Town Point, County of Essex; "aged about 23 years; 5 feet, 8 or 9 inches; walks a little stooping; much addicted to alcohol and swearing; of a light brown complexion; light brown hair, lately cut off on the top of his head; born in Bristol"; advertised *in The New York Journal or General Advertiser*, August 22, 1771

GEORGE ARIS [ARISON]an English servant man; runaway from BROUGHTON REYNOLDS, living at Elizabeth Town Point, County of Essex; "aged about 27 or 28 years; 5 feet, 7 or 8 inches; very red complexion; sandy hair; down look and round shouldered; walks very dull and heavy"; advertised in *The New York Journal or General Advertiser*, August 22, 1771

NATHANIEL LITTLE, an apprentice lad; runaway from JAMES BLACK and DANIEL PEARSON, living at Springfield, near Elizabeth Town; "aged about 18 years; 5 feet, 9 inches; fair complexion; light hair; by trade a weaver; had pretty thick legs and a down look"; advertised in *The New York Gazette and Weekly Mercury*, September 2, 1771

ICABUD FOSTER, an apprentice lad; runaway from

JAMES BLACK and DANIEL PEARSON, living at Springfield, near Elizabeth Town; "aged about 18 years; 5 feet, 9 inches; dark complexion; dark hair; by trade a tailor"; advertised in *The New York Gazette and Weekly Mercury*, September 2, 1771

Taken up on suspicion of being a runaway servant man, HUGH M'CAGE, says he belongs to WILLIAM MILLER and JOHN MILLER, living near Lancaster; "5 feet, 6 inches; pock marked"; advertised in *The Pennsylvania Gazette*, September 12, 1771

JOHN MITCHELL, a servant boy; runaway from MICHAEL GRAHAM, living in West Nantwell Township, Chester County; "aged about 17 years; 5 feet, 6 inches; straight black hair; bred near Trenton; writes with a good hand"; advertised in *The Pennsylvania Gazette*, October 3, 1771

JOHN COLGAN, an Irish servant man; runaway from SAMUEL DICK and CURTIS TRENCHARD, living in Salem; "aged about 28 or 30 years; 5 feet, 6 or 7 inches high; dark complexion; black eyes; short black hair which curls very much; a little pock marked; thick, well set fellow; a very remarkable cast with his eyes; sings a good song; has followed school keeping; is fond of company and apt to get into liquor"; advertised in the *Supplement to the Pennsylvania Gazette*, January 30, 1772

JOHN BARLOW, an English servant man; runaway from SAMUEL DICK and CURTIS TRENCHARD, living in Salem; "aged about 35 years; 5 feet, 9 inches high; sandy complexion; light hair which he wears tied; thin visaged with a hooked nose; stoops pretty much when he walks; went away with a woman he calls his wife; English born; thick short woman; much pock marked with a long nose and red hair; both fond of liquor and apt to quarrel when drunk"; advertised in the *Supplement to the Pennsylvania Gazette*, January 30, 1772

HOWELL DAWDY, a servant man; runaway from SAMUEL DICK and CURTIS TRENCHARD, living in Salem;

"aged about 26 years; 5 feet, 9 inches high; sandy complexion; red beard with a hair mole on the right side of his chin; sandy hair which he wears tied; thin visaged; pretends to be a carpenter; is a well made fellow; sings a good song; and is very fond of company"; advertised in the *Supplement to the Pennsylvania Gazette*, January 30, 1772

PETER WOODFORD [BENJAMIN DAVIS], a servant man; runaway from URIAH PAUL; "aged about 21 or 22 years of age; darkish complexion; straight hair; thin visage; very much addicted to liquor; a great boaster and very quarrelsome; chews tobacco to a great excess;" advertised in *The Pennsylvania Gazette*, February 13, 1772

WILLLIAM BIRD, a servant lad; runaway from JAMES LAWRIE, living in Upper Freehold Township, Monmouth County; "aged 21 years; 5 feet, 4 inches high; fair complexion; red hair"; advertised in *The Pennsylvania Gazette*, February 13, 1772

Taken up and committed to Trenton gaol on suspicion of being a runaway, THOMAS HENRY ENMAN; "5 feet, 9 inches high; lost one of his eyes; long light hair; fair complexion"; advertised by PETER HANKINSON, Gaoler in *The Pennsylvania Gazette*, February 13, 1772

Taken up and committed to Trenton gaol, Hunterdon County on suspicion of being a runaway, ROBERT JACKSON [WILLIAM MOORE]; "5 feet, 9 inches high; well set; full faced with black curled hair"; advertised by PETER HANKINSON, Gaoler in *The Pennsylvania Gazette*, February 13, 1772

RICHARD TEACLE, an English servant man; runaway from CHRISTOPHER BISHOP, living in Springfield Township, Burlington County; "aged about 22 years; 5 feet, 8 or 9 inches high; pretty well set; dark complexion; round faced; very talkative; has been a soldier and had a bullet shot through his left arm, in or near the elbow, which causes it to be stiff"; advertised in *The New York Journal or General Advertiser*, February 27, 1772

DANIEL M'SHANE, a servant man; runaway from JACOB STARN, living at Change Water forge, in Sussex County; "5 feet, 10 inches high; black complexion; black beard; very fond of strong liquor; very quarrelsome when drunk; left with a woman, ANN GRAZIOUS, who lives with him as his wife"; advertised by in *The Pennsylvania Gazette,* March 12, 1772

Taken up on suspicion of being a runaway, THOMAS HARRIS, an Englishman who has been in the country for two years; "short; belongs to HENDRICK VINIGAR at the Oblong, near Poughkeepsie; aged about 19 years; by trade a nail maker"; advertised by in *The Pennsylvania Gazette,* March 5, 1772

JACOB EDMONDS, American born servant man; runaway from THOMAS STEVENS, living in Maidenhead Township, Hunterdon County; "aged about 21 years; 5 feet, 10 inches high; stout well made man; fair complexion; sandy hair; gray eyes; large nose; scar on his right leg that is very remarkable; lost one of his upper foreteeth"; advertised in *The Pennsylvania Packet and General Advertiser,* March 9, 1772

JOHN SMITH, servant man; runaway from THOMAS STEVENS, living in Maidenhead Township, Hunterdon County; "short, thick man; 5 feet, 4 inches high; fair complexion; light hair; is a great singer and lover of company"; advertised in *The Pennsylvania Packet and General Advertiser,* March 9, 1772

JOHN GREEN, apprentice lad; runaway from CHARLES ELLET; "aged about 20 or 21 years; 5 feet, 3 inches high; brown hair; stole clothes from SAMUEL AUSTIN; by trade a tanner"; advertised in *The Pennsylvania Gazette,* March 9, 1772

WILLIAM BUTLER, an American born servant man; runaway from Greenwich Township, Glouster County; "5 feet, 9 or 10 inches high; artful; grand rogue; can write a middling good hand; New York born; slim; thin visaged; wears his own dark hair; by trade a tailor"; advertised by in *The Pennsylvania Gazette,* April 9, 1772; *The New York Gazette and The Weekly Mercury,* April 13, 1772; *The Pennsylvania Packet and General Advertiser,*

July 16, 1772 *The Pennsylvania Chronicle and Universal Advertiser*, August 1, 1772

WILLIAM HOOD, a servant man; runaway from JOSEPH PAULLIN, living in Pilesgrove, Salem County; "5 feet, 8 or 9 inches high; slim build; dark hair; much given to liquor and gaming; his finger on his left hand next, to his little finger is crooked; has relations in Chester County, Pennsylvania; by trade a tailor"; advertised in *The Pennsylvania Gazette*, April 9, 1772

JOHN HUXELY, an American born servant man; runaway from JACOB PAULLIN and ABRAHAM RICHMAN, living at Pilesgrove, Salem County; "6 feet high; born in New England; a little knock kneed; a surly cross look; talks very thick and fast and has a stammer in his speech; sandy beard with long whiskers"; advertised in *The Pennsylvania Gazette*, April 23, 1772

JAMES KERN, an Irish servant man; runaway from DANIEL RUMSEY, living at Pilesgrove, Salem County; "about 23 years of age; 5 feet, 6 or 7 inches high; fair complexion; black hair which he wears clubbed with other hair tied to it; blue eyes; speaks good English; very thick for his height; very much given to company and gaming and a great boaster of his smartness; by trade a mason; took with him a woman named MARGARET DORREN"; advertised in *The Pennsylvania Gazette*, April 23, 1772

JAMES M'INTOSH, a servant man; runaway from MICHAEL JORDAN, living in Mannington Township, Salem County; "about 20 years of age; 5 feet, 6 or 7 inches high; fair complexion; light straight hair"; advertised in *The Pennsylvania Packet and General Advertiser*, April 27, 1772

HENRY SHARP, a servant man; runaway from MICHAEL JORDAN, living in Mannington Township, Salem County; "about 19 years of age; 5 feet, 7 or 8 inches high; well set; round shouldered; talks Dutch and English"; advertised in *The Pennsylvania Packet and General Advertiser*, April 27, 1772

WILLIAM M'CORMICK, an Irish servant man; runaway from HENRY RIDGWAY in Springfield, Burlington County; aged about 21 years; 5 feet, 8 or 9 inches high; short black hair; a little pitted with the small pox"; advertised *The Pennsylvania Chronicle and Universal Advertiser*, May 18, 1772

DANIEL M'LERNAN, a servant man; runaway from THOMAS LAMB at Aetna Furnace; "5 feet, 8 inches high; brown hair; hazel eyes; lightish colored beard; pretty fair skin; cut over one eye"; advertised in *The Pennsylvania Journal and the General Advertiser*, May 21, 1772

SAMUEL MANSFIELD, [also called JOHN M'FELLY], an American born servant man; runaway from SAMUEL SMITH of Alloways Creek, Salem County; "aged about 35 or 36 years; 5 feet, 10 or 11 inches high; born in Lancaster, Pennsylvania; looks indifferently smart; is remarkable for having his teeth all double; speaks good English; dark complexion"; advertised in *The Pennsylvania Chronicle and Universal Advertiser*, May 25, 1772

PETER WEISDORF, a German servant man; runaway from COXE and FURMAN and Aetna Furnace; "aged about 36 years; 5 feet, 8 inches; pretty well built; has brown hair; speaks but little English"; notice to CHARLES READ Esq. at Aetna Furnace or ADAM AKER in Philadelphia; advertised in *The Pennsylvania Gazette*, May 28, 1772. Also advertised in *The Pennsylvania Gazette* as a runaway from COXE and FURMAN or ADAM AKER; "had on his own straight hair and leather breeches; speaks but little English; he was delivered at the side of the Delaware river, about a mile above the mouth of the Anocus, in April last on the Jersey shore, with a letter, enclosing his indentures, assigned to CHARLES READ, ESQ., to go to Mr. FENEMORE'S at the mouth of the Anocus"

JOHN WARREN, an American born apprentice lad; runaway DAVID RIDGWAY in Springfield, Burlington County; "aged about 17 years; small of his age; dark hair; swarthy complexion; grey eyes; born in Princeton and apprenticed to JOHN SAUNDERS, who formerly traded in tin, at Philadelphia or

Wilmington"; advertised in *The Pennsylvania Gazette*, May 28, 1772

WILLIAM WRIGHT, a servant man; runaway from JOSEPH NICHOLSON of Glouster Town in Glouster County; "about 5 feet, 1 inch high; straight black hair; well set; dark complexion"; advertised in *The Pennsylvania Gazette*, June 11, 1772

PATRICK BICKUM, a Scotch servant man; runaway from DAVID CLAYTON in Penn's Neck on Oldman's Creek in Salem County; "aged about 23 years, 5 feet, 8 inches high; chunky, well set fellow; has a lock on his leg; short black hair"; advertised in *The Pennsylvania Gazette*, June 25, 1772

DANIEL M'GIVERON, an Irish servant man; runaway from ROBERT JOHNSON, living in Salem; "aged about 19 years; 5 feet, 7 or 8 inches high; down look; long sharp nose; three of his upper teeth stick out farther than the rest and he has a clumsy walk"; advertised in *The Pennsylvania Journal and General Advertiser*, June 25, 1772

HUGH BURNS, a servant man; runaway from LUKE M'CABE, living at Clomell in the Jersies; "5 feet, 6 or 7 inches high; dark complexion; short black hair; served part of his time with one CUMMINGS, a tinker in Bucks county and has often traveled through many parts of the country selling tin ware"; notice to THOMAS MULLAN in Front Street; advertised in *The Pennsylvania Packet and General Advertiser*, July 6, 1772

JOHN HARWOOD, an English servant man; runaway from JOSEPH CALDWELL, living in Kent County on the Delaware; "5 feet, 6 or 7 inches high; very smooth faced fellow; black complexion; wears his own hair timed behind; has a pretty large scar upon his face; has a Roman nose; has worked in many places in America; loves drink very much and when in liquor swears and sings; by trade a tailor"; advertised in *The Pennsylvania Packet and General Advertiser*, July 16, 1772

JOSEPH WILEY, a servant man runaway from NATHAN KIMSEY, Constable, living in Deptford Township, Glouster County; "aged about 20 years; 5 feet, 7 inches high; dark complexion; brown hair; long visage"; advertised in *The Pennsylvania Packet and General Advertiser,* July 16, 1772

DANIEL WHEATON, American born; runaway from his bail; "aged about 30 years; 5 feet, 8 or 9 inches high; fair sandy complexion; light curled hair; well made; very fond of strong liquor; little freckled in his face; took his wife with him who is a small woman of a dark yellow complexion"; advertised by CURTIS TRENCHARD in *The Pennsylvania Gazette,* July 22, 1772

ISAAC HILDERBRAND, runaway from his bail; "aged about 30 years; 5 feet, 7 or 8 inches high; dark complexion; black hair; seldom drinks strong liquor; gray blue eyes; marked with small pox"; advertised by CURTIS TRENCHARD in *The Pennsylvania Gazette,* July 22, 1772

JOHN COLEMAN, an American born servant man; runaway from his bail; "aged about 26 years; 5 feet, 8 inches high; ruddy complexion; bushy red hair, nose droops a little"; born in New Jersey, notice to FRANCIS WADE in Philadelphia, HEMPHILL AND GORDON in Wilmington and ROBERT MACK, Gaoler in New Castle; advertised in *The Pennsylvania Packet and General Advertiser,* July 27, 1772

WILLIAM HARRISON SIMPSON, an apprentice lad; runaway from BENJAMIN RAMBO, living in Woodbury, Glouster County; "aged about 19 years; by trade a shop joiner"; advertised in *The Pennsylvania Gazette,* July 29, 1772

BENJAMIN MATISON, a servant man; runaway from ROBERT CARTER, living at Egg Harbor, Glouster County; "aged about 23 or 24 years; 6 feet high"; advertised by in *The Pennsylvania Chronicle and Universal Advertiser,* August 1, 1772

MICHAEL WHEALON, an Irish servant man; runaway

from CURTIS TRENCHARD, living in Salem; "5 feet, 7 or 8 inches high"; advertised in *The Pennsylvania Journal and Weekly Advertiser*, August 5, 1772

RICHARD HENDMAN, a servant man; runaway from ALEXANDER ALLISON, living in Blue Rocks; "5 feet, 8 or 9 inches high; dark hair; pearl on one eye; down look; a mole on left cheek and an iron collar around his neck;" notice to SAMUEL CHESNUT, living at the Pennsylvania Farmer, Second Street, Philadelphia; advertised in *The Pennsylvania Gazette*, August 12, 1772

JAMES LEE, a servant boy; runaway from Aetna Furnace; "aged about 19 years; 5 feet high; spare made; dark complexion; has an impediment in his speech; by trade a nailor"; advertised by CHARLES READ in *The Pennsylvania Gazette*, August 12, 1772

WILLIAM ALLEN; "aged about 25 years, 5 feet, 10 inches tall, black hair, fair complexion"

JAMES JOHNSON, an English servant man; runaway from SAMUEL LIPPINCOTT, living at Evesham in Burlington County; "about 5 feet, 6 inches high; of a swarthy complexion; a little pitted with small pox; has black hair"; advertised in *The Pennsylvania Gazette*, August 26, 1772

Committed to custody of RICHARD JOHNSON, Gaoler of the county of Glouster, on suspicion of being a runaway, JOHN HANDLIN, Irish born; "about 30 years of age; a short well set fellow of a dark complexion and black curled hair"; advertised in *The Pennsylvania Gazette*, September 9, 1772

CHRISTAIN BASIER, a Dutch servant man; runaway from BENJAMIN ARCHER, Blacksmith, living in Evesham Township; "aged about 30 years; 5 feet, 6 or 7 inches high; light complexion; red hair; little or no beard; a wart or mole between his eyebrows; round shouldered; knock kneed; a clumsy walk"; advertised in *The Pennsylvania Gazette*, October 28, 1772

WILLIAM HOPKINS [WILLIAM WOOD], a servant man; runaway from his bail; "middle aged; 5 feet, 10 inches high; very black hair; dark complexion; wears his hair tied back; short fore teeth; stoop shouldered and commonly followed ditching"; advertised by WILLIAM M'CLUNE and JOHN MCEWEN in *The Pennsylvania Gazette,* December 23, 1772

JOHN HAMMER, an English servant man; runaway from JOHN GILL, living in Haddonfield, Glouster County; "aged about 20 years; 5 feet, 7 inches high; slim built; light brown hair; has a scar in the middle of his left cheek"; advertised in *The Pennsylvania Gazette,* December 30, 1772

THOMAS CARTER, a Irish servant man; runaway from JOHN KELLE, living opposite Marcus Hook, in Glouster County; "aged 30 years; 5 feet, 6 inches high; fresh colored; black bushy hair, tied behind; full face; gray eyes; a mole on his left cheek on a line with mouth; speaks good Dutch; has traveled a great deal in this country; expected to go to GRUBB's ironworks; by trade a currier"; advertised in *The Pennsylvania Gazette,* January 6, 1773

JOHN WARREN, a servant man; runaway from GEORGE NORRIS, living in Princeton; "5 feet, 5 or 6 inches high; swarthy complexion; dark brown hair; thin build; down look"; notice to JOHN W. SANDERS, near Princeton; advertised in *The Pennsylvania Gazette,* January 6, 1773

ICHABUD ROBERTS, an apprentice boy; runaway from ISAAC PLUME, living Newark; "aged about 19 years; well set; light brown hair; by trade a shoemaker and tanner and understands something about currying"; advertised in *The New York Gazette and Weekly Mercury,* January 18, 1773

THOMAS ROBINSON, an Irish servant man; runaway from WILLIAM GRAHAM, living at *The Sign of the Uicorn*, in Elizabeth Town; "short man; 5 feet, 3 inches high; brown complexion; wears on his own hair and seems to walk as if he was bow legged; by trade a hostler"; advertised in *The New York Gazette and Weekly Mercury,* January 18, 1773

JAMES KEEFE, an Irish servant man; runaway from EPHRAIM SHEPHERD and DANIEL MULFORD, living in Cumberland County; "aged about 24 years; 5 feet, 6 inches high; came with Capt. JAMES CURTIS from Waterford; speaks good English but says he can not read or write"; advertised in *The Pennsylvania Packet*, January 18, 1773

JACOB WARRINGTON, an American born servant man; runaway from EPHRAIM SHEPHERD and DANIEL MULFORD; "aged about 22 years; 5 feet, 5 inches high; well built; brown hair"; advertised in *The Pennsylvania Packet*, January 18, 1773

MICHAEL WHEALON, an Irish servant man runaway from CURTIS TRENCHARD, living in Salem; "5 feet, 6 or 7 inches high; pale complexion; down look; light sandy hair; stoops a good deal in his walk; talks with much of the brogue; is fond of liquor and is very impudent when drunk or sober; marked with small pox"; advertised in *The New York Gazette and Weekly Mercury*, January 28, 1773

BURGIS GAMBOL, American born; runaway from WILLIAM GERARD, living in Newtown Township, Glouster County; "aged 25 years; 5 feet, 6 inches high; born at Mount Holly; snaggle teeth; thick lips; thin beard and brown hair; by trade a cooper"; advertised in *The Pennsylvania Packet*, March 8, 1773

JOHN BROWN, a servant man; runaway from JEDEDIAH ALLEN, living in Manington, Salem County; "aged 35 to 40 years; 5 feet, 5 or 6 inches high; middling well built; thin face; the little toe on his right foot turns over the others"; advertised in *The Pennsylvania Gazette*, March 10, 1773

DAVID SMITH, a servant man; runaway from JEDEDIAH ALLEN, living in Manington, Salem County; "aged 20 years; 5 feet, 7 or 8 inches high; well set; down look; large scar on the back of one hand and a sore on one leg"; advertised in *The Pennsylvania Gazette*, March 10, 1773

CHARLES CAUSGROVE, a servant man; runaway from JOHN BURGIN living in Cumberland County; "aged 24 years; 5 feet, 5 or 6 inches high; fair complexion; light colored hair; is very fond of strong liquor"; advertised in *The Pennsylvania Journal*, March 10, 1773

JOHN KINSEY, a servant man; runaway from NATHANIEL ADAMS, living in Burdenton, Burlington County; "5 feet, 10 inches high; fair complexion; light hair; limps very much with his right leg which is about three inches shorter than the other; by trade a cooper"

Committed to my custody on suspicion of being a runaway, BARNEY KEAN; "5 feet, 6 or 7 inches high; pitted with the pox"; advertised by GEORGE EBERLY, Gaoler in *The Pennsylvania Gazette*, March 24, 1773

JOHN CAMBEL, a servant man; runaway from PHILIP JACOBS living in Swedesboro, Glouster County; "aged 35 years; 5 feet, 6 inches high; by trade a sailor"; advertised in *The Pennsylvania Gazette*, March 31, 1773

GEORGE GOFF, a servant man; runaway from THOMAS NORRIS and THOMAS SINNICKSON, living in Salem; "is of small stature, not exceeding 5 feet 2 or 3 inches high and proportionately made; commonly wears a sailor's habit and talks much of his knowledge of that business; he is a quarrelsome, surly fellow and swears much in conversation; most probable places to get intelligence of him is along the wharfs, of the watermen or sailors or about Irish Town in the Southern Liberties; by trade a waterman and known by all watermen on the Delaware"; advertised in *The Pennsylvania Gazette*, March 31, 1773

ADAM WATT, a northern Irish servant man; runaway from THOMAS LYELL, living in Willingborough, Burlington County; "aged 21 years; 5 feet, 7 inches high; dark complexion like an Indian; black lank hair; stoops a little; speaks very broad"; advertised in *The Pennsylvania Gazette*, April 14, 1773

JACOB LIPPENCOTT, an apprentice lad; runaway from FREDERICK ENGLE, living in Middletown, Chester County; "aged 19 years; 5 feet, 8 inches high; sandy complexion; thin curled hair; thin visage; a down look and slow motion; apprenticed by his guardian ABRAHAM HEWLING"; advertised in *The Pennsylvania Gazette*, April 21, 1773

JOHN OULDEN, an Irish servant man; runaway from PETER CHEESMAN, living in Glouster Town and Glouster County; "5 feet, 4 inches high; thick and well set; has a pretty broad face, with straight brown hair and speaks good English"; advertised in *The Pennsylvania Gazette*, April 28, 1773

JOHN WELLS, a servant man; runaway from JOHN BAINBRIDGE living in Newton; "5 feet 3, inches high; black hair; by trade a tailor; dark eyes; rather thin than fat; pretty talkative when merry, has a scar or bump on the middle of his nose; hurt about a year ago by a fall or blow"; advertised in *The Pennsylvania Journal*, April 28, 1773

JOHN ROSE, an English servant man; runaway from JOHN TATUM, living in Deptford Township, Glouster County; "aged 22 years; 5 feet,7 or 8 inches high; pretty well proportioned; fresh colored; had straight black hair; a round scar on the back of one of his wrists; shipped himself from Ireland; by trade a stocking weaver"; advertised in *The Pennsylvania Chronicle*, May 17, 1773

JOSEPH RICHARDS, an English servant man; runaway from CALEB SWEYZE, living in Roxbury Township, Morris County; "aged 35 years; 5 feet, 9 inches high; slim made; fair skinned, but of a tawny complexion in the face; dark brown hair; speaks broad; by trade a collier"; advertised in *The Pennsylvania Journal*, May 19, 1773

WILLIAM SMITH, an English servant man; runaway from MOSES YAMANS & Company, at Chalsey Forge, near the mouth of the Muscunnetcung in Sussex County; "about 5 feet, 9 inches high; fair complexion; red beard; very apt to get drunk and talks very saucy when in liquor; has a wife and two children, one of whom is dumb"; advertised in *The Pennsylvania Gazette*, May 26, 1773

ANDREW METS, a Dutch servant man; runaway from BENJAMIN POWELL; "about 18 years of age; 5 feet, 3 or 4 inches high; dark complexion; brown hair; stoops very much in walking, but is an active fellow and fond of showing it, especially in walking upon ropes"; advertised in *The Pennsylvania Gazette*, May 26, 1773

ADAM LINNEY, a Dutch servant man; runaway from THOMAS ANDERSON living in Sussex County; "about 16 years of age; dark complexion; short black hair; his honesty is far from being unquestionable; says his father lives in Philadelphia; by trade a tailor"; advertised in *The Pennsylvania Chronicle*, May 31, 1773

BENJAMIN SMITH, a servant man; runaway from JOHN SUMMERL, at Penn's Neck in Salem County; "fair hair and wears it tied;" in company with one JOHN RUSSEL; advertised in *RIVINGTON'S New York Gazetteer or The Connecticut, New Jersey, Hudson's River and Quebec Weekly Advertiser*, June 3, 1773

JOHN CRAWFORD, an Irish servant man; runaway from WILLIAM WILSON, in the town of Mansfield, Burlington County; "about 21 years of age; 5 feet, 6 or 8 inches high; brown curled hair; his back, if examined, will appear to have been lately under the discipline of the cat o' nine tails; it is supposed he will make for JACOB CHARLEY'S in Hartford Township, over Scuykill, as he left some clothes there"; advertised in *RIVINGTON'S New York Gazetteer or The Connecticut, New Jersey, Hudson's River and Quebec Weekly Advertiser*, June 3, 1773

JOHN RYAN [JOHN M'AHEE] an Irish servant man; runaway from SETH PANCOAST and THOMAS LEVIS, living at Springfield Township, Chester County; "about 20 years of age; 5 feet, 8 or 9 inches high; well set fellow; gray eyes; light complexion; brown sandy hair; impudent look; has been in the country for ten months; speaks with the brogue; thought to have gone to a cousin's, JOHN KIEF, who resides in the Jerseys"; advertised in *The New York Journal or General Advertiser*, June 3, 1773

BARTHOLOMEW MURPHY, an Irish servant man; runaway from SETH PANCOAST and THOMAS LEVIS, living at Springfield Township, Chester County; "about 20 years of age; 5 feet, 6 inches high; dark hair; gray eyes; bow legged; long feet; a silly looking fellow"; advertised in *The New York Journal or General Advertiser*, June 3, 1773

JESSE MONEY, a servant man; runaway from ISAAC MULFORD, living in Hopewell, Cumberland County; "about 33 years of age; 5 feet, 8 or 9 inches high; dark complexion; brown hair; round shouldered and a down look"; advertised in *The Pennsylvania Packet*, June 7, 1773

THOMAS WATSON, a servant man; runaway from his bail given by JACOB RHINEDOLLOR; "stout; well built; young fellow; 6 feet, 2 or 3 inches high; round shouldered; has a smooth tongue; can write a good hand of several sorts; black complexion; dark hair; marked with the pox; went with him MARY ANN WHEELER, the wife of JOHN WHEELER of Philadelphia; supposedly was at a school in Egg Harbor last winter; formerly followed the sea"; advertised in *The Pennsylvania Gazette*, June 16, 1773

JOHN ALFORD, American born servant man; runaway from Astion Furnace in Burlington County; "about 22 years of age; 5 feet, 7 inches high; fair complexion; has lately had the small pox; has a scar on his upper lip; is well set and wears his own hair, which is brown and short and curls all round his head"; advertised by LAWRENCE SALTAR, in *The Pennsylvania Journal*, June 16, 1773

JOHN WEIGKEL, a German servant man; runaway from WILLIAM LAWRENCE and DETRICK REES, Innkeeper in Philadelphia; "about 30 years of age; 6 feet high; tall, slim fellow;

brown straight hair; speaks the Low Dutch language very well; scar on his upper lip; light gray eyes; is bald on top of his head; has a very bold look; speaks little or no English; has been an old soldier and has a sore on his leg, occasioned by a wound he had received in the army"; advertised in *The Pennsylvania Gazette*, June 23, 1773

CHRISTIAN SMITH, a German servant man; runaway from WILLIAM LAWRENCE and DETRICK REES, Innkeeper in Philadelphia; "5 feet, 2 or 3 inches high; born in Saxony; short light hair; a scar on his nose and bandy legs; mostly shuts one of his eyes when he speaks; has an impediment in his speech; speaks little or no English; has an indenture for JOHN ADAM LOUBER"; advertised in *The Pennsylvania Gazette*, June 23, 1773

JAMES DICK, a Scottish servant man; runaway from THOMAS CARNEY, Jr. , living in Penn's Neck, Salem County; "about 30 years of age; 5 feet, 8 or 9 inches high; thick, well set fellow; sandy complexion with a very sandy beard; had on an iron collar when he ran away as this was the sixth time he has run away; coarse voice and a down look"; advertised in *The Pennsylvania Gazette*, June 23, 1773 ; advertised again in *The Pennsylvania Packet*, September 6, 1773, as runaway from JOHN POOL living in Upper Penn's Neck, Salem county; " down look and talks coarse; had on when he went away an iron collar (this being the eighth time he has run away)"; advertised again in "; advertised in *Dunlop's Pennsylvania Packet*, August 22, 1774 as having runaway, now with a red beard from THOMAS CARNEY, Jr. again and re advertised in *The Pennsylvania Gazette*, August 14, 1776, additionally described as "his beard almost red; marked with small pox"

MICHAEL FARREL, an Irish servant man; runaway from ANDREW RICHMAN, living in Glouster County; "5 feet, 9 or 10 inches high"; advertised in *The Pennsylvania Gazette*, July 7, 1773

JOHN BOLING, an English servant man; runaway from MAHLON WRIGHT, living in New Hanover Township, Burlington County; "about 21 years of age; thick set fellow; 5 feet,

7 or 8 inches high; wears his own sandy hair frized; has a down look and talks Yorkshire"; advertised in *The Pennsylvania Gazette*, July 7, 1773

Taken up on suspicion of being a runaway servant man, HUGH M'MANAN; "5 feet, 5 inches high; black beard; black hair; says he is the servant of WILLIAM BEAKS of Cecil County, Maryland"; advertised in *The Pennsylvania Journal and Weekly Advertiser*, July 28, 1773

JOHN LETTERIDGE, an Irish servant man; runaway from JOSEPH RIGGS, near Cranberry, Middlesex County; "about 20 years of age; 5 feet, 9 inches high; fair complexion; thin visaged; looks pale; dark hair; blue eyes; scar on left eye; scar on left hip by a pistol ball; has very good learning; marked with the pox; bought a few days before out of Amboy jail by JOHN PATTERSON of Philadelphia"; advertised in *The New York Gazette*, August 2, 1773

TIMOTHY SMAULES, an English servant man; runaway from WILLIAM HULET, living in Shrewsbury, Monmouth County; "4 feet, 10 inches high; light hair; thick set; talks quick; great singer by note; marked with the pox"; advertised in *Rivington's New York Gazetteer*, August 5, 1773

BENJAMIN SMITH, an English servant man; runaway from JOHN SUMMERL, living in Salem County; "about 26 or 27 years of age; 5 feet, 9 or 10 inches high; wears hair tied; slender; fair complexion; tailor but not perfect in cutting out; handy at knitting caps for women or silk purses for the men; given to drink and apt to talk; advertised in *The Pennsylvania Gazette*, August 11, 1773

WILLIAM DAY, a servant man; runaway from JONATHAN DAYTON, WILLIAM PARSONS, JONATHAN SKINNER, living at Elizabeth Town; "about 35 to 40 years of age; 6 feet high; short brown hair; stout, well made; axe and scythe maker by trade; very talkative; much addicted to drinking grog but seldom gets much intoxicated" supposed to have gone to New

England or to Poughkeepsie;

CORNELIUS CONINIE, a servant man; runaway from JONATHAN I. DAYTON, living in Elizabeth Town; "about 20 years of age; 5 feet, 8 or 10 inches high; stout build; light complexion; brown curled light hair and round shouldered; was whipped last fall in Essex for a felony and was purchased by his master to help defray the gaol expenses"; advertised in *The New York Gazette*, August 16, 1773

JAMES ETHERINGTON, a servant lad; runaway from ANDREW MITCHELL, living in Marlborough Township, Chester County, Pennsylvania; "about 17 years of age; 5 feet, 3 inches high; scar on one of his cheeks; supposed to be the left cheek; red hair; freckled"; advertised in *The Pennsylvania Gazette*, August 18, 1773

JAMES CAMBELL, a servant lad; runaway from ANDREW MITCHELL, living in Marlborough Township, Chester County, Pennsylvania; "about 17 years of age; 5 feet"; advertised in *The Pennsylvania Gazette*, August 18, 1773

JOHN BROWN, American born servant man; runaway from WILLIAM TOMLIN of Glouster county, near the headwaters of Mantua Creek; "about 31 years of age; 5 feet, 6 or 7 inches high; down look and apt to get drunk; has two brown marks, one on each side below his breast, the bigness of a penny, one rather smaller than the other"; advertised in *The Pennsylvania Journal and The Weekly Advertiser*, August 18, 1773

HENDRICK HESS, a Dutch servant man; runaway from GARRET VORHEES, living at Springfield, about three miles from Burlington; "about 40 years of age; 5 feet, 7 inches high; fresh complexion; well set; dark curled hair; marked with the pox; round faced; speaks broken English; by trade a butcher"; advertised in *The Pennsylvania Packet*, August 23, 1773

JOHN KEANE, a servant man; runaway from the Ship *Hannah*, JAMES MITCHELL, Master; "5 feet, 10 inches high;

stout and well made; long black hair;" advertised by BARCLAY and MITCHELL in *The Pennsylvania Journal and Weekly Advertiser*, August 25, 1773

DANIEL ROGAN, a servant man; runaway from the Ship *Hannah*, JAMES MITCHELL, Master; "5 feet, 6 inches high; smooth faced; long black hair, tied back"; advertised by BARCLAY and MITCHELL in *The Pennsylvania Journal and Weekly Advertiser*, August 25, 1773

WILLIAM KENNEDY, a servant man; runaway from the Ship *Hannah*, JAMES MITCHELL, Master; "5 feet, 10 inches high; has a speech impediment; very stout and thick boned; marked with the pox and freckled"; advertised by BARCLAY and MITCHELL in *The Pennsylvania Journal and Weekly Advertiser*, August 25, 1773

HENRY DRAIN, a servant man; runaway from the Ship *Hannah*, JAMES MITCHELL, Master; "4 feet, 6 inches high; smooth faced; well limbed"; advertised by BARCLAY and MITCHELL in *The Pennsylvania Journal and Weekly Advertiser*, August 25, 1773

ANDREW BOYD, a servant man; runaway from the Ship *Hannah*, JAMES MITCHELL, Master; "5 feet, 10 inches high; a large nose; smooth faced"; advertised by BARCLAY and MITCHELL in *The Pennsylvania Journal and Weekly Advertiser*, August 25, 1773

JOHN GREEN [WILLIAM JOHNSON], an Irish servant man; runaway from WILLIAM KELSO, in East Pennsborough, Cumberland County; "about 22 years of age; 5 feet, 8 inches high; reddish complexion; sour look; much freckled in the face and a scar on the right side of his head, near the crown; short red curled hair, which appears bushy, as he does not often curl it; cut on top of his head; he was kept some time at Mr. GRUBB'S Furnace, with wood cutters; is an artful fellow; a good scholar and a great rogue and much given to strong drink; he formerly lived with Mr. HUMPHREYS, on Schuylkill at the Middle Ferry; has been some time at sea"; advertised by BARCLAY and MITCHELL in *The Pennsylvania Gazette*, September 15, 1773

Was committed to Glouster Gaol on suspicion of being a runaway, THOMAS RIVERS; "5 feet, 6 inches high, pale complexion, sandy hair"; advertised by RICHARD JOHNSON, Gaoler in *The Pennsylvania Packet and the General Advertiser*, September 20, 1773

JAMES SPEDDY, a servant man; runaway from his bail; "about 19 years of age; 5 feet, 7 or 8 inches high; dark complexion; brown hair, tied"; advertised by JOHN M'CLELLAN, Jr. in *The Pennsylvania Packet and General Advertiser*, September 20, 1773

MICHAEL BURGESS, an Irish servant man; runaway from GRESHOM LEE, in Amwell, Hunterdon County; "5 feet, 8 inches high; well set; sandy complexion; hair cut short; has a down look and is subject to drink and swearing; says he has been in the army; is remarkably fond of exercising with a musket"; advertised in *The Pennsylvania Gazette*, September 29, 1773

JEDIAH ADAMS, apprentice boy; runaway from SAMUEL BOWKERA, living in Mount Holly; "about 17 years of age; 5 feet high; sandy complexion"; advertised in *The Pennsylvania Gazette*, September 29, 1773

DANIEL M'IMNIRY, an Irish indentured servant; ran away from RICHARD SMITH JR, living in Elsenborough, Salem County; "he is about 5 feet, 8 inches high; well set; light straight hair and very bald; has a large scar on one of his heels, cut by a scythe, and length way on his foot; full face; reddish complexion; small beard; is very apt to use the word "really"; talks very broken and backward and is fond of strong drink;" advertised in *The Pennsylvania Packet*, October 11, 1773

Taken up on suspicion of being a runaway from SAMUEL OWINGS, Jr.n. near Baltimore, says his name is SAMUEL COWAN

JOSHUA AGAN, an apprentice to GILBERT TICE of Johnstown; "5 feet, 5 inches high; slim made; fair complexion; much addicted to alcohol and a profane swearing man"; advertised in *The New York Gazette and Weekly Mercury*, October 18, 1773

PATRICK MORRIS, an Irish servant man; runaway from Mount Holly Iron works; "aged about 22 years; 5 feet, 6 inches high; dark complexion; short black hair; chews tobacco; marked with small pox; has worked as a collier"; advertised by THOMAS MAYBERRY in *The New York Gazette and Weekly Mercury*, October 18, 1773

THOMAS HOUSE, a servant man; runaway from Mount Holly Iron works; had been apprenticed to JAMES GREGORY, Jr. refiner at the Mount Holly Iron Works; "aged about 22 years; 5 feet, 10 inches high; walks very upright; curled hair; chews tobacco; has a full face pitted with small pox; by trade a collier"; advertised by THOMAS MAYBERRY in *The New York Gazette and Weekly Mercury*, October 18, 1773

THOMAS RIVERS, an Irish servant man; runaway from WILLIAM RAWSON, living in Glouster County; "aged about 20 or 21 years; 5 feet, 8 or 9 inches high; tall, slim fellow; pale complexion"; advertised in *The Pennsylvania Gazette*, October 20, 1773

MICHAEL ROFF, a German servant man; runaway from WILLIAM CORLIS and JOSHUA SHRIEVE, living in Springfield Township, Burlington County; "5 feet, 6 inches high; dark complexion; in country but 7 weeks; cannot speak English"; advertised in *Rivington's New York Gazetteer*, November 8, 1773

CHRISTOPHER HEIDECH, a German servant man; runaway from WILLIAM CORLIS and JOSHUA SHRIEVE, living in Springfield Township, Burlington County; "a short, well set fellow; dark complexion; light colored eyes; in country but 7 weeks; cannot speak English"; advertised in *Rivington's New York Gazetteer*, November 8, 1773

CHARLES MALLIN, a Dutch servant lad; runaway from JOHN DICKENSON living in Salem County; "age not known; is about 5 feet, 6 or 7 inches high; of a sandy complexion; by trade a butcher"; advertised in *The Pennsylvania Gazette*, November 10, 1773

Unnamed Irish servant man; runaway from CHRISTOPHER DIETRICK, living in Waterford Township, Glouster County; "aged about 28 years; 5 feet, 6 inches high; sickly and had the ague when he went away; of a dark ill looking visage and complexion; red beard"; advertised in *The Pennsylvania Gazette*, November 17, 1773

PATRICK CUFF, an Irish servant man; runaway from SAMUEL PURVIANCE and JOHN PURVIANCE in Philadelphia; "aged about 25 years; 5 feet, 9 inches high; dark complexion; stoops a little; speaks much with brogue; short black hair; wants a tooth in the fore part of his upper jaw; went off in the company of JOHN KEARNEY, a free man, who is 5 feet, 5 inches high; wears his own hair and has brogue also"; advertised in *The Pennsylvania Journal and The Weekly Advertiser*, November 17, 1773

DAVIS KIEFF, an Irish servant man; runaway from Basto Furnace, near the Forks of Little Egg Harbor; "aged about 28 years; 5 feet, 7 inches high; fair complexion; straight brown hair; gray eyes; thin visage; has a down look and stoops in his walk; chews tobacco very much and went off in company of THOMAS MURRAY"; advertised in *The Pennsylvania Journal and The Weekly Advertiser,* November 24, 1773

BARTHOLOMEW LIONS, an Irish servant man; runaway from Basto Furnace, near the Forks of Little Egg Harbor; "aged about 21 years; 5 feet, 4 inches high; tawny complexion; straight brown hair; gray eyes; down look; chews tobacco very much and went off in company of THOMAS MURRAY"; advertised in *The Pennsylvania Journal and The Weekly Advertiser*, November 24, 1773

ALBERT WILSON, an apprentice; runaway from GEORGE HENOLD, living in Haddonfield, Glouster County; "aged about 20 years; 5 feet, 10 inches high; by trade a wheelwright"; advertised in *The Pennsylvania Gazette*, December 1, 1773

JOHN BALSER KINSINER, a Dutch servant man; runaway from MICHAEL M'GUIRE, Jr. living at Great Pipe Creek, Frederick County, Maryland; "5 feet, 6 inches high; sandy beard; dark frized hair; black eyes, sunk in his head and very small; father lives in Philadelphia; was whipped at Lancaster at October Court, 1772, at Trenton last August and is well acquainted with the whipping post in Philadelphia; can work at the weaving business; by trade a tailor"; advertised in *The Pennsylvania Gazette*, December 8, 1773

HUGH M'KAIN, an Irish servant man; runaway from CONROD BONER, living in Taronytown, Frederick County, Maryland; "5 feet, 4 inches high; small and slender; of middle age; the fore part of his head almost bald; black hair; pale visage; a great snuffer; much given to liquor; has a small scar or mark under his left nostril; by trade a tailor"; advertised in *The New York Gazette and Weekly Mercury*, December 13, 1773

WILLIAM RICHARDSON, a servant lad; runaway from ANTHONY HOOPER, living in Greenwich, Glouster County; "about 17 years of age; 4 feet, 8 or 9 inches high; has a down, bashful look when in company; a round face and fresh complexion; advertised in *The Pennsylvania Gazette*, December 22, 1773

WILLIAM RICHELSON, an English servant man; runaway from GILES LOVERING, in Upper Alloway's Creek, Salem County; "about 22 years of age; 5 feet, 3 inches high; sandy complexion; red hair; has lost two of his fore teeth in his upper jaw; by trade a chimney sweep"; advertised in *The Pennsylvania Gazette*, December 22, 1773; also advertised in *The Pennsylvania Gazette*, January 5, 1774

Unnamed Irish servant man; runaway from CHRISTOPHER DIETRICK in Waterford Township, Glouster; "about 28 years of age; about 5 feet, 6 inches high; he was sickly and had the ague when he went away; dark ill looking visage and complexion and red beard"; advertised in *The Pennsylvania Gazette*, January 5, 1774

MICHAEL ROOF, a Dutch servant man; runaway from JOSHUA SHREVE and WILLIAM CURTIS, Jr. living in Springfield, Burlington County; "black hair; lately come to country and cannot speak English"; advertised in *The Pennsylvania Gazette*, January 5, 1774

CHRISTIAN HEIDIECH, a Dutch servant man; runaway from JOSHUA SHREVE and WILLIAM CURTIS, Jr. living in Springfield, Burlington County; "much freckled; lately come to country and cannot speak English"; advertised in *The Pennsylvania Gazette*, January 5, 1774

OWEN BOWEN, American born servant man; runaway from JOHN KILLE of Glouster County; "about 27 years of age; about 5 feet, 10 or 11 inches high; he was full mouthed; dark eyes; walks very straight and is slim to his height"; advertised in *Dunlop's Pennsylvania Packet*, January 17, 1774

THOMAS GRIFFITHS, an English indented man; runaway from Burlington;, "in a former part of his life, when resident in his Mother Country, kept a Tavern in the City of London known by the *Sign of the King's Arms*, in Leaden Hall Street, but for some year before he left England, rented a considerable farm near Bristol; a well looking man between the ages of 30 and 40; of a middle stature; stoops in his walk; and cannot, with the smallest degree of effrontery, look a man in the face; has an easy, soft, smooth manner of speaking"; advertised in *The New York Gazette*, February 7, 1774.

ALBERT WILSON, an apprentice lad; runaway from GEORGE HENHOLD, living in Haddonfield, Glouster County; "about 20 years of age; about 5 feet, 10 inches high; by trade a wheelwright";

HANCE ANDREW CHRISTIAN BREMER, a German indented servant; runaway from ARCHIBALD M'CLANY; "speaks broken English"; advertised in *Dunlop's Pennsylvania Packet*

JOHN BRADLEY, an Irish servant man; runaway from THOMAS POTTS, living near Chelsea Forge; "aged about 47 years; short, chunky fellow; short black hair; has lost one of his toes"; advertised in *The Pennsylvania Gazette*, April 13, 1774

unnamed servant boy; runaway from JACOB HALLET; "5 feet, 9 inches high; stout, hard favored man; dark brown or black hair"; advertised in *The New York Gazette and The Weekly Mercury*, April 18, 1774

WILLIAM NICKLE, a German born servant man; runaway from JOHN BEEMER, living in Bethlehem Township, Hunterdon County; "about 24 years of age; 5 feet, 7 or 8 inches high; slim built; long nose; thick lips; stoop shouldered; fresh complexion; fair hair; can speak but little English and says he used be a soldier in the German service; pock marked"; advertised in *The Pennsylvania Gazette*, April 20, 1774

WILLIAM RICHARDSON, an English servant man; runaway from ISAAC RAIN, living at Alloways Creek Neck; "about 22 years of age; 5 feet, 4 or 5 inches high; very musical; by trade a sweep chimney"; advertised in *Dunlap's Pennsylvania Packet*, April 25, 1774; advertised again in *The Pennsylvania Gazette*, December 21, 1774 as having runaway from ISAAC REIGN, living in Alloway's Creek, Salem county; " red hair; lost two of his upper teeth; very fond of strong drink and is very much given to singing; marked with small pox; by trade a chimney sweep, also tailor and breeches maker"

GOTTLIEB FUHRMAN, a German servant man; runaway from LEONARD JENAWEIN, living in Manheim Township, York County; "5 feet, 7 or 8 inches high; well set; one of his little fingers rendered useless by a shot, wherefore he hides it as best he can; is a native of Eisleben in the county of Mansfield in Saxony; is a great lover of strong liquor and a great smoker of tobacco and snuff taker"; advertised in *Dunlap's Pennsylvania Packet,* April 25, 1774

JAMES GERALD, an Irish servant man; runaway from ALEXANDER HILL, living in Lower Penn's Neck, Salem county; "about 30 years of age; 5 feet, 9 or 10 inches high; with a flesh mark in his right arm from his knuckles to his shoulder and of a claret color"

MICHAEL NUGENT, an Irish servant man; runaway from THOMAS TOBIN, residing near Princeton; "about 26 years of age, is pock marked, near 6 feet high; stout and well made; speaks much of the brogue and is addicted to strong liquor"; advertised in *Rivington's New York Gazette,* April 28, 1774

MICHAEL KEELLY, an Irish servant man; runaway from PATRICK COLVIN, living at Trenton Ferry; "about 5 feet, 6 inches high; 22 years of age; has brown hair; very thick legs and is fresh colored"; advertised in the *New York Gazette and Weekly Mercury,* May 9, 1774

WILLIAM INGLE, an English servant lad; runaway from ANDREW SINNICKSON and EZRA FIRTH, in Lower Penn's Neck, Salem County; "about 18 or 19 years of age; about 5 feet, 5 or 6 inches high; a thick well set fellow; fair complexion; smooth faced; straight black hair; has been in the country for four years"; advertised in *the Pennsylvania Gazette,* June 22, 1774

RICHARD BROWN, an American born servant lad; runaway from ANDREW SINNICKSON and EZRA FIRTH, in Lower Penn's Neck, Salem County; "about 18 years of age; about 5 feet, 4 or 5 inches high; a slight spare lad; dark brown hair; a down look and something near sighted"; advertised in *The Pennsylvania Gazette,* June 22, 1774

MICHAEL FEROL, a servant man; runaway from

ROBERT MENDENHALL, living in Concord, Chester County; "about 22 years of age; about 5 feet, 10 inches high; pale complexion; light brown hair; wangles in his walk"; advertised in *The Pennsylvania Gazette*, June 22, 1774

THOMAS HARVEY, an Irish servant man; runaway from ALEXANDER HILL, living in Lower Penn's Neck, Salem County; "about 20 years of age; short, thick full faced fellow"

JOHN OLDFORD, an American born servant man; runaway Mount Holly; " well set"

PETER MURPHY, an Irish servant boy; runaway from JONATHAN BALDWIN, living at Princeton; "5 feet, 10 inches high, reddish complexion; curled brown hair; speaks good English and very little on the Irish, his native language"; advertised in *Dunlap's Pennsylvania Packet*, July 4, 1774

EDWARD GRIFFY, an Irish servant man; runaway from SIMON ADDES, living in Middlesex County; "about 24 years of age; 5 feet, 4 or 5 inches high; short black hair; has a scar on his cheek; came to Philadelphia last year on the Ship *Narrow*, Capt. HILL; advertised in *The New York Gazette and The Weekly Mercury*, July 18, 1774

WILLIAM KERNS, an Irish servant man; runaway from PETER CHEESEMAN, living in Glouster Township ; "about 20 years of age; 5 feet, 6 inches high"; advertised in *The Pennsylvania Journal*, July 27, 1774

JOHN SIMPSON, an Irish servant man; runaway from JOHN JACOB FAESH, living at Mount Hope, Morris County; "about 25-30 years of age; 5 feet, 5 inches high; well set; dark complexion; short black hair; very sullen in his temper'; advertised in *The New York Gazette and The Weekly Mercury*, August 1, 1774

JOHN SMITH, an Irish servant man; runaway from THOMAS PAXEN, living at Mount Holly; "5 feet, 2 or 3 inches high; light complexion; apt to get disguised in liquor; by trade a saddler"; advertised in *The Pennsylvania Journal*, August 3, 1774

EDWARD DUMPHY, an Irish servant man; runaway from PHEBE MORTON, living in Philadelphia; "about 19 years of age; slim fellow; 5 feet, 6 or 7; fair complexion; long light hair tied back"; advertised in *The New York Gazette and The Weekly Mercury*, August 15, 1774

RICHARD BROWN, a servant man; runaway from ANDREW SINNICKSON, living in Lower Penn's Neck Salem County; "about 18 years of age; 5 feet, 4 inches high; brown complexion; straight dark hair; a sneaking down look and near sighted"; advertised in *The Pennsylvania Gazette*, August 24, 1774

JACOB REILEY, an American born servant man; runaway from GABRIEL DOWBROW, living at Racoon Creek; "about 26 or 27 years of age; 5 feet, 8 or 9 inches high; pale complexion; lightish hair and is very raw boned"; advertised in *The Pennsylvania Gazette*, August 24, 1774

MICHAEL TOLEN [STEPHEN SMITH], a servant man; runaway from KENDAL COLES and BENJAMIN MATLACK; "5 feet, 6 or 7 inches high; fresh faced; light brown hair; very talkative; has lately been whipped at Glouster"; advertised in *The Pennsylvania Journal*, August 24, 1774

JAMES LAND, a servant man; runaway from SAMUEL ELLIS, living in Greenwich Township, Glouster County; "about 30 years of age; 5 feet, 4 inches high; dark complexion; straight black hair"; advertised in *The Pennsylvania Journal*, August 24, 1774

JOHN MORGAN, an Irish servant man; runaway from JEREMIAH MANNING, living in Woodbridge; "about 20 or 21 years of age; 5 feet, 4 inches high"; notice to JOHN LEGG at WILLIAM BAKER's in Chestnut Street, between Third and Fourth streets, Philadelphia; advertised in *The New York Gazette*, August 31, 1774

DENNIS M'MULLEN, an Irish servant man; runaway from William Montgomery, living in Londonderry Township, Chester County; "about 22 years of age; 5 feet, 9 or 10 inches high; pretty well made; has short, brown curling hair; smooth red face and is fond of spiritous liquor; JON MOONEY, a journeyman blacksmith went with him"; notice to DANIEL MONTGOMERY, painter, in Philadelphia; advertised in *Dunlop's Pennsylvania Packet*, September 5, 1774

THOMAS BRADSHAW, an apprentice lad; runaway from DANIEL COATE, living in Evesham; "about 18 years of age; 5 feet, 3 inches high; dark hair and eyes; pretty well set"; advertised in *The Pennsylvania Gazette*, September 7, 1774

DANIEL JURNEY, an apprentice lad; runaway from HARTSHORNE FITZ RANDOLF, in Morris County; "about 18 years of age; about 5 feet, 4 inches high; middling well set; goes somewhat stooping; black hair; somewhat curled; a very swarthy complexion; has some black blood in him; speaks thick"; advertised in *The New York Gazette and the Weekly Mercury*, September 26, 1774

JOHN DICK, a Dutch born servant man; runaway from JOHN JARVIS, near Bordentown; came from London with Capt. STEPHEN JONES; "followed sugar baking business for some time in London where he lived for some time; speaks good English"; advertised in *The New York Journal and General Advertiser*, September 29, 1774 ; also advertised as "5 feet, 9 inches high; black hair; came with Capt. STEPHEN JONES from London to Philadelphia" in *The Pennsylvania Gazette*, November 2, 1774

NATHANIEL ANSTER, an Irish servant man; runaway from JOHN CHAMBERS, at Penacon Bridge, in Chester Town, Burlington County"; 5 feet, 6 or 7 inches high; thick; chunky, well made fellow; sandy hair; speaks much of the brogue and is fond of strong liquor"; advertised in *The Pennsylvania Journal and The Weekly Advertiser*, November 2, 1774

WILLIAM DELANY, an Irish servant man; runaway from THOMAS SCULLEY, living in Middletown, Newcastle County on Delaware; "5 feet, 8 or 9 inches high; dark complexion; black hair, tied back; fond of strong liquor and, when drunk, which will be as often as he can get rum, is fond of speaking much in his own praise, particularly his great abilities in school keeping, which he has done for some time in Precipany, near Elizabeth Town; served two years with ISAAC DECOU, Esq. attorney at law in Trenton but was obliged to flee for forging CHARLES OGDEN's hand; advertised in *Dunlap's Pennsylvania Packet or The General Advertiser,* November 14, 1774

JOHN WORT, an apprentice lad; runaway from ARNOLD BOMBARGER, living at Lancaster Borough; "5 feet, 3 or 4 inches high; thin pale complexion; black hair, tied back; mother lives in New German Town; by trade a tailor"; advertised in *The Pennsylvania Gazette,* November 23, 1774

JOHN M'GORK, an Irish servant man; runaway from JAMES MOLESWORTH; "5 feet, 6 inches high; well set; speaks good English and talks very fast; is given to liquor; used to work in an iron furnace"; notice to Widow YARIALL'S in Philadelphia; advertised in *The Pennsylvania Gazette,* November 23, 1774

JAMES M'BRIDE, an Irish servant man; runaway from DERICKL BARCALOW, living at Upper Frehold, Monmouth County; "about 20-30 years of age; 5 feet, 7 or 8 inches high; well set; came into country last spring; by trade a dish turner"; advertised in *The New York Gazette and The Weekly Mercury,* November 28, 1774

THOMAS MURPHY, an Irish servant lad; runaway from JOSHUA BUNTING, living at Chesterfield Town, Burlington County; "about 19 years of age; 5 feet, 6 or 7 inches high; thin visaged and raw boned; has a long chin; a full mouth; short, stumpy nose; brown hair; gray eyes, and a very down look; the joint of his left ankle bends out which occasions his treading awry as well as a hobbling walk; used to the plantation business especially threshing"; advertised in *The Pennsylvania Gazette,*

November 30, 1774

Taken up on suspicion of being runaway, JOHN PEMBERTON, who answers to the notice for JOHN M'GUIRE, master's name JOHN BOUCTHER; advertised by ELIAS WHITAKAR, gaoler of Cumberland County in *The Pennsylvania Gazette*, December 14, 1774

Taken up on suspicion of being runaway, JOHN GARDINER; "5 feet, 5 or 6 inches high; lost one eye"; advertised by ELIAS WHITAKAR, gaoler of Cumberland County in *The Pennsylvania Gazette*, December 14, 1774

NATHANIEL SHEPPERD, American born servant man; runaway from JONATHAN MALSBARY, living in Mansfield Township, Burlington County; "about 25 years of age; 5 feet, 4 inches high; swarthy complexion; light straight hair; round shouldered"; advertised in *The Pennsylvania Gazette*, December 28, 1774

Taken up on suspicion of being a runaway, JAMES PARSONS; "5 feet, 7 inches high; thin made; dark complexion; black hair and eyes; hair pinned to the ears with a fashionable high top powdered; says he is a farmer but more looks like a barber; very impertinent, abusive and insolent"; advertised in *The New York Journal and General Advertiser*, December 29, 1774

JOHN GARDINER, American born servant man; runaway from WILLIAM BRIGHT, living in Cumberland; "5 feet, 10 inches high; born in East New Jersey; dark complexion; advertised in *The Pennsylvania Gazette*, January 11, 1775

Was committed on suspicion of being a runaway servant, JOHN SMALLWOOD; runaway from WILLIAM DOYL, innkeeper in Doylstown, Bucks County, Pennsylvania; advertised in *The Pennsylvania Gazette*, January 11, 1775

JAMES RUSSEL, an apprentice lad; runaway from JAMES BLACK of Springfield; "about 19 years of age; 5 feet, 8 inches tall; by trade a weaver"; advertised in *The New York Gazette,* January 23, 1775

JOHN O'NEIL, an Irish servant man; runaway from LAWRENCE SALTAR at Astion Forge in Evesham Township, Burlington County; "about 23 years of age; 5 feet, 8 inches tall"; advertised in *The Pennsylvania Gazette,* January 25, 1775

JOHN PURSLEY, an Irish servant man; runaway from GEORGE CUNNINGHAM of Hopewell Township, Cumberland County; "about 23 years of age; 5 feet, 7 or 8 inches tall"; advertised in *The Pennsylvania Gazette,* January 25, 1775

EDWARD MOFFAT, an Irish servant man; runaway from THOMAS ANDERSON, living near Sussex Courthouse; "about 16 years of age"; advertised in *The New York Journal,* January 25, 1775

ISAAC LEWIS, a servant man; runaway from MARMADUKE COOPER of Newtown, Glouster county; "about 24 years of age; 5 feet, 10 or 11 inches tall; lived with JOHN IAMS, of the Western shore in Maryland, who is remarkable for keeping good racing horses and afterwards with ARCHIBALD DICK of Marcus Hook"; advertised in *The Pennsylvania Gazette,* February 1, 1775

OWEN WILLIAMS, a Welsh servant man; runaway from ENOCH EVANS of Evesham; "about 18 years of age; fresh colored; came with Captain COOK from London"; advertised in *The Pennsylvania Gazette,* February 9,1775

JOSEPH BURWELL, an apprentice lad; runaway from JAMES CAMPBELL of Springfield; "about 18 years of age"; advertised in *The New York Gazette,* February 13, 1775

JOHN M'DONALD, an Irish servant man; runaway from JOHN OLIVAR of Bordentown; "about 20 years of age; 5 feet, 5 inches tall; came from Cork in Ireland and talks in that dialect, by trade a house painter";advertised in *Pennsylvania Gazette,*

February 15, 1775

BILLY BRIAN [WILLIAM O'BRIAN], a servant man; runaway from ABRAHAM SHREVE of Mannington Township; "about 28 years of age; served part of his time with one JACKSON and part with NATHAN WRIGHT and the last with JOSEPH BULLOCK in Burlington County and then came to Salem County with CHRISTOPHER WHITE"; advertised in *The Pennsylvania Gazette*, February 22, 1775

FRANCIS TRASEY, a servant man; runaway from ABEL HARRIS of Penn's Neck, Salem County; "about 30 years of age; 5 feet, 9 or 10 inches tall"; advertised in *The Pennsylvania Gazette*, February 22, 1775

JAMES BROWN, an Irish servant man; runaway from WILLIAM HUDSON of Mendem, in Morris County; "about 23 years of age; 5 feet, 8 inches tall; came last fall from Ireland with Captain MOORE, by trade a shoemaker"; advertised in *The New York Gazette*, February 27, 1775

JOHN FOSTER, an English servant man; runaway from FRANCIS HUDSON of Waterford Township, Glouster County; "about 35 years of age; 5 feet, 5 or 6 inches tall; sandy complexion; brown, bushy head of hair"; advertised in *Dunlap's Pennsylvania Packet*, February 27, 1775

WILLIAM WESTBURN, an American born servant man; runaway from JOSEPH HARVEY of Upper Makefield, Bucks County; "5 feet, 4 inches tall; fair complexion; down look; says he was born in Morris County"; advertised in *The Pennsylvania Gazette*, March 1, 1775

DANIEL MURRIN, an Irish servant man; runaway from WILLIAM SMITH of Trenton; "5 feet tall; by trade a butcher" advertised in *Dunlap's Pennsylvania Packet*, March 6, 1775

MATTHIAS CANE, an Irish servant man; runaway from PETER GEYER of Racoon Bridge on the Salem Road, in Glouster

County; "about 23 or 24 years of age; 5 feet, 4 or 5 inches tall"; advertised in *Dunlap's Pennsylvania Packet*, March 6, 1775

BENEJAH HEWIT, an American born apprentice; runaway from AAROM LEAMING of Cape May; "about 19 years of age; born in Cape May and bred to plantation business"; advertised in *The Pennsylvania Gazette,* March 15, 1775

JOHN BRIXEY, an English servant man; runaway from FRANCIS DUDLEY of Evesham, Burlington County; "about 20 years of age; 6 feet tall; slim built"; advertised in *The Pennsylvania Gazette*, March 15, 1775

DANIEL TURRY, an apprentice lad; runaway from HARTSHORN FITX RANDOLPH of Morris county; "about 19 years of age; 5 feet, 5 inches; middling size"; advertised in *The New York Journal*, March 30, 1775

JAMES DAY, American born servant man; runaway from ROBERT MENDENHALL, living in Concord, Chester county; born near Trenton; "about 24 or 25 years of age; about 5 feet, 6 or 7 inches high; swarthy or brown complexion; brown hair; looks young"; advertised in the *Pennsylvania Gazette*, June 22, 1775

EBENEZER DARWIN; runaway from Jacob PAULLIN and ABRAHAM RICHMAN of Pilesgrove, Salem County; "21 or 22; American born; 5 foot, 6 or 7 inches"

ABRAHAM HENDRICKS; runaway from JACOB PAULLIN and ABRAHAM RICHMAN of Pilesgrove, Salem county; " aged 21 or 22; American born; 5 foot, 8 or 9inches tall"

JOHN DUNN, runaway from JOHN TOWN of Salem; "about 5 foot, 9 or 10 inches high; a house carpenter; fond of liquor"

JOHN FOY; runaway from JOHN TOWN of Salem; "about 5 foot, 5 or 6 inches high; a house carpenter; fond of liquor"

CHRISTOPHER FREDERICK STOITS, a Dutch servant man born in Mecklenburgh; runaway from JOHN VANCE of Cumberland County; "about 18 years of age; 5 foot, 6 or 7 inches high; he came from Germany about two years ago and was cook's mate on board the ship; believe that he had gone to the frontiers of New Jersey"; give notice to Rev. JAMES LANG or HENRY HELM or JAMES BICHAM; advertised in the *Pennsylvania Journal*, May 24, 1775

ISAAC JONES, a Jew, born in London; runaway from HARTSHORN FITZ RANDOLF in Morris County; "said his name was Solomon Isaac; came to this country ten years ago; served seven years in Virginia; was put in jail in New York and received 30 lashes for stealing and was arrested three time in Philadelphia for stealing; 36 years of age and about 5 feet, 4 inches high; is a grand villain and it is like that he will change his apparel; he can speak High Dutch and is pitted with pox; advertised in *Pennsylvania Journal* May 24, 1775

WILLIAM DUNMEAD, an English Servant man; runaway from FRANCIS KAY in Waterford Township in Glouster county; 5 foot, 4 inches tall; advertised in *The Pennsylvania Gazette* May 31, 1775

WILLIAM WARRREN, an English servant man; runaway from THOMAS HARRISON, living in Strawbrrry Alley; "about 24 years of age, 5 foot, 4 inches, a tailor by trade, advertised in *The Pennsylvania Gazette* May 31, 1775

HUGH M'DANIEL, an American born servant man; runaway from THOMAS HARRISON, living in Strawberry Alley; "about 30 years of age; brought up in husbandry"; advertised in *The Pennsylvania Gazette,* May 31, 1775

CORNELIUS BURBARY, a Swedish indentured servant runaway from Melyn MILLER, living in Westfield near Elizabeth; "speaks broken English; about 25 years of age; about 5 foot, 9 inches; came from London in the Ship *York*, Captain Ackland and is indented for four years"; advertised in *The New York Journal,*

April 13, 1775

JOHN O'NEILL, an Irish servant man; runaway from JAMES DYE, in Salem Town; "a weaver by trade; about 28 years old; 5 foot, 6 inches high; advertised in *The Pennsylvania Gazette*, April 19, 1775

WILLIAM FAR, an English servant man; runaway from BENJAMIN VANLEER, Newtown Township, Glouster; "about 22 years of age; a thick set fellow; about 6 feet high"; advertised in *The Pennsylvania Gazette*, April 19, 1775

JAMES BRYANT, servant man; runaway from BENJAMIN VANLEER, Newtown Township, Glouster; "about 17 years of age; smart lad"; advertised in *The Pennsylvania Gazette* April 19, 1775

NATHNIEL ANSTER, an Irish servant man; runaway from JOHN CHAMBERS of the Township of Chester, Burlington County; "about 32 years of age"; advertised in *The Pennsylvania Gazette*, April 19, 1775

HUGH SMITH, a servant man; runaway from THOMAS STOUT, JAMES VAN DER VEEER, CASPAR BURGER, JAMES VAN SICKLE, JOHN VAN SICKLE in Reading Town in Hunterdon; "about 5 foot, 6 inches";advertised *The New York Journal*, April 20, 1775

JOHN CASPERSON, a servant man; runaway from SAMUEL PAUL of Greenwich Township, Glouster County; "about 19 years of age"; advertised in *The Pennsylvania Gazette*, April 5, 1775

WILLIAM RICKET, a servant man; runaway from JOHN HARRIMAN of Pacquanack, Morris County; "about 24 years of age; 5 feet, 10 or 11 inches tall; father is JOHN RICKET of Brookland Ferry, Long Island"; advertised in *The New York Gazette,* June 5, 1775 unnamed servant man; runaway from GEORGE BROWN of the Falls Township, Bucks County, Pennsylvania; a sailor; advertised in *The Pennsylvania Gazette*, June 14, 1775

JAMES GREEN, an Irish servant man; runaway from SAMUEL BUNTING, Jr. of Chesterfield; "about 23 years of age; 5 feet, 9 inches tall"; advertised in *The Pennsylvania Gazette*, June 14, 1775

CHRISTOPHER DERRICK, an American born servant man; runaway from JONATHAN WOOD of Lower Alloways Creek, Salem county; "about 24 years of age; 5 feet 5, or 6 inches tall; Dutch ancestry"; advertised in *The Pennsylvania Journal*, June 14, 1775

JAMES HAMBLETON, a servant man; runaway from JOHN HILLIAS and JONAH WOOLMAN of Burlington County; "about 17 years of age; 5 feet, 3 or 4 inches tall "; advertised in *Dunlap's Pennsylvania Packet*, June 19, 1775

JAMES HALL, a servant man; runaway from JOHN HILLIAS and JONAH WOOLMAN of Burlington County; "about 17 years of age; 5 feet, 3 or 4 inches tall"; advertised in *Dunlap's Pennsylvania Packet*, June 19, 1775

JOHN WILSON, an English servant man; runaway from HENRY SPARKS, DAVID HENRY and URIAH PAUL of Penn's Neck, Salem County; "about 20 years of age; middling stature; well made; fair complexion; brown hair somewhat inclining to curl"; notice to GEORGE MONRO, Esq. in Newcastle; advertised in *The Pennsylvania Journal*, June 21, 1775

THOMAS PRESTON, an English servant man; runaway from CRISPI PEARSON of Solebury Township, Bucks County; "5 feet, 6 inches tall; fair faced; dark hair and eyes; marked with small pox; remarkable scar on one corner of his mouth; very talkative fellow; loves strong drink; by trade a silk weaver"; advertised in *The Pennsylvania Gazette*, June 21, 1775

JAMES LIBO, an Irish servant man; runaway from SAMUEL HENRY of Trenton; "about 20 years of age"; advertised in *The Pennsylvania Gazette*, June 21, 1775

unnamed Scotch servant man; runaway from THOMAS CARNEY, Jr. of Upper Penn's Neck, Salem County; "about 30 years of age; 5 feet, 8 or 9 inches tall; thick well set fellow; will try to pas as one of GAGE's deserters but he would rather be a foe to this country if he could"; advertised in *The Pennsylvania Gazette*, June 21, 1775

JOHN OGDEN, a servant man; runaway from JOHN CHIPS of Mendam Township, Morris County; "about 49 years of age; 5 feet, 10 inches tall; short gray hair; by trade a weaver"; advertised in *The Pennsylvania Gazette*, June 21, 1775

GEORGE GEE, a servant man; runaway from THOMAS M'NAGHTEN of Hopewell Township, Cumberland County; about 18 or 19 years of age; 5 feet, 2 or 3 inches tall"; advertised in *Dunlap's Pennsylvania Packet*, July 3, 1775

MATTHIAS CANE, [Michael Coda] an Irish servant man; runaway from PETER KIER; "about 5 feet, 6 or 7 inches high; about 28 to 30 years of age"

GEORGE CROWDER, [GEORGE M'GINNIS] an English servant lad; living in Piles Grove; had belonged to JOHN KIDD, a shallopman

MARSHALL HALL [THOMAS MARSHALL], an English servant man; runaway from RALPH ALLEN of New Hanover Township, Burlington county; "about 23 years of age; about 5 feet, 8 inches high; full faced; black curled hair, and slim legs; came from London last fall with Capt. GETSHENS and has been in Charleston South Carolina;" notice to ANDREW CRAIG of Philadelphia; advertised in *The Pennsylvania Journal*, March 13, 1776

JAMES MORRIS, an English servant man; runaway from

EDMUND HOLLINSHEAD of Chester Township, Burlington county; "about 5 feet, 8 inches high; dark bushy hair; dark complexion; talks in a West country dialect"; advertised in *The Pennsylvania Ledger*, May 25, 1776

JAMES WIGGINS, an apprentice lad; runaway from SAMUEL THOMPSON living in Woodbury, Glouster County; "about 17 or 18 years of age; about 4 feet. 9 inches high; pretty well set; has a fair complexion and a down look"; advertised in *The Pennsylvania Ledger*, June 1, 1776

PETER DENNY, a Low Dutch servant man; runaway from JOHN JESSUP; "black curly hair; pitted with small pox; surly"; advertised in *The Pennsylvania Journal*, July 3, 1776

ISAAC BROWN, an Irish servant man; runaway from JACOB STILLE, living near Oldman's Creek in the Township of Woolwich of the County of Glouster; "about 27 years of age; born near Springfield New Jersey; about 5 feet, 10 inches high"; advertised in *The Pennsylvania Journal*, July 24, 1776

JOHN FISHER, an English servant man; runaway from LAWRENCE SALTAR at Astionworks; "about 16 years of age; about 5 feet, 4 inches high; slender made; small legs; large feet; a little knock kneed; much marked with small pox; surly countenance"; advertised in *The Pennsylvania Ledger*, August 3, 1776

FRANCIS LAWRANCE PIDGINETT, a Portguese servant man; runaway from JOHN COX of the Basto Furnace; "about 5 feet, 7 or 8 inches high; stoops in his walk; yellow complexion; middling long black hair; chews tobacco"; advertised by JOSEPH BALL in *The Pennsylvania Journal*, September 11, 1776

MATTHEW SHFRONE, a French servant man; runaway from JOHN COX of the Basto Furnace; "about 30 years of age; about 5 feet, 7 or 8 inches high; black hair tied behind; dark complexion; gray eyes; black beard and has a scar across the lower part of his jaw"; advertised by JOSEPH BALL in *The Pennsylvania Journal*, September 11, 1776

EMANUEL RODRIGUES, a Spanish servant man; runaway from JOHN COX of the Basto Furnace; "about 30 years of age; about 5 feet, 6 or 7 inches high; short, black hair; black eyes; dark complexion"; advertised by JOSEPH BALL in *The Pennsylvania Journal*, September 11, 1776

FRANCIS BERRARA, a Spanish servant man; runaway from JOHN COX of the Basto Furnace; "about 30 years of age; about 6 feet, 2 inches high; black hair; brown eyes; thin visage; takes a great deal of snuff; his fore teeth remarkably wide; has a down look";advertised by JOSEPH BALL in *The Pennsylvania Journal*, September 11, 1776

JOSEPH RODRIGO, a servant man; runaway from JOHN COX of the Basto Furnace; "about 5 feet, 5 or 6 inches high; black hair; black eyes; yellowish complexion"; advertised by JOSEPH BALL in *The Pennsylvania Journal*, September 11, 1776

JOSEPH LOVETT, a French servant man; runaway from JOHN COX of the Basto Furnace; "about 5 feet, 9 or 10 inches high; long brown hair; fair complexion; thin visage; gray eyes; marked with small pox"; advertised by JOSEPH BALL in *The Pennsylvania Journal*, September 11, 1776

DANIEL SULLIVAN, a servant man; runaway from Glouster, County; "about 35 years of age"; advertised in *The Pennsylvania Gazette*, June 19, 1776

JAMES WIGGINS, an apprentice lad; runaway from SAMUEL THOMPSON of Glouster County; "about 17 years of age; about 4 feet, 9 inches high; pretty well set and of a fair complexion"; advertised in *The Pennsylvania Gazette*, June 19, 1776

ENGEL BERTCLASEN, a Dutch servant man; runaway from JAMES BROWN of Deptford Township, Glouster County;

"about 29 years of age; about 5 feet, 7 or 8 inches high; bushy hair of a ligthish color; light complexion; lately had a cut on his right instep, not quite well"; advertised in *The Pennsylvania Gazette*, July 24, 1776

RICHARD SNELL, an English servant lad; runaway from JACOB ROBERTS of Glouster Town; "about 17 years of age; about 5 feet, 3 or 4 inches high; straight brown hair; very dark complexion"; advertised in *The Pennsylvania Gazette*, September 11, 1776

JOHN SMITH, a servant man; runaway from PETER ROSE, brewer, of Burlington; "about 21 years of age; middle stature and bushy hair; understands country work pretty well; large scar down his forehead; pretty full faced"; advertised in *The American Weekly Mercury*, October 1, 1776

JOSEPH GARISON, an apprentice lad; runaway from CORNELIUS AUSTIN, Pittsgrove Township in Salem County; "about 20 years of age, but small for his age; dark hair; blue eyes; it is supposed he in enlisted in the provincial militia, where he can do some good, if he cannot help it; reward of two pence and one penny for his trouble"; advertised *The Pennsylvania Gazette*, February 5, 1777

ROBERT DOWNS, an apprentice lad, runaway from JOHN MATTS living in Woodbury, Glouster County; "aged about 18 years; about 5 feet, 4 inches high; slender built; has a pretty bold countenance; wears own black hair; and can talk quite enough for one of his station"; advertised in *The Pennsylvania Journal*, April 16, 1777

LEVI BISHOP, an apprentice lad; runaway from JABEZ WOOLSTON, near Mount Holly; "aged about 19 or 20 years; 5 feet 7 or 8 inches high; down look; bushy hair; marked with the small pox; by trade a tailor; was drafted out in the Northhampton Militia with Capt. WEAVER, but left him; has a brother at the Squan Salt works that goes by the name JOSEPH BISHOP"; advertised in *The New Jersey Gazette*, February 25, 1778

NICHOLAS PECK, a servant man; runaway from ADAM AULBERGER, at Trenton; "aged about 18 years; 5 feet high; dark complexion; marked with the small pox"; advertised in *The New Jersey Gazette*, February 25, 1778

ENOCH JONES, an apprentice lad; runaway from ABRAHAM SKIRM, living at Nottingham, Burlington; "aged about 17 years; middle sized; by trade a fuller"; advertised in *The New Jersey Gazette*, April 7, 1778

JOSEPH PATERSON, an American born servant boy; runaway from WILLIAM EVANS, living in Evesham, Burlington County; aged about 15 years; short; well built; has lost one eye which is entirely sunk"; advertised in *The Pennsylvania Packet*, August 20, 1778

HENRY STEENHAAGEN, a Dutch servant man; runaway from NATHANIEL LEWIS; "aged about 17 years; 5 feet, 6 inches high; dark complexion; slender made; thin visage; dark bushy hair; speaks a little on the German dialect; recently purchased from GODFREY TWELVES"; advertised in *The Pennsylvania Packet*, November 17, 1778

JONATHAN SHOARS, a servant man; runaway from HENRY LISHMAN, living in Springfield Township; "aged about 18 years; 5 feet, 8 inches high; fresh complexion; light straight hair; a very large nose; stoops in walking and something knock kneed"; advertised in *The New Jersey Gazette*, June 10, 1778

BERNARD ROBERTS, an apprentice lad; runaway from WILLIAM HEPPARD, living in Newtown Township; "aged about 14 years; middle sized"; advertised in *The Pennsylvania Evening Post*, June 25, 1778

HENRY MEINHAUGEN, a Dutch servant lad; runaway from WILLIAM GAMBLE, in Bordentown; advertised in *The Pennsylvania Gazette*, January 6, 1779

JOHN GEORGE WANNER, a Dutch servant man,

runaway from JOSHUA DUDLEY of Evesham Township, Burlington County; "aged about 21 years; about 5 feet, 8 or 9 inches high; well built. but somewhat clumsy and speaks broken English; his father JACOB WANNER, lives near Allen Town, Northhampton County, Pennsylvania"; advertised in *The Pennsylvania Packet*, February 20, 1779

JUSTUS CRAMMER, a Dutch servant man, runaway from EPHRAIM HAINES, Moore's Town, Burlington County; "aged about 21 years; about 5 feet, 6 or 7 inches high; a well built likely fellow with black curled hair; dark eyes; has a scar betwixt his upper lip and chin; speaks tolerable good English and 'tis thought he speaks Dutch, but imperfectly"; advertised in *The Pennsylvania Packer*, February 23, 1779

RICHARD HOGG, an English servant lad, runaway from ARNEY LIPPINCOTT; "aged about 16 or 17; is wanting to get into the English army"; advertised in *The Pennsylvania Packet*, March 16, 1779

BRYANT ROBINSON, an apprentice lad, runaway from CONSTANT KING, living Roxbury in Morris County; "aged about 19 years; well looking lad"; advertised in *The New Jersey Journal*, March 23, 1779

JOHN BIRD, an English servant lad; runaway from SAMUEL JAMES, living in Hanover Township, Burlington County; "aged about 19 years; 5 feet high; very much knock-kneed; very much marked with the small pox"; advertised in *The New Jersey Gazette*, May 12, 1779

ELISHA OSBIN, a servant man; runaway from JOSEPH HARTLEY, living in Manington Township, Salem County; "5 feet, 11 inches high; fair complexion; pitted with small pox" notice to BENJAMIN MIERS in Strawberry-Alley, Philadelphia"; advertised by in *The Pennsylvania Packet*, October 2, 1779

WILLIAM MALICE, an American born apprentice lad; runaway from JAMES HINCHMAN, living at Deptford, Glouster County; "aged about 18 years; 5 feet, 2 or 3 inches high; chunky, well made lad; short brown hair; round faced, black eyes, glissens much when he smiles; something freckled; a cunning smart active fellow; advertised in *The Pennsylvania Gazette*, September 22, 1779

SAMUEL LIPPINCOT, an apprentice, runaway from DANIEL POTTS, near Pitts-Town; "aged about 18 years; about 5 feet, 5 or 6inches high; yellow hair; a remarkable spot on his forehead resembling a pear"; advertised in *The New Jersey Gazette*, February 2, 1780

JAMES RUTH, an apprentice boy; runaway from CHARLES CLUNN, living; "aged about 11 years; fair complexion; short, light hair; gray blue eyes; marked with small pox;"

ANDREW COUNTRYMAN, a Low Dutch servant man; runaway from HENRY APGAR, living in Bethlehem Township, Hunterdon County, near the Hickory tavern; "aged about 22 years; sandy complexion; some of his upper fore teeth are missing; very vain and fond of strong liquor"; advertised in *The New Jersey Gazette*, February 14, 1781

Was committed to the gaol of Burlington county, JOHN TEANIS, who had broken out of Easton gaol; advertised by RALPH PRICE, Gaoler, in *The New Jersey Gazette*, February 28, 1781

WILLIAM WORSTILL, an apprentice lad; runaway from JOSEPH JENKS living in Middletown, Bucks County; "aged about 19 years; 5 feet, 6 inches high; light complexion; well set and full faced; remarkably fond of playing the fife; by trade a weaver; went off with JOSEPH GILLAM, a weaver, and JOHN TWINING, a laborer"; advertised in *The New Jersey Gazette*, May 30, 1781

RUNAWAY SLAVES of NEW JERSEY

JERSEY, a Negro man servant; runaway from Mistress GILL, Widow, of Boston; is about 6 feet high; speaks little or no English; advertised in *The Boston News Letter*, August 27, 1711

NIM, an Indian man, runaway from DAVID LYELL in New York or in Amboy; he was aged about 21 years; had lately belonged to JAMES MOORE; depicted as a short, broad shouldered fellow, whose hair had been lately cut off; marked with a swelling on the back of his right hand; it was said that "he can do something at the carpenter's trade"; advertised in *The Boston News Letter*, July 23, 1716

POMPEY, an Indian man; runaway from THOMAS HILL of Salem; aged about 30 years; of middle stature and pretty much pox broken; advertised in *The American Weekly Mercury*, September 28, 1721

FRANSH MANUEL, a Negro man; runaway from WILLIAM YARD of Trenton; tall; speaking indifferent English; belonged to JOHN RAYMOND of Fairfield in New England; notice to be given to WILLIAM BRADFORD of New York or WILLIAM BURGE of Philadelphia; advertised in *The American Weekly Mercury*, November 15, 1722

POPAW, taken at the house of JOHN LEONARD at South River Bridge, near Amboy, a Negro man; forced to said house for want of subsistence; a middle sized man; "talks no English or says that he cannot; his teeth seem to be filed or whet sharp; will not tell his Masters name"; advertised in *The American Weekly Mercury*, July 14, 1726

WILL, a Negro man; runaway from JAMES LEONARD of Somerset; aged about 26 years, "speaks good English"; advertised in *The American Weekly Mercury*, June 1, 1727

ISAAC GUNNITT, an Indian servant man; runaway from

BENJAMIN AETON of Salem; "of a middle size and has very thick lips; speaks good English"; advertised in *The American Weekly Mercury*, September 4, 1729

Unnamed Negro male slave; runaway from DANIEL ALLEN, of Great Egg Harbor in West New Jersey; "a short, squat fellow; pitted with the small pox"; advertised in *The American Weekly Mercury*, September 18, 1729

CLAUSE, a Negro slave; runaway from SOLOMON BATES of Elizabeth Town; aged about 27 years of age; middle stature; speaks English and Dutch; sometimes calls himself NICHOLAS, "he can play on a fiddle tolerably well;" formerly belonged to DANIEL BAGLEY; advertised in *The New Jersey Gazette*, May 25, 1730

JAMES SMITH, a Negro servant man; runaway from ROBERT CUMMINGS of Trenton; a thick, short black fellow; pretty elderly; he is so prodigious liar that if observed he may be discovered by it; has a mark on the side of his head a little above his eyebrows; advertised in *The American Weekly Mercury*, November 12, 1730

Taken up, a Negro man by name of JOHN; thick; he had nothing on but a crocus shirt; he can speak no English"; advertised in *The American Weekly Mercury*, August 2, 1733

JACK, a Negro man; runaway from ROBERT PEIRSON of Notingham, near Trenton; about 30 years of age; a lusty, stout, well set fellow; a little pock marked; advertised in *The New York Gazette*, October 8, 1733

STOFFELS, an Indian man; runaway from JUDITH VINCENT of Monmouth County; about 40 years of age; speaks good English; is a house carpenter; wheel wright, cooper and butcher; advertised in *The New York Gazette*, July 8, 1734

Unnamed half Indian and half Negro man; runaway from JUDITH VINCENT of Monmouth County; advertised in *The New York Gazette*, July 8, 1734

Unnamed Mulatto man; runaway from JUDITH VINCENT of Monmouth County; "about 30 years of age; plays upon the violin and has it with him"; advertised in *The New York Gazette*, July 8, 1734

WAN, a half Negro, half Indian man; runaway from SAMUEL LEONARD of Perth Amboy; "thick short fellow having but one eye; black as most Negroes; can play on the fiddle and speaks good English and this country Indian"; advertised in *The American Weekly Mercury*, October 24, 1734

TOM, a Negro man; runaway from ZEBULON STOUT of Somerset County; about 35 years old; is a well set fellow, middle stature; a thin visage; he speaks good English; advertised in *The New York Gazette*, November 3, 1735

CESAR, a Negro man; runaway from ALEXANDER MORGAN of Waterford township of county of Glouster; about 24 years of age; "tall and slim with small legs and great feet"; has run off before and tried to sail on ship as sailor to Barbados; advertised in *The American Weekly Mercury*, November 3, 1737

LAZARUS KENNY, a Mulatto servant man; runaway from JOSEPH JAMES of Cohansey; "swarthy fellow, his father being a mulatto and his mother a white woman; pretty tall stature; his hair cut off; well set"; advertised in *The American Weekly Mercury*, June 22, 1738

PEET [PETER WALDREN], an American born Negro man; runaway from JOHN HUNT of Hopewell, Hunterdon County; aged about 28 years; "lusty; born on Long Island; speaks good English; well set"; advertised in *The American Weekly Mercury*, July 31, 1738

Unnamed Madagascar Negro man; runaway from JAMES THOMPSON of Piscattaway; "lusty; formerly belonged to JOHN REID of Monmouth county; has a small scar on his nose and talks good English; yellowish complexion"; advertised in *The New York Gazette*, July 31, 1738

SIMON, a Negro Man; runaway from JAMES LEONARD of Kingston of Middlesex County; aged about 40 years; about 5 foot, 10 inches high; "is a well set fellow; has large eyes and a foot 12 inches long; he was born and bred in the country; talks good English; can read and write; is very slow in his speech; can bleed and draw teeth, pretending to be a great doctor and very religious; says he is a churchman"; advertised in *The Pennsylvania Gazette*, September 11, 1740.

JAMES, a lusty Negro fellow; runaway from THOMAS WHITE of Shrewsbury in Monmouth County; "has right shoulder out and is still so, which, by lifting up his arm may soon be discovered"; advertised in *The New York Weekly Journal*, June 23, 1740

ROBIN, a Negro slave; runaway from JOHN JACKSON in Whippany Township in Morris County; "about 40 years of age; a short, thick and well set fellow with a round fat face"; advertised in *The New York Weekly Journal*, May 11, 1741

CAESAR, a half Spanish Indian, half Negro slave; runaway from JOHN JACKSON in Whippany Township in Morris County; "about 20 years of age; a very likely fellow; has lost a piece of one of his ears bit off by a horse"; advertised in *The New York Weekly Journal*, May 11, 1741

CLAUS, a Negro man; runaway from PHILIP FRENCH of New Brunswick; "of middle stature; yellowish complexion; about 45 years of age; speaks Dutch and good English; he is a fiddler and took his fiddle with him; he uses the bow with his left hand"; advertised in *The American Weekly Mercury*, August 27, 1741

ROBIN; a lusty Negro Man; runaway from JOSEPH TAYLOR of Freehold, Monmouth County; aged 20; "wart on his neck; large hands and feet"; advertised in *The Pennsylvania Gazette*, April 5, 1744.

JAMES BELL, a Negro Man; runaway from JOHN WILLIAMS of Trenton Ferry; 30 years of age; middle stature; "speaks very good English and very fluent in his talk; he formerly belonged to SLATOR CLAY"; advertised in *The Pennsylvania Gazette*, May 17, 1744.

GEORGE, a Mulatto Spanish Slave; runaway from BENNET BARD of Burlington; about 24 years of age; five foot, ten inches high; "smooth faced; well set; has his hair lately cut off; speaks tolerable good English; born in Havana; says he was several years with DON BLASS and is a good shoemaker"; advertised in *The Pennsylvania Gazette*, August 1, 1745.

MOSES WILLIAMS, an Indian Mulatto servant man, being half Indian and half Irish; runaway from SAMUEL SHIVERS of Greenwich of Glouster county; "of a swarthy complexion; no hair; middle stature; a bold or rather a surly look and speaks good English being this country born"; advertised in *The Pennsylvania Gazette*, September 26, 1745

SAM, a Negro man; runaway from THOMAS CADWALADER of Trenton; aged about 26 years; "likely fellow; speaks very good English; was enticed to run away by ISAAC RANDALL, an apprentice to THOMAS MARRIOT; went to board privateer"; advertised in *The Pennsylvania Gazette*, October 31, 1745; he was re advertised in *The Pennsylvania Gazette*, April 9, 1747 as a "runaway from THOMAS TINDALL of Trenton; had formerly belonged to Dr. CADWALADER of Trenton; aged about 26 years; middle stature; speaks very good English. He was advertised a third time in *The New York Gazette revived in the Weekly Post Boy* as "about 28 years of age; a tall likely fellow; has lately had the small pox and is pitted pretty much.

JACK, a mulatto slave; runaway from ALEXANDER LOCKART of Trenton; aged about 35 years; "middle stature; well made; long wooly hair"; advertised in *The New York Weekly Post Boy*, November 18, 1745

POMPEE, a Negro man; runaway from WESSEL TENBROOK living near Rocky Hill; "aged about 25 years; very black hair; a tall well set fellow; 6 feet long; speaks English well and tolerable good Dutch"; was brought up in Westchester; advertised in *The New York Evening Post*, May 5, 1746

JACK, a Negro man; runaway from HUGH MARTIN of Lebanon, Hunterdon County; aged about 22 years; "short stature; well made; pitted with the small pox"; advertised in *The Pennsylvania Gazette*, July 3, 1746

WILLIAM COLSON, a Bermudian born Negro man; runaway from WILLIAM HUGG of Glouster Town; middle stature; "talks very good English; by trade a sailor"; advertised in *The Pennsylvania Gazette*, July 10, 1746

UNNAMED Negro man, now in Gaol in Burlington; says he is from Albany and his master's name is Millor; "he is a middle sized fellow; aged about 28 or 30 years; has cuts in his face and laughs much"; advertised by JOSEPH HOLLINSHEAD, Sheriff in *The Pennsylvania Journal*, October 23, 1746

ISAAC, a Negro man; runaway from ANDREW REED of Trenton; aged about 30 years, "middle stature, well set, likely fellow, he can play upon a fiddle"; advertised in *The New York Gazette rivived in the Weekly Post Boy,* June 15, 1747

SAMPSON, a Negro man; runaway from SILAS PARVIN of Cohansie; aged about 58 years; "very lusty; he is hip shot and goes very lame; has some Indian blood"; advertised in *The Pennsylvania Journal*, October 1, 1745

SAM, a Negro lad; runaway from SILAS PARVIN of Cohansie; aged about 12 or 14 years; "was born of an Indian woman and looks very much like an Indian"; advertised in *The Pennsylvania Journal*, October 1, 1745

JAMES ROUSE, a Negro man; runaway from JOHN CORYELL of Amwell; "is lame in one of his knees and has a scar on his upper lip"; advertised in *The New York Gazette, revived in the Weekly Post Boy*, December 27, 1747

DAN, a Negro man; runaway from EMMANUEL COCKER of Newark; "about 35 years of age; speaks broken English"; advertised in *The New York Gazette revived in the Weekly Post Boy*, November 28, 1748.

CHARLES, a Negro man; runaway from EMMANUEL COCKER of Newark; about 35 years of age; speaks broken English; advertised in *The New York Gazette revived in the Weekly Post Boy*, November 28, 1748

MANDO, a Negro man; runaway from SAMUEL MOORE and FRANCIS BLOOD of Woodbridge Township, "about 20 years of age; lusty young black fellow"; advertised in *The New York Gazette, revived in the Weekly Post Boy*, May 1, 1749

TOM, a Madagascar Negro man; runaway from SAMUEL MOORE and FRANCIS BLOOD of Woodbridge Township, "about 40 years of age; of middle stature; well set; can read; a yellow Madagascar fellow; is a cunning fellow; the person who takes him up is desired to be careful lest he deceive them"; advertised in *The New York Gazette, revived in the Weekly Post Boy*, May 1, 1749 and again in May 15, 1749 issue

Unnamed half Indian and half Negro man; runaway from SAMUEL NEVILL of Woodbridge Township, "about 20 years of age; of short stature; well set"; advertised in *The New York Gazette, revived in the Weekly Post Boy*, May 1, 1749

PETER, an American born Negro man; runaway from ELISABETH BILES of Trenton; "about 19 years of age, has with a large dog with a short tail; understands farming in all its branches; talks good English"; advertised in *The Pennsylvania Gazette*, June 8, 1749

TITUS, a Negro man; runaway from THOMAS CLARK of Little Egg Harbor; "about 27 years of age; six feet high; can read and speaks good English; he was brought up in Lyme in Connecticut and it is supposed he will make that way"; advertised in *The New York Gazette revived in the Weekly Post Boy*, June, 12, 1749

ROBIN, a Negro man ; runaway from JOHN ZABRISKIE of Hackinsack; "about 20 years of age; yellow complexion"; advertised in *The New York Gazette, revived in The Weekly Post Boy*, July, 3 1749

TONY, a Negro fellow; runaway from CORNELIUS VANDERVERE of Middletownship, Monmouth; "a middle sized fellow; pretty full face; can do all manner of farm labor; can play pretty well on the fiddle"; advertised in *The New York Gazette, revived in the Weekly Post Boy*, July, 10, 1749

SAMSON, a Negro man; runaway from SAMUEL LYNCH of Penn's Neck Township, Salem County; "about 21 years of age; of middle stature; a likely fellow; his hair cut short; modest look; can read middling well and took with him a hymn book and a testament"; advertised in *The Pennsylvania Gazette*, August 24, 1749.

GEORGE, a Spanish Mulatto servant man; runaway from GEORGE MARPOLE, of Goshen Neck Township, Burlington County; "a short, thick, well set with thick curled hair; formerly ran away from CHARLES READ of Burlington and went a privateering and may attempt to get on some vessel"; advertised in *The Pennsylvania Gazette*, June 29, 1749; in a later advertisement, he is described as of middling stature; no hair; speaks but indifferent English; a shoemaker by trade; re-advertised in *The New York Gazette, revived in the Weekly Post Boy*, October 2, 1749

Unnamed Negro man; runaway from JONATHAN SARGEANT, Newark, County of Essex; "about 20 years of age; has a long face; straight nose; of a middle stature"; advertised in *The New York Gazette revived in the Weekly Post Boy*, April 9, 1750

LOT, a Negro; runaway from THOMAS HOOTON of Trenton Ferry in Burlington County; "about 5 foot, 6 inches high; talks very good English; formerly lived in Allen Town and Great Egg Harbor with one HIGBEE and JOSEPH SOOY"; advertised in *The Pennsylvania Gazette*, August 9, 1750.

ISHMAEL, a Negro boy; runaway from JACOB FORD of Morris-Town, Morris County; "aged about 16 years; short and thick; full faced; has a very large foot; born in the country and has a sly look"; departed with another unnamed Negro belonging to

SHADRECK HATHEWAY; advertised in *The New York Gazette revived in the Weekly Post Boy*, August 13, 1750

BILL, a Negro man, runaway from WILLIAM BIRD of the Union Iron Works in Hunterdon County; 30 years of age; "a case hardened horse lock on one of his legs; is a very talkative fellow in liquor and apt to swear"; formerly belonged to NATHANIEL IRISH, deceased; advertised in *The Pennsylvania Gazette*, September 6, 1750

ROBIN, a Negro man, runaway from WILLIAM BIRD of the Union Iron Works in Hunterdon County; 40 years of age; "a small slender fellow with several warts on his face; talks bad English"; advertised in *The Pennsylvania Gazette*, September 6, 1750

JAMES, a Spanish Mulatto slave; runaway from JACOB PRICKET of Burlington; "aged about 25 or 30 years; a tall slender fellow; has lost one or both of his upper teeth; speaks good English and understands a sawmill"; advertised in *The Pennsylvania Journal*, November 8, 1750.

LONEN GENENS, a Negro man; runaway from MOUNCE KEEN, Jr. of Pilesgrove, Salem County; aged about 35 years; "pretends to be a skinner and is very talkative; lately belonged to PETER RAMBO of Manto Creek"; advertised in *The Pennsylvania Journal*, November 29, 1750

Now in custody of THOMAS SMITH, Sheriff of Cape May County, JUPITER HAZARD, a runaway Negro man; "aged about 27 years; not very black; of middle stature; well built; speaks English like a country born Negro who has lived some time among the Dutch; seems to have traveled pretty much for he gives a good account of Rhode Island, New York, Pennsylvania, Shrewsbury and other places; says his master's name is JOHN BANNISTER and lives in Piscataway in Rhode Island Government"; advertised in *The Pennsylvania Gazette*, June 13, 1751

FRANK, a Negro man; runaway from JOSEPH JAMES of Cohanesey Bridge in Cumberland County; "about 5 feet, 6 inches high; aged about 26 or 28 years; speaks good English"; advertised in *The Pennsylvania Gazette,* June 18, 1752

CAESAR, a Negro man; runaway from DAVID KENT of Woodbridge; aged about 22 years; middling thick fellow; of short stature; right foot twisting and the toe of the same inclining to turn outward a she walks and his right knee bending inwards toward the left; talks but poor English; advertised in *The Pennsylvania Gazette,* October 26, 1752

JACK, a Negro man; runaway from ABRAHAM VAN BUSHKIRK of Bergen County; "aged about 25 years; middle sized; not very black; pretty thick lips; speaks very slow; speaks both English and Dutch"; advertised in *The New York Gazette Revived in The Weekly Post Boy,* October 30, 1752

BRISTOL, a Negro man; runaway from JOSEPH HEDDIN, living at Newark Mountain; "aged about years; 5 feet, 6 inches high; not very black; was bred at the east End of Long Island and lately belonged to DAVID OGDEN, Esq. of Newark"; advertised in *The New York Gazette or the Weekly Post Boy,* December 10, 1752

BOOT, a Mulatto slave; runaway from THOMAS HUNT of Amwell; aged about 25 years; "5 feet, 9 inches high, and has had the small pox"; advertised in *The Pennsylvania Gazette,* May 3 1753

JACK, a Mulatto slave; runaway from ROBERT NEWELL of Hunterdon County; "aged about 22 years; pretty tall and lusty; by trade a cooper"; advertised in *The Pennsylvania Gazette,* May 3,1753

ANTHONY, a Mulatto fellow; runaway from SAMUEL MORRIS of Morris County; "aged about 22 years; 6 feet high; well set with remarkably large feet; his hair cut off; talks good English; is very ingenious and he has probably forged a pass of his own writing"; advertised in *The New York Gazette or Weekly Post Boy,* June 18, 1753

ASH, a Negro fellow; runaway from JOHN WARDELL of Shrewsbury, Monmouth county; small; advertised in *The New York Gazette or the Weekly Post Boy*, March 22, 1754

PRIMUS, a Negro servant man; runaway from JOHN MARTIN of Piscataway; "yellow complexion; near 6 foot high; speaks good English"; advertised in *The New York Gazette or the Weekly Post Boy*, April 15, 1754

JACK, a Negro man; runaway from DERRICK ATEN, of Readens Town, Hunterdon County; aged about 30 years; near 5 feet high; much pock marked; has a flat nose; a lover of white women and a great smoker; advertised in *The Pennsylvania Gazette*, August 8, 1754

ROBIN, a Negro man; runaway from GEORGE REYERSE [RYERSON] of Pequanek, Bergen county; aged about 40 years; middle stature; not very black; advertised in *The New York Gazette or the Weekly Post Boy*, October 22, 1754

TOM, a mulatto fellow; runaway from JOHN SHEPHERD of Shrewsbury; "aged about 24 years; middling long hair; middle stature;" formerly belonged to Dr. MILLS; advertised in *The New York Gazette or the Weekly Post Boy*, August 18, 1755

ESOP, a Negro man; runaway from JONATHAN SERGEANT; "middle sized; round forehead; straight nose; down guilty look; he can write"; departed with JOHN SMITH, a white man with long face and nose and straight brown hair"; later advertised as being runaway from JAMES VAN BUSHERK, near Hackinsack; advertised in *The Pennsylvania Gazette*, August 28, 1755

SAM, a Mulatto slave; runaway from WILLIAM STOCKTON, living in Springfield Township, Burlington County; "about 19 years of age; of a middle size; somewhat freckled i his face and his hair cut off

SANDY, an African born Negro man; runaway from JOHN ATKINSON of Mount Holly, Burlington County; "aged about 25 year; about 5 feet, 5 inches; a 'new' Negro, but speaks good English"; belongs to PETER BARD and Company at Mount Holly iron works; advertised in *The Pennsylvania Gazette*, October 2, 1755

CATO [TOBY], a Negro man; runaway from RICHARD STILLWELL of Middletown; "aged about 30 years; a lusty well set fellow; full faced; was branded as a boy in Jamaica with a 'B' and 'C' on his left shoulder blade; he is a sly artful fellow and he deceives the credulous by pretending to tell fortunes; pretends to be free and speaks English as well as if he were country born; plays on the fiddle"; advertised in *The Pennsylvania Gazette*, April 15, 1756

WAN, an Indian slave; runaway from FRIND LUCAS, at the mines near Second river, about 30 years of age; a little slim fellow; about 4 foot, 4 or 5 inches; short thick hair which was cut off last summer; he was seen at Elizabeth, trying to enlist as a soldier and then at Amboy;

BRISTOL, a Negro man; runaway from NATHANIEL DALGLISH, of Hanover in Morris County; "about 30 years old; is of a middle stature and speaks good English"; advertised in *The New York Mercury*, July, 18, 1757

CATO, a Jamaica born Negro man; runaway from RICHARD STILLWELL, of Middletown in Monmouth County; "a short well set fellow; understands husbandry in all its parts; an excellent hand with a scythe in grass or grain; speaks English as well as country born and pretends to be free; underneath his right shoulder blade he was branded in Jamaica as a boy, with the letter BC, which are plain to be seen; he plays poorly on the fiddle and pretends to tell fortunes"; advertised in *The Pennsylvania Gazette*, August 18, 1757

JOHN JUSTER a Spanish Negro man; runaway from JOHN REID, Jr. living in Cranberry of Middlesex County; "5 feet, 7 or 8 inches high; yellow complexion; well built fellow; served four years at Lawrence's Farm in the county"; advertised in *The Pennsylvania Gazette*, December 15, 1757

PRINCE, a Negro man; runaway from WILLIAM PEARTREE SMITH of Elizabeth Town; "speaks English and Dutch; has lived in Jamaica, the West Indies, with SIMON PARSCO and in Dutchess County, New York"; advertised in *The New York Mercury*, August 21, 1758

JACK, a Mulatto servant; runaway from JOSEPH BURR of Burlington County; "aged about 30 years; goes stooping in his shoulders; is a well made man; has a sore on the right side of his under lip"; advertised in *The Pennsylvania Gazette*, January 5, 1758

BRISTOL, a Negro man; runaway from BENJAMIN WILLIAMS, living at Newark; "aged about 26 years; 5 feet, 7 inches tall"; give notice to DANIEL NAP; advertised in *The New York Mercury*, October 9, 1758

FORDE, a Negro fellow; runaway from SAMUEL COLES, of Glouster County; "a stout, able fellow; aged about 25 or 26 years; about 5 feet, 8 or 10 inches high; can talk Dutch well; is apt to stutter if he speaks in haste; has a scar on his right shin"; advertised in *The Pennsylvania Gazette*, August 23, 1759

MOSES, a Negro man; runaway from WILLIAM CLAYTON of Trenton; "about 16 years of age; well set and stoops a little as he walks"; advertised by in *The Pennsylvania Journal*, May 31, 1759

BOOD, a Mulatto man servant man; runaway from WILLIAM HUNT in Hopewell; "about 5 feet, 10 inches high; pretty well set"; advertised in *The Pennsylvania Gazette*, June 21, 1759

BRISTOL, a Negro man servant man; runaway from WILLIAM HUNT in Hopewell; "about 5 feet, 10 inches high; pretty well set"; advertised in *The Pennsylvania Gazette*, June 21, 1759

JACK, a Negro man servant man; runaway from JOHN HART in Hopewell; "thick and well set"; advertised in *The*

Pennsylvania Gazette, June 21, 1759

TOM, a Negro man servant man; runaway from JOSEPH GOLDER in Hopewell; "short and well set"; advertised in *The Pennsylvania Gazette*, June 21, 1759

MOSES, an American born Negro lad, runaway from GEORGE KEEN, in Oxford Township in Philadelphia; "aged about 18 years; born in Trenton; has a remarkable scar across the toes of his right foot"; advertised in *The Pennsylvania Gazette*, April 22, 1762

HARRY, a Negro man, runaway from MOORE FURMAN of Trenton; "aged about 20 years; speaks low, but proper and can read English; about 5 feet, 9 inches high; slender made and stoops a little or rather hangs his head down and suspicious when he is spoke to; his legs are small and his feet appear flatter than common, tho not large; when he walks he turns his toes out pretty much and walks heavy"; advertised by ROBERT LETTIS HOOPER, Jr. in *The Pennsylvania Journal*, July 1, 1762

JAMES, a Mulatto slave, runaway from BENJAMIN MULFORD in Cumberland County; "aged about 34 years; about 5 feet, 4 inches high; tanner by trade"; advertised in *The Pennsylvania Journal*, September 2, 1762

JACK JOHNSON [JOHN JOHNSON], a Mulatto servant man, runaway from JOHN SMITH of Burlington; "aged about 24 years; has a bushy head of hair; stoops as he walks; splaw footed; formerly lived with JAMES BIDDLE of Springfield; supposed that he wants to go aboard a privateer"; advertised in *The Pennsylvania Gazette*, September 9, 1762

SAMPSON, a Negro man; runaway from SAMUEL MEEKER; "aged about 24 years; 6 feet, 4 inches tall; speaks good English"; advertised in *The Pennsylvania Journal*, May 12, 1763

JACK, a Guadaloupe born Negro man; runaway from the Ship *Sarah*; "6 feet tall; very slim make; a very smooth face; formerly belonged to Mr. PENNEL of Guadaloupe Island; eyes bloodshot; speaks tolerably good English"; advertised in *The Pennsylvania Journal*, May 23, 1763

Committed to the Cumberland gaol on suspicion of being a runaway, a unnamed Negro man, "aged about 50 years; middle stature; well set; says he was born in Virginia and belongs to JOSHUA FISHER of Philadelphia; speaks good English and is a blacksmith by trade"; advertised by HOWELL POWELL, Sheriff, in *The New York Gazette*, September 26, 1763

MOSES, a Negro man; runaway from ABRAHAM HEWLINGS, living in Evesham; "aged about 18 years, 5 feet, 3 or 4 inches tall; has a scar on the upper side of one of his feet"; formerly belonged to GEORGE KEEN; advertised in *The Pennsylvania Gazette,* September 29, 1763

CATO, an American born Mulatto slave; runaway from CORNELIUS LOW in Raritan Landing; "aged about 20 years; wide mouth; bushy hair, lately cut off; walks with his knees bending forward; extremely handy fellow at any type of common work, especially with horses or carriages of almost any sort, having been bred to it since a little boy, to the loading and unloading of boats; a good deal used to a farm; can do all sorts of house work and very fit to wait upon a gentleman; speaks very good English and Low Dutch; also pretty good High Dutch; is noted for his sense, and particularly for his ability at anything he takes in hand"; advertised in *The Pennsylvania Journal*, October 13, 1763

SAMBO, a Negro man; has come to the house of THOMAS LETSON of Black Point; "5 feet, 6 inches tall; talks English very indifferently; says he belongs to one ALLEN; now sick"; advertised in *The New York Gazette*, November 7, 1763

JACK, an American born Negro fellow; runaway from EDWARD AGAR; "about 5 feet, 8 inches high; his hair pretty long and stares very much; very black complexion; pretty much pitted with small pox; born in Hackensack; when he talks, he speaks quickly"; advertised in *the New York Mercury*, March 12, 1764

JAMES DONBAR, a Spanish Indian servant man; runaway from RICHARD WESCOT of Great Egg Harbor; "5 feet, 3 or 4 inches high; his hair tied behind"; advertised in *The Pennsylvania Gazette,* April 12, 1764

OSBORN, a Negro man, runaway from Powles Hook; "aged about 27 years; about 5 feet, 4 inches high; has a remarkably strong waist and bad legs; pretends to a knowledge of cooking; has a down cast look when he is spoke to by strangers, seemingly the effect of bashfulness"; advertised in *The New York Gazette and Weekly Mercury,* April 21, 1764

HARRY [TRASO], a Negro man; runaway from SAMUEL COCK of Mansfield Wood House of Sussex County; "about 25 or 26 years of age; 5 feet, 10 inches high; very black complexion; understands playing on a fiddle; brought up in this country"; advertised in *The New York Mercury,* May 14, 1764

FORTUNE, a Negro fellow; runaway from FRANCIS BEARD, living at Bound Brook, Somerset County; "a lusty fellow"; advertised in *The New York Mercury*, May 28, 1764

Committed to the Gaol of Cumberland county on suspicion of being a runaway, AMOS, a Negro, property of Colonel HOPPER of Queen Anne's County in Maryland; "about 30 years old; 5 feet, 5 inches high; says he was born in Guiney [Guinea]"; advertised in *The Pennsylvania Gazette,* May 31, 1764

Committed to the Gaol of Cumberland County on suspicion of being runaways, DANIEL ROGERS, a Negro, who says he is a free man and who came from Cambridge in Dorset County; advertised in *The Pennsylvania Gazette,* May 31, 1764

TOBY, a Negro man; runaway from JOSEPH GROVER and JOSEPH COWARD living in Upper Freehold, Monmouth County; "about 21 or 22 years of age; 5 feet, 5 or 6 inches high; well set; of a pleasant countenance for a Negro; shows his teeth frequently which are very white; is square built with bow legs; all the toes on one foot are short as they have been froze; the toe next to his great toe on the other foot lies over his great toe; he can play on the violin, but not extraordinary well"; advertised in *The Pennsylvania Gazette,* May 31, 1764

ABRAHAM, a Negro man; runaway from JOSEPH GROVER and JOSEPH COWARD living in Upper Freehold, Monmouth County; once belonged to Mr. EMLEN in Philadelphia, JOSEPH STANIARD and JOSEPH COX of Upper Freehold, in Monmouth County; "he can write and read and understands Plantation work; 5 feet, 9 or 10 inches high; well built"; advertised in *The Pennsylvania Gazette,* May 31, 1764

TONY, a Negro man; runaway from WILLIAM LISTER, living in Trenton; "about 30 years of age; 5 feet, 7 or 8 inches high; has a remarkable way of walking, as if he was a little lame and stoops a little forward; had a bad cut on his left thumb, fresh cut just before he went away; advertised in *The Pennsylvania Gazette,* June 28, 1764

Unnamed Negro man; runaway from Dr. BERN BUDD of Hanover in Morris County; "5 feet, 9 inches high; yellow complexion; speaks good English and understands all parts of Farmer's work and something of the sea"; advertised in *The Pennsylvania Gazette,* August 9, 1764

Committed on the suspicion of being a runaway, an unnamed Negro boy; "aged about 17 or 18 years; appears to be a new Negro; says his master's name is ANDREW"; advertised in *The Pennsylvania Gazette,* August 9, 1764

JACOB [JAMES SMART, JAMES PRATT], a Negro slave; runaway from GILBERT SMITH of Upper Freehold, Monmouth County; "aged about 23 years; 5 feet, 4 or 5 inches high; his mother was a Negro and his father an Indian and he passes himself off as an Indian and is like one, yellowish tawny complexion; his hair cut short on the crown, but curls around his neck; has a remarkable scar on one of his cheek bones, occasioned by a scald or a burn; speaks good English; is much addicted to smoking and drinking; left from his work at the plough, without shoes or stocking"; came to New York with AARON BUCK; notice to JOHN TALMAN in New York, Butcher, or to FRANCIS

FIELD, Golden Hill; advertised in *The New York Mercury*, September 10, 1764

JOHN JOHNSON, a Mulatto servant man; runaway from ABIA BROWN and JOSEPH CLAYTON, living at Brown's Mills in Nottingham Township; aged about 25 or 26 years; "5 feet, 8 or 10 inches high; has a lump on his lip, thought to be the under one; has a down look; very talkative fellow; given to drink;" lived some time ago with JOSEPH BIDDLE, then JAMES SMITH of Burlington, afterwards with RICHARD BROWN, then with subscribers; advertised in *The Pennsylvania Gazette*, January 2, 1766

TONEY, a Negro man; runaway from ELIJAH BOND, living in Trenton; "aged about 36 years; 5 feet, 4 inches high; has lost the first joint of one of his thumbs; speaks pretty good English"; advertised in *The Pennsylvania Gazette*, January 30, 1766

BENJAMIN MOORE, an indented Negro servant man; runaway from HENRY ROBINSON and JOSEPH ROBINSON, living in Freehold, Monmouth County; "aged about 40 years; 5 feet, 6 inches high; a likely, spry fellow"; formerly an indented servant to JOB THROCKMORTON and GEORGE RHEA of Freehold; advertised in *The New York Gazette or Weekly Post Boy*, February 6, 1766

TOM, a Negro man; runaway from SAMUEL HENRY of Trenton; aged about 24 years; 5 feet, 5 inches high"; formerly belonged to GERADUS BEEKMAN of New York; notice to JOHN BEEKMAN in New York; advertised in *The New York Gazette or Weekly Post Boy*, February 20, 1766

BILL, a Negro man; runaway from JOHN KLEIN, living at Raritan Landing; "aged about 20 or 22 years; 5 feet, 6 inches high"; formerly belonged to CORNELIUS CLOPPER at Raritan Landing; speaks good English and Low Dutch fluently; advertised in *The New York Gazette or Weekly Post Boy*, May 1, 1766

TOM, [JACOB] Mulatto slave; runaway from JOHN VANDORN, living in Passacak in Morris County; "5 feet, 6 inches high; very bushy hair; has a small scar on forehead"; advertised in *The New York Gazette or Weekly Post Boy*, May 1, 1766

POMPEY, a Negro servant man; runaway from JOHN MORRIS, living in Shrewsbury, Monmouth County; "aged about 35 years; 5 feet, 8 or 9 inches high; lusty fellow; speaks pretty good English"; advertised in *The New York Gazette or Weekly Post Boy*, May 1, 1766

NERO, a Negro servant man; runaway from JOHN MORRIS, living in Shrewsbury, Monmouth county; "aged about 25 years; slender, young fellow; speaks pretty bad English"; advertised in *The New York Gazette or Weekly Post Boy*, May 1, 1766

LEWIS, a Mulatto servant man; runaway from SAMUEL HOW, living in city of Burlington; "5 feet, 10 inches tall; stoops in his walk; round shins; the calves of his legs very high up to his hams; long visaged; grey eyes; very much freckled; supposed to have gone off with JOHN SIDENHAM, lately enlisted in Royal American Battalions; so white that he would only be taken for a mulatto by his hair"; advertised in *The Pennsylvania Gazette*, June 19, 1766

BILL, a Negro fellow; runaway from JOHN KLEIN; "aged about 20-22 years; 5 feet, 6 inches tall; speaks good English and Low Dutch fluently; has a scar across the bridge of his nose; by trade a baker and understands his business very well"; advertised in *The New York Gazette or Weekly Post Boy*, June 19, 1766

HANNABALL, a Negro man; runaway from EMORY FUETTER, "5 feet, 7 or 8 inches tall; likely black fellow; has a pert look and when talking, is always either laughing or smiling; walks proper and straight without limping, but, if examined, will find that one of his feet stiff and scarce able to bend it from his ankle to his toes"; advertised in *The Pennsylvania Journal*, June 19, 1766

JACOB, a Negro man; runaway from WILLIAM COOPER, living in Glouster County at the ferry opposite Philadelphia; "aged about 22 years; 5 feet, 8 inches tall; has sharp filed teeth and is very apt to stammer when talks fast"; advertised in *The Pennsylvania Gazette*, June 26, 1766; advertised two years later for running away from the same master; now 24 years of age; *The Pennsylvania Journal*, June 9, 1768

JOE, [Lewis] a Negro man; runaway from AUGUSTIN REID, living in Roxbury Township; "aged about 20 years; 5 feet, 8 or 10 inches tall; sprightly nimble fellow; yellowish complexion; has a scar on his forehead; speaks good English; plays the fiddle, since running away has hired himself to a butcher in New York; has gone to one OAKLEY in Westchester"; notice to HUGH GAINE; advertised in *The New York Gazette or Weekly Post Boy*, June 26, 1766

CUFF, a Negro man; runaway from JONATHAN CLAWSON, living in Woodbridge; "aged about 22 years; 5 feet, 9 inches tall; has a scar on his right toe and the ends of some of his other toes are cut off"; advertised in *The New York Gazette or Weekly Post Boy*, July 3, 1766

CATO, a Negro man; runaway from JOSEPH JOHNSON, living at Great Egg Harbor; "aged about 22 or 23 years; 5 feet, 2 or 3 inches tall"; advertised in *The Pennsylvania Gazette*, July 10, 1766

JEMMY, a Negro man; runaway from JOHN HILLIER, living in Northampton Township; "aged about 35 years; 6 feet tall; well limbed fellow; stutters much in his speech, which is bad English"; advertised in *The Pennsylvania Gazette*, July 17, 1766

Taken up and committed on suspicion of being a runaway, unnamed Negro man, "aged about 30 years; middle stature and speaks good English; says he came out of Queen Anne's County in Maryland and that his master's name is WILLIAM COOSEY"; advertised by THEOPILUS ELMER, Sheriff of Cumberland County in *The Pennsylvania Gazette*, July 24, 1766

PRINCE, an American born Negro man; runaway from THOMAS PLUMSTED, at Mt. Clement between East and West Jersey; "5 feet, 10 inches; remarkably black complexion; little pitted with small pox; speaks poor English"; advertised in *The Pennsylvania Gazette*, August 7, 1766

BEN, a Negro man; runaway from NATHANIEL RICHARDS, living at Newark; "aged about 28 years; 5 feet, 8 or 9 inches; slim man, thin visaged; yellow complexion; a likely lively cunning fellow; speaks good English and can speak Low Dutch"; formerly belonged to THOMAS BUDDLE, living at Morris county and sold to Mrs. ELIZABETH FINN, at Prakenas in Bergen County, pretended he had drowned so as to run away; advertised in *The New York Gazette or Weekly Post Boy*, September 4, 1766

GLASCO, a Negro man; runaway from ALEXANDER MOORE, living at Cohansey bridge, Cumberland County; "about 18 years of age; a well set fellow; has a scar on his left cheek and speaks good English"; advertised in *The Pennsylvania Journal*, November 20, 1766

PERRO SMITH, an American born Mulatto slave; runaway from GEORGE ARMSTRONG, living in Morris County; "about 35 years of age; 5 feet, 8 inches high; handsome; well looking man; can play on the violin and sings at the same time; is a sensible fellow; can read, write and cypher; he plays with his left hand and is much addicted to liquor; bred and born near Boston"; advertised in *The New York Mercury,* January 5, 1767

Committed to the City of Burlington gaol on suspicion of being a runaway, CHARLES CORNISH, a Negro man; "can read and write"; advertised by EPHRAIM PHILLIPS, Gaoler in *The Pennsylvania Gazette,* January 8, 1767

JOE, a Negro man; runaway from WILLIAM HENDRICKSION, living at Middletown Point in Monmouth County; "about years of 30 age; 6 feet; long visage; large eyes; a smooth tongued fellow"; advertised in *The New York Mercury*,

May 18, 1767

LINDEN, a Negro man; runaway from GIZEBERT LANE, living near Princeton; "about 33 years of age; 5 feet, 9 or 10 inches high; fore finger stiff; addicted to strong liquor and troublesome when drunk; pretends to be a doctor; remarkably stout; a cunning artful fellow"; advertised in *The Pennsylvania Gazette*, May 21, 1767

JACK, a Musquitto Shore Indian; runaway from ROBERT FIELD of Whitehill in Burlington; "aged about 21 years; 5 feet, 6-7 inches high; thick set; long black hair which he usually wears tied behind him; took with him a fiddle which he plays badly"; advertised in *The Pennsylvania Journal*, June 18, 1767

RICHARD [DICK], a Negro man; runaway from ROBERT FIELD of Whitehill, Burlington; "aged about 25 years; 5 feet, 9 inches high; very stout and well set; grave countenance; walks a little stooping; is a good farmer; probably in company with JACK, Indian servant previously noticed"; advertised in *The Pennsylvania Journal*, June 25, 1767

CHARLES, a Negro lad; runaway from SAMUEL HARKER of Oldman's Creek, Glouster County; "aged about 15; middle stature; talks good English; was lame in the right leg by the bite of a boar; has a scar in the forehead from the kick of a horse"; advertised in *The Pennsylvania Gazette*, July 16, 1767

SWACARNOCKUM [aka JACK] a Negro man, taken up and brought to Trenton Gaol; "about 40 to 50 years of age; speaks very bad English; is 5 feet, 8 inches high; stout built and has a down look"; advertised by GEORGE BROWN, Gaoler, in *The Pennsylvania Gazette*, July 23, 1767

CHARLES QUITE, half Negro, half Indian man; runaway from RICHARD JAMES of Upper Freehold, Monmouth County, near Imlay's Town; "aged about 28 years; 6 feet, 2 inches high; yellow complexion; long hair very much curled and thin on the top of his head; something knock kneed; large feet; a scar on one of his cheeks near his temple; well set"; advertised in *The Pennsylvania Gazette,* August 6, 1767

GARRET HARBOUR, a servant Negro man; runaway from SAMUEL FORMAN, in Kildair of Freehold; "aged about 28 years; low, squat, well set fellow; very much marked with the small pox; with black curled hair"; advertised in *The New York Mercury,* August 17, 1767

HARRY, a Mulatto slave; runaway from LEVIN CRAPPER, Three Run Mills, Sussex County, on Delaware; "aged about 40 years; 5 feet, 6 inches high; well set; much given to strong drink and playing on the fiddle; by trade a miller and understands very well how to manufacture flour and can invoice the same; understands the carpenter's and mill wright businesses middling well"; was removed from East Jersey in 1762 by NICHOLAS VEIGHT, who lived at Rocky Hill where he kept a mill; has a mulatto free born wife named PEG and two children; notice to CHARLES WHARTON, Merchant in Philadelphia; his wife has run away from her bail at Lewis Court in Sussex County; advertised in *The Pennsylvania Chronicle,* September 28, 1767

CATO, a Negro man; runaway from JOHN HENDRICK, living at Middletown Point; "short, thick fellow"; advertised in *The New York Journal or General Advertiser,* October 8, 1767

CORNELIUS GALLAHON, a mulatto man; runaway from WILLIAM HUGG of Glouster; aged about 24 years; advertised in *The Pennsylvania Gazette,* December 3, 1767

Was committed to Burlington gaol on suspicion of being a runaway, JACK HAMMAN, a Negro, says he belonged to WILLIAM COURSEY, of Queen Ann's County, Maryland; "aged about 32 years"; advertised by EPHRAIM PHILLIPS, Gaoler in *The Pennsylvania Gazette,* December 10, 1767

LANK, a Negro fellow; runaway from WILLIAM HENDRICKS of Middletown, Monmouth county; "aged about 25 years; about 5 feet, 8 or 9 inches high; slender made"; advertised in *The Pennsylvania Gazette*, March 3, 1768

    JACK HAMMOND, a Negro man; runaway from JOSEPH HAIGHT in the city of Burlington; "about 5 feet, 8 inches high; nose remarkably large and sharp"; advertised in *The Pennsylvania Journal*, April 28, 1768

    YORK, a Negro man; runaway from CYRENIUS VAN MATER of Middletown, Monmouth County; "aged about 18 years; about 5 feet, 9 inches high; well set; has one of his fore teeth broke off near the gum"; advertised in *The New York Journal or General Advertiser*, May 19, 1768

    PETER, a Negro man; runaway from ISAAC ANTRIN and EPHRAIM SEELY of Cumberland County; "artful fellow; about 5 feet, 10 or 11 inches high"; advertised in *The Pennsylvania Gazette*, May 26, 1768

    WILL, a Negro man; runaway from ISAAC ANTRIN and EPHRAIM SEELY of Cumberland County; "artful fellow; stout, well set fellow; shorter than 5 feet, 10 inches"; came from Carolina; advertised in *The Pennsylvania Gazette*, May 26, 1768

    BUNCE [TOM], a Negro, a servant man; runaway from CHARLES EVERSOLE of Reading in Hunterdon County; "aged about 30 years; about 5 feet, 2 or 3 inches high; very nimble in walking and talks broken English and low Dutch"; advertised in *The New York Gazette and Weekly Mercury*, June 6, 1768

    PETER [JACK SHARP], a Negro man, runaway from EPHRAIM SEELY living in Cumberland county; "aged about 30 years; about 5 feet, 10 inches high; has a large scar on one of his arms cut by a sickle"; advertised in *The Pennsylvania Journal*, June 9, 1768

    CUFF, a Negro man, runaway from JONATHAN CLAWSON, in Woodbridge; "about 5 feet, 10 inches high; full faced; thick set; has a large scar on his right great toe, cut within"; advertised in *The Pennsylvania Chronicle*, June 13, 1768

HARRY, a Negro man, runaway from JOHN ACTON living at Pumpton; "aged about 40 years; much pitted with small pox; can speak both Dutch and English; plays on the violin and loves grog"; advertised in *The New York Gazette and Weekly Mercury*, June 20, 1768

SAMUEL WRIGHT, an American born Mulatto man, runaway from RICHARD FRY, living near Great Egg Harbor in Glouster Township; born near Hampton in Virginia; "aged about 30 years; about 5 feet, 8 inches high; well set; his hair bushy and rather red; much marked with small pox; has a down look; when angry very apt to turn up the white of his eyes; one of his thumbs greatly bruised; has been whipped and pilloried at Philadelphia last year for horse stealing"; advertised in *The Pennsylvania Chronicle*, July 25, 1768

ISHMAEL, a Negro fellow, runaway from HENDRICK COYLER at Horse Neck; "by trade a black smith; is much pitted with small pox; has a blemish in one eye; is a great fiddler and often showing sleight of hand tricks; has a squaw for a wife"; deliver to Capt ELIAS DAYTON in Elizabeth Town; advertised in *The New York Gazette and Weekly Mercury*, August 22, 1768; re advertised in *The Pennsylvania Journal*, April 6, 1769

Taken up on suspicion of being a runaway, and committed to the Elizabeth Town gaol, by the order of JOHN SITES, an unnamed Negro, "about 24 years old; very thick lips; can speak English and Dutch; says he is a free man"; notice to gaoler BENJAMIN MILLER; advertised in *The New York Gazette and Weekly Mercury*, October 3, 1768

BENJAMIN KIPP, a Negro man; runaway from JOHN WOOD, living in Little Egg Harbor; advertised in *The Pennsylvania Gazette*, November 3, 1768

JAMES WILSON, a Mulatto boy; runaway from JOHN WOOD, living in Little Egg Harbor; "a lock of white hair on the back part of his head"; advertised in *The Pennsylvania Gazette*, November 3, 1768

FRANK, a Negro man; runaway from P. DARCEY, living in Hanover, Morris County; "a stout, able fellow; talks the English, Dutch, Spanish and Danish languages; has lost one of his eyes and wears a rag over it; escaped with the assistance of two of Capt. KENNEDY's Negroes; very artful and cunning and has escaped two times before"; notice to Mr. KELLY in New York; advertised in *The New York Gazette or Weekly Mercury*, December 5, 1768

JIM, a Negro man; runaway from WILLIAM HYER, living at Middletown Point, Monmouth County; "aged about 30 years; slim fellow; speaks both English and Dutch; much pitted with small pox"; advertised in *The New York Gazette and Weekly Mercury*, January 23, 1769

Committed to the Westchester gaol on suspicion of being a runaway; JIM, a Negro man, master's name is ERWIN in New Jersey, formerly belonged to lawyer OGDEN; "tall and very black"; advertised in *The New York Gazette and Weekly Mercury*, May 1, 1769

ANNEY'S JOE, a Negro man; runaway from EMER JACKSON of Upper Freehold, Monmouth County; "aged about 50 years; 5 feet, 10 or 11 inches high; well set; arch cunning rogue; wants his fore teeth; plays on the fiddle; is very much given to strong drink and pretends to be free"; advertised in *The Pennsylvania Gazette*, May 13, 1769

BENJAMIN, a Negro man; runaway from NATHANIEL RICHARDS, living in Newark; "5 feet, 9 inches high; has a mole on his cheek; down look, yellow cast; a lively fellow"; advertised in *The New York Gazette and Weekly Mercury*, May 22, 1769

An unnamed Mulatto, runaway from LEFFERT WALDRON and ERNEST VAN HARLIGEN; "aged about 19 years; 5 feet, 2 inches high; speaks good English and Dutch; yellowish complexion"; advertised in *The Pennsylvania Gazette*, June 29, 1769

JACK, a Mulatto, runaway from LEFFERT WALDRON

and ERNEST VAN HARLIGEN; "aged about 21 years; 5 feet, 9 inches high; speaks good English and Dutch; yellowish complexion; plays the fiddle"; advertised in *The Pennsylvania Gazette,* June 29, 1769

EBEN, a Negro man; runaway from WILLIAM CROOK; "aged about 30 years; speaks English and Dutch; can read and write"; advertised in *The New York Journal or General Advertiser,* July 6, 1769

Unnamed Negro man; runaway from WILLIAM COOKE in Somerset county; "a likely fellow; 5 feet, 10 inches high; has a nose more like a white than a black; speaks good English and writes a good hand"; advertised in *The Pennsylvania Chronicle,* July 10, 1769

BRUNCE, a Negro man; runaway from JACOBUS VAN DERVEER, living in Reading Town, Hunterdon County; "aged about 30 years; 5 feet, 6 inches high; speaks English and Low Dutch"; advertised in *The New York Gazette and Weekly Mercury,* July 10, 1769

FRANK, a Negro man; runaway from DANIEL VAN METER, living in Freehold, Monmouth County; "aged about 24 years; 5 feet, 7 inches high; walks nimble and light; small round scar on his cheek"; advertised in *The New York Gazette and Weekly Mercury,* July 10, 1769

PETER, a Negro man; runaway from JOHN HUNT of Hopewell, Hunterdon County; "5 feet, 6 or 7 inches high, well built"; advertised in *The Pennsylvania Gazette,* July 20, 1769

Committed to Burlington county gaol on suspicion of being a runaway, SAM, a Barbados born Negro man; "says his master's name is Capt. JOHNSON and that one WILLIAM THOMAS and JAMES BROWN sailed with the captain on a sloop loaded with rum and molasses; 22 or 23 years of age"; advertised by EPHRAIM PHILLIPS, Gaoler in *The New York Gazette or Weekly Post Boy,* August 14, 1769

Taken up on suspicion of being a runaway, BEN KIPPS, a Mulatto; "says he belongs to NICHOLAS SMITH of Egg Harbor"; advertised by JONAS PIERSON, Keeper of the Gaol at Newark in *The New York Gazette and Weekly Mercury*, August 28, 1769

Taken up on suspicion of being a runaway, JEM, a Negro man, says he belongs to THOMAS SEVERNS, who keeps the ferry at Elk River, Maryland; advertised by JOHN SMOCK, Keeper of the Gaol in Somerset county in *The Pennsylvania Gazette*, August 31, 1769

TONEY, a Negro man; runaway from ISRAEL WRIGHT, living in Bordentown; formerly the property of WILLIAM LESTER; advertised in *The Pennsylvania Gazette*, September 7, 1769

JOHN, a Negro fellow; runaway from WILLIAM P. SMITH at Elizabeth Town; "likely, young fellow; considerably upon the tawny color; bred in the family of HENRY BROCKHOLST at Pompton"; advertised in *The New York Gazette and Weekly Mercury*, September 11, 1769

GRIG, a Negro fellow; runaway from JOSEPH HUGG, living near Glouster; "lusty fellow; once belonged to Mr. WILCOX and to Mr. MULLUN, Innkeeper in Philadelphia;" notice to JAMES DELAPLAIN in Market Street; advertised in *The New York Journal or General Advertiser,* September 21, 1769

Unnamed Negro man; runaway from ISAAC WOODRUFF, Merchant of Elizabeth Town; advertised in *The New York Journal or General Advertiser,* September 21, 1769

BEN, a Negro man; runaway from NATHANIEL RICHARDS of Newark; "aged about 30 years; 5 feet, 8-9 inches high; tawny color; crafty fellow; well made; has a hair mole on his cheek and lost two of his fore teeth; walks very quick; sometimes stooped over"; advertised in *The New York Gazette and Weekly Mercury*, October 2, 1769

JAMES MORE, a Negro man; runaway from JAMES HILLIARD in Northampton Township, of Burlington county; "aged about 40 years; 6 feet high; walks straight and swings his arms partly behind him; pretends to be a free man and a fortune teller and it is not unlike that he will get some ill minded person to write him a pass"; advertised in *The New York Gazette and Weekly Mercury*, October 2, 1769

SYRON, a Negro man; runaway from RICHARD BRITTAIN of Upper Freehold, Monmouth County; "middle aged; 5 feet, 10 inches high; a stout; well set; bold looking fellow; very talkative; smooth face and remarkable large feet"; advertised in *The Pennsylvania Gazette*, December 7, 1769

PEN [JAMES PEMBERTON], a Negro servant man; runaway from THOMAS SAVIN, living in Cecil County, in Maryland Province; "aged about 25 years; a chunky, well set, black fellow; very talkative and pretends to be very religious"; advertised in *The Pennsylvania Chronicle*, January 22, 1770

SILAS, a Negro lad; runaway from ISAAC COATS, Brickmaker, living on Vine Street, Philadelphia; "aged about 17 years; 5 feet tall; yellowish cast; well set; by trade a chimney sweep and seen in company with several Negro lads, also chimney sweeps; oily tongued chap; much inclined to drink"; advertised in *The Pennsylvania Journal*, April 19, 1770

ROBIN, a Negro man; runaway from WILLIAM CLEAYTON of Trenton; "aged about 36 years; 5 feet, 2 inches tall; he was brought up at OWEN OWEN'S and is fond of strong liquor; talkative; very handy fellow; understands farming and milking"

WILL, a Negro man; runaway from DANIEL COOPER, living opposite to Philadelphia; "aged about 30 years; 6 feet tall; lusty; of the blackest cast"; advertised in *The Pennsylvania Chronicle*, October 1, 1770

SY [CYRUS], an American born Negro slave; runaway

from ISAAC COATS, brick maker, living in Vine Street, Philadelphia; "aged about 16 years; 5 feet high; yellow or copper colored complexion; well set; chews tobacco and loves strong liquor; can sweep chimneys; seen at house of RICHARD TENNANT, innkeeper in Trenton"; advertised in *The Pennsylvania Chronicle,* March 4, 1771

BRIT, a Negro man; runaway from JECAMIAH SMITH, living at Springfield, near Elizabeth Town; "aged about 30 years; 6 feet high; well made and stout; was taken by execution at the suit of ELIAS DESBROSSES of New York and sold at Vendue by the Sheriff of Essex County; former master was NATHANIEL SALMON at Wyoming, where he may now be"; advertised by in *The New York Gazette and Weekly Mercury,* March 25, 1771

JAMES, a Mulatto slave; runaway from Lower Penn's Neck; "aged about 40 years; 5 feet, 6 inches high"

TOM, a Negro man; runaway from HANCE LAMBSON, living in Lower Penn's Neck, Salem County; "5 feet, 4 or 5 inches high; a thick, well set fellow; has a large scar on his right cheek"; advertised in *The Pennsylvania Chronicle,* August 5, 1771

HUMPHREY, a Mulatto fellow; runaway from ELIJAH BOND, near Trenton; "aged about 30 years; very near sighted; a lusty fellow"; advertised in *The Pennsylvania Gazette,* September 5, 1771

WILL, a Negro man; runaway from Captain STOFFEL PROBASCO and HENDRICK PROBASCO, living in Millstone, near Somerset Courthouse, in Somerset County; "about 30 years of age; 5 feet, 8 or 9 inches; can read, write and cypher; plays very well upon the fiddle and has taken one with him"; advertised in *The New York Gazette and Weekly Mercury,* September 30, 1771

PRYM, a Negro man; runaway from Captain STOFFEL PROBASCO and HENDRICK PROBASCO, living in Millstone, near Somerset Courthouse, in Somerset County; "aged about 25 years; 5 feet, 8 or 9 inches; pretty long hair and one of his toes is cut off; speaks very good English and Dutch"; advertised in *The New York Gazette and Weekly Mercury*, September 30, 1771

KENT, a Negro man; runaway from WILLIAM COOPER, living in Glouster County; "aged about 24 years; middle sized fellow; pock marked; chimney sweep"; advertised in *The Pennsylvania Gazette*, October 3, 1771

CORNELIUS GALLAGHAN, a Mulatto servant man; runaway from WILLIAM HUGG, living in Glouster; "aged about 26 years; 5 feet, 6 inches high; middling well set; red beard; has lost the first joint off the forefinger of his left hand and part of the one next to it"; advertised in the *Supplement to the Pennsylvania Gazette, January 30, 1772*

Taken up on suspicion of being a runaway, DANIEL M'ANITINIE; advertised by BATEMAN LLOYD, Sheriff of Salem county in *the Pennsylvania Gazette*, February 6, 1772

Taken up on suspicion of being a runaway, JACOB, a Negro man, who came from Snow Hill in Maryland; "smart active, lively Negro; has been caught in several lies; about 22 years of age"; advertised by BATEMAN LLOYD, Sheriff of Salem county in *The Pennsylvania Gazette*, February 6, 1772

EZEKIEL, a Negro man; runaway from JAMES MILLER, at Bladensburgh in Maryland; "30 years old; 5 feet 10 or 11 inches high; thin faced; slim made; very active; speaks good English and Low Dutch; is very plausible in his talk and crafty in his behavior; whoever takes him must use great care or he will give them the slip; can make coarse shoes; has worked at Starr Forge, on Still Water in Sussex County"; notice to JAMES MACCUBBIN or JAMES WHITEHEAD, Philadelphia; advertised in *The Pennsylvania Journal and the Weekly Advertiser*, February 6, 1772

JOB, a Mulatto fellow; runaway from THOMAS FORMAN, living in Arnistown, Burlington County; "6 feet high; well set; bushy hair"; advertised in *The New York Gazette and The Weekly Mercury*, April 13, 1772

BRISTOL, a Negro man; ranaway from PETER TALLMAN, living in Town of Mansfield, in Burlington County; "pretty black; has thick lips and a hitch in his walk; he is 5 feet, 9 or 10 inches high; slim built;" advertised in *The New York Journal*, June 11, 1772

CATO, a Negro man; runaway from JOHN DE PEYSTER, Jr. living in New York; aged about 22 years; about 5 feet, 9 inches tall; is very black; straight, well limbed; looks grum; speaks pretty good English; a little lisping; three months ago he belonged to CHARLES TOOKER of Elizabeth, Essex county; advertised in *The New York Gazette and Weekly Post Boy*, August 31, 1772

GRIG, a Negro man; runaway from JOSEPH HUGG; "about 5 feet, 10 or 11 inches tall and well set; had an iron collar arond his neck when he went away"; advertised in *The Pennsylvania Packet and the General Advertiser*, September 7, 1772

Committed to custody of RICHARD JOHNSON, Gaoler of the county of Glouster, on suspicion of being a runaway; ANTHONY WELSH, a Negro man; says he belongs to BENJAMIN CLARK in Hanover Township, Lancaster County and says he was born in Burlington county in New Jersey; advertised in *The Pennsylvania Gazette*, September 9, 1772

MINGO [JIM], a Negro man; runaway from SAMUEL OGDEN; "aged about 30 years; 5 feet, 7 or 8 inches high; has a scar on his nose; plays on the violin; speaks good English and Dutch and is much addicted in strong drink; formerly the property of ISAAC WILKINS, of Westchester"; advertised in *The Pennsylvania Gazette,* December 30, 1772

JACK, a Negro man; runaway from PETER KETELTAS; "aged about 33 years; a short spare fellow; purchased from HENDRICK EMONS of Rocky Hill about 9 years ago; has a wife at ANTHONY TEN EYCK at Albany"; advertised in *The New York Gazette and Weekly Mercury*, January 18, 1773

Unnamed West Indian Negro man; runaway from WILLIAM HOLDCRAFT; "aged about 34 years; 5 feet, 10 inches high"; advertised in the Supplement to *The New York Gazette and Weekly Mercury*, January 18, 1773

BRIT, a Negro man; runaway from JACAMIAH SMITH, living near Elizabeth Town; "aged 33 years; 6 feet high; very stout; well made fellow; same fellow the SALMONS had at Wyoming for 3 years"; advertised in *The Pennsylvania Gazette*, April 7, 1773

PERO, a Negro man; runaway from ELIJAH CLARK, living at Great Egg Harbor in Glouster County; "aged 28 years; 5 feet, 8 inches high; hobbles in his walk; his left foot having been frozen, the great toe of which is considerably shorter than the other; speaks broken English"; advertised in *The Pennsylvania Packet*, May 10, 1773

POMPEY, a servant man; runaway from DAVID OGDEN, living in Newark; "5 feet, 8 inches high; well set; speaks both English and Dutch, but something broken; 35 years of age"; notice to Captain JOSIAH BANKS, at Hackinsack;

HARRY, a Mulatto fellow; runaway from THOMAS BROWN, living in Newark, Essex County; "about 22 years of age; 5 feet, 2 inches high; black straight hair, which he generally wears tied back; speaks good English and understands the pot ash business"; advertised in *The Pennsylvania Gazette*, June 16, 1773

BONTURAH, an American born Negro man; runaway from SAMUEL STOUT, Sr., BENJAMIN STOUT, Jr. and SAMUEL STOUT, Jr. living in Hopewell Township, Hunterdon County; "about 22 years of age; well set; shoemaker by trade; 5 feet, 6 inches high; of the blackest kind; can read"; notice to THOMAS SHIELDS in Philadelphia; advertised in *The Pennsylvania Journal*, June 16, 1773

JACK, an American born Negro man; runaway from SAMUEL STOUT, Sr, BENJAMIN STOUT, Jr. and SAMUEL STOUT, Jr. living in Hopewell Township, Hunterdon County;

"about 23 years of age; exceeds the others in stoutness; of the blackest kind; can read; 5 feet, 6 inches high"; notice to THOMAS SHIELDS in Philadelphia; advertised in *The Pennsylvania Journal*, June 16, 1773

FRANK, an American born Negro man; runaway from SAMUEL STOUT, Sr. BENJAMIN STOUT, Jr. and SAMUEL STOUT, Jr. living in Hopewell Township, Hunterdon County; "about 19 years of age; 5 feet, 6 inches high; of the blackest kind; can read"; notice to THOMAS SHIELDS in Philadelphia; advertised in *The Pennsylvania Journal*, June 16, 1773

CAESAR, a Negro man; runaway from, runaway from THOMAS SKILLMAN, living in Kingston, Somerset County; "about 23 years of age; 5 feet, 9 or 10 inches high; slim fellow; has an old sore on the small of one of his legs; speaks broken English; advertised in *The Pennsylvania Gazette*, June 23, 1773

PETER, a Negro man; runaway from JOHN M'CALLA; "about 20 years of age; 5 feet high; a clumsy looking fellow; stoops a little in his walk; is a cunning artful fellow; has a mother who lives in Trenton whose name is VIOLET, a Free woman"; advertised in *The Pennsylvania Gazette*, June 30, 1773

BEN [CIP], a Negro man; runaway from STEPHEN TALLMAN, Jr., living in Shrewsbury; "about 30 years of age; 5 feet high; yellow complexion; he has been in the army and talks much when he has been elevated by liquor"; advertised in *The New York Journal or General Advertiser*, July 17, 1773

PETER, a Mulatto man; runaway from SAMUEL PURVIANCE, in Pitts Grove, near the Mud Meeting House, in Salem; "about 33 years of age; 5 feet 10 inches high; very likely; active; lusty and well made; has been used to drive a coach and understands town and country work well; fond of cyder and strong liquor and is apt to get drunk; artful fellow; formerly lived with DAVID FRANKS in East New Jersey and Philadelphia"; advertised by in *The Pennsylvania Journal and Weekly Advertiser*, July 28, 1773; re advertised three years later in *The Pennsylvania*

Journal, September 13, 1776, as running away from same Master but age now "about 35 years of age", height given as "about 5 feet, 6 or 7 inches high; stout; is fond of strong liquor, and, when drunk, very saucy, and talks a great deal about his abilities as a farmer; he formerly lived with DAVID FRANKS, Esq of Philadelphia"

JAMES, a Negro man; runaway from ELIJAH BOND; advertised in *The Pennsylvania Gazette,* August 4, 1773

LEB [SAM], an American born Negro servant man; runaway from ANDREW BARRAT, living in Cecil County, Maryland, near the Mouth of the Susquehannah River; "short, thick, well set, lusty looking fellow; yellow complexion"; advertised in *The Pennsylvania Journal and The Weekly Advertiser*, August 4, 1773

BRISTOL, a Negro man; runaway from JOHN RICHARDS, living at Barbados Neck; "about 25 years of age; 5 feet, 10 inches high; a stout strong fellow; very black; plays well on the fiddle and carries one with him"; advertised in *The New York Gazette and Weekly Mercury*, September 27, 1773

JACK, a Negro man; runaway from SAMUEL OKESON, livng on Longbridge farm in Middlesex; 5 feet, 11 inches high; brown color; rather slim made"; advertised *Rivington's New York Gazzteer*, October 21, 1773

JACK, a servant man; runaway from ISAAC TAPPEN, living in Woodbridge; "aged about 32 years; 5 feet, 7 inches high; Indian look; bushy hair; can read; has lost his upper fore teeth and is to be seen on his left hand a bruise done formerly with a stone; pretends to be a freeman, but is a proper slave born in this province; often runs away by drinking too much and other misdemeanors"; advertised in *"Rivington's New York Gazetteer*, April 7, 1774

GEORGE, a Negro man; runaway from ABRAHAM LAWRENCE living in Flushing, New York and TALMAN

SMITH, near Bordentown; "about 35 years of age; yellowish complexion; black bushy hair which he commonly wears tied behind; remarkable scar on one of his cheeks; is apt to get drunk"; advertised in *The Pennsylvania Gazette*, September 14, 1774

Was committed in New Castle gaol on suspicion of being a runaway, PRINCE, a Negro man, belonging to Doctor ANTHONY YELDALL; advertised by THOMAS PUSEY, Gaoler in *The Pennsylvania Gazette*, September 14, 1774

Was committed in Lancaster gaol on suspicion of being a runaway, JOHN SOLOMON, an American born Negro; "about 5 feet, 11 inches high; marked with the pox; is a mill-wright by trade; says he was born in Millstone, New Jersey"; advertised by GEORGE EBERLY, Gaoler in *The Pennsylvania Gazette*, September 7, 1774

FRANK, a Negro man; runaway from BALDWIN WAKE, at Franklin Park, near Burlington; "likely fellow; 5 feet, 10 inches high; Indian cast to him; bushy hair; has had several masters, the last one being JOHN DAVAN; living in Hackensack, Bergen County; stole horse from SAMUEL QUICK, near Borden Town"; advertised in *Dunlop's Pennsylvania Packet*, September 26, 1774

CONSTANT, a Negro man; runaway from JOHN WILLIAMS SANDERS, living near Princeton; "about 26 years of age; well built; likely, black, active, sensible fellow; has been accustomed to attend on a gentleman"; notice to Dr. SAMUEL DUFFIELD at Philadelphia, LLOYD DAUBNEY at New York or to Dr. BATES WILLIAMS PETERSON, near Elizabeth Town"; advertised in *Rivington's New York Gazetteer*, November 3, 1774

MARK, a Negro man; runaway from MARK PREVOST, in Bergen county; "about 40 years of age; serious; civil; slow of speech; rather low of stature; reads well and is a preacher among the Negroes"; notice to ARCHIBALD CAMPBELL in Hackensack or THOMAS CLARKE, near New York; advertised in *The New York Journal or The General Advertiser*, November 10, 1774advertised jointly with his wife as "MARK and JENNY, a

Negro man and his wife" in *The New York Journal*, June 5, 1775 as being he is a middle aged man; a preacher; well set; both are dressed as Indians"

PEET, a Negro man; runaway from AARON LONGSTREET,Jr., living at Princeton; "about 27 years of age; 5 feet, 6 inches high; yellow complexion; large scar on one side of his neck and another on his head occasioned by a cut with a knife

Taken up on suspicion of being a runaway, PETER BROWN, a Mulatto, runaway from JAMES TALMAN in New Jersey; advertised by JOEL WILLIS, Gaoler of Chester County in *The Pennsylvania Gazette*, December 28, 1774

Taken up on suspicion of being a runaway, a Negro fellow, DANIEL KENT; "about 32 years of age; 5 feet, 4 or 5 inches high; bandy legged; very black complexion;" enquire of JOSIAH BANKS at Hackensack Ferry; advertised in *Rivington's New York Gazetteer*, December 29, 1774

PEET, a Negro man; runaway from DIRICK LONGSTREET of Princeton; "about 27 years of age"; advertised in *The New York Gazette*, March 27,1775

JOE, a Negro man; runaway from ISAAC VAN BLRCUM, of Paramus of Bergen county; "5 foot, 6 inches high"; advertised in *Rivington's The Pennsylvania Gazette,* May 29, 1775

BEN, a Negro man; runaway from HENRY SPARKS, DAVID HENRY and URIAH PAUL of Penn's Neck, Salem county; 6 feet 2 inches tall, stout, well made, notice to GEORGE MONRO, Esq. in Newcastle; advertised in *The Pennsylvania Journal*, June 21, 1775

Committed to the Burlingon gaol on suspicion of being a runaway, WILLIAM BROWN, a Negro man, of Princess Anne County, Virginia; "about 30 years of age; 5 feet, 5 inches tall; had been a preacher among the Indians"; advertised by EPHRAIM PHILLIPS, Sheriff in *The Pennsylvania Gazette*, July 5, 1775

PRINCE, a Negro man, runaway from AUGUSTINE REID of Roxbury, Morris county; "aged about 23 years; about 5 feet, 8 or 9 inches high; he is pretty broad shouldered and walks loose in the knees; has a scar on his thumb, it being split open, as was his leg, by an axe last year; he has just been inoculated with the small pox, not yet cleaned up, his arm still sore and is very liable to spread that infection"; advertised in *The Pennsylvania Journal*, April 9, 1777

CUFF, an American born Negro man, runaway from HENRY BURR, Sr. living in Northampton Township, Burlington County; "aged about 25 years; about 5 feet, 5 or 6 inches high; has been bred to plantation work and stock built; he has had the small pox by inoculation and is not marked with it"; advertised in *The Pennsylvania Evening Post*, June, 5, 1777

SIM, a Negro man, runaway from JAPHETH IRELAN, living in Egg Harbor Township; "aged about 24 years; about 6 feet high; well made; can read and write; has a remarkable large foot"; advertised in *The Pennsylvania Journal*, June 25, 1777

QUASH, a Negro man, runaway from JOHN JONES of Mount Holly; "aged about 26 years; about 5 feet, 8 or 9 inches high; plain speaking; by trade a cooper; thought he will go to the American camp as he is fond of soldiery"; advertised in *The New Jersey Gazette*, December 5, 1777

LEVI, a Mulatto lad, runaway from ABIJAH HOLMES, Cumberland County, West New Jersey; "aged about 18 years; has a down look; slim and straight build"; advertised in *The New Jersey Gazette*, January 21, 1778

LUN, a Negro man; runaway from ISAAC JOHNSON, living in Amwell township; "aged about 30 years; 5 feet, 8 or 9 inches high; a thick well set fellow; has a remarkable scar of a cut on his upper lip;" formerly belonged to JOHN SEVERNS; advertised in *The New Jersey Gazette*, February 8, 1778

NEAN, a Negro man; runaway from WILSON HUNT, JOHN HUNT and JOSEPH BURROWES; "aged about 25 years; a middle sized fellow; has thick lips and stutters very much in his speech; when he speaks in a hurry"; advertised in *The New Jersey Gazette*, February 25, 1778

JAMES, a Negro man; runaway from WILSON HUNT, JOHN HUNT and JOSEPH BURROWES; "aged about 20 years; short, chunky fellow; likes much to play much upon the fife"; advertised in *The New Jersey Gazette*, February 25, 1778

CUFF, a Negro servant man; runaway from WILSON HUNT, JOHN HUNT and JOSEPH BURROWES; "aged about 30 years; 5 feet, 8 inches high; well set fellow; very fond of playing on the fiddle"; advertised in *The New Jersey Gazette*, February 25, 1778

DORUS, a Negro lad, taken by Hessians from his master HENRY BUDD, of New Mills; notice to JAMES ESDALE at Burlington or THOMAS WATSON at Bordentown; advertised in *The New Jersey Gazette*, April 23, 1778

SAMBO, a Negro boy; runaway from WILLIAM LAWRENCE near Cooper's Ferry; "about 11 or 12 years of age; had a scar over one of his eyes; thick lips and is small for his age"; advertised in *The Pennsylvania Packet* August 25, 1778

HARRY, a Mulatto boy; runaway from JACOB GARRASON at Aquackananck, in Essex, "light complexion; dark brown hair; about 5 foot 4 inches; 18 years of age; a scar on one of his eyebrows and one of his little fingers crooked; speaks Dutch"; supposed to have gone off with WILLIM SUTLIFF, former British soldier; information to Mr. JOSEPHSON, on Market Street, Philadelphia; advertised in *The Pennsylvania Packet*, August 25, 1778

BEN, a Negro man; runaway from ELISHA LAWRENCE; "aged about 22 years; remarkably stout and well made"; advertised in *The New Jersey Gazette*, April 1, 1778

Taken on suspicion of being a runaway from Staten Island and now in Amboy, HACK, a Negro fellow; "sturdy; about 60 years of age; 6 feet high"; advertised by Capt. JAMES MORGAN, Second Regiment, in *The New Jersey Gazette*, March 25, 1778

Taken on suspicion of being a runaway from Staten Island and now in Amboy, JOE, a Negro fellow, "sturdy; aged about 26 years; 5 feet, 10 inches high"; advertised by Capt. JAMES MORGAN, Second Regiment, in *The New Jersey Gazette*, March 25, 1778

SAMBO, a Negro man; runaway from JOSEPH M'CULOH; "aged about 27 years; well built"; advertised in *The New Jersey Gazette*, May, 6, 1778

TOM, a Negro man; runaway from SAMUEL HENRY; "well set; 5 feet, 8 or 9 inches high"; advertised in *The New Jersey Gazette*, April 7, 1778

PRINCE [ADAM DICK], a Negro man; runaway from JOHN DANIELS, living in Fairfield Township, Cumberland County; "aged about 22 years; 5 feet, 8 or 9 inches high; lusty; walks somewhat crippled his feet having been frozen and he has lost some of his toe nails"; advertised in *The Pennsylvania Packet*, April 13, 1778

JACK, a Mulatto Negro man; runaway from THOMAS FORMAN, in Arney's Town, Burlington County; "pretty well set; 5 feet, 5 inches high; exceedingly scarred in the face, especially about the eyes"; advertised in *The New Jersey Gazette*, February, 1778

HARRY, an American born Negro man; runaway from ROBERT JOHNSON, at Salem; "aged about 28 years; 5 feet, 8 or 9 inches high; stout; well made fellow; large nose"; advertised in *The Pennsylvania Packet*, August 20, 1778

TOM, a Negro man; runaway from STEPHEN HUMPHREYS, living in Hopewell, Hunterdon County; "short and well set; his face cut much on both sides"; advertised in *The New Jersey Gazette,* August 26, 1778

FRANK, an American born Negro lad; runaway from SARAH RAMSAY, living in Hopewell, Cumberland County; "aged about 16 years; slim made"; advertised in *The New Jersey Gazette,* December 23, 1778

Was taken up on suspicion of being a runaway slave, BEN, a Negro man; "says he was formerly called HARRY; aged about 25 years; taken up in Hacket's Town"; advertised by PHILIP BRIGHT in *The New Jersey Gazette,* June 10, 1778

JEM, a Negro man; runaway from CHARLES COXE living in Kingwood, Hunterdon County; middle stature; marked with the pox; advertised in *The New Jersey Gazette,* June 10, 1778

TOM, a Negro man; runaway from TOBIAS SHULL, living in New Britain, Bucks County; "well made; 6 feet high; he also took a fiddle with him and plays with his left hand; was bought from WILLIAM BROWN at or near Ten Mile Run in New Jersey";advertised in *The Pennsylvania Gazette,* January 6, 1779

CHELS, a Negro man; runaway from the house of JESSE WILLIAMS in Philadelphia; "aged about 22 years; 5 feet, 8 inches high; very black and well set"

MARK, a Negro man; runaway from the house of JESSE WILLIAMS in Philadelphia; "aged about 24 years; 5 feet, 5 inches high; yellow complexion; chunky; has hair like an Indian, except that it curls"

JOE, a Negro fellow; runaway from EBENEZER BLACHLY, Jr. , living in Mendam, Morris County; "aged about 28 years; 5 feet, 6 inches high; well made; something lame in one of his legs"; advertised in *The New Jersey Journal,* April 13,1779

PHILL, a Negro boy; runaway from AARON KITCHEL; "aged about 13 years; short, thick set fellow"; advertised in *The*

New Jersey Journal, April 27, 1779

JUPITER, a Mulatto servant man; runaway from DAVID JONES, Capt. Living in Hunterdon county; aged about 20 years; likely; tall, slim fellow; advertised in *The New Jersey Gazette,* April 28, 1779

CUFF, a Negro man; runaway from HEZEKIAH HOWELL, living in Trenton; aged about 27 or 28 years; 5 feet, 9 inches high; has a small blemish in one eye and is marked on the cheek with a circle or round "O"; by trade a blacksmith; advertised in *The New Jersey Gazette,* June 9, 1779

CATO, a Negro man; runaway from WALTER RUTHERFORD, living in Lebanon, Hunterdon County; "aged about 20 years; 5 feet, 9 inches high; straight; well built; a little lame occasioned by a cut in his left ankle"; advertised in *The New Jersey Gazette,* June 23, 1779

PETER, a Negro man; runaway from aboard the prize sloop *Retrieve* at the Forks, Egg Harbor; "aged about 16 years; pretty tall and slender"; advertised by JOSEPH BALL in *The Pennsylvania Packet,* July 1, 1779

TONE, a Negro man; runaway from CORNELIUS VANHORN, living in the Town of Reading, Hunterdon County; "aged about 30 years; 5 feet, 10 inches high; well built; talks good English and low Dutch"; advertised in *The New Jersey Gazette,* September 1, 1779

CHARLES, a Negro man; runaway from CORNELIUS VANHORN, living in the Town of Reading, Hunterdon County; "aged about 17 years; 6 feet high; well set; yellow complexion; squints very much with his eyes; can talk good English and Low Dutch"; advertised in *The New Jersey Gazette,* September 1, 1779

SCIPIO, a Negro man; runaway from JOHN LEARY of Chatham; "aged about 35 years; 5 feet, 9 inches high; flat face and nose; large eyes and gray hair in his head"; notice to Capt. JACOB

ARNOLD at Morris Town and JOHN BARRERE

    WILL, a Negro fellow; runaway from JOHN SHAW, living in Bernard's Town, Baskenridge; "aged about 23 years; stout man; was formerly owned by WILSON HUNT of Maidenhead and was called MINCK; advertised in *The New Jersey Gazette*, November 17, 1779

    CUDGE, a Negro man; runaway from Somerset, two miles above the landing on Raritan River; "aged about 28 years; short and thick

    PRINCE, a Negro man; runaway from JOHN BLANCHARD, living in Hanover, Morris County; "aged about 24 or 25 years; very thin; very black; can speak low Dutch; formerly belonged to one VAN RIPER at Second River; if he gets a little liquor, he is talkative; 5 feet, 7 or 8 inches high"; advertised in *The New Jersey Journal*, June 21, 1780

    JACK, a Negro man; runaway from LUCAS VON BEVERHOUDT at Beverwyck, near Morris Town; "low stature; very black; limps a little in his walk, although not lame; speaks broken English and Negro Dutch"; notice to PATRICK DARCY; advertised in *The New Jersey Journal*, October 11, 1780

    WILL, a Negro boy, runaway from MARTIN WYCKOFF in Reading Town, Somerset County; "aged about 15 or 16 years; about 5 feet high; left under the pretense of going to JACOB WYCKOFF'S house in Mendham, Morris County"; advertised in *The Pennsylvania Gazette*, February 9, 1780

    BILL, a Negro boy; runaway from MEDCEF EDEN, Brewer, living at Golden Hill; "aged about 14 years; thick set; lately belonging to Mr. WATSON of Amboy"; advertised in *The New York Gazette and Weekly Mercury*, October 2, 1780

    CAESAR, a Negro man; runaway from JOHN DENTON; "aged about 25 years; 5 feet, 8 inches high"; advertised in *The New Jersey Journal*, November 15, 1780

BRISS, a Negro man; runaway from ROBERT JOHNSON, living in Salem; "aged about 35 years; remarkably large feet; formerly belonged to Major HUGG of Glouster County"; advertised in *The Pennsylvania Gazette*, December 6, 1780

JOE, a Negro man; runaway from EBENEZER BLACKLY, Jr.; "aged about 30 years; 5 feet, 8 inches high; one leg shorter than the other; part of one big toes cut off; lost some teeth; back is much scarified and in lumps by whipping"; advertised in *The New Jersey Gazette*, December 27, 1780

JOE, a Negro man; runaway from ROBERT L. HOOPER and ROBERT HOOPS, living in Trenton; "5 feet, 6 or 7 inches high; well set; full faced; was formerly a servant to a British officer and speaks the German language well"; advertised in *The New Jersey Gazette,* January 17, 1781

CAIN, a Negro man; runaway from GARRET COWENHOVEN, living in Penn's Neck, Windsor Township, Middlesex County; "aged about 40 years; 5 feet, 5 or 6 inches high; remarkably bald on his head; very talkative; well set; fond of trading"; advertised in *The New Jersey Gazette*, February 14, 1781

FRANK, a Negro man; runaway from Mrs. WILSON, living in Hackett's Town, Sussex county; aged about 40 years; notice to Col. THOMPSON at Trenton, Mr. BRAY at Raritan Landing or Col. STEWART at headquarters, New Windsor; advertised in *The New Jersey Gazette*, April 25, 1781

unnamed Negro man; runaway from Mrs. WILSON, living in Hackett's Town, Sussex County; "aged about 25 years;" notice to Col. THOMPSON at Trenton, Mr. BRAY at Raritan Landing or Col. STEWART at headquarters, New Windsor; advertised in *The New Jersey Gazette*, April 25, 1781

TONEY, a Negro man runaway; from ANDREW BLACKWELL, living in Hopewell; "aged about 35 years; 5 feet, 6 inches high"; advertised in *The New Jersey Gazette*, May 9, 1781

JACK, a Mulatto; runaway from ANDREW CALDWELL, living in Philadelphia; "5 feet, 2 or 3 inches high; fair complexion; bushy black hair; good tempered fellow when sober, but sulky or quarrelsome in liquor; well acquainted with the country; had been a servant to Dr. HUTCHINSON, when the army was at Valley Forge; good tailor;" notice to GEORGE DAVIS at Trenton; advertised in *The New Jersey Gazette*, May 31, 1781

JACK, A Negro boy; "aged about 15 years; down look; is a very great liar; advertised in *The New Jersey Gazette*, July 11, 1781

JACK, a Negro boy, runaway from PATRICK COLVIN, living at Trenton Ferry; "aged about 15 or 16 years; slim built; yellowish complexion;" lately the property of General PHILEMON DICKINSON; advertised in *The New Jersey Gazette*, September 12, 1781

NED, a Negro man; runaway from WILLIAM M'CALLA, living in Bucks County, Pennsylvania; "about 20 years of age; likely; well built fellow;" advertised in *The New Jersey Gazette*, September 26, 1781

Taken up on suspicion of being a runaway and going over to the enemy, PRINCE FORSBERG a Negro; "6 feet high; says he was out in the Privateeer Ship *Congress* on the last cruise"; advertised by PETER HULICK, gaoler in New Brunswick in *The New Jersey Gazette*, November 7, 1781

Taken up on suspicion of being a runaway and going over to the enemy, JACK WILLIAMS, a Negro; "5 feet 9 inches high; says he was out in the Privateeer Ship *Congress* on the last cruise"; advertised by PETER HULICK, gaoler in New Brunswick in *The New Jersey Gazette*, November 7, 1781

Taken up on suspicion of being a runaway and going over to the enemy, ENOS PATTERSON, a Mulatto man, 5 feet, 10 inches high, says he was out in the Privateeer Ship *Congress* on the last cruise; advertised by PETER HULICK, gaoler in New

Brunswick in *The New Jersey Gazette*, November 7, 1781

Taken up on suspicion of being a runaway and going to New York, JOSEPH, a Negro man; "5 feet, 10 inches high; says he formerly belonged to Mrs. CATLE, of Charles Town, South Carolina, but now of New York and that for some time since he has lived with Capt. MERCER of Philadelphia"; advertised by PETER HULICK, gaoler in New Brunswick in *The New Jersey Gazette*, November 28, 1781

GEORGE, a dark Mulatto slave; runaway from JOHN BLEDSOE, BENJAMIN CRAIG, JEREMIAH CRAIG, living near Racoon Ford, Orange county, Virginia; "17 years of age; 6 foot high; sour down look"; advertised in *The New Jersey Gazette*, November 21, 1781

HARRY, a Negro slave; runaway from JOHN BLEDSOE, BENJAMIN CRAIG, JEREMIAH CRAIG, living near Racoon Ford, Orange county, Virginia; "17 years of age; low; well set fellow; sprightly and quick spoken"; advertised in *The New Jersey Gazette*, November 21, 1781

CHARLES, a Negro slave; runaway from JOHN BLEDSOE, BENJAMIN CRAIG, JEREMIAH CRAIG, living near Racoon Ford, Orange county, Virginia; "16 years of age; thinner than HARRY with whom he had runaway; has a very pleasant countenance and speaks slow; he spins well on the foot wheel"; advertised in *The New Jersey Gazette*, November 21, 1781

JOE, a Negro man; runaway from JOHN RUNYAN and JACOB WILLIAMSON, living near Ringo's Tavern, near Hunterdon; "aged about 22 years; six foot high"; advertised in *the New Jersey Gazette,* January 16, 1782.

WOMEN RUNAWAYS

ANNA RICHARDSON, a servant woman; runaway from DAVID STRAHAN of New Jersey, she about 40 years of age, of middle stature, having a swarthy complexion with a scar over her right eye; notice was directed to be made to SAMUEL KIRK of Brandy Wine Ferry; advertised in *The American Weekly Mercury*, June 16, 1720

SARAH PARLER, a servant woman; runaway from Doctor JOHN BROWNE, on York road, West Jersey; supposed to be inveigled or conveyed away by one RICHARD SARTIN, who served his time at French Creek in Pennsylvania, at the iron works; he pretends he is her husband, but is not; "she is a little thin person"; advertised in *The American Weekly Mercury*, August 25, 1726

Broke out of the Gaol of Monmouth, at Freehold, ELEANOR WHITE, under sentence of death for the murder of her bastard child; tall and slender; round faced; freckled with black hair and black eyes; advertised by JOHN WILLIAMS, Under Sheriff and BUBRYCK, Sheriff in *The Pennsylvania Gazette* of May 1, 1735 and *The New York Gazette* of May 12, 1735

Assisted in the escape of ELEANOR WHITE from the Gaol of Monmouth, at Freehold, MARY BOWMAN, English born servant to JOHN WILLIAMS, Gaol Keeper; "thick, short and fat; pockfretten and of brown complexion"; advertised by JOHN WILLIAMS, Under Sheriff and BUBRYCK, Sheriff in *The Pennsylvania Gazette* of May 1, 1735 and *The New York Gazette* of May 12, 1735

MARTHA BARNES, a servant woman; runaway from DAVID HELDRETH of Middletown in Monmouth county; "aged about 36 years; lusty and well set; long, thin visaged; tawny complexion; light hair and blue eyes; with one tooth out before and great ringworms on her breast and arms"; advertised in *The Pennsylvania Gazette*, July 24, 1735

unnamed woman in the company of JAMES HAGEN, an Irish servant man; a short young woman that has a hump back"; advertised in *The Pennsylvania Gazette*, November 17, 1737

SUSAN, a Negress; runaway from ROBERT FIELD of Burlington county; "between 40 and 50 years of age; a tall woman; her hair is cut short"; advertised in *The American Weekly Mercury*, December 28, 1736

ELIZABETH PERRY, a servant woman; runaway from CORNELIUS VAN HORNE and others in Upper Freehold, Monmouth County; aged about 20 years; middle sized; "fresh colored and squints"; advertised in *The American Weekly Mercury*, April 20, 1738

ELIZABETH PRICE, an Irish servant maid; runaway from JOHN THACKERY of Newtown, in Glouster County; aged about 23 years; advertised in *The Pennsylvania Gazette*, March 20, 1740

KATHERINE M'KEW, an Irish servant woman; runaway from JOHN GILL and SAMUEL BOGGS of Hattonfield in Glouster County; fair complexion; long visage; will suppose that she and JOHN GREEN will attempt to pass for man and wife, which they are not; advertised in *The Pennsylvania Gazette*, September 16, 1742.

MARY GRIMES, an Irish servant woman; runaway from HENRY COOPER of New Hanover Township, Burlington County; "very well set, but of short stature; fair complexion; pitted with small pox"; advertised in *The Pennsylvania Gazette*, June 25, 1747

SARAH DAVIS, a Welsh servant woman; runaway from WILLIAM PLASKETT of Trenton; "about 27 years of age; of middle stature; somewhat freckled; has a small scar on her forehead and is slow of speech"; advertised in *The Pennsylvania*

Gazette, September 17, 1747

 MARY MUCKLEROY, an Irish servant maid; runaway from SAMUEL LIPPINCOTT of Northhampton, Burlington County; middle stature; advertised in *The Pennsylvania Gazette*, April 16, 1748

 MARGARET KANE, an Irish servant woman; runaway from JOSEPH REED of Trenton; middle stature, black hair, down look; advertised in *The Pennsylvania Gazette*, May 12, 1748

 MARY SULLIVAN, an Irish servant woman; runaway from JOHN VANNORDEN of New Brunswick; aged about 22 years, "short set stature, child of 14 months, which she calls Billy; he has black eyes"; advertised in *The New York Gazette revived in the Weekly Post Boy*, June 20, 1748

 KATHERINE ANDERSON, an Irish servant maid; runaway from MARTIN BICKHAM of Greenwich Township, Glouster County; aged about 23 years; "middle stature; well set; fresh complexion; full faced; speaks good English"; advertised in *The Pennsylvania Gazette*, July 7, 1748

 MARGARET PHILIPS, a servant maid; runaway from JOHN EGLINGTON of Glouster County; "about 30 years of age; of middle stature; with large breasts and can sing well and dance the ropes with many other tricks; she calls herself MARY SMITH; she has a brindle dog with her and is known by the name of Bellanamony"; advertised in *The Pennsylvania Gazette*, December 1, 1748

 HECATISSA, alias SAVINA, a Negro wench; runaway from NICHOLAS BEARCRAFT of Hunterdon County; "about 27 years of age; of short stature; gloomy down look; short; often troubled with Cholick"; advertised in *The Pennsylvania Journal*, June 8, 1749

 MARY KELLY, an Irish servant woman; runaway from SAMUEL BOGGS, near Haddonfield of Glouster County; "aged about 20 years; low stature; fresh; has a large scar on her arm and another on the back part of one of her legs"; advertised in *The Pennsylvania Gazette*, June 1, 1752; advertised in *The New York Gazette revived in the Weekly Post Boy*, November 29, 1752 as having run away from Capt. JONATHAN HAMPTON of Elizabeth Town; a likely girl; aged about 20 years; short and well set; has run away twice before, once from New-Castle and the other time from Glouster; used to travel at night and steal fowl"

CATHERINE MAGAHEY, an Irish servant woman; runaway from WILLIAM WOODWARD of Crosswicks; about 5 feet 5 inches high; fresh complexion; likely woman; notice to JOHN ALLEN of Trenton; advertised in *The Pennsylvania Gazette*, August 13, 1752

MRS. RICHARD MALONE, runaway together with her husband, from Piscataway; and suppose to have gone to Rockaway or Barnegat"; advertised in *The New York Gazette Revived in the Weekly Post Boy*, November 20, 1752

NELL, a Negro wench; runaway from ISAAAC KINGSLAND of Saddle River in Bergen County; a tall, slim wench; has three diamonds on her face, one on each side and the other on her forehead; formerly belonged to ROBERT LIVINGSTON, merchant in New York; advertised in *The New York Gazette Journal or Weekly Post Boy*, May 14, 1753

MRS. ISAAC GARRISON, runaway with her husband and living at Cohansy bridge in Cumberland County; "they had but no children as they never had any; notice to J. JAMES, Jr. or JOHN LASEY; advertised in *The Pennsylvania Gazette*, June 14, 1753

MRS. HENRY CLARK, tall; slender; of a pale complexion; dull countenance; with a lusty boy of about 18 months; went down the river to Philadelphia advertised in *The Pennsylvania Gazette*, August 9, 1753

MARIA KUMMERSFIELD, a Dutch servant woman; runaway from JOHN CUMING of Trenton; "aged about 26 years;

sandy complexion; thick and fat; talks very bad English; has a hobbling walk and stoops pretty much"; advertised in *The Pennsylvania Gazette*, April 14, 1754

RUTH ORR, an Irish servant woman; runaway from ELISHA BOND of Trenton; aged about 35 years; "thin visage; born in Dublin; light hair; small stature; squints"; advertised in *The New York Gazette or the Weekly Post Boy*, April 15, 1754

MOLLY, a Negro woman born in Bermuda; "about three weeks out of the small pox; is about 32 years of age; speaks good English; has been used in the house; supposed to have gone to the Jerseys"; advertised in *The Pennsylvanoia Journal*, November 18, 1756

ELIZABETH BURK, [aka BETTY BRIN and BETTY DAWSON], an Irish servant girl; runaway from Work House in Chester and belongs to THOMAS BLAIR of the Township of Woodhouse in Sussex County in West Jersey; "born in Ireland but denies her country; is about 18 years of age; small stature; dark complexion and speaks much through her nose; is suppose to have gone to Annapolis Maryland; she stoops much as she walks; not to believe what she says because she certainly will tell many lies"; advertised in *The Pennsylvania Gazette*, June 3, 1756 and again by GEORGE KEITH in *The Pennsylvania Gazette*, December 2, 1756;

SARAH ALLEN, an apprentice servant girl; runaway Maidenhead Township in West Jersey; "aged about 17 years; of a swarthy complexion; hollow eyed; down look; with brown hair of a reddish cast"; lived at Mr. MULLOCK's in New Brunswick

Taken up and confined in Glouster Gaol under suspicion of being a runaway servant MARY HEADEN; "young woman of a fair complexion; landed with Capt. COLE at Annapolis" advertised by ROBERT FRIEND PRICE, Sheriff, in *The New York Gazette*, October 27, 1757

ANNA CATHERINA MICHTILIN, a high Dutch servant

woman; runaway from WILLIAM SNOWDEN of Amwell, Hunterdon County; "a down cast; woman of middle stature;well set; aged about 25 or 26 years; black eyes and black hair; much freckled; has a female child with her about a year and ten months old with dark eyes"; advertised in *The Pennsylvania Gazette*, November 3, 1757

HANNAH DOROTHY SCOUSS, a Dutch servant woman; runaway from JAMES SEXTON, living in Monmouth County; "thick set; full face; fair complexion; very much marked with small pox; speaks good English; supposed to be secreted near Philadelphia"; advertised in *The Pennsylvania Gazette*, August 23, 1759

BARBARYS AGER, an Irish servant woman; runaway from ROBERT RUTHERFORD of Trenton, Hunterdon County; "of middle size; takes a great deal of snuff and speaks pretty good English"; advertised in *The Pennsylvania Gazette*, January 5, 1758

MARY MACMEIN, a servant woman, runaway from JONATHAN FOX and JAMES GINIS of Springfield in Burlington County; "aged about 30 years; a short, thick set woman; flat faced; reddish hair; supposed to be going to Kent County"; advertised in *The Pennsylvania Gazette*, January, 7 1762

CATHERINE BARCLAY, she is exceedingly pock marked; very brown; about 40 years of age but looks much older; a very neat woman; advertised by Sheriff JONATHAN HAMPTON and SYLVESTER COLER in *The Pennsylvania Gazette*, July 8, 1762

SARAH READING, an Irish servant girl, runaway from WILLIAM RUDDEROW living by Pensawkin Creek, about a mile above the Bridge, in Burington County; "about 5 feet, 2 inches high; well set; has a small scar or seam from her left nostril down to the corner of her mouth; sandy hair; marked with the small pox"; advertised in *The Pennsylvania Gazette*, September 27, 1762

From the Trenton gaol, VENUS, a Negro wench, formerly

the property of SAMUEL STOUT, Jr., in Amwell; advertised by JOHN ALLEN High Sheriff in *The Pennsylvania Gazette*, October 14, 1762

MARY HEANY, an Irish servant girl, runaway from JAMES WHITALL; "short and thick"; advertised in *The Pennsylvania Gazette*, November 25, 1762

ELIZABETH RAINEY, an Irish servant girl; runaway from JAMES JACKSON, of Upper Freehold, Monmouth County; "aged about 17 or 18 years; very short stature; very thick; full faced; speaks very broad; born in Belfast; marked with the small pox;" notice to ANDREW STEUART, Printer, in Philadelphia; advertised in *The Pennsylvania Gazette*, October 6, 1763

NELL, a Negro wench, runaway from BROOKE FARMER, Esq., Post Master in New Brunswick; aged about 30 to 40 years; "middle sized; well set; a very little pitted with small pox; is very handy and talkative"; formerly lived at the Widow PRITTONS in Trenton; advertised in *The Pennsylvania Journal*, February 23, 1764

BETTY, a Negro woman; runaway from JANE BLACKWOOD, living at the Falls of Schuykill; has a husband at Mr. BARD's Iron Works at Mt. Holly; advertised in *The Pennsylvania Gazette,* April 26, 1764

LUCY [SUE], a Negro woman; runaway from PATRICK HANLON, living in Cranberry, Middlesex County; "about 30 years of age, slender; small woman; wants some of her teeth; full eyed"; supposed she went to Bucks county where one LAMBERT VANDYKE, near Shaminy Meeting House, where she has a daughter; her mother and brother live with Mr. KEMBLE in Brunswick; speaks Dutch well; advertised in *The Pennsylvania Gazette*, June 14, 1764

Was committed in the Cumberland County gaol on the suspicion of being a runaway, MARY YATES; advertised by HOWELL POWELL, Sheriff in *The Pennsylvania Journal*,

September 6, 1764

JOHANNA DUNAGAN, an Irish servant girl; runaway from Dr. THOMAS WARE in Burlington; "aged about 20 years; middle stature; brown complexion; grey eyes; a down look; short black curled hair, much like a mulatto; pretty much marked with small pox; has a very short walk and is given to liquor"; advertised by THOMAS WARE in *The Pennsylvania Journal*, March 13, 1766

ELIZABETH LOUISA WILSON, an English servant woman; runaway from JACOB TAYLOR, shoemaker, of Princeton; "aged about 25 years; middle sized; fair complexion; light hair and eyes; has a remarkable mole on her face and a very sour look; went in company of SIMON ROGERS and ISAIAH"; advertised in *The New York Mercury*, August 10, 1767

MARY CROANE, an Irish servant girl; runaway from WILLIAM MOUNTEER of Princeton; "aged about 26 years; middle sized; supposed to be secreted by ROBERT NEMINS at Princeton and conveyed to his son WILLIAM NEMINS living at Brandwine Rocks near Christeen Ferry"; had been challenged by JAMES SAUNDERS at the house of HENRY BRACKEN; about 5 miles from New Port in New Castle County, but escaped; advertised in *The Pennsylvania Journal*, August 13, 1767

MARY ANN O'BRYAN [MARY BRYAN], an Irish servant girl; runaway from JOHN FIRTH of Salem County; aged about 17 or 18 years; short and thick; fair complexion; light brown hair; much given to drink and very impudent when so"; advertised in *The Pennsylvania Gazette*, November 5, 1767; also advertised in *The Pennsylvania Gazette*, February 11, 1768 as "MARY BRIAN, "middle sized; born in Dublin; fair complexion; aged about 18 or 19 years; dark brown hair and pretty full mouth; very talkative and apt to get drunk and very impudent when in drink".

unnamed woman English born thick short woman, much pock marked with a long nose and red hair; fond of liquor and apt to quarrel when drunk"

unnamed small woman of a dark yellow complexion

MARGARET JOYCE, a servant woman; runaway from JOSEPH HAIGHT, of the city of Burlington; "5 feet, 5 or 6 inches high; black hair and eyes; rosy cheeks and thick lips; had formerly lived with JOSEPH PARKER, Tailor of Philadelphia"; advertised in *The Pennsylvania Chronicle*, July 17, 1769; also advertised in *The Pennsylvania Chronicle*, October 2, 1969 as "aged about 19 years; 5 feet, 6 inches high; down cast look; fresh complexion"; notice to be given to CHARLES BASSONET in Bristol, Bucks County, Pennsylvania.

MARY HAWKES, an apprentice girl; runaway from JOHN GYLESE, living in Wilmington, Delaware; "aged about 9 years; full face; black eyes and large teeth; mother is JANE HAWKES of Penn's Neck, Salem County"; advertised in *The Pennsylvania Journal*, September 30, 1770

MARGARET ELTON, wife of THOMAS ELTON, a very likely, round favored woman; short thick body; black hair; a little flat nose; her eyes stand at a greater distance from one another than women's eyes commonly do; her cheeks very rosy; has a small scar under her right nostril, something resembling a cross; has lost two of her fore teeth; talkative and very fond of singing; about 22 years of age; supposed to be gone to Baltimore; advertised in *The Pennsylvania Chronicle*, April 15, 1771

RACHEL SCOTT, American born; she is a lusty, strong hussey and is apt to be light fingered"; advertised in The Pennsylvania Gazette, May 9, 1771

ELEANOR BUTLER, wife of JOHN BUTLER of Pittsgrove, an Irish woman, about 35 years of age, small pock marked, speaks with the brogue and is very fond of strong liquor"; advertised in The Pennsylvania Gazette, August 8, 1771

ANN GRAZIOUS, runaway with DANIEL M'SHANE

who lives with him as her husband"; advertised by in *The Pennsylvania Gazette,* March 12, 1772

MARGARET DORREN, ran away with JAMES KERN, at Pilesgrove, Salem County advertised in *The Pennsylvania Gazette,* April 23, 1772

ANN MILLER, an Irish servant woman; runaway from ALEXANDER LESLIE, near the New Dutch Church, New York; "aged about 25 or 30 years; swarthy complexion; black hair and a black beard on her upper lip; went off with HENRY USTICK's nailer"; advertised in *The New York Journal and General Advertiser,* July 30, 1772

ELIZABETH CURRY, an Irish servant woman; runaway from ALEXANDER LESLIE, near the New Dutch Church, New York; "aged about 18 years; fair complexion and hair; freckled in the face; went off with HENRY USTICK's nailer"; advertised in *The New York Journal and General Advertiser,* July 30, 1772

PHOEBE, a Negro woman; runaway from JOHN HAZELWOOD, living in Philadelphia; "short with scar on her right eye; brown; has a 2 year old female child with her"; advertised in *The Pennsylvania Gazette,* January 6, 1773

CAROLINA DE POOL, a Dutch servant woman; runaway from JOSEPH KAIGHIN; "aged about 23 years; short chunky body; one shoulder is higher than the other; light colored hair; a large humped nose and a hardy bold look"; advertised in *The Pennsylvania Gazette,* February 10, 1773; also advertised in *The Pennsylvania Gazette,* April 17, 1777, as a runaway from JOHN BISPHAM, living in Mount Holly; "a little body with a hump back; high nosed and marked with the small pox; last seen about Trenton and Princeton".

HAGER, a Negro wench; runaway from JACOB MORRELL, living in Morris County; "aged 20 years"; advertised in *The New York Gazette and The Weekly Mercury,* May 24, 1773

ANNA MARGARETTE FRELUHEN, a Dutch servant woman; runaway from JOHN POOL in Burlington; "aged about 22 years; well looking woman; black hair; swarthy complexion; pockmarked; cannot talk a word of English; she came in the *Brittania*, Capt. Peters, from Rotterdam two weeks ago"; advertised in *The Pennsylvania Journal and the Weekly Advertiser*, October 6 1773

ELIZABETH EDGWORTH, an indented servant girl; runaway from EDWARD HENDERSON living at the upper end of Hunterdon County; "tall and slim built; brown hair; she is suppose to be near or at Philadelphia"; advertised in *The Pennsylvania Gazette*, November 10, 1773

Was committed in New Castle gaol on suspicion of being a runaway, MARY MENTOR, belonging to WILLIAM KEE of New Jersey; short thick person; brown hair; red face; marked with the pox"; advertised by THOMAS PUSEY, Gaoler in *The Pennsylvania Gazette*, September 14, 1774

JENNIE, a Negro woman; runaway from MARK PREVOST, in Bergen County; "about 36 years of age; smart, active, and handy; rather lusty; has bad teeth and a small cast in one eye; she is likely to look upon; reads and writes; brought up in the house of the late Mr. SHOCKMAPLE of New London"; notice to ARCHIBALD CAMPBELL in Hackensack or THOMAS CLARKE, near New York; advertised in *The New York Journal or The General Advertiser*, November 10, 1774; advertised jointly with her husband as "MARK and JENNY, a Negro man and his wife" in *The New York Journal*, June 5, 1775 as being " smooth tongued and very artful; both are dressed as Indians"

SUSANNA YOUNG, a Dutch servant woman; sought by JOHN MASON and HUGH SHARP of Evesham, Burlington County; "about 21 years of age; a likely black haired woman; served her time with ABRAHAM ELDRIDGE of Evesham and was now free; left her 2 year old son with the Overseers of the Poor"; advertised in *The Pennsylvania Gazette,* June 21, 1775

CHRISTINA BERYON, a Dutch servant woman; runaway from DAVID COOPER of Glouster County; about 28 years of age; heavy made; in height rather above the middle size; has lost most of her single teeth; speaks broken English"; advertised in *The Pennsylvania Gazette,* June 21, 1775

HESTER CAVANAGH, an Irish servant girl; runaway from JOHN SHIELDS at Mount Holly; "about 18 years of age; about 5 feet high; stout build and looks remarkably innocent; has light brown hair; full grey eyes and a remarkable burn, which she got lately upon her right arm, near the elbow"; advertised in *The Pennsylvania Gazette,* February 19, 1777

SARAH M'GEE, an American born but of Irish descent servant woman, runaway from BARZILLAI COAT in Evesham Township, Burlington County; "aged about 23 years; about 5 feet, 7 inches high; very lusty made in proportion; has a cross on her right arm, put in with gun powder and the first two letters of her name and the date of the year; last seen with her mother who lives in Shippen Street, where it is supposed she is concealed"; advertised in *The Pennsylvania Gazette,* April 30, 1777

CHRISTIANNA GUNN, a Scotch servant lass; runaway from SAMUEL ROBBINS, living in Bibury; "aged about 16 years; 5 feet high; fresh complexion; long nose; dark brown hair; little eyes; broad shoulders; a little pitted with the small pox; supposedly gone to Philadelphia where her mother lives"; advertised in *The New Jersey Gazette,* April 1, 1778

SARAH [RACHAEL], a Mulatto slave; runaway from MORDECAI GIST; "aged about 34 years; lusty wench; had 6 year old son BOB; who has amazingly fair complexion and flaxen hair"; notice to BLAIR M'CLENACHAN of Philadelphia, Capt. BENJAMIN BROOKS of the 3rd Maryland regiment or to JAMES STERRET in Baltimore

DINAH, a Negro wench; runaway from BENJAMIN VAN CLEAVE, living in Maidenhead; "aged about 28 or 30 years; 5 feet, 6 or 7 inches high; black and very lusty; lately bought from

PARSON VAN ARSDALL at Springfield and has a brother with Colonel SCUDDER in Freehold"; give notice to Mr. PHILLIPS, innkeeper at Maidenhead or WILLIAM CRAB; advertised in *The New Jersey Gazette*, December 31, 1778

    MASSY DOYL, an apprentice girl; runaway from JOHN BARKLEY, living in Bedminster Township, Somerset County; "aged about 14 or 15 years; sandy complexion; brown hair; down look"; advertised in *The New Jersey Journal*, December 14, 1779

    MARIA [AMORITTA], a Negro wench, runaway from JOHN DUFFIELD, living in Philadelphia; "aged about 34 years; tall and well made; her face long and her features more regular than are common with her color; once lived with THOMAS LOWREY of Flemington in New Jersey; took with her female child named JANE, about 4 years old, well made, fat, round faced and lively"; advertised in *The New Jersey Gazette*, January 10, 1781

    HESTER, a Negro wench; runaway from ROBERT L HOOPER and ROBERT HOOPS, living in Trenton; "small. though well made; has a lively eye; bred in Carolina but has the manners of a West Indian slave"; advertised in *The New Jersey Gazette*, January 17, 1781

    AGNES BEAT, a Mulatto girl; runaway from ADAM VANHART; advertised in *The New Jersey Gazette*, February 7, 1781

    PHOEBE, a Negro woman; runaway from Mrs. WILSON, living in Hackett's Town, Sussex County; "aged about 40 years; has a child with her;" notice to Col. THOMPSON at Trenton, Mr. BRAY at Raritan Landing or Col. STEWART at headquarters, New Windsor; advertised in *The New Jersey Gazette*, April 25, 1781

    FANN, a Negro woman; runaway from SAMUEL YARDLEY living in Newtown, Buck's County; "aged about 18 or 19 years; short; thick wench; very black; thick lips; advertised in

The New Jersey Gazette, June 6, 1781

BET, a Negro woman; runaway from JACB PHILLIPS; aged about 21 years, took with her child of about 3 years; advertised in *The New Jersey Gazette,* July 11, 1781

ESCAPED PRISONERS

Escaped from Salem county gaol, REYNER JOHNSON; "a tall thin man; 6 feet, 6 inches tall;, aged about 22 years; short black hair; sometimes uses name of JOHN LEE, a bookbinder by trade and a servant to Mr. BRADFORD of Philadelphia"; advertised in *The American Weekly Mercury*, April 21, 1720

Escaped from Salem county gaol, THOMAS MEHEW, an Irish servant man; "short hair"; advertised in *The American Weekly Mercury*, April 21, 1720

Escaped from Salem county gaol, unnamed servant man belonging to REIGNER LOWDEN of Salem; "middle sized; down look; smooth face; advertised in *The American Weekly Mercury*, April 21, 1720

Escaped from Salem county gaol, HENRY COULTON; "a middle sized man; down look; black curled hair, very like a perriwig; a printer by trade and a servant to Mr. BRADFORD of Philadelphia"; advertised in *The American Weekly Mercury*, April 21, 1720

Escaped from Salem county gaol, HENRY BROWN; "a lusty tall man; aged about 30 years; light brown, short, curled hair; quick of speech; broke into house of BENJAMIN HOLM"; advertised in *The American Weekly Mercury*, September 8, 1720

Escaped from Salem county gaol, EDWARD HARDIN; "a thick, well set, short man; black hair"; advertised by WILLIAM GRIFFIN, High Sheriff in *The American Weekly Mercury*, September 14, 1720

Escaped from Monmouth county gaol, EDMUND MACKANDRES: "aged about 30 years; a lusty round shouldered man; dark brown hair; pale faced"; advertised in *The American Weekly Mercury*, September 27, 1722

Escaped from Monmouth county gaol, WILLIAM CONNAR; "aged about 24 years; a short, thin favored man; a little bandy legged; wears a wig; advertised in *The American Weekly Mercury*, September 27, 1722

Escaped from Monmouth county gaol, JOHN EMANS, a Dutchman; "aged about 30 years; well set; dark brown, bushy hair; ruddy complexion; Dutch accent; short, thin favored man; a little bandy legged; wears a wig; advertised in *The American Weekly Mercury*, September 27, 1722

THOMAS WRIGHT, taken as a fugitive; weaver by trade, who used to go by the name of THOMAS SMITH; says he was born in Maryland but has lived on Long Island and New England and "has traded from one end of the country to the other"; in prison on suspicion of horse theft; contact ANDREW BRADFORD; advertised in *The American Weekly Mercury*, August 31, 1727

Broke out of the gaol of the County of Burlington, JAMES CARVER; "tall man; bushy hair; a millwright by trade; aged about 40 years"; notice to JOHN ALLEN, SAMUEL BUSTILL AND RICHARD ELLISON, Esqrs.; advertised by Sheriff THOMAS HUNLOKE in *The American Weekly*, August 8, 1728

Broke out of the gaol of the County of Burlington, JOHN BRIGHTWELL; "short, thick, squat man; brown complexion; aged about 28 years; has his hair cut off; is mean in habit; by trade a tailor and stay maker"; notice to JOHN ALLEN, SAMUEL BUSTILL AND RICHARD ELLISON, Esqrs.; advertised by Sheriff THOMAS HUNLOKE in *The American Weekly*, August 8, 1728

JOSEPH ROBINS, of the County of Monmouth, Yeoman; escaped from the custody of WILLIAM NICHOLS, High Sheriff of the said county; "he being a tall slender man; thin faced; bottle nosed; light, lank hair and about thirty years of age"; advertised in *The Pennsylvania Gazette*, July 4th, 1729

ARISTOBLUS CHRISTOPHER escaped from the gaol of Burlington; "about thirty years of age; of a swarthy complexion; thick brown hair; about 5 feet, 8 inches high; shipwright by trade"; advertised in *The American Weekly Mercury*, October 16, 1729

MALATO JOHN, a Mulatto, from the gaol of Burlington; "about forty years of age; of a swarthy complexion; short brown hair; about six feet, two inches high and well set; soothed faced; he pretends to be house carpenter"; advertised in *The American Weekly Mercury*, October 16, 1729

JAMES BURNSIDES, Irish, escaped from the gaol in Burlington, THOMAS HUNLOCK, Sheriff; "about 26 years of age; of middle stature; sanguine complexion; short red hair, curled; has the brogue upon his tongue; a shoemaker by trade"; advertised in *The American Weekly Mercury*, December 16, 1729

ISAIAH FOLKS, escaped from the gaol in Burlington, THOMAS HUNLOKE, Sheriff; "about 30 years of age; about 5 foot, 10 inches high; pale face; round visage; black curled hair with a black beard; gray eyes"; advertised in *The New York Gazette*, July 13, 1730

Broke out of the Glouster gaol, WILLIAM CUNNINGHAM; "aged about 24 years; a lusty, well set fellow; light complexion; short brown hair"; advertised by SAMUEL HARRISON, Sheriff in *The Pennsylvania Gazette*, October 15, 1730

Broke out of the Glouster gaol, RICHARD GREY, a West Country man; "aged about 40-45 years; dark complexion; thin straight black hair; by trade a butcher"; advertised by SAMUEL HARRISON, Sheriff in *The Pennsylvania Gazette*, October 15, 1730

Broke out of the gaol at Trenton, JOHN LANGFORD, English man; "a tall and pretty thick man, lately followed butchering in or about Allenstown and Trenton; middle aged and lover of drink"; advertised by ENOCH ANDERSON, Jr., Sub-

Sheriff in *The Pennsylvania Gazette*, July 24, 1732

Broke out of the gaol at Trenton, EDWARD BUTLER; "of middle stature; short hair; drawling in his speech; pretends to be a shoemaker and turner by trade; has lived on Long Island; middle aged and lover of drink"; advertised by ENOCH ANDERSON, Jr., Sub-Sheriff in *The Pennsylvania Gazette*, July 24, 1732

Broke out of the gaol, at Trenton, WARREN BARR, an Irish man; "formerly kept the ferry next above Delaware Falls, on the Jersey side; by trade a cooper; of shorter stature; his hair cut; middle aged and lover of drink"; advertised by ENOCH ANDERSON, Jr., Sub-Sheriff in *The Pennsylvania Gazette*, July 24, 1732

Broke out of Burlington gaol, JOHN SMITH; "a turner by trade; about 24 years of age; of middle stature; short brown hair"; advertised by THOMAS HUNLOKE, Sheriff in *The American Weekly Mercury*, January 11, 1733

Broke out of Monmouth gaol, SIMON GILLMAN, a West Country man; "short well set fellow; sandy brown hair; red beard with hazel eyes; talks broadly; by trade a fuller"; advertised by JOHN WILLIAMS, Gaol-Keeper in *The Pennsylvania Gazette*, July 5, 1733

Broke out of Perth Amboy gaol, CORNELIUS SOLEM, late of New Brunswick; "aged about 40 years; a thick, swarthy, well set fellow; lame of one hand and wants the thumb of his right hand"; advertised by W. CROSBY, Sheriff in *The American Weekly Mercury*, January 22, 1734

Broke out of Bergen gaol, CORNELIUS MATTYSEN, of Hackensack; "aged 35 years or thereabouts; middle stature but somewhat inclining to fat"; advertised by PAR. PARMYTER, Sheriff in *The New York Weekly Journal*, June 10, 1734

Broke out of Bergen gaol, JACOB POWELSE, Mulatto of Hackensack; "aged 40 years or thereabouts; middle stature; lame in one of his fingers"; advertised by PAR. PARMYTER, Sheriff in *The New York Weekly Journal*, June 10, 1734

Broke out of the gaol of the County of Salem County, JOHN GALLOWAY, English servant man belonging to CORNELIUS TOBIT; "he is about 22 years of age; pretty tall and pretty slender; fresh colored; a Roman nose; wears his own hair and has a down look"; advertised by WILLIAM TUFFT, Sub-Sheriff in *The Pennsylvania Gazette*, April 22, 1736

Broke out of the gaol of Salem County, JOSEPH LEE; "a short thick man; dark complexion; black hair"; notice to JOHN HUNT, Sheriff; advertised in *The American Weekly Mercury*, October 21, 1736

Broke out of the gaol of Salem County, JOHN SAVAGE, an Irish man; "tall man; very short black dark hair; dark complexion; has a little of the brogue"; notice to JOHN HUNT Sheriff; advertised in *The American Weekly Mercury*, October 21, 1736

Broke out of the gaol of Glouster County, THOMAS GEOGBEGAN, an Irish man; "of middle stature; black hair lately cut off and wears a gray wig; pretends to be a schoolmaster; has a horse lock on one of his legs"; notice to WILLIAM TATUM, Sheriff; advertised in *The American Weekly Mercury*, November 4, 1736

Broke out of the gaol of Salem County, JAMES MacPETERS; "of middling stature; brown short curled hair; sandy complexion; pock fretten"; notice to JOHN HUNT Sheriff; advertised in *The American Weekly Mercury*, April 7, 1737

Broke out of the gaol of Salem County, HENRY ROBINSON; "a tall, pale faced man; wears dark brown hair"; notice to JOHN HUNT Sheriff; advertised in *The American Weekly Mercury*, April 7, 1737

Broke out of the gaol of Burlington County, JOHN

CRUES; " of middle stature; hollow mouthed, that is his nose and chin inclining to meet; a weaver by trade, but pretends to be a Quaker Preacher; he is supposed to have gone to New England to preach again where he has preached before"; notice to CHARLES TONKIN, Under Sheriff; advertised in *The Pennsylvania Gazette*, August 4, 1737

Broke out of Somerset gaol, GILBERT MILLER, Irish; "about 50 years of age; lame in one hand and arm; tall and thin; a shoemaker by trade and wears a leather apron"; advertised by Sheriff WILLIAM HOLLINSHEAD in *The Pennsylvania Gazette*, May 22, 1740

Broke out of Somerset gaol, EDWARD HOPPER, Long Island; "New York born; full faced; pretty thick and of a middle stature; a blacksmith by trade"; advertised by Sheriff WILLIAM HOLLINSHEAD in *The Pennsylvania Gazette*, May 22, 1740

Broke out of Somerset gaol EDWARD BONNEL; "New Jersey born; a lusty full faced young man; a blacksmith"; advertised by Sheriff WILLIAM HOLLINSHEAD in *The Pennsylvania Gazette*, May 22, 1740

Broke out of Somerset gaol, EVAN HARRY; "Pennsylvania born, of a middle stature; black complexion; short hair or wig; a saddler"; advertised by Sheriff WILLIAM HOLLINSHEAD in *The Pennsylvania Gazette*, May 22, 1740

BENJAMIN FARRINGTON; escaped from High Sheriff THOMAS HUNLOKE of the City of Burlington; "about 44 years of age; a short, thick, full faced man; with short light curled hair; is pretty full of talk; is a plaister by trade"; advertised in *The Pennsylvania Gazette*, April 29, 1742.

JOHN TOOL; escaped from High Sheriff THOMAS HUNLOKE of the City of Burlington; about 25 years of age; "a short thick man; with blackish curled hair; advertised in *The Pennsylvania Gazette*, April 29, 1742; a JOHN TOOL, described as an "Irish servant man; runaway from GEORGE MUNROW of

Evesham Township, Burlington county; a short well set fellow; with short dark brown hair and gray eyes" and advertised in *The American Weekly Mercury*, October 14, 1742.

TIMOTHY RYLEY; escaped from High Sheriff THOMAS HUNLOKE of the City of Burlington; "about 35 years of age; a pretty slim man; fair complexion; no hair"; advertised in *The Pennsylvania Gazette*, April 29, 1742.

JOHN LYCAN, a Swede; escaped from High Sheriff THOMAS HUNLOKE of the City of Burlington; "about 50 years of age; a short, well set man; with short brownish, straight hair"; advertised in *The Pennsylvania Gazette*, April 29, 1742.

WILLIAM BRITTON escaped by force of arms from Constable JOHN OPDIKE of Amwell; "BRITTON is an Irishman; aged about 25 years; a weaver by trade; supposed to wear his own hair of a sandy color; has light eyes"; advertised in *The Pennsylvania Gazette*, March 21, 1743

Broke out of the gaol of New Brunswick, PETER VANURDER; "a lusty tall man; a baker by trade"; advertised by JOHN DEARE, Sheriff in *The Pennsylvania Gazette*, June 23, 1743.

Broke out of the gaol of New Brunswick, LAWRENCE HORTWICK, a German; "short and thick with long hair; he has followed boating for a long time"; advertised by JOHN DEARE, Sheriff in *The Pennsylvania Gazette*, June 23, 1743

Broke out of Trenton gaol, JAMES JOHNSON; Irish, "lusty, strong built man about six feet high; of a fresh complexion and fair insinuating speech; right name is WHITE; had lately run from his bail and entered upon the *Dreadnought*, Capt. CUNNINGHAM, who, upon application, caused him to be set on shore and brought to Trenton gaol"; advertised by WILLIAM BROWN, Under Sheriff in *The Pennsylvania Gazette*, November 7, 1745

Broke out of the Salem gaol, JOHN RAMPOON of Salem; "5 foot, 9 inches high; poxed"

Broke out of Glouster gaol, HUGH COFFY; "5 feet, 10 inches high; house carpenter by trade; slim built and of a pale countenance; pock marked; long face; long chin and short dark hair"; advertised by FRANCIS HADDOCK, Under Sheriff in *The Pennsylvania Gazette*, February 24, 1747

Broke out of Burlington gaol, JEREMIAH CARPENTER, [*aka* AMOS FULLER] American born (New England); "committed for uttering counterfeit money; 6 feet high and pale complexion"; advertised by JOS. HOLLINSHEAD, Sheriff in *The New York Gazette, revived in the Weekly Post Boy*, October 12, 1747

Escaped from JOHN HOLME, Constable of the Town of Waterford in Glouster County, JAMES WILSON, an Englishman; "middle stature; dark bushy hair; thick lips and a round visage; taken in custody for abusing a servant and was found guilty of homicide by the coroner's inquisition for the same"; *advertised in The Pennsylvania Gazette*, December 12, 1747

Broke out of Burlington gaol, BENJAMIN MARFORD; "about 5 feet, 6 inches high; pale faced and black eyes"; advertised by JOS. HOLLINSHEAD, Esq. Sheriff in *The New York Gazette, revived in The Weekly Post Boy*, July, 24, 1749.

Broke out of Burlington gaol, DAVID DUNDORSE, a Scotch man; "about 6 feet high; well set; square shouldered; broad faced; pock marked and short curled brown hair; stole horse from CALEB SHINN"; advertised by JOS. HOLLINSHEAD, Esq. Sheriff in *The Pennsylvania Gazette*, November 2, 1749.

Broke out of Trenton gaol, WILLIAM TUTTLE, American born in Pennsylvania, "5 foot ,8 inches high; thin faced; sandy complexion; bushy hair; bred to farming; burnt on the hand with the letter "T" but hard to be seen"; advertised by JOHN ALLEN, Sheriff, in *The New York Gazette revived in the Weekly Post Boy*,

October 29, 1750

Broke out of Trenton gaol, JOSEPH WILSON [aka ABRAHAM TAYLOR] [aka GIBBONS], an Englishman; "about 5 feet, 7 inches high; of a black complexion and no hair on; he has been trying to learn the shoemaker's trade; fresh colored; round faced; has a sty under his right eye; burnt on the hand with the letter "T" but hard to be seen; about 30 years of age"; advertised by JOHN ALLEN, Sheriff, in *The New York Gazette revived in the Weekly Post Boy,* October 29, 1750

Runaway from his bail given by EBENEZER BROWN, an Irish man who calls himself WILLIAM HACKETT, but his correct name is BRIAN DORON of Glouster; "about 35 years of age; of middle stature; sandy complexion"; advertised in *The Pennsylvania Gazette,* November 1, 1750

Broke out of Monmouth gaol, JAMES WILSON, born in Monmouth County and a prisoner for debt; "about 23 years of age; 5 feet, 10 inches; thick; well set man; pretends to be a great horse jockey"; advertised by JOHN REDFORD, Sheriff, in *The Pennsylvania Gazette,* November 29, 1750

Broke out of Glouster gaol, DAVID PARK, an Irishman; " 6 feet high; committed for felony"; advertised by SAMUEL HARRISON, Sheriff, in *The Pennsylvania Gazette,* December 11, 1750

Broke out of Glouster gaol, HENRY BATE, an Englishman "5 feet, 10 inches high; well set; committed for felony; pale complexion and talks much about being a sailor"; advertised by SAMUEL HARRISON, Sheriff in *The Pennsylvania Gazette,* December 11, 1750

From the Burlington gaol, JOHN SMITH [PHILIP CANTLEN]; "6 feet high; slim; down looking fellow; dark complexion; slow of speech except when in drink and then very talkative; was a servant to THOMAS RAMBO of Waterford Township, Glouster County and is a deserter"; advertised by

THOMAS SHINN, Sheriff in *The Pennsylvania Gazette*, April 16, 1761

From the Essex County gaol, JOHN BARCLAY; "a short, chunky, well set fellow; of a sandy complexion; talks thick and palavering when in liquor which is often; an Irish man; about 50 years of age; a clothier by trade and has been long in New Jersey around Basking Ridge; forged document with his brother in-law's name, ANDREW ARMSTRONG, assisted by one ANDREW M'GOWN to escape; CATHERINE BARCLAY, his wife accompanied him; she is exceedingly pock marked; very brown; about 40 years of age but looks much older; a very neat woman; advertised by Sheriff JONATHAN HAMPTON and SYLVESTER COLER in *The Pennsylvania Gazette*, July 8, 1762

From the Essex County gaol, WILLIAM HAMILTON [Hambleton], an Irish man; "about 55 years of age; a stout, lusty, ill looking fellow; ill favored; dirty; slouching; much sun burnt; wig, seldom combed; took his 14 year old son and daughter with him in a cart bound for Susquehanna; is a butcher; has sore eyes; son is impudent; he is sheep thief; advertised by High Sheriff JONATHAN HAMPTON and SYLVESTER COLER in *The Pennsylvania Gazette*, July 8, 1762

Broke out of Salem gaol, MARTIN CORNETT; "about 22 years of age; well set; pale countenance; black hair, sometimes tied; advertised by JOSEPH BURROUGH, Sheriff, in *The Pennsylvania Journal*, July 14, 1763

Broke out of Salem gaol,, JOHN HARDING OTTWAY; "about 5 feet, 4 inches high; has a stoppage in his speech as if he had a great cold; wears bushy hair, somewhat sandy; 22 years of age; well set; pale countenance; black hair; sometimes tied; advertised by JOSEPH BURROUGH, Sheriff, in *The Pennsylvania Journal*, July 14, 1763

Broke out of the Somerset County, MICHAEL SULLIVAN; "a middle sized man; about 5 feet 5 or 6 inches high; short, brown hair with red beard"; advertised GEORGE REMER or WILLIAM MILLAN, gaoler in *The Pennsylvania Gazette*, August 11, 1763

Broke out of the Trenton gaol, JAMES BRAY; "about 5 feet, 9 inches high; short, black hair; marked with small pox; has a blemish in one eye; is much inclined to drink strong liquors"; advertised by GEORGE BROWN, Gaoler, in *The Pennsylvania Gazette*, September 1, 1763

Broke out of Trenton gaol, THOMAS FOWLER, a felon; "about 5 feet high; thick set; pock marked; pretends to be a Limner"; advertised GEORGE BROWN, Gaoler, in *The Pennsylvania Gazette*, October 6, 1763

Made his escape from the Constable of the Town of Deptford, Glouster County, JOHN BOAN; "about 5 feet, 6 inches high; well set; sandy complexion; speaks bold"; advertised by JOSIAH CHATTIN, Constable, in *The Pennsylvania Gazette*, November 10, 1763

Made his escape from the Constable of Penns Neck, in Salem County; "WILLIAM M'GROERTY; committed on suspicion of a felony; about 5 feet, 8 inches high; long black hair cued behind; a tailor by trade"; advertised by EDWARD MOORE, Constable, in *The Pennsylvania Journal*, November 17, 1763

WILLIAM FRAZIER, a Scotch man; 25 years of age; 5 feet, 7 inches; bushy brown hair

Made his escape from the Sheriff of Somerset County, JACOB TOSTBINDER; "American born, but High Dutch; cooper by trade; well built man; about 5 feet, 8 inches high; fair colored hair; red beard; pale face"; advertised by GEORGE REMER, Sheriff in *The New York Mercury*, January 23, 1764

Made his escape from Hunterdon gaol, SAMUEL PELTON; "a person of infamous character and a disturber of the peace in general; committed upon an accusation of forgery; aged about 30 years; about 5 feet, 6 or 7 inches tall; well built; pock broken; black eyes and short curled hair; has lost some of his upper fore teeth; has a bold, impudent countenance; a joiner by trade; advertised by SAMUEL TUCKER, Sheriff, in *The Pennsylvania Gazette*, January 30, 1764

Made his escape from Hunterdon gaol, JOHN MOORE; "a person of infamous character and a disturber of the peace in general; committed upon an accusation of forgery; aged about 25 years; about 5 feet, 5 or 6 inches tall; smooth face; black hair tied behind and sandy colored whiskers"; advertised by SAMUEL TUCKER, Sheriff, in *The Pennsylvania Gazette*, January 30, 1764

Made his escape from Glouster gaol, JOHN HOLLAND, an Irish man; "about 5 feet, 9 or 10 inches tall; wears his own black hair curled; is of a ruddy complexion; very low spoken"; advertised by JOHN CRAWFORD, Constable, in *The Pennsylvania Journal*, March 13, 1764

Made his escape from Salem gaol, JOHN VERNON; "a cooper by trade; about 5 feet, 10 inches tall"; advertised by EDWARD TEST, Sheriff, in *The Pennsylvania Gazette*, May 1, 1764

Made his escape from Kent County on the Delaware gaol, BENJAMIN ARROWSMITH; "about 5 feet, 10 inches tall; slender; usual place of abode is said to be in the Jerseys"; advertised in *The Pennsylvania Journal*, May 31, 1764

Made his escape from Somerset gaol, GEORGE BUCHELOW, American born; "about 5 feet, 9 inches tall; swarthy complexion; pock broken; black hair; speaks good English; born near South River; pretends to be an honest fellow"; advertised by QILLIAM MILLAN, sub sheriff and gaoler in *The New York Mercury*, June 4, 1764

Made his escape from Monmouth county gaol, SAMUEL EDWARDS; "a thick well set man; a tailor by trade; wears his own hair"; advertised by JOHN TAYLOR, Sheriff, in *The Pennsylvania Journal*, June 7, 1764

Made his escape from Salem County gaol, JOHN CLEAVER; "5 feet, 8 inches high; pock marked; has brown hair; tailor by trade and plays on the fiddle; is very talkative and much addicted to drink"; advertised by JOHN BUDD, Sheriff, in *The Pennsylvania GAZETTE*, August 23, 1764

Made his escape from Burlington gaol, ROBERT HOLLAND; "about 5 feet, 3 or 4 inches tall; brown complexion; dark brown hair; has a remarkable lump or wart on his right thumb and has lost most of his fore teeth; a breeches maker by trade"; advertised by DANIEL ELLIS, Sheriff, in *The Pennsylvania Gazette*, August 30, 1764

Made his escape from the Perth Amboy gaol, JOHN HUGHES; "about 5 feet, 5 inches tall; short, thick; square shouldered man; has sore eyes and has lost one or two of his fore teeth; is supposed he went away with JAMES MOORE, a servant to PHILIP KERNEY, it is thought he has gone to Brandywine, Chester County or towards Gunpowder, Baltimore County; by occupation a ditcher and laborer"; advertised by JAMES BROOKS, Sheriff of the City of Perth Amboy in *The Pennsylvania Journal*, September 6, 1764

Made his escape from the Perth Amboy gaol, JAMES MOORE; a servant to PHILIP KERNEY; "a tall spare young fellow, about 24 years old; long black hair, tied behind; is supposed he went away with JOHN HUGHES to Brandywine, Chester County or towards Gunpowder, Baltimore County"; advertised by JAMES BROOKS, Sheriff of the City of Perth Amboy in *The Pennsylvania Journal*, September 6, 1764

CHRISTOPHER BURNS; an Irish man; aged 18 years; 5 feet, 5 inches high

Broke out of Cape May County gaol, JOHN BUCK; aged about 50 years; lusty man; took his wife and child with him and went to Delaware Bay and Lewes"; advertised by SYLVANUS TOWNSEND, Sheriff, in *The Pennsylvania Gazette*, June 19, 1766

Broke out of Somerset gaol, Doctor ANANIAS RANDALL, American born in Long Island; "aged about 25 years; 5 feet, 6 inches high; dark brown hair; commonly wears it cued; fair skin; black eyes"; advertised by JOB STOCKTON, High Sheriff, and CORNELIUS LOTT, Sub Sheriff in *The Pennsylvania Gazette,* June 19, 1766

Broke out of Somerset gaol, ROBERT MOUSTON, a Scotch born tailor; "5 feet, 6 inches high; fair skin; black hair"; advertised by SAMUEL BREWER, gaoler, in *The Pennsylvania Gazette,* June 19, 1766

Broke out of Salem gaol, JOSEPH BEESLEY; "aged about 25 years; tall, slim man; fair complexion; black hair"; advertised by CHRISTOPHER SMITH, Constable, in *The Pennsylvania Gazette,* June 26, 1766

Broke out of Salem gaol, ANDREW KING, born in Scotland; "about 5 feet, 5 inches high; fair complexion; stole clothing from NATHAN BOY's house on the Salem road"; advertised in *The Pennsylvania Journal,* September 11, 1766

Absconded from his bail, SAMUEL EVANS, an Irishman; about 22 years of age; 5 feet, 9 or 10 inches high; somewhat slender built; fresh colored; a little bit freckled on his hands and face; pock marked; reddish hair; speaks on the Scotch Irish order"; notice to DANIEL ELLIS, Esq. at Burlington or JOHN FORKER; advertised in *The Pennsylvania Gazette,* September 18, 1766

Runaway from his bail, DAVID DAVIS; "about 28 years of age; 5 feet, 9 inches high; pock mocked; a thick, well set fellow; wears his hair tied behind; a talkative fellow; apt to tell of what he has done and what he has seen; pretends to be a house carpenter"; reward paid by MICHAEL POWER, ROBERT WOOD, WILLIAM HAMPTON; advertised in *The Pennsylvania Gazette,* October 2, 1766

Broke out of the common gaol at Morris Town, TONY, a Negro man belonging to JOHN VAN DORIN; "lately burnt his master's house; is 5 feet, 6 inches high; pretty well proportioned; is a likely, smart fellow"; advertised by JOCOB FORD, Jr., Sheriff of Morris Town; advertised in *The Pennsylvania Journal*, October 16, 1766

Made his escape from Trenton gaol; JAMES M'DANIEL; "aged about 23 years; fond of liquor; short, brown curled hair; much marked with small pox; speaks very low; recently come into country"; advertised by GEORGE BROWN, Gaoler in *The Pennsylvania Gazette*, November 6, 1766

Made his escape from Trenton gaol; RICHARD WARREN, committed for debt; "aged about 26 years; 5 feet, 3 inches high; fond of liquor; light brown curled hair; is a pretty likely fellow but has a pale look; pretends to show the sleight of hand and has been in the army'; advertised by GEORGE BROWN, Gaoler in *The Pennsylvania Gazette*, November 6, 1766

Made his escape from Glouster gaol, JAMES ABIT; "aged about 40 years; 5 feet, 6 inches high; pale complexion; marked with small pox; by profession a house carpenter"; advertised by SAMUEL BLACKWOOD, Sheriff, in *The Pennsylania Gazette*, November 20, 1766

Made his escape from gaol of Philadelphia; DAVID SMITH; "aged about 36 years; 5 feet, 5 inches high; dark, thin visage; his hair lately cut off; lately kept a store in Reckless Town, New Jersey; by trade a shipwright"; advertised by WILLIAM PARR, Sheriff in *The Pennsylvania Journal*, December 18, 1766

JOHN GALLAHAN [*aka* M'DANIEL, *aka* READ]; a tanner by trade; 18 or 19 years of age

Escaped from the Cumberland County gaol, WILLIAM HAWKINS; committed for debt; "middle age and stature; wears his natural hair which is dark colored and is tied behind; was of late an innkeeper in the City of Philadelphia"; advertised by THEOPHILUS ELMER, Sheriff in *The Pennsylvania Journal*, January 12, 1767

Broke out of the gaol in the Town of Elizabeth; JOHN HARDY, American born; "about 26 years of age; short, but well set; fresh complexion; somewhat Roman nose; has a short neck and dark hair; by trade a fuller"; advertised by ABRAHAM CLARK, Sheriff, in *The New York Mercury*, May 18, 1767

Broke out of the gaol in the Town of Elizabeth; THOMAS GORDON, Scotch born; "about 40 years of age; 6 feet high; spare and raw boned; long visaged; hair of a light or sandy colored; by trade a school teacher"; advertised by ABRAHAM CLARK, Sheriff, in *The New York Mercury*, May 18, 1767

Broke out of the gaol in the Town of Elizabeth; CHARLES GARRET; advertised by ABRAHAM CLARK, Sheriff in *The New York Mercury*, May 18, 1767

Broke out of Morris County Gaol, ALEXANDER M'CORMICH, Irishman; "about 40 years of age; 5 feet, 10 inches high; with short black curled hair; has much of the brogue on his tongue; pretends to play on the bag pipes and is suppose to have gone to New York as his wife is there"; advertised by DANIEL COOPER, Sheriff in *The New York Mercury*, July 27, 1767

Made his escape from the gaol of Cumberland County, FREDERICK OTTO; "a slender fellow; thin faced and much marked with the pox; wears his own hair long and tied behind; he has for some time practiced physic in Cumberland County"; advertised by THEO. ELMER, Sheriff, in *The Pennsylvania Journal* October 8, 1767

Made his escape from the Sheriff of Sussex County, EDWARD DOUGHTY; "40 years of age; reddish hair; 5 feet, 9 inches; fair complexion; well built; formerly lived near Walpack on Delaware and is very much given to drinking strong liquor"; advertised in *The Pennsylvania Gazette*, October 8, 1767

Escaped from the Monmouth Gaol, NICHOLAS WILLIAMS, Dutch born; "about 5 feet and a half high; well set; of a swarthy complexion; wears his own straight brown hair;

suppose to be at Germantown where his mother lives or at CHARLES READ, Esq's ironworks"; advertised by THOMAS LEONARD, Sheriff, in *The Pennsylvania Chronicle*, February 1, 1768

Broke out of the Gaol of Glouster County, HUGH WILSON, Irish born; "aged about 30 years; 5 feet, 3-4 inches high; well set; black hair; marked with the small pox; pleasant countenance; has lived lately in Chester and New Castle Counties; by trade a tanner; much inclined to strong liquor and apt to be intoxicated"; advertised by SAMUEL BLACKWOOD, Sheriff, in *The Pennsylvania Gazette*, February 11, 1768

Escaped from the Glouster gaol, DAVID COCHRAN, an Irish man; "about 5 feet, 6 inches high; aged about 25 years; red short hair; freckled face; fuller by trade; has lived in Allentown and Haddonfield; much inclined to strong liquor and apt to be intoxicated"; advertised by Sheriff SAMUEL BLACKWOOD in *The Pennsylvania Gazette*, February 11, 1768; re advertised by JOSIAH CHATTIN, Gaoler in *The Pennsylvania Gazette*, October 20, 1768 adding "long visaged; sandy beard and eyebrows; has had the bridge of his nose cut through";

From the Morris County gaol, JOHN SMITH, an Irish man; "about 45 years of age; 5 feet, 10 inches high; long visaged; hair somewhat gray"; advertised by DANIEL COOPER, Jr., Sheriff in *The New York Gazette or Weekly Post Boy*, October 10, 1768

Escaped from the Sussex gaol, WILLIAM DAVIDSON, debtor; "small man; yellowish hair and is somewhat baldheaded"; advertised by High Sheriff JACOB STARN in *The New York Journal or General Advertiser*, March 31, 1768

Escaped from the Sussex gaol, EBENEZER DRAKE, debtor; "a small man with black hair somewhat curled"; advertised by High Sheriff JACOB STARN in *The New York Journal or General Advertiser*, March 31, 1768

Escaped from the Sussex gaol, JOHN SCANTLING, an

Irish servant man belonging to DAVID GOLD, a stout, lusty fellow with black hair; loves drinking and seems fond of the water; it is supposed he will endeavor to get to sea; advertised by High Sheriff JACOB STARN in *The New York Journal or General Advertiser,* March 31, 1768

Escaped from the Sussex gaol, THOMAS BEALIE, an Englishman; "small man; large eyes; says he knows a Mr. HIGGINS in [New York] city"; advertised by High Sheriff JACOB STARN in *The New York Journal or General Advertiser*, March 31, 1768; subsequently described as THOMAS BEAL; "35 years of age; 5 feet, 6 inches; light colored hair tied behind; remarkable large full blue eyes; advertised in *The Pennsylvania Gazette*, April 21, 1768

Escaped from the Somerset gaol, PETER GRAHAM, an Irish man; counterfeiter; "about 5 feet, 10 inches high; thick set fellow; talks broad; black hair; fair complexion; weaver by trade"; advertised by his victims, JOHN COOPER, HUGH CALWELL, THOMAS BURGIE in *The New York Gazette or Weekly Post Boy*, May 23, 1768

From the Trenton gaol, JACOB HOOVER [JACOB MATTHEWS]; "5 feet, 11 inches high; well built; speaks French and High Dutch; but indifferent English"; advertised by GEORGE BROWN, gaoler in *The Pennsylvania Gazette*, September 1, 1768

From the gaol for Chester county, ROBERT SCOTT; "about 24 years of age; 5 feet, 9 inches high; full faced; pock pitted; has light brown hair; apt to swear and get drunk; very quarrelsome; generally makes his home at one RALSON's near Newark"; advertised by JOSEPH THOMAS, Constable in *The Pennsylvania Gazette*, September 8, 1768

From the gaol for Chester County, ANDREW CRAWFORD, an Irish man; "about 25 years of age; 5 feet, 11 inches high; stoop shouldered; pock pitted; pale faced; has black hair tied behind; apt to swear and get drunk; very quarrelsome; generally makes his home at one RALSON's near Newark";

advertised by JOSEPH THOMAS, Constable in *The Pennsylvania Gazette*, September 8, 1768

From the Perth Amboy gaol, CHARLES LEE, English born mulatto man; "5 feet, 9 inches high; slim built; has a scar on one side of his nose and wears his own hair; watch maker by trade"; advertised by NATHANIEL HEARD in *The New York Gazette or Weekly Mercury*, September 19, 1768

From the Glouster County gaol, HENRY BIDDLE; "about 45 years of age; 5 feet, 10 inches high; straight hair; dark complexion; slim built and has a sour look"; advertised by JOSIAH CHATTIN, gaoler, in *The Pennsylvania Gazette*, September 29, 1768

From the Morris County gaol, JOHN HARBOR, an Irish man; "a likely young fellow; 5 feet, 3 inches high; has the letter "D" marked on one of his hands with gun powder"; advertised by DANIEL COOPER, Jr. , Sheriff in *The New York Gazette or Weekly Post Boy,* October 10, 1768

Made his escape from Glouster gaol, PATRICK NEWLIN, an Irish man; "aged about 34 years; 5 feet, 6 or 7 inches high; sandy complexion; straight sandy hair; flat broad face; a peeked nose; marked with small pox; by trade a soldier; very apt to get drunk"; advertised by JOSIAH CHATTIN, Gaoler in *The Pennsylvania Gazette*, October 20, 1768

Made his escape from Glouster gaol, WILEY WOOD; "aged about 21 years; 5 feet, 8 inches high; round faced; black straight hair; dark complexion; has a hardy countenance; well set; lisps in his talk and drinks no rum"; advertised by JOSIAH CHATTIN, Gaoler in *The Pennsylvania Gazette*, October 20, 1768

Made his escape from JOSEPH GALPIN and JOHN GREEN, one WILLIAM GREEN, a prisoner for theft, an English man by birth and a fuller by trade; "slender, middle sized man"; advertised in *The New York Journal or General Advertiser*, November 17, 1768

Escaped from the Gaol at Mill Stone in Somerset County, THOMAS STILES; "under sentence of death; well set young fellow; about 20 years of age and 5 feet, 6 inches high; has black hair and a swarthy complexion"; advertised by ROBERT STOCKTON, Sheriff, in *The New York Gazette or Weekly Post Boy*, December 26, 1768

Broke out of the Gaol of Glouster County, ROBERT JONES, Irish born; "aged about 30 years; 6 feet; strong made; has a rugged look; has a large black beard and short black curled hair; round shouldered and stoops in his walk; has a remarkably sore leg; was jailed for house burglary and is galled about the ankles for being ironed; very fond of strong drink"; advertised by JOSEPH HUGG, Sheriff, in *The Pennsylvania Gazette*, November 9, 1769

Was committed in Jamaica Gaol in Queen's County, New York on suspicion of being an escaped prisoner from Morris County gaol; JOHN SMITH, notice given to DANIEL COOPER, Jr., Sheriff of Morris County by SAMUEL SMITH, Esq.; advertised in *The New York Gazette and Weekly Mercury*, January 16, 1769

Absconded from his bail, MATTHEW JOHNSON; "of a fair complexion; 5 feet, 10 or 11 inches high; much give to drink and stoops a little in his walk

Made his escape from ROBERT MAGEE, living near Cranberry, DAVID LINDSEY; arrested for theft; "thin; pale visaged man; has long brown hair; gray eyes; pitted with small pox; letters "D.L." tattooed on his hand; has pass from Justices of the Peace SKILTON and EMBLY of New Jersey"; advertised in *The New York Gazette and Weekly Mercury*, February 20, 1769

Made his escape from THOMAS NORRIS, Constable, living in Prince Town, JAMES KEARNEY; "a well built fellow; about 5 feet, 9 inches high; short, black hair and fresh colored"; advertised in *The Pennsylvania Journal*, May 18, 1769

Made his escape out of the prison in Trenton,

CORNELIUS BENNET; "about 23 years of age; a stout well built fellow; 5 feet, 8 inches or thereabouts; black complexion; short black hair; of a down look; large gray eyes with a remarkable degree of white in them; a short face; his nose rather long and rising; has lost one or more of his teeth in his upper jaw; speaks low Dutch; very talkative and fond of liquor; convicted of horse stealing; feared that he will join a gang on the frontiers"; advertised by JOHN BARNES, Sheriff in *The Pennsylvania Gazette*, August 10, 1769

DR. THOMAS OGLE, an Irish man; "5 feet, 6-7 inches; pitted from the pox; given to liquor and, when in drink, talks much of his skill in Physic and Surgery; has had one of his legs broken"

WILLIAM YOUNG; 20 years of age; middle stature; a tailor by trade

DESERTERS

THOMAS RYMER, an Englishman; deserted from American Regiment of Foot, commanded by WILLIAM GOOCH and enlisted in West Jersey by ANTHONY PALMER; "5 foot, 7 inches high; fair complexion with light short hair; well set; talks much of his strength; worked lately about Trenton and, sometimes since, Cape May in slatting and sawing"; advertised in *The Pennsylvania Gazette*, July 22, 1742

THOMAS FURY from North Ireland; deserted from American Regiment of Foot, commanded by WILLIAM GOOCH and enlisted in West Jersey by ANTHONY PALMER; "about 21 years of age; 5 foot, 10 inches high; a laborer; well set; fair complexion with very fair eye brows and grey eyes; much pockfretten"; advertised in *The Pennsylvania Gazette*, July 22, 1742

JOHN JOHNSON; a Jersey Man; "about 30 years of age; round visage; six feet high; cast with one eye"; advertised in *The Boston Weekly Post Boy*, December 3, 1744

Deserted from Capt. NATHANIEL RICHARD'S Company of Foot, JOHN COX, living in Basken-Ridge; "a tall fellow with bushy hair; aged about 40 years"; advertised in *The New York Evening Post*, September 8, 1746

Deserted from Capt. NATHANIEL RICHARD'S Company of Foot, MARTIN PALMER; "by trade a shoe maker; 5 feet, 8"; advertised in *The New York Evening Post*, November 24, 1746

Deserted from Capt. NATHANIEL RICHARD'S Company of Foot, HENDRICK SICKELS; "kept tavern formerly in Freehold; about 5 feet, 9 inches"; advertised in *The New York Evening Post*, November 24, 1746

Deserted from Capt. NATHANIEL RICHARD'S Company of Foot, JOHN STILLWILL; "a well set likely fellow; when he talks, lisps pretty much; kept the ferry formerly at the Narrows";

advertised in *The New York Evening Post*, November 24, 1746

TERENCE MULFORD; Deserter; Irish; "5 foot, 6 inches in height; short, brown hair; poxed; by trade a weaver

ALEXANDER DANE; Deserter

DAVID FITZRANDOLPH, Deserter; American born in New Jersey; "26 years of age; 5 foot, 10 inches tall; long dark hair; stoops when he walks

THOMAS COOK, Deserter; American born in New Jersey; 26 years of age; 5 feet, 9 inches tall; well made man

BARTHOLMEW HALL, Deserter; American born in New Jersey; 17 years of age; 5 feet, 7 inches tall; a riddle maker by trade

Deserted from the New Jersey Regiment, commanded by Col. PETER SCHUYLER, Capt. NATHANIEL RUSCO's Company, HENRY DAVIS, "by trade a turner and has formerly kept school at a place called Short Hills; about 5 feet, 10 inches high; slender; walks very upright; is very sprightly and active; of a fair complexion; his nose somewhat flattened at the end; sharp chin; is about 22 years of age"; advertised in *The New York Gazette*, July 21, 1755

Deserted from the New Jersey Regiment, commanded by Col. PETER SCHUYLER, Capt. NATHANIEL RUSCO's Company, FRANCIS BRADLEY; advertised in *The New York Gazette*, July 21, 1755

Deserted from the New Jersey Regiment, commanded by Col. PETER SCHUYLER, Capt. NATHANIEL RUSCO's Company, ALEXANDER M'KINE; advertised in *The New York Gazette*, July 21, 1755

Deserted from the New Jersey Regiment, commanded by Col. PETER SCHUYLER, Capt. NATHANIEL RUSCO's Company, JOHN STEWART; advertised in *The New York*

Gazette, July 21, 1755

Deserted from the New Jersey Regiment, commanded by Col. PETER SCHUYLER, Capt. NATHANIEL RUSCO's Company, WILLIAM CARR; advertised in *The New York Gazette,* July 21, 1755

Deserted from Capt. HERBERT's Company, Fourth Battalion, 62nd Regiment of foot, in Burlington, called the Royal Americans; THOMAS CAMPBELL, soldier; "about 18 years of age; 5 foot, three and ½ inches high; has brown hair and face and is pretty much marked with the smallpox"; apply to Lieutenant MACKEY at Widow ULRICK in Second Street, Philadelphia, near the George Tavern"; advertised in *The Pennsylvania Gazette,* February 10, 1757

Deserted from Captain POLSON's 44th Regiment, EDWARD SMITH, a Scottish born soldier; "36 years of age; about 5 foot, nine inches tall; fair complexion; by trade a shoemaker; has his tools with him; he wants one or two of his fore teeth; advertised in *The Pennsylvania Journal,* February 17, 1757

Deserted from Lieutenant COWART of the 48th Regiment of Foot WILLIAM WILSON, soldier; "between 34 and 35 years of age; about 5 foot, 4 inches high; his hair near of a black color; well set; gray eyes; wide mouth; a large round forehead; thick legs; walks well and upright and looks a little wrinkled in the face; is of a yellow complexion"; advertised in *The Pennsylvania Gazette,* March 24, 1757

Deserted from a recruiting party, ROBERT AENSWORTH, an Irish soldier; "brown complexion; about 27 years of age; 5 foot, 8 inches high; served his time with Mr. COXE in Trenton; taken up a deserter at RICHARD MAYBURTY's and had a pair of handcuffs put on, but escaped; was later seen on ferry to Pennsylvania side"; apply to PETER VAN BUSCURK, near the Union Iron Works or to JOHN POLSON; advertised in *The Pennsylvania Journal,* March 31, 1757

Deserted from THOMAS SHAW'S Company of New Jersey Provincials, JOHN THOMAS, born in Wales; "5 foot, 4 inches high; his hair is light brown; about 21 years of age; talks fast and is apt to stammer in his speech; he is very apt to crow when in liquor; it is supposed he went towards Lancaster, Pennsylvania"; advertised in *The Pennsylvania Gazette*, May 19, 1757

Deserted from THOMAS SHAW'S Company of New Jersey Provincials JAMES DAY, an American born soldier; "5 foot, 8 inches high; light brown hair which curls; fair complexion"; advertised in *The Pennsylvania Gazette*, May 19, 1757

Deserted from Cape May Regiment, HENRY HARTMAN; "a short man; sandy complexion; red beard; pretty much pox marked; his nose flat in the middle"; give notice Lieutenant SAMPSON HAWK; advertised in *The Pennsylvania Gazette*, September 1, 1757

Deserted from the Recruiting Company of the 22nd Regiment, commanded by Ensign BRERTON, JOHN WOOTON, Corporal; "dark complexion; broad; well made; 32 years of age; 5 feet, 8 inches tall"; advertised in *The Pennsylvania Journal*, February 2, 1758

Deserted from the Recruiting Company of the 44th Regiment of Foot, JAMES DICKENSON; "of a remarkable florid complexion and clean made; assumes the dialect and behavior of a Quaker; 5 feet, 10 inches tall"; advertised in *The Pennsylvania Gazette*, March 30, 1758

Deserted from the forces of the Lower counties in Delaware, Captain RICHARD WELLS's Company, RICHARD GRANT, American born, born at Squan, "a laborer; aged about 24 years; 5 feet, 6 inches high; fair complexion; brown hair; well set; suspected to have gone to Maurice river in West New Jersey"; advertised in *The Pennsylvania Gazette*, May 11, 1758

Deserted from JOSEPH ELLIS' Company of the New

Jersey regiment, WILLIAM ALLEN, West Country born; "5 feet, 7 inches high; dark complexion; has a hair mole on one of his cheeks"; advertised in *The Pennsylvania Gazette*, May 18, 1758

Deserted from JOSEPH ELLIS' Company of the New Jersey regiment, JOHN HANNA, an Irishman; "5 feet, 5 inches high; dark complexion; bushy hair; large nose and thick lips; advertised in *The Pennsylvania Gazette*, May 18, 1758

Deserted from Capt. CHARLES GARRAWAYS'S Company of the First Battalion of the Pennsylvania Regiment; JONATHAN HILL, New Jersey born; "6 feet high"; advertised in *The Pennsylvania Gazette*, June 15, 1758

Deserted from Capt. CHARLES GARRAWAYS'S Company of the First Battalion of the Pennsylvania Regiment; JOHN MILLER, New England born; "5 feet, 7 inches high"; advertised in *The Pennsylvania Gazette*, June 15, 1758

Deserted from Capt. CHARLES GARRAWAYS'S Company of the First Battalion of the Pennsylvania Regiment; BARTEMIUS PACK, American born; "5 feet, 10 inches high"; advertised in *The Pennsylvania Gazette*, June 15, 1758

Deserted from Capt. CHARLES GARRAWAYS'S Company of the First Battalion of the Pennsylvania Regiment; JOSEPH M'MAHON, New Jersey born; "6 feet high"; advertised in *The Pennsylvania Gazette*, June 15, 1758

Deserted from the recruiting party of Captain SKEY, WILLIAM ROBERTSON; English born; "aged about 30 years; 5 feet, 7 inches; dark brown complexion; a laborer; gray eyes; slender made; a great talker"

Deserted from Captain BARNARD's Company of the New Jersey Regiment, a certain PETER BENNET; "about 22 years of age; about 5 feet, 3 inches high; a sailor"; advertised in *The Pennsylvania Journal*, May 10, 1759

Deserted from Captain WILLIAM M'DONALD Company of the New Jersey Regiment, a certain JOHN M'DERMONT; "about 5 feet, 10 inches high; has a sore leg; has a wife in Chester County"; advertised *The New York Mercury*, May 14, 1759

Deserted from Captain WILLIAM M'DONALD's Company of the New Jersey Regiment, a certain SAMUEL WEST; "about 5 feet, 5 inches high; dark complexion and has black eyes; said to have a wife in Burks County"; advertised *The New York Mercury*, May 14, 1759

Deserted from Captain WILLIAM M'DONALD's Company of the New Jersey Regiment, a certain WILLIAM WATTS; "about 5 feet, 4 inches high; well set; has been a sailor"; advertised *The New York Mercury,* May 14, 1759

Deserted from a recruiting party of the Pennsylvanians, DANIEL BRAYTON; "aged about 30 years; 5 feet, 3 inches high; brown complexion; black hair"; lived near Haddonfield; advertised by THOMAS LOYD, Lieut. Colonel in *The Pennsylvania Gazette*, September 6, 1759

Deserted from Lieutenant SHUTE of the New Jersey Regiment, JOHN RINGAR, a German servant man, living in Greenwich at Cumberland County; "about 26 years of age; 5 feet, 3 inches high; speaks pretty good English; commonly called "Prussia" because of his country of birth and is supposed to have gone toward Readingtown in New Jersey"; advertised in *The Pennsylvania Gazette*, March 18, 1762

Deserted from Captain ELIAS DAYTON's Company of the New Jersey Regiment, a certain JOHN GRENWOOD; "about 5, feet 9 inches high; likely well built fellow; something round shouldered and lightly pitted with the pox"; advertised in *The Pennsylvania Journal*, April 15, 1762

Deserted from the New York Troops, commanded by Maj. WILLIAM W. HOGAN, of RICHARD REA'S Company; ABRAHAM SUTHARD; "aged 30 years; 5 feet, 10 inches high;

born in New Jersey"; advertised in *The New York Mercury*, May 14, 1764

Deserted from the New York Troops, commanded by Maj. WILLIAM W. HOGAN, of Capt. DAWSON's Company; ROGER GIDDONS; " born in New Jersey; 5 feet, 8 inches high; light colored hair; blue eyes"; advertised in *The New York Mercury*, May 14, 1764

Deserted from the New York Troops, commanded by Maj. WILLIAM W. HOGAN, of Capt. WHITE's Company; OLIVER WESTOVER; "by trade a blacksmith; born in New Jersey; 5 feet, 9 inches high; fair complexion; short black hair; round visage; brown eyes"; advertised in *The New York Mercury*, May 14, 1764

Deserted from the Pennsylvania Regiment, from Capt. JOHN WEBB's Company; JOHN RUSSEL; born in New Jersey; "5 feet, 6 inches high; about 22 year of age; brown complexion; a cooper by trade"; advertised in *The Pennsylvania Gazette*, July 9, 1764

Deserted from the Pennsylvania Regiment, from Capt. JOHN WEBB's Company; DANIEL COLE, born in new Jersey; 5 feet, 6 inches high; about 20 year of age; brown complexion"; advertised in *the Pennsylvania Gazette*, July 9, 1764

Deserted WILLIAM SIMPSON; "aged 19; 5 foot, 8 inches high; short brown hair; blue eyes; fifer; born in the regiment; straight and well made; thin visage; fair complexion; large nose; large limbs; speaks short; pretty much an Irish accent; large hole or hollow on top of skull from fracture at Castle Island; plays well flute, fife and a little on violin and French horn"; advertised in *The New York Gazette or Weekly Post Boy*, September 10, 1770

Deserted from His Majesty's 29th Regiment of Foot, JAMES GORDON, born in Enniskillen, Ireland; "aged about 21 years; 6 feet high; swarthy complexion; dark brown hair; hazel eyes; pock marked; by trade a laborer; round small visage; straight and well made; an old deserter and was in the Royal Americans";

advertised in *The New York Gazette and Weekly Mercury*, August 5, 1771

Deserted from His Majesty's 29th Regiment of Foot, JOHN LOVELL, born in Enniskillen, Ireland; "aged about 27 years; 5 feet, 10 and 3/4 inches high; brown complexion; brown hair; light grey eyes; a little pock marked; by trade a laborer; long and full visage; stoop shouldered; stout made"; advertised in *The New York Gazette and Weekly Mercury*, August 5, 1771

Deserted from His Majesty's 29th Regiment of Foot, JOHN GIBBONS; "aged about 27 years; 5 feet, 11 and 3/4 inches high; ruddy complexion; brown hair; light grey eyes; thin visaged and much carbuncled straight and light made"; advertised in *The Pennsylvania Journal*, September 5, 1771

Deserted from His Majesty's 29th Regiment of Foot, THOMAS JONES, was born in town of Burrisakane, county of Tipperary in Ireland; "aged about 21 years; 6 feet and 1/4 inches high; fresh complexion; dark brown hair; light grey eyes; long visage; a large mole on his left cheek; heavy limbed; in kneed, turns in his toes when he walks; a little pitted with the small pox and well made"; advertised in *The Pennsylvania Journal*, September 5, 1771

Deserted from His Majesty's 29th Regiment of Foot, JOHN HART, born in the city of Limerick in Ireland; "aged about 22 years; 5 feet, 10 and 1/4 inches high; pale complexion; light brown hair, inclined to curl; dark brown eyes; thin but round visage; straight and well made"; advertised in *The Pennsylvania Journal*, September 5, 1771

The following deserted during 1776

JOHN KEANE; "5 foot 10, inches high; long black hair; poxed; stout and well made; by trade a sailor"

DANIEL ROGAN; "5 foot, 6 inches high; long black hair;

smooth faced; by trade a sailor"

WILLIAM KENNEDY; "5 feet, 20 inches high; poxed; stout and thick boned; speech impediment; freckled; by trade a sailor"

HENRY DRAIN; "4 feet, 6 inches tall; smooth faced; sailor by trade

ANDREW BOYD; "5 feet, 10 inches high; smooth faced; large nose; by trade a sailor"

JOSEPH MILES, English born; "5 feet, 8 inches high; fair; carbuncles; hazel eyes; by trade a gardener; well made, straight man"

THOMAS DUNN, Irish; "30 years of age; 5 foot, 8 inches high; black hair; strong; well built; very fond of getting drunk and very abusive when he is so; dark complexion"

EPHRAIM CRAMNER, American born; "30 years of age; 5 foot, 9 inches tall; black hair; tolerably well built; has been sick for some considerable time and looks thin in the face"

LEVI BISHOP, American born; "23 years of age; 5 foot, 7 inches; brown complexion"

JACOB INGMAN; "22 years of age; 5 feet, 8 or 9 inches; light hair; pale complexion; gray eyes"

JOHN PETTERSON; 22 years of age; 5 feet, 10 inches high; dark hair; dark complexion; blue eyes; very active and civil and was little suspected of desertion"

JOHN CLARKE; "6 foot high; black curled hair; stutters; nail maker by trade"

JOHN LYNCH; Irish born; 40 years of age; 5 feet, 5 inches high; black hair"

JOSHUA DULY, American born in Essex County, New Jersey; "5 feet, 10 inches long; long sandy hair; shows upper teeth"

ISAAC TOBY; " aged 28; 5 feet, 5 inches tall; slim; poxed; sober looking fellow"

PATRICK NIXSON; American born in Bethlehem in Hunterton Township; "5 feet, 6inches high"

JOHN MCBRIDE; Irish; "35 years of age; a down looking fellow; a true votary to Bacchus; very talkative and impertinent"

ABRAHAM THOMPSON; American born in Amwell township, New Jersey; 21 years of age; 5 feet, 6 inches high"

THOMAS BEVERLY [SWINDLE]; born in England at Derbyshire; "5 feet, 7 inches high; slender; very fond of strong liquor; talkative; knock kneed"

ADIAN POIST; American born; " 5 feet, 9 inches high; thin faced"

JAMES DAILY; "5 feet, 5 inches high; black hair; pox; scar on face"

ROBERT FIELD; "5 feet, 4 inches high; well set; pox; not talkative; sailor; is very civil"

JOHN EMERY; "5 feet, 9 inches high; thick, light colored, curled hair; full faced"

JOHN KELLY; "5 feet, 5 inches high"

WILLIAM RICHARDSON; "20 years of age"

JAMES BRITT; "5 feet, 9 inches high; short black hair; crooked nose; ill looking; dark complexion; seems to be very still"

JOHN HIMES; Amer born; "5 feet, 9 inches high; dark

colored hair; brown complex; full faced; well set; round shouldered"

WILLIAM BRYAN; "5 feet, 6 inches high; dark complexion; well set"

THOMAS VANDERSLICE; "6 foot; straight, young man"

CADWALADER JONES; "6 foot; straight, young man"

JOSEPH SHAMBOUGH; "6foot; straight, young man"

ANDREW BELL; "6 foot; straight, young man"

ABRAHAM SKEEN; "6 foot; straight, young man"

WILLIAM GLOVER; "6 foot; straight, young man"

JOHN SHRACK; "6 foot; straight, young man"

JOHN BRYAN; "thick, well set"

JOHN BATHHURDST; "swarthy"

JACOB TANEY; "well set"

DANIEL TANEY; "fresh colored"

MICHAEL WARE; "5 feet, 8 inches; slender; missing some fingers; given to drink; seldom looks a man in the face"

NICHOLAS SMITH; "5 feet, 8 or 9 nine inches; at times very saucy"

JOHN ARES; " 5 foot, 5 inches ; possessed of every bad quality without any of the goods ones"

GEORGE SPARLIN, deserted from the American forces; born in Middlesex, New Jersey; aged 23 year; 5 feet, 10 and 1/2 inches; brown hair; brown complexion; downcast look; a laborer

PETER SUTTON; deserted from the American forces; born in Middlesex, New Jersey; "17 years of age; 5 feet, 5 and 1/2 inches high; dark brown hair; brown complexion; a laborer

Deserted from Captain MATTHEW SMITH'S Company, a certain JAMES MELLONE; "about 50 years of age; about 5 feet, 10 inches high; dark looking fellow; brown hair; hollow eyes; has been fighting and has a black eye"; advertised by Lieut. MICHAEL SIMPSON in *The Pennsylvania Gazette*, October 9, 1776

Deserted from Captain MARTIN SWINK's company, a certain EDWARD ROBERTS; "about years of 20 or 21 age; about 5 feet, 5 or 6 inches high"; advertised in *The Pennsylvania Gazette*, August 21, 1776

Deserted from Captain EPHRAIM ANDERSON'S company of the Second New Jersey regiment, commanded by Colonel ISRAEL SHREVES, a certain CHARLES DOWNS; "about 26 years of age; full faced; about 5 feet, 7 or 8 inches high; swarthy complexion"; advertised in *The Pennsylvania Packet*, February 11, 1777

Deserted from Captain EPHRAIM ANDERSON'S company of the Second New Jersey regiment, commanded by Colonel ISRAEL SHREVES, a certain JAMES BOYD; "about 29 years of age; full faced and fair hair; has one sore toe and cannot wear a shoe on his left foot"; advertised in *The Pennsylvania Packet*, February 11, 1777

Deserted from Captain JAMES DILLON's company of the Second New Jersey regiment, commanded by Colonel ISRAEL SHREVES, a certain WILLIAM GLINN; "about 5 feet, 10 or 11 inches high; light blue eyes; says he belongs to Marcus Hook, Pennsylvania; fresh complexion"; advertised by NATHANIEL BOWMAN, Lieut. in *The Pennsylvania Gazette*, February 12, 1777

Deserted from Captain JAMES DILLON's company of the Second New Jersey regiment, commanded by Colonel ISRAEL SHREVES, a certain EDWARD EVENDEN; "about 5 feet, 5 inches high; pale complexion; thick set; a worthless ordinary fellow; pretends to beat on a drum"; advertised by NATHANIEL BOWMAN, Lieut. in *The Pennsylvania Gazette*, February 12, 1777

Deserted from Captain JAMES DILLON's company of the Second New Jersey regiment, commanded by Colonel ISRAEL SHREVES, a certain GEORGE GETTILL; "a Dutch man; about 5 feet, 6 inches high; gray eyes; dark complexion; short curled hair"; advertised by NATHANIEL BOWMAN, Lieut. in *The Pennsylvania Gazette*, February 12, 1777

Deserted from Captain JAMES DILLON's company of the Second New Jersey regiment, commanded by Colonel ISRAEL SHREVES, a certain THOMAS WHITE; " a short thick fellow; fresh colored; light blue eyes; much given to liquor; this fellow makes a practice of defrauding the continent by enlisting in several different companies"; advertised by NATHANIEL BOWMAN, Lieut. in *The Pennsylvania Gazette*, February 12, 1777

Deserted from Captain JAMES DILLON's company of the Second New Jersey regiment, commanded by Colonel ISRAEL SHREVES, a certain BARNABY HIGGINS; "about 5 feet, 4 inches high; blue eyes; fresh complexion; short, curled hair; by trade a baker"; advertised by NATHANIEL BOWMAN, Lieut. in *The Pennsylvania Gazette*, February 12, 1777

Deserted from the Fourth New Jersey Battalion, commanded by Colonel EPHRAIM MARTIN and Captain JOHN ANDERSON, a certain WILLIAM WOOD; "about 5 feet, 8 or 9 inches high; very slim; small faced and black hair"; advertised in *The Pennsylvania Gazette*, February 26, 1777

Deserted from the Fourth New Jersey Battalion, commanded by Colonel EPHRAIM MARTIN and Captain JOHN ANDERSON; a certain GEORGE POWER; about 5 feet, 6 or 7 inches high; brown complexion; short brown hair"; advertised in *The Pennsylvania Gazette*, February 26, 1777

Deserted from the Fourth New Jersey Battalion, commanded by Colonel EPHRAIM MARTIN and Captain JOHN ANDERSON, a certain JOHN M'COLOMN; "about 5 feet, 6 or 7 inches high; round faced; dark complexion; short black hair"; advertised in *The Pennsylvania Gazette*, February 26, 1777

Deserted from the Fourth New Jersey Battalion, commanded by Colonel EPHRAIM MARTIN and Captain JOHN ANDERSON, a certain RICHARD CHEW; "about 5 feet, 7 or 8 inches high; brown complexion; slim waisted; small face; short brown hair; his nose is long and slim; advertised in *The Pennsylvania Gazette*, February 26, 1777

Deserted from the Fourth New Jersey Battalion, commanded by Colonel EPHRAIM MARTIN and Captain JOHN ANDERSON, a certain JAMES SMITH; "frequently goes by the name Jack the Sailor; about 5 feet, 6 or 7 inches high; middling slim waist; round faced; pock marked; knock-kneed and long black hair"; advertised in *The Pennsylvania Gazette*, February 26, 1777

Deserted from the Fourth New Jersey Battalion, commanded by Colonel EPHRAIM MARTIN and Captain JOHN ANDERSON, a certain HENRY M'NEAL; "about 5 feet, 9 inches high; very round face; very much pock marked; long brown hair and a little bandy legged"; advertised in *The Pennsylvania Gazette*, February 26, 1777

Deserted from the Fourth New Jersey Battalion, commanded by Colonel EPHRAIM MARTIN and Captain JOHN ANDERSON, a certain JOHN WILLIAMS; "about 5 feet high; red hair; thin visage; has followed the water some time past and now lives in Kensington"; advertised in *The Pennsylvania Gazette*, February 26, 1777

Deserted from Captain JAMES HALLITT's company, belonging to Colonel EPHRAIM MARTIN's Regiment of foot, of the State of New Jersey, the following: WILLIAM RANE, PETER ROSS, JOHN LAUGH, THOMAS CROTHERS, NATHANIEL LARRENCE, JOHN THARE, SAMUEL TURNER, THOMAS BENNET, BENJAMIN ROBESON, JOHN FALLS, ROBERT STEWART, CHARLES MONDAY, JOHN CASSOCK, WILLIAM FAGAN, JOHN RODDEN, COMMESOLE FARRARY, WILLIAM ASHMIN, MELSHER MILLER, GEORGE CAMPBELL, ROGER CLEIL, ELIJAH BURNES, DANIEL CLEM, WILLIAM JENKINS, THOMAS HATHERLY, FRANCIS MORRIS, JOHN M'DONNALD, JAMES JOHNSON, JOHN YOUNG, ALEXANDER MONTGOMERY, WILLIAM ROBESON, WILLIAM DODD; advertised in *The Pennsylvania Packet*, February 25, 1777

Deserted from Captain of Artillery, SAMUEL HUGG's company in the Train of Artillery, THOMAS GREEN, of Penn's Neck, Salem county, New Jersey; "about 5 feet, 7 or 8 inches high; is much inclined to strong liquor"; advertised in *The Pennsylvania Journal*, April 2, 1777

Deserted from Captain JOHN NOBLE CUMMING's company of the Second New Jersey regiment, commanded by Colonel ISRAEL SHREVES, a certain VALENTINE ROCHESTER; "aged about 25 years; about 5 feet, 4 inches high; grey eyes; dark complexion; brown hair; enlisted at Ticonderoga"; advertised in *The Pennsylvania Journal*, April 23, 1777

Deserted from Captain JOHN NOBLE CUMMING's company of the Second New Jersey regiment, commanded by Colonel ISRAEL SHREVES, a certain WILLIAM WOOD; "aged about 30 years; about 5, feet 9 inches high; blue eyes; fair complexion; black hair; enlisted at Albany; remarkably squinted eyed"; advertised in *The Pennsylvania Journal*, April 23, 1777

Deserted from Captain JOHN NOBLE CUMMING's company of the Second New Jersey regiment, commanded by Colonel ISRAEL SHREVES, a certain CONSIDER ADITION; "aged about 35 years; about 5 feet, 10 inches high; blue eyes; fair complexion; red hair and beard; enlisted at Albany"; advertised in

The Pennsylvania Journal, April 23, 1777

    Deserted from Captain JOHN NOBLE CUMMING's company of the Second New Jersey regiment, commanded by Colonel ISRAEL SHREVES, a certain CHARLES SALTER, enlisted in Ticonderoga; advertised in *The Pennsylvania Journal*, April 23, 1777

    Deserted from Captain JOHN NOBLE CUMMING's company of the Second New Jersey regiment, commanded by Colonel ISRAEL SHREVES, a certain PATRICK M'MULLIN, enlisted in Wood's Town, Salem county; advertised in *The Pennsylvania Journal*, April 23, 1777

    Deserted from Captain JOHN NOBLE CUMMING's company of the Second New Jersey regiment, commanded by Colonel ISRAEL SHREVES, a certain GEORGE POWERS; "aged about 35 years; about 5 feet, 5 inches high; swarthy complexion; light brown hair, enlisted at Glouster"; advertised in *The Pennsylvania Journal*, April 23, 1777

    Deserted from Captain JOHN NOBLE CUMMING's company of the Second New Jersey regiment, commanded by Colonel ISRAEL SHREVES, a certain EDWARD PARKER; "aged about 25, about 5 feet, 11 inches high; dark eyes; complexion and hair; enlisted in Glouster"; advertised in *The Pennsylvania Journal*, April 23, 1777

    Deserted from Captain JOHN NOBLE CUMMING's company of the Second New Jersey regiment, commanded by Colonel ISRAEL SHREVES, a certain THOMAS BURNS, enlisted at Cross Roads of Cumberland; advertised in *The Pennsylvania Journal*, April 23, 1777

    Deserted from Captain JOHN NOBLE CUMMING's company of the Second New Jersey regiment, commanded by Colonel ISRAEL SHREVES, a certain OWEN WARD; "a native Irishman; aged about 39 years; about 5 feet, 4 inches high; his fore teeth gone; knock kneed; has the letters "O W" pricked out with gun powder along his arm; supposed to have gone through Mount Holly"; advertised in *The Pennsylvania Journal*, April 23, 1777

Deserted from Captain JOHN NOBLE CUMMING's company of the Second New Jersey regiment, commanded by Colonel ISRAEL SHREVES, a certain JOHN STEPHENSON; "an Irishman; about 23 years of age; about 5 feet, 9 inches high; well made; brown complexion; dark brown hair which curls naturally on his neck; enlisted in Glouster where he had lived many years; last intelligence he was over Delaware river"; advertised in *The Pennsylvania Journal*, April 23, 1777

Deserted from Captain JOHN NOBLE CUMMING's company of the Second New Jersey regiment, commanded by Colonel ISRAEL SHREVES, a certain HENRY BISHOP; "about 22 years of age; about 5 feet, 11 inches high; gray eyes; fair complexion; brown hair"; advertised in *The Pennsylvania Journal*, April 23, 1777

Deserted from Captain JOHN NOBLE CUMMING's company of the Second New Jersey regiment, commanded by Colonel ISRAEL SHREVES, a certain WILLIAM MILLER; "about 23 years of age; about 5, feet 10 inches high; dark complexion; much pock marked; short brown hair; sandy beard; talkative; speaking much in his own praise; father lives in Bucks Town Pennsylvania and he has stolen money from him in his escape; also took with him a servant girl to WILLIAM GRENDINE, late of Burlington"; advertised in *The Pennsylvania Journal*, April 30, 1777

Deserted from Captain JOHN HAMMIT's company in Col. OLIVER SPENCER's Regiment of Guards, a certain JOHN SMITH; "a shoe maker by trade; about 27 years of age; about 5 feet, 10 inches high; swarthy complexion; brown hair; a waterman by trade"; advertised in *The Pennsylvania Packet*, April 22, 1777

Deserted from Captain JOHN HAMMIT's company in Col. OLIVER SPENCER's Regiment of Guards, a certain STEVEN STEWARD, American born; "about 35 years of age; about 5 feet,

10 inches high; swarthy complexion; straight brown hair"; advertised in *The Pennsylvania Packet*, April 22, 1777

Deserted from Captain JOHN HAMMIT's company in Col. OLIVER SPENCER's Regiment of Guards, a certain MORRIS WELCH, Irish born; "about 5 feet, 6 inches high; straight fair hair; a waterman; enlisted with Captain M'FARTREDGE, on board the *Washington Galley*"; advertised in *The Pennsylvania Packet*, April 22, 1777

Deserted from Captain JOHN HAMMIT's company in Col. OLIVER SPENCER's Regiment of Guards, a certain JAMES MELSOM, an English man; "a tanner; about 22 years of age; about 5 feet, 5 inches high; dark complexion; straight brown hair"; advertised in *The Pennsylvania Packet*, April 22, 1777

Deserted from Captain of Artillery, SAMUEL HUGG's company in the Train of Artillery, WILLIAM RAWLINS, born in Glouster, New Jersey: "by trade a shoe maker; a likely well set fellow; about 5 feet, 5 inches high; black hair tied behind"; advertised in *The Pennsylvania Journal*, April 2, 1777

Deserted from First Lieutenant WILLIAM PARROTT, a certain CHARLES MIRES, American born; "about 5 feet, 8 inches high; fair complexion and formerly lived in Broad Neck in the county of Salem"; advertised *The Pennsylvania Journal*, May 21, 1777

Deserted from the 1st New Jersey Regiment, JOHN BARLOW; "aged about 27 years; 5 feet, 8 or 9 inches high; well set"; advertised in *The New Jersey Gazette*, March 18, 1778

Deserted from the 1st New Jersey Regiment, HUGH WELSH; "5 feet, 8 or 9 inches high; dark complexion; down look"; advertised in *The New Jersey Gazette*, March 18, 1778

Deserted from the Fourth Regiment of Light Dragoons, JAMES WATSON; "aged about 25 years; 5 feet, 6 inches high; well set; fair complexion; light hair; formerly lived in

Bordentown"; advertised by ANTHONY W. WHITE in *The Pennsylvania Packet*, April 5, 1778

Deserted from Capt. JONATHAN PHILLIPS's company, Col. SHREVE's Second New Jersey regiment, GEORGE COOK; "aged about 20 years; 5 feet, 7 inches high; likely fellow; by trade a tailor; advertised in *The New Jersey Gazette*, April 29, 1778

Deserted from Quarter Guard of the Fourth regiment of Light Dragoons, commanded by Col. STEPHAN MOYLAN, JOHN CHEAK; "5 feet, 10 inches high; dark complexion; black hair; confined for embezzlement and high treason"; advertised by ZEBULON PIKE, in *The New Jersey Gazette*, May 13, 1778

Deserted from Col JOHN MUNSEN's Battalion, Morris county, an Irish man, "aged about 22 years, a small fellow, 5 feet high, curled hair; down look; much marked with the pox"; advertised by SAMUEL SAYRE, Major in *The New Jersey Gazette*, June 10, 1778

Deserted from Col JOHN MUNSEN's Battalion, Morris county; ANDREW CONNARD, an Irish man; "aged about 25 years; 5 feet, 8 inches high; well set; apt to take a *large drink* and often uses those words; light complexion"; advertised by SAMUEL SAYRE, Major in *The New Jersey Gazette*, June 10, 1778

Delivered as a deserter from the Continental Army, JOHN CURTIS; "aged about 28 years; 5 feet, 3 inches high; slim built; has been a servant to EDWARD EDWARDS, Lieutenant in the 4th Maryland battalion"; advertised by JOHN OSBORN, Trenton gaoler, in *The New Jersey Gazette*, July 8, 1778

Deserted from Count PULASKI's Legion, ANDREW NELSON; "aged about 18 years; 5 feet, 8 inches high; black hair and eyes; supposed to be in the pines, near Imlay's Town, making tar or at the salt works in Monmouth"; advertised by Major HENRY BEDKIN in *The New Jersey Gazette*, July 15, 1778

Deserted from Capt. JOHN BURROWES, CORNELIUS BARCALOW; advertised in *The New Jersey Gazette*, August 12, 1778

Deserted from Capt. JONATHAN PHILLIPS's company of the 2d New Jersey regiment, BENJAMIN VOGLUM; "5 feet, 9 inches high; marked with small pox; down look"; advertised in *The New Jersey Gazette*, August 12, 1778

Deserted from Capt. JONATHAN PHILLIPS's company of the 2d New Jersey regiment, HUGH M'CLANE, an Irishman; "5 feet, 8 inches high; a square set and bushy curled hair"; advertised in *The New Jersey Gazette*, August 12, 1778

Deserted from Capt. JONATHAN PHILLIPS's company of the 2d New Jersey regiment, JOHN THOMPSON; "a 19 months man; formerly a galleys man; 5 feet, 8 inches high; swarthy complexion; marked with small pox"; advertised in *The New Jersey Gazette*, August 12, 1778

Deserted from Capt. JONATHAN PHILLIPS's company of the 2d New Jersey regiment, GEORGE COOK, American born; "aged about 20 years; 5 feet, 5 inches high; a likely young man"; advertised in *The New Jersey Gazette*, August 12, 1778

Deserted from Capt. JOHN V. ANGLIN's company of the 1st New Jersey regiment, THEOPHILUS CUMMINS; "aged about 21 years; 5 feet, 6 inches high; supposed to be near New German town"; advertised in *The New Jersey Gazette*, September 2, 1778

Deserted from Capt. JOHN V. ANGLIN's company of the 1st New Jersey regiment, WILLIAM ERWIN; "aged about 17 years; 5 feet, 6 inches high"; advertised in *The New Jersey Gazette*, September 2, 1778

ELISHA OSBORNE, from EPHRAIM MARTIN, 4th Jersey Regiment; "about 25 years of age; pock marked, blue eyed; short, light colored hair; about 5 foot, 10 inches high"; *The New Jersey Gazette*, December 2, 1778

The following were noticed as deserters during the first half of 1779:

OWEN WILLIAMS; "5 feet, 9 inches high; bombardier"

PETER PETERSON; a German; "5 feet, 8 inches high; poxed"

ANDREW SCOTT; an Irish man

JOHN GREEN; an Irish man

THOMAS JOHNSON; an Irish man

ROBERT ARMSTRONG; an Irish man

PATRICK ASHLEY; "26 years of age; 5 feet, 7 inches high; his left cheek is swelled and he has a black patch on it"

JOHN WHITE; "26 years of age; 5 feet, 8 inches high; slim; well dressed"

JAMES CARROLL; "30 years of age; 5 feet, 6 inches high; dark complexion"

CHARLES HALL; "25 years of age; 5 feet, 6 inches high; light complexion; well made; a saddler; very fond of strong drink and talks much when drunk"

JOHN FOY; an Irish man; "5 feet, 9 inches high

ISAAC JOHN JOHNSON; "5 feet, 5 inches high

JAMES DAVIS; 5 feet, 10 inches high; bald"

JOHN COX; "5 feet, 10 inches high; short black hair; slim; has had the pox; swarthy complexion; down look"

JOHN SALMON; American born; "26 years of age; 5 feet

8 inches high; fair complexion; well made; artful, sly fellow and writes an excellent hand"

JOSEPH FOWLER; an Irish man

MOTTID MILES; "40 years of age; 5 feet 6 inches high; well set"

STEVEN HAWKINS; American born; "5 feet 8 inches high; dark complexion; well made

Deserted from Capt. JOHN DAVIS's Company of the New Jersey State regiment, whereof Col. FREDERICK FREELINGHAUSON is commander, ANDREW BELCHER; "aged about 33 years; 5 feet 10 inches high; dark complexion; brown hair which is tied;, by trade a shoemaker"; notice to Col. JOHN TAYLOR at Elizabeth Town; advertised in *The Pennsylvania Journal*, September 22, 1779

Deserted from Capt. JOHN DAVIS's Company of the New Jersey State regiment, whereof Col. FREDERICK FREELINGHAUSON is commander, JOSEPH GIFFORD; "aged about 29 years; 5 feet 6 inches high; dark complexion; supposed to be around Egg Harbor"; notice to Col. JOHN TAYLOR at Elizabeth Town; advertised in *The Pennsylvania Journal*, September 22, 1779

Deserted from Capt. JOHN DAVIS's Company of the New Jersey State regiment, whereof Col. FREDERICK FREELINGHAUSON is commander, THOMAS DOUGHTY; "aged about 20 years; 5 feet 9 inches high; dark complexion; supposed to be around Egg Harbor;" notice to Col. JOHN TAYLOR at Elizabeth Town; advertised in *The Pennsylvania Journal*, September 22, 1779

Deserted from Capt. JOHN DAVIS's Company of the New Jersey State regiment, whereof Col. FREDERICK FREELINGHAUSON is commander, ABRAHAM PETERSON; "aged about 27 years; 5 feet 11 inches high; fair complexion;

supposed to be at Egg Harbor"; notice to Col. JOHN TAYLOR at Elizabeth Town; advertised in *The Pennsylvania Journal*, September 22, 1779

Deserted from Capt. JOHN DAVIS's Company of the New Jersey State regiment, whereof Col. FREDERICK FREELINGHAUSON is commander, NATHANIEL AVIS; "aged about 17 years; 5 feet 4 or 5 inches high; sandy complexion; supposed to be about Swedesboro"; notice to Col. JOHN TAYLOR at Elizabeth Town; advertised in *The Pennsylvania Journal*, September 22, 1779

Deserted from Capt.DOUGHTY's company, Col. LAMB's regiment of Artillery, MICHAEL ROE; "aged about 20 years; 6 feet; dark complexion; short black hair; grey eyes; full faced"; advertised by THOMAS THOMPSON, Capt. Lieut. Art. in *The New Jersey Journal*, June 8,1779

Deserted from Capt.DOUGHTY's company, Col. LAMB's regiment of Artillery, BEZELIEL ACKLY; "aged about 25 years; brown complexion; light brown hair; grey eyes; advertised by THOMAS THOMPSON, . in *The New Jersey Journal*, June 8,1779; re advertised in *The New Jersey Gazette*, June 12, 1781

Deserted from Colonel JOHN LAMB of the Second Regiment of Artillery, "on their rout from Trenton to Head of Elk, a certain BAZALIEL ACKLEY, a matross, about 29 years of age, about 5 feet 9 and one half inches high, brown hair, fair complexion; by trade a founder, was born in Connecticut and resided for some time in Springfield. East New Jersey; advertised by EBENEZER STEVENS, Lieutenant Col.

Deserted from Capt. MOTT's company, Col. LAMB's regiment of Artillery, WILLIAM HELNIT, matross; "aged about 22 to 26 years, 5 feet 5 inches high, fair complexion, light hair, short and curls, blue eyes, blooming cheeks, stout build, whipt for theft which his back now shows sufficient proof; advertised by GERSHOM MOTT in *The New Jersey Journal*, June 8, 1779

Deserted from the first New Jersey regiment, Lieut. BOUROUGH's company, NATHAN HALL; "elderly man, 5 feet 10 or 11 inches high; advertised by Lt. SAMUEL SEELY in *The New Jersey Journal*, November 30, 1779

Deserted from the first New Jersey regiment, Lieut. BOUROUGH's company, BENJAMIN LISK; 5 feet 10 inches high; by trade a blacksmith"; advertised by Lt. SAMUEL SEELY in *The New Jersey Journal*, November 30, 1779

JAMES WATSON, American born in New Jersey; "aged 25 years; 5 feet 6 inches high; light hair; fair complexion; well set";

JAMES LUCAY, deserted from a company of boat men; "aged about 19 years; 5 feet 10 inches high; dark complexion; black hair; formerly from North Carolina"; advertised by SAMUEL BOND, Superintendent of the Ferry, in *The New Jersey Gazette*, August 23, 1780

Deserted from Capt. Mead's company of the 1st Regiment, JOHN BURNETT; advertised in *The New Jersey Journal*, December 27, 1780

Deserted from Capt. Mead's company of the 1st Regiment, JOHN YHERTS; advertised in *The New Jersey Journal*, December 27, 1780

Deserted from Capt. Mead's company of the 1st Regiment, BENJAMIN BONNEL; advertised in *The New Jersey Journal*, December 27, 1780

JOHN BROWN; "5 feet 9inches tall; long brown hair, black complexion; long visage; one of his upper fore teeth is broke off; stout, active fellow";

Deserted from Colonel JOHN LAMB of the Second Regiment of Artillery, on their route from Trenton to Head of Elk, a certain ANTHONY BREMER, a fifer; "about 18 years of age;

about 4 feet 9 inches high; yeoman; fair hair; light complexion; born in Philadelphia and resided some time in Warwick, State of New York"; advertised by EBENEZER STEVENS, Lieutenant Col. in *The New Jersey Gazette*, June 12, 1781

Deserted from Colonel JOHN LAMB of the Second Regiment of Artillery, on their route from Trenton to Head of Elk, a certain ALLEN M'CLEAN, a matross; "about years of 31 age; about 5 feet 5 and one half inches high; yeoman; brown hair; ruddy complexion; pitted with the small pox; born in Scotland and resided some time in Kahiatt, State of New York"; advertised by EBENEZER STEVENS, Lieutenant Col. in *The New Jersey Gazette*, June 12, 1781

Deserted from Colonel JOHN LAMB of the Second Regiment of Artillery, on their route from Trenton to Head of Elk, a certain JOSEPH HUGG, a matross; "about 25 years of age; about 5 feet 6 inches high; brown hair; fair complexion; born at Greenwich in Glouster county, New Jersey and resided some time in Philadelphia"; advertised by EBENEZER STEVENS, Lieutenant Col. in *The New Jersey Gazette*, June 12, 1781

Deserted from Colonel JOHN LAMB of the Second Regiment of Artillery, on their route from Trenton to Head of Elk, a certain DAVID LEARD, a matross; "about 30 years of age; about 5 feet 10 inches high; black hair; fair complexion; born in Phillipsburg in the State of New York"; advertised by EBENEZER STEVENS, Lieutenant Col. in *The New Jersey Gazette*, June 12, 1781

Deserted from Colonel JOHN LAMB of the Second Regiment of Artillery, on their route from Trenton to Head of Elk, a certain ABRAHAM M'KILLUP, a corporal; "about 38 years of age; about 5 feet 9 inches high; yeoman; dark hair and complexion; born in Ireland and resided some time in Stillwater in the state of New York"; advertised by EBENEZER STEVENS, Lieutenant Col. in *The New Jersey Gazette*, June 12, 1781

Deserted from Colonel JOHN LAMB of the Second

Regiment of Artillery, on their route from Trenton to Head of Elk, a certain RICHARD WILLIAMS, a corporal; "about 35 years of age; about 5 feet 5 and a half inches high; yeoman; brown hair; fair complexion; born and resided in Greenfield, Connecticut"; advertised by EBENEZER STEVENS, Lieutenant Col. in *The New Jersey Gazette*, June 12, 1781

Deserted from Colonel JOHN LAMB of the Second Regiment of Artillery, on their route from Trenton to Head of Elk, a certain MATTHIAS CHRISTY, a bombardier; "about 24 years of age; about 5 feet 7 and a half inches high; by trade a black smith; born and resided in Elizabeth Town, New Jersey"; advertised by EBENEZER STEVENS, Lieutenant Col. in *The New Jersey Gazette*, June 12, 1781

Deserted from Colonel JOHN LAMB of the Second Regiment of Artillery, on their route from Trenton to Head of Elk, a certain BENJAMIN COLE, a matross; "about 25 years of age; about 5 feet 7 inches high; yeoman; black hair; dark complexion; born in Essex county, New Jersey and resided for some time near the North Redoubt on Hudson's River, where he has a wife and family"; advertised by EBENEZER STEVENS, Lieutenant Col. in *The New Jersey Gazette*, June 12, 1781

Deserted from Colonel JOHN LAMB of the Second Regiment of Artillery, on their route from Trenton to Head of Elk, a certain JAMES M'BRIDE, a sergeant; "about 24 years of age; about 5 feet 8 inches high; yeoman; dark hair; dark complexion; well made; born in Ireland and resided for some time at New Windsor in the state of New York"; advertised by EBENEZER STEVENS, Lieutenant Col. in *The New Jersey Gazette*, June 12, 1781

Deserted from Colonel JOHN LAMB of the Second Regiment of Artillery, on their route from Trenton to Head of Elk, a certain WILLIAM M'BRIDE, a corporal; "about 27 years of age; about 5 feet 6 inches high; yeoman; dark hair; dark complexion; well made; born in Ireland and resided for some time at New Windsor in the state of New York"; advertised by EBENEZER

STEVENS, Lieutenant Col. in *The New Jersey Gazette*, June 12, 1781

ENDNOTES

1. The importance of indentured servants can be seen in Virginia, where in 1618 the colony offered the planter a head right, a grant of 50 acres per servant, as an incentive to import more of them from England.

2. Not included were either women or slaves of either sex. Their origins are discussed *infra*.

3. The Scotch Irish emigrant was America's gain. Both as soldiers and patriots, they would be instrumental in the upcoming war against Britain. Indeed, at the time of the Revolution, almost 15% of the colonists were descendants of this Ulster migration. Ten per cent of today's American population claims ancestry from these same Scotch-Irish indentured servants. At least, eighteen of their descendants would become presidents of the United States. Theodore Roosevelt referred to this group as "the kernel of the distinctly and intensely American stock who were the pioneers of our people in their march westward.".

4. The Irish migrated steadily through the time of the Revolution and by then were numerous. However, as the practice of Catholicism was banned everywhere but Maryland and Rhode Island, many of them by then had abandoned their Roman Catholic beliefs and with it their ethnic identity.

5. Ringwood, was an iron furnace, with three forge operations, a grist mill, saw mill, worker's houses, stores, and farms. It dates back to the 1740s when Cornelius Board and, after him, the Ogden family, began to smelt the local iron ore. By 1765, Peter Hasenclever, from whom these nine German miners had fled, made Ringwood the center of his iron making empire which included 150,000 acres in New Jersey, New York and Nova Scotia. He also imported more than 500 workers from Germany and England. . This iron making technology transfer from Germany to the Colonies is said to have had a huge effect on America's iron and steel industry over the next two centuries.

6. In addition to Ringwood, they fled from Change Water Forge in Sussex County, Union Iron Works in Hunterdon County, Etna Furnace in Burlington County, and Tanton Forge, also in Burlington County. [EXPAND]

7. In 179?, Moses Brown, later founder of Brown University, and a William Almy convinced their fellow Quaker, Samuel Slater, newly arrived from England, to reconstruct from memory an automatic textile mill, the first in the United States. This broke an English monopoly and hastened America's change from being an agricultural to an industrial nation. It was the beginning of the Industrial Revolution.

8. The factories were in New England where the natural resources, including the soils, had become depleted, and were fed, via the new railroad, the raw materials of the rest of the nation. Using immigrants and girls from the over populated countryside, whom the agricultural society no longer could support, the factories sent back, on the return trains, manufactured goods of all kinds, consumer and industrial, for the rest of the country to buy. The method of constructing houses well illustrates this change. Prior to 1830, houses, barns and other structures of similar size were built on site by *local* carpenters using *local* building materials. Nearby trees would be felled and brought to the closest sawmill converted into planking, paneling and shakes and brought back to the building site. The house was in effect *home made*. After 1830, however, the building materials were mostly of a standard size and machine made. Often, items like doors or window frames were prefabricated. Nails produced and used after 1830 were all machine made, heads and shaft. Hand wrought, forged nails were a thing of the past.

9. New Jersey was an agricultural economy at the eve of the Revolution -- a sea of farms with waves of wheat and corn. Good land was available at reasonable prices, the climate favorable. An average farm was a hundred acres in size and was worked by a single family. The brute force of harnessed oxen helped clear the land. The soil was readied by hand and mule, often with barely effective wooden plows. Harvesting was by means, such as

scythes, unchanged since Biblical times. Hired hands were scarce. The abundance of available land allowed every man to have his own farm. Thus, indentured servants and slaves were needed.

Winter wheat was a big crop in both the eastern and western divisions of the Province of New Jersey as were barley, oats, rye, buckwheat, flax, vegetables and fruits of many varieties, including apple, plum, peaches and cherries. Livestock on the typical farm consisted of hogs, horses, "horned" cattle, sheep and poultry. In the southern counties, like Cape May and Cumberland, with their extensive meadows of salt hay, cattle raising was also a principal industry. Herds of these animals would be driven by men, called "cowboys," to Philadelphia and New York for sale in their markets. Hogs were slaughtered, packed in barrels of brine and shipped to the islands of the Caribbean. The produce of the orchards was distilled into ciders and brandies, for personal consumption as well as export. They made linen from flax, boots and shoes from leather and homespun wool. In short, most of what was produced on the Jersey farm of the 1770's was consumed there by the farm families.

Sometimes, farms expanded beyond agriculture. A few had blacksmith operations, saw mills and grist mills associated with them. Gradually, they provided enough employment to non family members as to become the hub of a village

10. According the Federal Reserves of Dallas 1992 report " *The Churn, The Paradox of Progress*, as America changed, so did its jobs. In 1900, it took nearly 40 out of every 100 Americans to feed the country(now it requires just three). In addition to the farmers and farm workers, general laborers, servants, merchants, clerks, sales people, carpenters, railroad workers and miners were the most popular occupations. The transportation industry – trains, cars, trucks and planes –ousted the hostlers and harness makers, the watermen and the carters.

By 1960 retail sales workers, farmers, teachers, truck and tractor drivers, secretaries, private household workers, farm labor, manufacturing labor, bookkeepers and carpenters
were the top jobs and, 1990, it was retail workers, teachers, secretaries, truck drivers farmers, janitors and cleaners, bookkeeper engineers, cooks and auto mechanics.

The popular occupations in 2000 include shop staff, teachers, nurses and other health care workers, child-care workers, helper and cleaners, commercial and technical and carpenters.

11. In 1880, a century later, John still led with William, Charles, George, James, Joseph, Frank, Henry, Thomas and Harry following in that order. By 1920, it had changed, but not by much. John, William, James, Robert, Joseph, Charles, George, Edward, Thomas and Frank were the top choices.

12. John, Robert and James slipped to 3rd, 4th, and 5th places, replaced on top by David and Michael. Another newcomer Mark slipped into 6th place, followed by William, Richard, Thomas and Steven.

13. This might seem old in a society, like England, where the average life expectancy at birth for English people in the 1600s was just under 40 –39.7 years. However, over 12% of all children born would die and this skewers the statistics . A man or woman who reached the age of 30 could expect to live to 59. Life expectancy in New England was much higher, where the average man died in his mid-sixties and women lived on average to 62. Today, a male child has a life expectancy of 73 and a female child 79.

14. Do not confuse what they ate with a healthy diet. A typical breakfast in pre-1900 America would be pork, served salted, boiled or as bacon. Salted fish was also a staple, as was corn pone, well kneaded with grease and eggs and hoecake, a coarse strong bread and hominy, a pounded Indian corn boiled together with milk. By the 1850s, people each consumed about a ton of foodstuffs each a year, with heavy emphasis on meats. It was also poorly prepared in frying pans and wolfed down without any of the ritual we observe at table today.

15. Gerald Carson, *The Cornflake Crusade* (1957). The averages height for modern American men is just over 5' 9".

16. There was a single advertisement that had the runaway's

height as 5 foot seven inches and later in the advertisement described him as a "short, well set fellow.

17. The author is aware that taking the mean and comparing it to the average of another set can be flawed. However, selecting the mean age rather than the average height in feet and inches is much more convenient and any distortions minor.

18. *The New York Gazette*, December 6, 1773

19. . Smallpox outbreaks have occurred from time to time for thousands of years, but now have been eradicated by a successful worldwide vaccination program.

20. For example, county fairs were closed to minimize infection:" At a Petty session of the Peace, held for the County of Burlington, at Burlington, the 16th Day of April, 1731, it was consider'd that Fairs generally occasion great Concourse of People, from the most adjacent Places, and that at present it was not Meet for keeping the Fair at Burlington, as usual, by reason of the great Mortality in Philadelphia and other Parts of Pennsylvania, where the Small-Pox now violently Rages. Therefore, to prevent, to the utmost Power of the Justices of the said Sessions, the further spreading of so Epidemical and Dangerous of a Distemper, and more especially, for that the approaching Heat of Summer may be more malignant and fatal, it is Ordered that May Fair next be, and hereby is, Prohibited to be kept in the said Town of Burlington and all Persons are hereby strictly required to take Notice hereof accordingly as they will answer for their Contempt at their Peril. *The American Weekly Mercury,* April 15, 1731.

21. It is rare in the United States today because of the elimination of tubercle from the milk and the prevention of mass infections in childhood. Heliotherapy --getting outside in the sun -- was a traditional method of treatment.

22. Attempts at describing being knock kneed were :"knees bending somewhat inward"; "turns out his feet much as he walks and his knees are inclined to strike one another and "throws his

feet very much out and bends his knees as he goes".

23. As of the year 2000 and provided by the National Institute on Alcohol Abuse and Alcoholism.

24. See4Ala Galway in his *The Indian Slave Trade: the Rise of the British Empire in the American South (1670 -1717)*. The motive for some slave owners was economic gain. Slaves created wealth fo their owners. In other cultures, they were a sign of the master's power.

25. Ironically, it seems likely that this "Antoney" who was on the first boat might be the same Antoney, who, after serving his term as an indentured servant, became a prosperous farmer and himself owned slaves.

26. The building is more notable for being George Washington's tavern of choice uring his first term as President when New York was the Capital. It still stands today, more than two centuries after that later, on the same corner of Pearl Street and Broad at the foot of Manhattan Island and enjoying the same use as a tavern and restaurant.

27. The pass read:
New York
This is to certify to whomever it may concern that the bearer hereof
[name],
a Negro, reported to the British Lines in consequence of the Proclamations of Sir William Howe and Sir Henry Clinton, late Commanders in Chief in America, and that the said Negro hereby has his Excellency Sir Guy Carleton's permission to go to Nova Scotia or where else [he or she] thinks proper.
By order of the Brigadier General
[Samuel Birch]

28. It was a difficult relocation for the Blacks. But it was better than slavery. Some, calling themselves Black Pioneers, gleefully accepted a special settlement for the "black gentry" and named it

Birchtown, in honor of the General who had signed the pass that gave them liberty, free to go wherever and do whatever they wanted. A second settlement was on the other side of Nova Scotia at the Bay of Fundy, at a black township named Brindley Town. Some, led by a Thomas Brownspriggs, went even further north to Chedabucto Bay and Cape Breton Island. It is in Guysborough county in the Cape Breton Islands where one still can find the pure lineage, descendants of the group, led by Thomas Brownspriggs, in 1784.

29. There were more slaves in New Jersey than the New England states, New York, Pennsylvania and Ohio combined. In fact, in 1830, of the 3,568 Northern blacks who remained slaves, more than two-thirds were in New Jersey.

30. At the start of the Civil War, New Jersey citizens owned 18 "apprentices for life" (the federal census listed them as "slaves") -- legal slaves by any name.

31. Few, if any, of these Native American slaves were probably from New Jersey. When the first Europeans had arrived, the Atlantic coastline from the southern portion of Long Island down to the Virginia Capes and inland for hundreds of miles had been the domain of a tribe of Indians who had named themselves the Lenni Lenape, meaning in their tongue, "the real people." They were a peaceful nation and relations between the Indians and the white settlers had generally been good. As their number waned, the Lenni Lenape were given a reservation, called Brotherton, in the Western Province of New Jersey. Before the American Revolution, they had sold it and moved to upstate New York, beginning a journey that eventually took them to Oklahoma where their descendants, called the Delaware, can still be found.

32. Nine were listed as tall, 25 as being middle sized and 27 as short.

33. In a *New York Journal or General Advertiser,* June 21, 1770 advertisement under the heading " INNOCULATION", George Pugh, Surgeon, "lately arrived from Jamaica" claimed to have been "the first Person [to] introduce the Suttonian Method of Inoculation for the Small Pox in that part of the West Indies,

where he has been instrumental in almost eradicating that loathsome Disease." He gave a list of Plantations in Jamaica, each with 400 slaves on average, whom he had inoculated "without the loss of a patient".

Dr. Pugh proposed to "carry on that Branch of his Profession, every Spring and Fall in Elizabeth Town, New Jersey, where he has opened a Commodious House for the Reception of Patients. Any Person, Family, or Company, desirous of being inoculated by him at New York, Philadelphia or elsewhere, may depend upon his strictest Care and Attendance to conduct them through the Small Pox, and upon Terms agreeable to their Circumstances, and what may justly be added with little Loss of Time or Hindrance

INDEX

A

ABBERNATHY, John - 68

ABIT, Burroughs - 134, 135
ABIT, James - 281
ABRAHAM - 223
ABZICHER, Paulus - 145
ABZICHER, Peter - 145
ACKLAND, Capt. (first name not given) - 197
ACKLY, Bezeliel - 311
ACTON, John - 231
ADAMS, Alexander - 132
ADAMS, Jedidiah - 182
ADAMS, Nathaniel - 174
ADAMS, Samuel - 115
ADAMS, Thomas - 115
ADITION, Consider - 303
ADLEY, Thomas - 129
AENSWORTH, Robert - 291
AETON, Benjamin - 50, 208
AGAN, Joshua - 183
AGAR, Edward - 221
AHIERN, Morris - 77
AINSWORTH, Robert - 101
AKER, Adam - 168
ALBERTSON, William - 85
ALBURTIS, Benjamin - 88
ALCUT, John - 162
ALFORD, John - 177
ALLAN, Robert - 100
ALLEN, Aaron - 103
ALLEN, Daniel - 208
ALLEN, Jedediah - 173
ALLEN, John - 90, 256, 259, 268, 274, 275
ALLEN, Moses - 103
ALLEN, Ralph - 200
ALLEN, Sarah - 257
ALLEN, William - 102, 171, 293
ALLEN, no first name given - 221
ALLEN & TURNER - 60
ALLISON, Alexander - 171
AMBLER, Peter - 154
AMORITTA - 37, 265
AMOS - 222
ANDERSON, Eliacom - 54
ANDERSON, Jr. Enoch. - 269, 270
ANDERSON, Ephraim Capt. - 300
ANDERSON, James - 78, 117
ANDERSON, John - 109, 301, 302
ANDERSON, Katherine - 255
ANDERSON, Thomas - 194
ANDREW, James - 83
ANDREWS, Thomas - 99
ANGLIN, John V. Capt. - 308
ANNEY'S JOE - 30, 232
ANSTER, Nathaniel - 191, 198
ANTHONY - 216
ANTRAM, Thomas - 106
ANTRIN, Isaac - 230
APGAR, Henry - 206
APPLETON, John - 57
ARCHER, Benjamin - 171
ARCHIBOLD, Christopher - 152
ARIS, George - 163

ARISON, George - 163
ARISTOBLUS, Christopher 269
ARMSTRONG, Andrew - 276
ARMSTRONG, George - 227
ARMSTRONG, Robert - 309
ARNEY, Joseph - 95
ARNOLD, Jacob Capt. - 249
ARREL, Richard - 110
ARROWSMITH, Benjamin 278
ASH - 30, 217
ASHLEY, Patrick - 309
ASHMIN, William - 303
ASHTON, Edward - 133
ASHTON, John - 110
ATEN, Derrick - 217
ATKINSON, John - 217
ATKINSON, Samuel - 80
ATTERBURY, Francis - 79
AULBERGER, Adam - 204
AUSBORN, Joseph - 149
AUSTIN, Amos - 60
AUSTIN, Cornelius - 203
AUSTIN, Samuel - 166
AVIS, Nathaniel - 311

B

BACK, John - 129
BACKMAN, John - 127
BACON, Daniel - 52
BAGLEY, Daniel - 208
BAGLY, James - 125
BAIN, James - 127
BAINBRIDGE, John - 175
BAKER, Thomas - 111
BAKER, William - 190
BALDWIN, James - 93
BALDWIN, Jonathan - 157
BALDWIN, William - 189
BALFORD, Joseph - 60
BALL, Andrew - 82
BALL, Joseph - 201, 202, 248
BANBURY, Edward - 73
BANKS, James - 86
BANKS, Joseph Stone - 119
BANKS, Josiah - 239, 243
BANNISTER, John - 215
BANTLENT, Joseph - 129
BARCALOW, Cornelius - 308
BARCALOW, Derick - 192
BARCLAY, Catherine - 258, 276
BARCLAY, John - 49, 276
BARCLAY & MITCHELL 181, 182
BARD, Bennet - 85, 94, 211
BARD, Peter - 90, 218
BARD, (first name not given) 259
BARETT, Absalom -155
BARGOLT, Philip Jacob - 127
BARKER, Peter - 141
BARKLEY, Hugh - 120
BARKLEY, John - 265
BARLOW, John - 164, 306
BARNARD, Capt.(first name not given) - 293
BARNES, John - 287
BARNES, Martha - 253
BARR, Warren - 270
BARRA, Peter - 103
BARRAT, Andrew - 241
BARRAT, Michael - 125

BARRERE, John - 249
BARTON, Jonathan - 162
BASIER, Christian - 171
BASSET, Elisha - 104
BASSET, Phebe - 157
BASSET, William - 137
BASSONET, Charles - 261
BATE, Henry - 275
BATES, Solomon - 208
BATES, Dr. - 242
BATH, John - 71
BATHHURDST, John - 299
BATTEN, Francis - 95
BAUM, Bartholomew - 131
BEACH, Epenetus - 117
BEAKES, Edmund - 118
BEAKES, Nathan - 57
BEAKS, William - 179
BEAL, Thomas - 284
BEALIE, Thomas - 284
BEARCRAFT, Nicholas- 255
BEARD, Francis - 222
BEAT, Agnes - 265
BEATIE, Isaac - 136
BEDKIN, Maj. Henry - 307
BEEKMAN, Christopher -17
BEEKMAN, Geradus - 224
BEEKMAN, John - 224
BEEMER, John - 187
BEESLEY, Joseph - 280
BELCHER, Andrew - 310
BELL, Andrew - 299
BELL, James - 30, 210
BEN, -227, 234, 240, 243, 245, 247
BENJAMIN, - 232
BENNET, Cornelius - 287
BENNET, Joseph - 152

BENNET, Peter - 293
BENNET, Thomas - 85, 303
BENNIN, Joseph -152
BERNARD, - 126
BERRARA, Francis - 202
BERTCLASEN, Engel - 202
BERYON, Christina - 264
BESSONET, John - 156
BET, - 266
BETTY, - 259
BEVERLY, Thomas - 298
BICHAM, James- 197
BICKHAM, Martin - 255
BICKUM, Patrick - 169
BIDDLE, Henry - 285
BIDDLE, James - 220
BIDDLE, Joseph- 84, 224
BILES, Elizabeth - 213
BILL, - 215, 224, 225, 249
BILLIN, Abraham - 63
BIRD, John - 205
BIRD, William - 165, 215
BISHOP, Christopher - 165
BISHOP, Henry - 305
BISHOP, Joseph - 203
BISHOP, Levi - 203, 297
BISPHAN, Benjamin - 99
BISPHAM, John - 262
BLACHLY, Jr. Ebenezer - 247
BLACK, James - 163, 164, 193
BLACK, John - 52, 158
BLACK, Mary - 162
BLACKLY, John - 250
BLACKWOOD, Hugh - 70
BLACKWOOD, Jane - 70, 74, 259
BLACKWOOD, Samuel - 282, 283
BLAIR, Samuel - 71

BLAIR, Thomas - 88, 102, 257
BLAKE, William - 91
BLANCHARD, John - 249
BLASS, Don - 211
BLEDSOE, John - 252
BLOOD, Francis - 213
BOAN, John - 277
BOATMAN, Matthias - 113
BOB, - 39, 264
BOELS, Thomas - 48
BOGGS, Samuel - 55, 72, 254, 255
BOHAM, John - 92
BOLING, John - 178
BOMBARGER, Arnold - 192
BOND, Elijah - 224, 236, 241
BOND, Elisha - 257
BOND, Samuel - 312
BONER, Conrad - 185
BONNEL, Benjamin - 312
BONNEL, Edward - 272
BONTURAH - 239
BOOD - 219
BOOT - 216
BORDEN, Richard - 142
BOUCTHER, John - 193
BOUDENHAGEN, John- 110
BOURN, Anthony - 137
BOURN, Merica - 42, 215
BOURNS, Anthony - 137
BOUROUGH, Lt. - 312
BOWEN, Owen - 186
BOWEN, William - 124
BOWERS, Lemuel - 113
BOWES, Frances - 73, 74

BOWKERA, Samuel - 182
BOWLS, John - 65
BOWMAN, Mary - 40, 253
BOWMAN, Nathaniel Lt.- 300, 301
BOWNE, Samuel - 112
BOY, Nathan - 280
BOYD, Andrew - 181, 297
BOYD, James - 300
BOYD, Robert - 127
BOZORTH, Andrew - 126
BRACKEN, Henry - 260
BRADFORD, Andrew - 48, 49, 50, 52, 53, 268
BRADFORD, Hugh - 81
BRADFORD, William - 48, 49, 53, 207
BRADFORD, Mr. - 267
BRADLEY, Francis - 290
BRADLEY, John - 187
BRADSHAW, Thomas -191
BRADY, Michael - 153, 155
BRANIN, Michael - 67, 107
BRAY, David - 63
BRAY, James - 277
BRAY, Mr. - 250, 265
BRAYTON, Daniel - 294
BREACH, John - 58
BREASTLAND, Patrick - 126
BREEDING, John - 133
BREINTNAL, John - 49
BREMER, Anthony - 312
BREMER, Hance - 187
BREWER, Edward - 108
BREWER, Samuel - 280
BRIAN, Billy [William] - 195
BRIAN, Mary - 260
BRICK, Joshua - 68
BRIEN, Daniel - 74

BRIGHT, Jacob - 138
BRIGHT, Philip - 247
BRIGHT, William - 193
BRIGHTWELL, John - 268
BRIN, Betty - 257
BRINAN, Nell - 58
BRINCKERHOFF, Dirck - 154
BRISS - 30, 250
BRISTOL - 30, 216, 218, 219, 238, 241
BRIT - 30, 236, 239
BRITAIN, Joseph - 50, 51
BRITT, James - 298
BRITTAIN, Abraham - 161
BRITTAIN, Joseph - 47
BRITTAIN, Richard - 235
BRITTON, William - 273
BROADLEY, Thomas - 50
BROCK, Burbage - 115, 116
BROCKHOLST, Henry- 234
BRODRICK, Darby - 47
BROOKS, Capt. Benjamin 264
BROOKS, James - 269, 279
BROWN, Abia - 224
BROWN, David - 120
BROWN, Ebenezer - 78, 275
BROWN, George -134, 199, 227, 281, 284
BROWN, Henry - 267
BROWN, James - 195, 202, 233
BROWN, John - 89, 173, 180, 253, 312
BROWN, Moses - 318
BROWN, Patrick - 83
BROWN, Peter - 243

BROWN, Richard -92, 139, 188, 190, 224
BROWN, Thomas - 93, 116, 239
BROWN, William - 243, 247, 273
BROWNE, Dr. John - 253
BROWNSPRIGGS, Thomas 323
BRUDERLIN, Carl - 130, 233
BRUPSTES, Patrick - 69
BRUST, Adrian - 158
BRYAN, Abraham - 66
BRYAN, John - 106, 299
BRYAN, Mary - 260
BRYAN, Thomas - 50
BRYAN, William - 299
BRYANT, James - 198
BRYANT, Valentine - 113
BUBRYCK, (first name not given) - 253
BUCHELOW, George - 278
BUCK, Aaron - 223
BUCK, John - 279
BUDD, Dr. Bern - 223
BUDD, Henry - 245
BUDD, John - 125, 279
BUDDLE, Thomas - 227
BULLINGHAM, Elisha - 84
BULLOCK, Joseph - 175
BULLOCK, William - 76
BUNCE - 230
BUNN, Thomas - 89
BUNTING, John - 64
BUNTING, Joshua -161, 192
BUNTING, Jr. Samuel - 199
BURBARY, Cornelius - 197
BURGE, William - 207

BURGER, Caspar - 198
BURGESS, Michael -182
BURGIE, Thomas - 284
BURGIN, John -174
BURIS, Peter - 118
BURK, Elizabeth - 90
BURK, John - 257
BURNES, Elijah - 303
BURNET, Mathias - 148
BURNETT, John - 312
BURNS, Christopher - 127, 279
BURNS, Hugh - 169
BURNS, John - 77, 146
BURNS, Thomas - 304
BURNS, William - 112
BURNSIDES, James - 269
BURR, Henry - 244
BURR, John - 65
BURR, Joseph - 80, 219
BURROUGHS, John - 94
BURROUGH, Joseph - 276
BURROUGHS, Samuel - 158
BURROUGHTS, Thomas - 73
BURROWES, John Capt. - 308
BURROWES, Joseph - 245
BURROWS, Evan - 73
BURROWS, Matthew - 57
BURROWS, Samuel - 186
BURROWS, Stephen - 73
BURWELL, Joseph - 194
BUSH, William - 58
BUSTILL, Samuel - 268
BUTLER, Edward - 270
BUTLER, Eleanor - 163, 261
BUTLER, John -163, 261

BUTLER, William - 166
BUTTERWORTH, William- 114
BYARD, Joseph - 123
BYRN, George B. - 102

C

CADWALADER, Thomas - 211
CADWALADER, Dr. (first name not given) - 211
CAESAR [Cesar] - 27, 30, 210, 216, 240, 249
CALDWELL, Andrew - 251
CALDWELL, Joseph - 169
CALWELL, Hugh - 284
CAMBEL, John - 174
CAMBELL, James - 180
CAMPBELL, Archibald - 242, 263
CAMPBELL, Cornelius - 119
CAMPBELL, George - 123, 303
CAMPBELL, James -125, 194
CAMPBELL, Thomas - 291
CANADA, John - 80
CANADA, Philip - 75
CANBY, Thomas - 96
CANE, Matthias - 195, 200
CANNON, John - 115
CANTLEN; Philip - 275
CAREY, John - 151
CARMACK, Robert - 148
CARMAN, John - 91
CARNAGIE, William - 97
CARNEY Jr.,Thomas - 178,

CARNEY, Thomas - 85, 178
CARNS, Jr., Richard - 149
CARPENTER, Jeremiah - 274
CARR, Robert - 66
CARR, William - 291
CARROLL, James - 309
CARTER, Asher - 153
CARTER, Robert - 170
CARTER, Thomas - 172
CARTY, Henry - 77
CARVEL, Jacob - 155
CARVER, James - 268
CASPERSON, John - 198
CASSAMOUR, Ephraim - 159
CASSOCK, John - 303
CASTEN, Hambleton - 79
CATLE, Mrs. - 252
CATO - 30, 218, 221, 226, 238, 248
CATON, William - 60
CAUSGROVE, Charles - 174
CAVANAGH, Hester - 264
CHALANER, John - 91
CHAMBERS, John - 191, 198
CHAMIER, Daniel - 147
CHANDLER, Jacob - 91
CHAPMAN, Robert - 51
CHARLES, - 213, 228, 262, 248
CHARLEY, Jacob - 176
CHATTIN, Josiah - 152, 277, 283, 288
CHEAK, John - 307
CHEESMAN, Peter - 175
CHELS -30, 247
CHESNUT, Samuel - 171
CHEVERS, William - 129
CHEVERS, Capt. - 4
CHEW, Richard - 72, 302
CHIPS, John - 200
CHRISTY, Charles - 55
CHRISTY, Matthias - 314
CIP - 30, 240
CLARK, Benjamin - 238
CLARK, David - 108
CLARK, Elijah - 259
CLARK, Henry - 95
CLARK, Henry Mrs. - 256
CLARK, James - 85
CLARK, John - 55, 87
CLARK, Michael - 80
CLARK, Richard - 118
CLARK, Thomas - 213
CLARK, Walter - 157
CLARKE, Benjamin - 139
CLARKE, Isaac - 145
CLARKE, John - 297
CLARKE, Thomas - 242, 263
CLAUS [CLAUSE, CLAUSS] 30, 208
CLAVE, Philip - 98
CLAWSON, Jonathan - 226, 230
CLAY, Slator - 211
CLAY, Thomas - 157
CLAYTON, David - 169
CLAYTON, Joseph - 224
CLAYTON, William - 219
CLEARWATER, Peter - 88
CLEAVER, John - 279
CLEAYTON, William - 235
CLEIL, Roger - 303
CLEM, Daniel - 303

CLEMANS, Judah - 126
CLEMONS, Edward - 158
CLINTON, Charles - 104
CLINTON, Henry - 25, 322
CLIZBE, Samuel - 108
CLOPPER, Cornelius - 224
CLOWSON, Francis - 113
CLUNN, Charles - 206
COAT, Barzillai - 264
COATE, Daniel - 191
COATS, Isaac - 235, 236
COCHRAN, David - 283
COCK, Samuel - 202
COCKER, Emmanuel - 212, 213
COCRAN, Peter - 78
CODA, Michael - 200
COFFY, Hugh - 274
COLAM, Ephraim - 72
COLE, Benjamin - 295
COLE, Daniel - 314
COLE, Henry - 120
COLE, Kendal - 111
COLE, William - 141
COLE, Samuel - 93
COLER, Sylvester - 258, 276
COLEMAN, John - 170
COLES, Kendal - 190
COLES, Samuel - 83
COLGAN, John - 164
COLLAGEN, Thomas - 146
COLLARD, Thomas - 160
COLLINGS, Michael - 70
COLLINGS, Richard - 140
COLLINS, Cornelius - 93
COLLINS, John - 159
COLLINS, Michael - 70, 82
COLLINS, Nathan - 145
COLPEN [CALVIN],

Malachiah [Melchor] - 86
COLSON, William - 30, 212
COLVIN, Patrick - 188, 251
COMES, Solomon - 86
COMPTON, Joseph - 150, 155
CONALLY, William - 47
CONGER, John - 141
CONINIE, Cornelius - 180
CONLIN, John - 87
CONLIN, Peter - 85
CONNAR, William - 267
CONNARD, Andrew - 308
CONNER, Bryan - 79
CONNER, Charles - 149
CONNER, William - 268
CONOR, Lawrence - 47
CONROE, Isaac - 93
CONSTANT - 30, 242.
COOK, George - 307, 308
COOK, Thomas - 290
COOK, Walter - 108
COOK, William - 76
COOK, Zebulon - 76
COOK, Capt.) - 194
COOKE, William - 233
COONS, Adam - 112
COOPER, Ann - 57
COOPER, Benjamin - 28, 102, 103, 113
COOPER, Daniel - 238, 282
COOPER Jr., Daniel - 283, 285, 286
COOPER, David - 264
COOPER, Henry - 80, 254
COOPER, James - 126
COOPER, John - 284
COOPER, Marmaduke - 194
COOPER, Samuel - 91
COPE, John - 49

COPPNER, Gabriel - 104
CORLIS, William - 183
CORNETT, Martin - 276
CORNISH, Charles - 227
CORTNEY, John - 69
CORWELL, Capt. - 152
CORYELL, John - 100, 212
COSTIGIN, Francis - 74
COULTON, Henry - 267
COUNTRYMAN, Andrew - 206
COURLEY, Abraham - 135
COURLEY, Richard - 135
COURSEY, William - 229
COWALT, Nicholas - 83
COWAN, Samuel - 182
COWARD, John - 66
COWARD, Joseph - 222, 223
COWART, Lieut. - 291
COX, David - 157
COX, John - 76, 112
COX, Samuel - 77
COX, Thomas - 134
COXE, Charles - 247
COXE (first name unknown) - 33, 291
COXE and FURMAN - 168
COYLER, Hendrick - 231
COYNE, Thomas - 138
CRAB, William - 265
CRAIG, Andrew - 200
CRAIG, Benjamin - 252
CRAIG, Jeremiah - 252
CRAIG, William - 148
CRAIGE, Archibald - 47
CRAMMER, Justus - 205
CRAMNER, Ephraim - 297
CRANE, Josiah - 113

CRANE, Mrs. - 14
CRAPPER, Levin - 229
CRAWFORD, Andrew - 284
CRAWFORD, John - 176, 278
CRAWFORD, William - 148
CRAZE, James - 125
CREEL, Manuel - 72
CREELY, Peter - 60
CRESSY, William - 141
CRISMON, Charles - 132
CRISPIN, Silas - 58
CROANE, Mary - 260
CROASDALE, Thomas - 58
CROOK, John - 64
CROOK, William - 233
CROSBY, W. - 270
CROSS, John - 75
CROSWEL, James - 54
CROTHERS, Thomas - 303
CROWDER, George - 200
CRUES, John - 272
CRUMMEL, Joseph - 149
CUDGE - 30, 249
CUFF - 30, 226, 230, 244, 245, 248
CUFF, Patrick - 148
CUFFEY, John - 67
CUMING, John - 256
CUMMING, Capt. John Noble 303, 304, 305
CUMMINGS, Robert - 208
CUMMINGS, (first name not given) - 169
CUMMINS, Theophilus - 308
CUNNINGHAM, George - 194
CUNNINGHAM, John - 84
CUNNINGHAM, Capt. - 4, 273
CURRY, Edward - 66

CURRY, Elizabeth - 262
CURRY, William - 116
CURTIS, James - 173
CURTIS, John - 307
CURTIS, Jr., William - 186
CYRUS - 235

D

DAILEY, George - 130
DAILY, Andrew - 68
DAILY, James - 298
DALGLISH, Nathaniel - 218
DAN, - 212
DANE, Alexander - 290
DANIELS, John - 246
DARBEY, William - 99
DARBY, Benjamin - 127
DARCEY, P. - 232
DARCY, Patrick - 249
DARWIN, Ebenenzer - 196
DAUBNEY, Lloyd - 242
DAVAN, John - 242
DAVID, Joseph -5, 119
DAVIDS, Benjamin -162
DAVIDSON, William -162, 283
DAVIES, William - 61
DAVIS, Benjamin - 45, 165
DAVIS, David - 280
DAVIS, Elijah - 124
DAVIS, George -123, 251
DAVIS, Henry - 290
DAVIS, James - 49, 309
DAVIS, John - 113, 151,
DAVIS, John Capt .- 310, 311
DAVIS, Philip - 90

DAVIS, Sarah - 254
DAVIS [DAVIDSON], William - 89, 91
DAWDY, Howell - 164
DAWSIT, Philip - 45
DAWSON, Betty - 257
DAWSON, J .- 122
DAWSON, Capt. -295
DAY, James -196, 292
DAY, Humphrey - 48
DAY, William - 170
DAYLEY, Daniel - 151
DAYTON, Capt. Elias - 231, 294
DAYTON, Jonathan - 179, 180
DE PEYSTER, Jr. John -238
DEAL[E], Thomas - 51, 98
DEALY, Joseph - 111
DEAN, Thomas - 98
DEARE, John - 273
DEBOW, Lawrence - 96
DECOU, Isaac - 192
DECOW, Joseph - 65, 69
DEGNAR, Peter - 135
DEHART, Dr. Mathias - 91
DELANEY, Cornelius - 63
DELANY, William - 192
DELAPLAIN, James - 234
DENCK, Simon - 131
DENIM, William - 53
DENNET, William - 149
DENNIS - 78
DENNIS, John 110, 141
DENNISTON, William - 158
DENNY, Peter - 201
DENORMANDIE, John Abraham - 90
DENTON, John - 140, 249
DE POOL, Carolina - 262

DERICKSON, Folkart - 69
DERRICK, Christopher - 199
DESBROSSES, Elias - 236
DEWEES, Jr., William - 142
DICK, Adam - 246
DICK, Archibald - 194
DICK, James - 178
DICK, John - 191
DICK, Samuel -137, 164
DICK - 30, 228
DICKENSON, James - 292
DICKENSON, John - 184
DICKINSON; Gen. Philemon - 251
DIETRICK, Christopher - 184, 186
DILLON, James Capt.- 300, 301
DINAH - 264
DOBSON, James - 123
DODD, William - 303
DOLIN, John - 66
DOLTON, William - 137
DONBAR, James - 222
DONELSON, Joseph -118
DONOYL, Thadymack -59
DORON, Brian - 275
DORREN, Margaret - 167, 262
DORRINGTON, William - 53, 55
DORUS- 245
DOUD, Richard - 71
DOUGHTY, Edward - 282
DOUGHTY, Henry - 54
DOUGHTY, Thomas -310
DOUGHTY, Capt. - 311
DOUGLASS; George - 150

DOVE, Samuel - 68
DOWBROW, Gabriel - 190
DOWDEN, William - 162
DOWDLE, Michael - 76
DOWEL, Thomas - 150
DOWELL, William - 74
DOWNEY, James - 76
DOWNEY, John - 134
DOWNS, Charles - 300
DOWNS, Robert - 203
DOWNS, William - 146
DOWNY, Terence - 153
DOYL, Massy - 265
DOYL, Philip - 57
DOYL, William - 193
DOYLE, Darby - 137
DOYLING; John - 63
DOZ, Andrew - 96
DRAIN, Henry - 181, 297
DRAKE, Ebenezer - 283
DRAPER, William - 65
DRESSNER, William - 85
DRISCOL, Jeremiah - 151
DUCKWORTH, George - 73
DUDLEY, Francis -102, 196
DUDLEY, Joshua - 205
DUEL, John -123
DUFFIELD, Isaac - 265
DUFFIELD, John - 265
DUFFIELD, Dr. Samuel - 242
DUGRAY, Charles -117
DULY, Joshua - 298
DUMPHY, Edward - 190
DUN, Andrew - 92
DUN, James - 95
DUNAGAN, Johanna - 260
DUNCAN, James - 53
DUNDAS, David - 82
DUNDORSE, David - 274

DUNLOP, Capt. - 121, 122
DUNMEAD, William - 197
DUNN, Hugh - 111
DUNN, James - 54
DUNN, John -196
DUNN, Martin - 81
DUNN, Thomas - 297
DUNNEBO, James - 95
DUNNING, Thomas- 57
DUNPHY,Thomas - 59
DURCK, John - 131
DURELL, Darby - 116
DURHAM, John M. - 90
DWYER, John - 100
DYE, James - 198

E

EARLINGTON, Widow - 50
EATTON, Daniel - 92
EBEN, - 30, 233
EBERLY, George - 174, 242
EDEN, Medcef - 249
EDEY, Ebenezer - 58
EDGWORTH, Elizabeth - 263
EDIMISTON, John - 134
EDMONDS, Jacob - 166
EDWARDS, Daniel - 136
EDWARDS, Lt. Edward - 307
EDWARDS, John - 46, 73
EDWARDS, Samuel - 278
EGLINGTON, John - 255
ELDRIDGE, Abraham - 263
ELLET, Charles - 166
ELLIS, Daniel- 279, 280
ELLIS, Jonathan - 81

ELLIS, Joseph - 84, 292, 293
ELLIS, Robert - 48
ELLIS, Samuel - 190
ELLIS, William - 56, 85
ELLISON, Richard - 268
ELMER, Theophilus - 226, 281, 282
ELTON, Margaret - 261
ELTON, Ruel - 162
ELTON, Thomas - 261
EMANS, John - 268
EMER Jackson - 232
EMERY, John - 298
EMLEY, John - 61, 65
EMLEY, Robert - 120
EMONS, Hendrick - 238
ENGLE, Frederick - 175
ENGLE, John - 100
ENGLISH, James - 51, 81
ENMAN, Thomas Henry - 165
ERMUS, John - 97
ERWIN, William - 308
ERWIN (first name unknown)- 232
ESDALE, James - 245
ESOP-30, 217
ESTILL, Samuel - 115, 116
ETHERINGTON, James -180
EVANS, Caleb - 112
EVANS, Enoch - 194
EVANS, John - 88
EVANS, Morgan - 96
EVANS, Samuel - 280
EVANS, William - 204
EVENDEN, Edward - 301
EVERSOLE, Charles - 230
EYRES, George - 59
EZEKIEL-30, 237

F

FAESH, John Jacob - 189
FAGAN, Daniel - 140
FAGAN, William - 303
FALLS, John - 303
FANN - 265
FANTON, William - 160
FAR, William - 198
FARMER, Brooke - 259
FARMER, Nicholas - 145
FARRARY, Commesole - 303
FARREL, Michael - 178
FARRINGTON; Benjamin- 272
FENTON, John - 57
FENTON, Thomas - 128
FERGUSON, David - 133
FEROL, Michael - 188
FERRY, William - 47
FIELD, Benjamin - 77
FIELD, Francis - 223, 244
FIELD, Robert - 228, 254, 298
FILER, Thomas - 99
FINLEY, John - 49
FINLY, David - 62
FINN, Elizabeth - 227
FINN, William - 57
FIRTH, Ezra - 188
FIRTH, John - 143, 260
FIRTH, William - 133
FISHBURN, William - 148
FISHER, John - 201
FISHER, Joshua - 221
FITHIAN, Aaron - 151
FITZ RANDEL, James - 78
FITZ RANDOLF, Benjamin 109
FITZ RANDOLF, Hartshorne - 191, 197
FITZGERALD, James - 75
FITZGERALD, Nicholas -156
FITZGERALD, Philip - 99
FITZHUGH, William - 133
FITZRANDOLPH, David - 290
FITZRANDOLPH, Nathaniel - 104
FIZELER, Jacob - 126
FLANNIGAN, James - 143
FLATT, Christian - 109
FLATT, Paultus - 109
FLENTHAM, William - 119
FLOOD, Francis -129
FLOWER, Samuel - 107
FLOYD, Richard - 54
FOLKS, Isaiah - 269
FOLWELL, Nathan - 120
FOORD, William - 278
FORBUSH, William - 60
FORD, Jacob - 70, 98, 214
FORD, Jacob Jr. - 140, 281
FORD, Jonathan - 159
FORDE, - 30, 219
FORKER, John - 280
FORMAN Elizabeth - 108
FORMAN, Isaac - 71, 74
FORMAN, Joseph - 47, 79
FORMAN, Thomas -117, 237, 246
FORMAN, Samuel - 229
FORSBERG, Prince - 251
FORSTER, Thomas - 79
FORSYTH, Matthew - 84
FORTUNE, - 30, 242
FOSTER, David - 123
FOSTER, Icabod -163

FOSTER, Jacob - 142
FOSTER, John - 195
FOSTER, William - 106, 126
FOWLER, Joseph - 310
FOWLER, Thomas - 277
FOX, Jonathan - 114, 258
FOX William - 114
FOY, John -196, 309
FRANK,- 30, 215, 232, 233, 240, 242, 247, 250
FRANKLIN, Benjamin -72
FRANKS, David - 240, 241
FRAZIER, Andrew - 159
FRAZIER, Joseph - 89
FRAZIER, William - 120, 277
FREELINGHAUSON, Col. Frederick - 310, 311
FREEMAN, Samuel - 52
FREEMAN, Thomas - 107
FREEMILLER, Joseph - 86
FRELUHEN, Anna Margarette - 263
FRENCH, John - 88
FRENCH, Philip - 210
FRITS, Christian - 100
FRY, Richard - 231

FRY, Thomas - 132
FUETTER, Emory - 225
FUHRMAN, Gottlieb - 187
FULLER, Amos- 274
FULLERTON, James - 142
FURMAN, Joseph - 110
FURMAN, Moore - 220
FURR, William - 98
FURY, Thomas - 289

G

GAINE, Hugh - 110, 226
GALLAGHAN, Cornelius - 30, 237
GALLAHAN, John - 281
GALLAHON, Cornelius - 229
GALLOWAY, John - 271
GALPIN, Joseph - 285
GAMBLE, John - 83
GAMBLE, William - 204
GAMBOL, Burgis - 173
GARDINER, George - 69
GARDINER, John - 193
GARISON, Joseph - 203
GARNET, William - 111
GARRAGAN, Peter - 85

GARRASON, Jacob - 245
GARRAWAYS, Capt. Charles - 293
GARRET, Charles - 282
GARRISON, Isaac - 94
GARRISON, Isaac Mrs. - 256
GARRISON, Samuel - 163
GASKELL, Jacob - 82
GAULEHER, Niel - 125

GEE, George - 200
GEISINGER, Charles - 139, 145
GEIST, George Leonard - 111
GENENS, Lonen - 30, 215
GENGE, George - 155
GEOGBEGAN, Thomas - 271
GEORGE - 30, 211, 214, 241, 252
GERALD, James - 188

GERARD, Daniel - 157
GERARD, William - 173
GETSHENS, Capt. - 200
GETTILL, George - 301
GEYER, Peter - 195
GIBBON, John - 124
GIBBONS, (first name unknown) - 275
GIBBONS, John - 296
GIBBS, Aaron - 144
GIBSON, Joseph - 114
GIDDONS, Roger - 295
GIFFORD, Joseph - 310
GILL, John -72, 103, 172, 254
GILL, William - 149
GILL, Widow, - 207
GILLCREACE, James - 142
GILLMAN, Simon - 270
GINIS, James - 114, 258
GIPSON, James - 157
GIST, Mordecai - 264
GLASCO - 30, 227
GLASS, Daniel - 129
GLINN, William - 300
GLOVER, William - 299
GODDARD, Nicholas - 98
GODFREY, Edward - 137, 139
GOFF, George - 174
GOLDER, Joseph - 220
GOOCH, William - 289
GOODING, Jacob - 146
GOODSON, Andrew - 77
GORDON, James - 295
GORDON, John - 52, 135
GORDON, Thomas - 77, 282
GORMAN, Henry - 123
GOSLING, David - 162

GOULD, Alexander - 135
GOULD, William - 135, 151
GOULDING, Joseph - 45
GOWEN, John - 53
GRAHAM, David - 122
GRAHAM, Peter - 284
GRAHAM, Michael - 164
GRAHAM, William - 172
GRANT, James - 66
GRANT, John - 82
GRANT, Richard - 292
GRAVES, Thomas - 120
GRAY, James - 123
GRAYBILL, Jacob - 124
GRAZIOUS, Ann - 161, 261
GREEN, Edward - 48
GREEN, George - 70
GREEN, James - 199
GREEN, John - 72, 166, 181, 254, 285, 309
GREEN, Thomas - 303
GREEN, William - 285
GREENSTREET, Benjamin - 55
GREENWOOD, David - 92
GREENWOOD, James - 81
GREGORY, James - 183
GRENWOOD, John - 294
GREY, Richard - 269
GRIFFE, Thomas - 46
GRIFFIN, William - 267
GRIFFITH, Catherine - 94
GRIFFITH, Samuel - 94
GRIFFITHS, Thomas -186
GRIG, slave -30, 234, 238
GRIMES, Mary - 254
GROCK, Morgan - 82
GROMMON, Ichabud - 108
GROVER, James - 98

GROVER, Joseph - 222, 223
GRUMBLE, Honos Yerwack 85
GUILMAN, Simon - 56
GUIN, Samuel - 65
GUNN, Christianna - 264
GUNNITT, Isaac - 27, 207
GWIN, William - 52
GYLESE, John - 261

H

HACK, - 30, 246
HACKET, John - 74, 113
HACKET, Richard - 138
HACKETT, William - 275
HACKETT, first name not given - 103
HACKNEY, Joseph - 112
HADDOCK, Francis - 274
HAGEN, James - 61, 254
HAGENER, Frederick - 128
HAGER - 262
HAGLIN, John - 96
HAIGHT, Joseph - 152, 230, 261
HAINES, Anthony - 81
HAINES, Ephraim - 205
HAINES, Hugh - 81
HAINES, John - 84
HAINES, Nathaniel - 91, 155
HAINS, Isaac - 152
HAINS, John - 84
HAINS, William - 68
HALINSHEAD, F. - 90
HALL, Bartholomew - 290
HALL, Charles - 309

HALL, Clement - 105
HALL, Francis - 90
HALL, James - 198
HALL, John - 160
HALL, Marshall - 200
HALL, Nathan - 312
HALLET, Jacob - 187
HALLITT, James - 302
HALSTEAD, Josiah O. - 106, 119
HALTER, Martin - 139
HAMBLETON, James - 199
HAMBLETON, Michael - 51
HAMBLETON, William - 276
HAMBRICHT, James - 100
HAMELS, George Leonard - 105
HAMILTON, Archibald - 97
HAMILTON, George - 100
HAMILTON, James - 89
HAMILTON, John - 76
HAMILTON, William - 276
HAMMAN, Jack - 229
HAMMER, John - 172
HAMMIT, John Capt. - 305, 306
HAMMOND, Jack - 230
HAMPTON, Jonathan - 125, 256, 258, 276
HAMPTON, William - 280
HANCE, John - 100
HANES, Joseph - 150
HANDLIN, John - 171
HANKINSON, James - 102
HANKINSON, Peter - 165
HANLEY, Richard - 147
HANLON, Patrick - 259
HANNA, John - 293
HANNABALL - 295

HANNALY, Richard - 138
HANNIGAN, Cornelius - 59
HANSMAN, Christopher - 128, 133
HARBER, Thomas - 148
HARBOR, John - 285
HARBOUR, Garret - 30, 229
HARDBURN, Thomas - 123
HARDIN, Edward - 267
HARDY, John - 282
HARKER, Daniel - 157
HARKER, Samuel - 228
HARKINS, John - 150
HARRIMAN, John - 198
HARRIS, Abel - 93, 195
HARRIS, Jacob - 116
HARRIS, John - 160
HARRIS, Robert - 45
HARRIS, Thomas - 269
HARRISON, John - 48, 160
HARRISON, Samuel - 197, 275
HARRISON, Thomas - 269
HARRISON, William - 48, 58, 60, 1704
HARRY - 30, 220, 222, 229, 231, 239, 245, 246, 247, 252
HARRY, Evan - 272
HART, John - 219, 296
HART, Nicholas - 140
HARTLEY, Joseph - 205
HARTLEY, Thomas - 154
HARTMAN, Henry - 292
HARTSHORN, John - 159
HARVEY, Arthur - 86
HARVEY, Edward - 107
HARVEY, Joseph - 195
HARVEY, Thomas - 189
HARWOOD, John - 169

HASENECLEVER, Peter -130, 131, 132
HASSEY, William - 55
HATHERLY, Thomas - 303
HATHEWAY, Shadreck - 215
HATNES, Richard - 54
HAULBEET, Ebenezer - 127
HAVENS, John - 94
HAVERSACH, John - 56
HAWK, Lt. Sampson - 292
HAWKES, Jane - 261
HAWKES, Mary - 261
HAWKINS, Steven - 310
HAWKINS, William -281
HAWXHURST, William - 115, 127
HAY, William - 92
HAZARD, Jupiter - 30, 215
HAZELWOOD, John - 262
HEADEN, Mary - 257
HEADEN, Thomas - 111
HEANY, Mary - 259
HEARD, Nathaniel - 151, 285
HECATISSA - 37, 255
HEDAY, Joseph - 98
HEDDIN, Joseph - 216
HEGEMAN, Benjamin - 129
HEGEMAN, Jacobus - 55
HEIDECH, Christopher - 183
HEIDIECH, Christian - 186
HEIGHT, Joseph - 130
HELDRETH, David - 253
HELM, Henry - 197
HELNIT, William - 311
HEMPHILL & GORDON - 170
HENDERSON, Edward - 263
HENDERSON, John - 61, 75 -
HENDMAN, Richard - 171

HENDRICK, Edward - 82
HENDRICK, John - 229
HENDRICKS, Abraham - 58, 196
HENDRICKS, William - 229
HENDRICKSON, William - 227
HENHOLD, George - 186
HENRY - 162
HENRY, David - 199, 243
HENRY, John - 47
HENRY, Samuel - 120, 135, 156, 200, 224, 246
HEPPARD, William - 204
HERITAGE, Benjamin - 82
HERRON, James - 145
HESS, Hendrick - 180
HESTER - 265
HEWES, Joseph - 133
HEWES, Samuel - 121
HEWIT, Benejah - 196
HEWLING[S], Abraham 175, 221
HICKS, Edward - 111
HIDE, William - 45
HIGBEE - 214
HIGGINS, Barnaby - 301
HIGGINS, (no first name given) 284
HILDERBRAND, Isaac - 170
HILL, Alexander - 95, 188, 189
HILL, John - 49
HILL, Jonathan - 293
HILL, Thomas - 207
HILL, Capt. - 189
HILL, (no first name given) - 120

HILLIARD, James - 235
HILLIAS John - 199
HILLIER, John - 226
HILMAN, Joab - 133
HIMES, John - 298
HINCHMAN, James - 158, 205
HINDS, Jeremiah - 78
HINES, Patrick - 107
HINGHAM, Benjamin - 87
HINSON, John - 110
HINSON, Joseph - 105
HIRETON, Obadiah - 171
HODGES, James - 127
HOGAN, Maj. William W.- 294, 295
HOGE, Zebulon - 148
HOGG, Richard - 205
HOLCOMBE, John - 64
HOLDCRAFT, William - 239
HOLLAND, Arthur - 61
HOLLAND, Edward- 51
HOLLAND, John - 278
HOLLAND, Richard - 78
HOLLAND, Robert - 279
HOLLER, Jacob - 145
HOLLINSHEAD, Edmund - 201
HOLLINSHEAD, Jacob - 137
HOLLINSHEAD, Joseph - 212, 274
HOLLINSHEAD, William - 272
HOLLOWAY, Isaac - 141, 142, 156
HOLLOWAY, John - 141, 142
HOLM, Benjamin - 267
HOLME, John - 274
HOLMES, Abijah - 244
HOLMES, Samuel - 64

HOLT, Magistrate - 69
HOME, Archibald - 72
HOOD, William - 167
HOOPER, Anthony - 185
HOOPER, Jr. Robert Lettis - 220, 250, 265
HOOPS, Robert - 250, 265
HOOTEN, Thomas - 106
HOOVER, Jacob - 284
HOPKINS, John Estaugh - 120, 127
HOPKINS, William - 172
HOPPER, Edward - 272
HOPPER, Col. - 222
HORNER, John - 84, 85
HORTWICK, Lawrence - 273
HOUGH, Jonathan - 82
HOUSE, Thomas - 183
HOUSE, Captain - 109
HOW, Samuel - 225
HOW, Micajah - 60
HOWARD, Lawrence - 107
HOWE, Sir William - 272
HOWEL, Thomas - 154
HOWELL, Benjamin - 118
HOWELL, Hezekiah - 248
HOWELL, John - 117
HRUBB, Henry - 97
HUCKABACK, John - 97
HUDSON, Francis - 195
HUDSON, William - 195
HUES, John - 51
HUGG, Jacob - 105
HUGG, Joseph - 143, 234, 238, 286, 313
HUGG, Capt. Samuel - 303, 306
HUGG, William - 212, 229, 237
HUGG, Major (first name unknown) - 250
HUGHES, John - 117, 140, 279
HUGHES, Joseph - 128
HUGHES, Peter - 159
HULET, William - 179
HULICK, Peter - 251, 252
HUMPHREY - 236
HUMPHREYS, Stephen - 246
HUMPHREYS (first name unknown) - 181
HUNLOCK, Thomas - 269
HUNLOKE, Thomas - 268, 269, 270, 272, 273
HUNT, Charles - 86
HUNT, John - 209, 233, 245, 271
HUNT, Thomas - 216
HUNT, William - 219
HUNT, Wilson - 146, 245, 249
HUNTER, Peter - 114
HURRY, Cornelius - 154, 163
HUSSEY, Patrick - 138
HUTCHINSON, John - 139
HUTCHINSON, Jonathan - 135
HUTCHINSON, Dr. (first name unknown) - 251
HUTSCHLARA, Peter - 131
HUXELY, John - 167
HYER, William - 232

I

IAMS, John - 194
IMLAY, Peter - 136
INGLE, John - 129

INGLE, William - 188
INGMAN, Jacob - 297
INSKAPE, John- 81
INSPEEK, Benjamin -160
IRELAN, Japaheth - 244
IRISH, Nathaniel - 252
ISAAC - 212
ISHMAEL - 30, 36, 214, 231
ISAIAH - 260
IVINS, Moses - 129

J

JABIL, Peter - 160
JACK - 27, 30, 208, 211, 212, 216, 217, 219, 220, 221, 228, 232, 238, 239, 246, 249, 251
JACKSON, Benjamin - 157
JACKSON, Emer - 232
JACKSON, James - 259
JACKSON, John - 210
JACKSON, Margaret - 67
JACKSON, Robert - 165
JACKSON, Thomas - 23
JACKSON, (no first name given) - 195
JACOB - 28, 223, 225, 226, 237
JACOBS, Philip - 141
JAMES, Jr. J. - 95, 256
JAMES, John - 48
JAMES, Joseph - 209, 215
JAMES, Richard - 228
JAMES, Samuel - 205
JAMES, Thomas - 94
JAMES - 210, 215, 220, 236, 241, 245

JANE - 39, 265
JARRAD, Thomas - 96
JARVIS, John - 191
JEM - 234, 247
JEMMY - 30, 226
JENAWEIN, Leonard - 187
JENKINS, John - 152
JENKINS, William - 150, 303
JENKS, Joseph - 206
JENNIE - 263
JENNY - 242, 263
JESSUP, John - 201
JEWELL, Nathaniel - 108
JOB - 237
JOE - 30, 226, 227, 243, 246, 247, 250, 252
JOHN - 208, 234
JOHNSON, Cornelius - 59
JOHNSON, George - 115
JOHNSON, Isaac - 23, 244, 309
JOHNSON, Jack - 30, 220
JOHNSON, Jacob - 54
JOHNSON, James - 70, 71, 72, 171, 273, 303
JOHNSON, John - 30, 132, 134, 220, 224, 289
JOHNSON, Joseph - 226
JOHNSON, Matthew - 286
JOHNSON, Reyner - 267
JOHNSON, Richard - 171, 182, 238
JOHNSON, Robert - 169, 246, 250
JOHNSON, Thomas - 309
JOHNSON, William - 109, 181
JOHNSON, (first name unknown - 128
JOHNSON, Capt. (first name

unknown) - 233
JOHNSTON, Andrew - 145
JOHNSTON,, James - 68
JOHNSTON, John L. - 145
JOHNSTON, Richard - 160
JOLLY, William - 153
JONES, Cadwalader - 299
JONES, Capt. David - 56, 248
JONES, Edward - 45
JONES, Enoch - 204
JONES, Evan - 61
JONES, Isaac - 197
JONES, Griffie - 53
JONES, John - 142, 152, 154, 156, 244
JONES, Joseph - 116, 134
JONES, Morgan - 48
JONES, Peter - 98
JONES, Reuben - 88
JONES, Robert - 286
JONES, Stephen - 191
JONES, Thomas - 118, 296
JONES, William - 68
JORDAN, Michael - 167
JORDAN, Richard - 87
JOSEPH - 252
JOSEPHSON, (first name unknown) - 245
JOYCE, Margaret - 261
JUPITER - 30, 248
JURNEY, Daniel -191
JUSTER, John - 30, 218

K

KAIGHIN, John - 118
KAIGHIN, Joseph - 76, 262

KANE, Margaret - 255
KARRAGAN, William - 158
KAY, Francis - 197
KEAFF, Timothy - 153
KEAN, Barney - 174
KEANE, John - 180, 290
KEARNEY, James - 184
KEARNEY, John - 286
KEASEY, William - 71
KEE, William - 263
KEEFE, James - 173
KEELLY, Michael - 188
KEEN, George - 220, 221
KEIGHN, David - 106
KEITH, George - 257
KELLE, John - 172
KELLEY, Joseph - 67
KELLY, Cornelius - 64
KELLY, John - 117
KELLY, Mary - 255
KELLY, Patrick - 72
KELLY, William - 108
KELLY, (no first name given) 232
KELSO, William - 181
KEMBLE, Edward - 49
KEMBLE (first name unknown) - 259
KEMPTON, Samuel - 98
KENDALL, Benjamin - 152
KENNEDY, William - 181, 297
KENNEDY, Capt. - 232
KENNY, Lazarus - 30, 209
KENT, Daniel - 30, 216, 243
KENT, David - 216
KENT, Joseph - 161
KENT - 30, 237
KENTLING, Philip - 126

KERN, James - 167, 262
KERNEY, Philip - 279
KERNS, William - 189
KETELTAS, Peter - 238
KEY, Simon - 140
KIDD, John - 200
KIEF, John - 177
KIEFF, Davis - 184
KIER, Archibald - 62
KIER Peter - 200
KIGER, Matthia - 110
KILLE, John - 186
KILLE, William - 118
KILLING, Thomas - 89
KILLSEY, James - 89
KIMSEY, Nathan - 170
KING, Andrew - 280
KING, Constant - 205
KING, John - 62, 78
KING, Joseph - 127
KING, Marcus - 146, 153
KING, Matthew -146, 153
KING, Robert - 52
KING, Thomas - 75, 101
KINGSLAND, Isaac - 256
KINGSLAND, John - 196
KINNERSLY, Richard - 105
KINNICUT, Hezekiah - 62
KINSEY, John - 174
KINSINER, John Balser- 185
KIPP, Benjamin - 30, 231
KIPPS, Ben - 234
KIRBY, Richard - 48
KIRK, Samuel - 253
KITCHEL, Aaron - 247
KITCHEN, William - 90
KLEIN, John - 224, 225
KNICKERBACKER,
Harman - 146
KOLLOCK, Magistrate - 69
KONIG, Wilholm - 132
KOSADY, William - 115
KOTTS, Conrad - 142
KOUL, Paul - 75
KUMMERSFIELD, Maria - 256

L

LADD, John - 97
LADD, John Jr. - 66
LAMB, Col. John - 311, 312, 313, 314
LAMB, Patrick - 150
LAMB, Thomas - 168
LAMBSON, Hance - 236
LAND, James - 190
LANE, Gizebert - 228
LANE, Richard - 74
LANE, Thomas - 101
LANG, Rev. James - 197
LANGEIDER, Joseph - 130
LANGFORD, John - 269
LANGLEY, John - 95
LANIN, Andrew - 99
LANK - 229
LAPSLEY, James - 114
LARRENCE, Nathaniel - 303
LASANT, Jacob - 66
LASEY, John - 95, 256
LAUGH, John - 303
LAWRENCE, Abraham - 241
LAWRENCE, Elisha - 245
LAWRENCE, John - 113
LAWRENCE, Robert - 56
LAWRENCE, William - 177,

178, 245
LAWRIE, James - 165
LAWSON, William - 161
LEAMING, Aaron - 127, 196
LEAN, Thomas - 100
LEARD, David - 313
LEARY, John - 248
LEB - 241
LEE, Charles - 149, 285
LEE, Greshom - 182
LEE, James - 171
LEE, John - 267
LEE, Joseph - 271
LEE, Michael - 124
LEE, Purmot - 154
LEER, Chritian - 119
LEGERGER, Adam - 111
LEGG, John - 190
LEIGH, Joseph - 151
LEITCH, Thomas - 99
LEONARD, James - 207, 210
LEONARD, John - 67, 207
LEONARD, Nathaniel - 46
LEONARD, Samuel - 103, 209
LEONARD, Thomas - 283
LESLIE, Alexander - 262
LESTER, William - 234
LESTRANGE, James - 80
LETHERMON, John - 132
LETSON, Thomas - 221
LETTERIDGE, John - 179
LEVI - 244
LEVIS, Samuel - 153
LEVIS, Thomas - 176, 177
LEWIS, Isaac, - 194
LEWIS, John - 46

LEWIS, Nathaniel - 204
LEWIS - 30, 225, 226
LIBO, James - 200
LINCH, Timothy - 95, 106
LINDSEY, David - 286
LINDY, Walter - 143
LINNEY, Adam - 176
LIONS, Bartholomew - 184
LIPPINCOT, Samuel - 171, 206, 255
LIPPINCOT, Thomas - 69
LIPPINCOTT, Arney - 205
LIPPINCOTT, Jr. Daniel - 124, 157
LIPPENCOTT, Jacob - 88
LIPPINCOTT, Job - 123
LISHMAN, Henry - 204
LISK, Benjamin - 312
LISTER, William - 223
LITHGOW, Daniel - 154
LITTLE, Nathaniel - 163
LIVINGSTON, Philip J. - 136
LIVINGSTON, Robert - 256
LLOYD, Bateman - 237
LLOYD, William - 121
LODGE, Benjamin - 162
LOGAN, William - 83
LONGSTREET, Jr., Aaron - 243
LONGSTREET, Dirick - 243
LONGWORTH, Thomas - 109
LORD, Abraham - 87, 123
LORD, Joshua - 125
LOT - 30, 214
LOTT, Cornelius - 280
LOUBER, John Adam - 178
LOUZADA, Aaron - 112
LOVELL, John - 296
LOVERING, Giles - 185

LOVETT, Joseph - 202
LOW, Cornelius - 61, 221
LOWDEN, Reigner - 267
LOWREY, Thomas - 265
LOYD, Thomas, Lt. Col.- 294
LUCAS, Frind - 218
LUCAY, James - 312
LUCY - 37, 259
LUDERMAN, Christian - 104
LUDLAM, Joseph - 90
LUDLAM, Thomas - 160, 162
LUN - 30, 244
LUPTON, John - 136
LYELL, David - 207
LYELL, Thomas - 174
LYCAN, John - 273
LYNCH, John - 297
LYNCH, Samuel - 214

M

M'AFEE, Daniel - 128
M'AHEE, John - 176
M'ANITINIE, Daniel - 237
M'BRIDE, James - 192
M'CABE, John - 97
M'CABE, Luke - 109
M'CABE, William - 161
M'CAGE, Hugh - 164
M'CAGHRY, Thomas - 134
M'CALLA, John - 240
M'CALLA, William - 251
M'CINDRED, Bernard - 124
M'CLANE, Hugh - 308
M'CLANE, Patrick - 69
M'CLANY, Archibald - 187
M'CLAUGHLIN, John - 90
M'CLEAN, Allen - 313
M'CLEAN, Hugh - 99
M'CLELLAN, John, Jr. - 182
M'CLENACHAN, Blair - 264
M'CLONE, Patrick - 69
M'CLOUGHLAND, Mark - 128
M'CLUNE, William - 172
M'COLOMN, John - 302
M'CORD, William - 132
M'CORMACK, Robert - 148
M'CORMICK, Alexander - 282
M'CORMICK, William -1 68
M'COY, John - 85
M'COY, William - 150
M'CULLAM, Andrew - 158
M'CULLEN, William - 160
M'CULLOUGH, John - 136
M'CULOH, Joseph - 246
M'CUNY, James - 90
M'DANIEL, Daniel - 84
M'DANIEL, Hugh - 197
M'DANIEL, James - 281
M'DANIEL, John -129
M'DANIEL, Matthew - 67
M'DANIEL, (first name not known) - 281
M'DERMONT, John -194
M'DONALD, John - 294
M'DONALD, Randle -141
M'DONALD, William - 294
M'DONNALD, John - 303
M'DONNAUGH, Alexander - 126
M'DONNELL, Alexander - 126
M'DONNOUGH, James - 147
M'DOWEL, John - 57
M'FARTREDGE Capt. (first

name not known) - 306
M'FELLY, John - 168
M'GEE, Sarah - 264
M'GINNIS, George - 200
M'GIVERON, Daniel - 169
M'GLAUGH, Dennis - 66
M'GORK, John - 192
M'GOWN, Andrew - 276
M'GRADY, James - 129
M'GROERTY, William - 277
M'GUIRE, John - 193
M'GUIRE, Jr. Michael - 185
M'IMNIRY, Daniel - 182
M'INTOSH, James - 167
M'KAIN, Hugh - 185
M'KILLUP, Abraham - 313
M'KINE, Alexander - 290
M'LAUGHLIN, Michael - 95
M'LERNAN, Daniel - 168
M'LLVEEN, Arthur - 88
M'MAHON, Joseph - 293
M'MAHAN, Dennis - 115
M'MANAN, Hugh - 179
M'MULLEN, Dennis - 191
M'MULLIN, Patrick - 304
M'NAGHTEN, Thomas - 200
M'NEAL, Henry - 302
M'NEAL, Samuel - 112
M'NEIL, Thomas - 134
M'PETERS, John - 124
M'SHANE, Daniel - 166, 261
M'VERMIK, Terry - 121
MACBON, Samuel - 60
MACCUBBIN, James - 237
MACDONALD, Randal - 149
MACHON, Thomas - 58
MACK, Robert - 170
MACKBRIDE, James - 54

MACKEY, Lieut.(first name unknown)- 291
MACKINNEY,William - 79
MACKINTOSH, John - 66
MACKMANNERS, Constantine - 51
MACLANE, Alexander - 51
MACMEIN, Joseph - 114
MACMEIN, Mary - 258
MACNEIL,John - 60
MACPETERS, James - 271
MACWIER, John - 93
MAFFET, Archibald - 150
MAGAHEY, Catherine - 256
MAGAHEY, Nicholas - 90
MAGEE, Abraham - 287
MAGEE, Robert - 86
MAGWIGIN, Turrence - 101
MAHANY, John - 70
MAHONY, Timothy - 147
MALATO, John - 269
MALICE, William - 205
MALLIN, Charles - 184
MALONE, Richard - 91
MALONE, Mrs. Richard - 256
MALONEY, Timothy - 78
MALSBARY, Jonathan - 193
MALTSBURY, John - 51
MANDO - 30, 213
MANNING, Jeremiah - 190
MANSFIELD, Samuel - 168
MANUEL, Fransh - 28, 207
MANWARRING, Richard - 65
MAQUOD, Brian - 133
MARFORD, Benjamin - 274
MARIA - 265
MARK - 30, 232, 247
MAROT ,Philip - 87
MARPOLE, George - 214
MARRIOT, Thomas - 211
MARSH, Peter - 125
MARSH, Susannah - 33
MARSHALL, John - 71, 74

MARSHALL, Thomas - 200
MARTIN, Ephraim Col.- 301, 302, 308
MARTIN, Hugh - 212
MARTIN, Jacob - 137, 139
MARTIN, James - 69, 120
MARTIN, John - 115, 217
MASON, John - 263
MASTER, George Frederick 103
MATHAS, Joseph - 67
MATISON, Benjamin - 170
MATLACK, Abraham - 126
MATLACK, Benjamin - 190
MATLACK, John - 49
MATLOCK, Timothy - 77
MATTHEWS, Francis - 139
MATTHEWS, Jacob - 284
MATTS, John - 203
MATTYSEN, Cornelius - 270
MAY, Edward - 117
MAY, George - 100
MAYBE, Edward - 105, 111
MAYBERRY, Thomas - 183
MAYBURTY, Richard - 291
MAYHALL, Joseph - 143
MAYHEW, Thomas - 119
MCBRIDE, John - 298
MCCAUSLAND, Capt. - 159
MCDANNOLD, Daniel - 82
MCDERMOT, Michael - 56
MCDONAGH, James - 137
MCDONALD, Alexander - 122
MCDONNEL, Bryan - 66
MCEWEN, John - 172
MCKABE [MCKAPE], William - 119
MCKAY, John - 121
MCKNIGHT, William - 99
McNEAL, Neal - 49

MCQUEEN, William - 121
MCCUNY, James - 90
MEAD, Capt.(first name unknown) - 312
MEAGHER, John - 155
MEDCALF, Jacob - 55
MEDDIN, Roger - 80
MEDLEY, John - 54
MEEK, Tobias - 103
MEEKER, Samuel - 220
MEHEW, Thomas - 267
MEINHAUGEN, Henry - 204
MELLONE, James - 300
MELSOM, James - 306
MENDENHALL, Robert - 189, 196
MENNEL, Peter - 157
MENTOR, Mary - 263
MERCER, Capt. (first name unknown) - 252
MERK, John - 162
MERSHON, Thomas - 73
MESHA, John Clode - 102
METS, Andrew - 176
MICHTILIN, Anna Catherina - 257
MICKEL, John - 56
MICKLE, Archibald - 105
MICKLE, Joseph - 109
MIDDLETON, Aaron - 54
MIDDLETON, George - 85
MIERS, Benjamin - 205
MILBURN, Robert - 91, 92
MILES, Bartholomew - 80,
MILES, Joseph - 297
MILES, Mottrid - 310
MILL, John - 77
MILLAN, William - 278
MILLAR, Alexander - 134
MILLER, Alexander - 90
MILLER, Ann - 262
MILLER, Benjamin - 231
MILLER, Daniel - 88

MILLER, George - 145
MILLER, Gilbert- 272
MILLER, James - 237
MILLER, John - 45, 102, 164, 293
MILLER, John Christian - 107
MILLER, Melsher - 303
MILLER, Melyn - 197
MILLER, Peter - 135
MILLER, William - 164, 305
MILLOR (no first name given) - 212
MILLS, Dr. - 217
MINCK - 249
MINGO - 238
MIRES, Charles - 306
MITCHEL, Patrick - 80, 82
MITCHELL, Andrew - 180
MITCHELL BARCLAY & 181, 182
MITCHELL, James - 180, 181
MITCHELL, John - 164
MOFFAT, EDWARD- 194
MOLESWORTH, James - 192
MOLLY - 37, 257
MONDAY, Charles - 303
MONEY, Jesse - 177
MONRO[W], George- 89, 199, 243
MONROW, John - 150
MONTGOMERIE, William- 59, 168
MONTGOMERY, Alexander - 303
MONTGOMERY, Catherine 110
MONTGOMERY, Daniel - 191
MONTGOMERY, William- 191
MONTGOMERY, Capt.- 4
MOODY, Henry - 59
MOON, John - 160
MOONEY, JON - 191
MOOR, John - 135
MOORE, Alexander - 227
MOORE, Benjamin - 224
MOORE, Daniel - 77
MOORE, Edward - 277
MOORE, James - 81, 207
MOORE, John - 150, 270
MOORE, Mary - 144
MOORE, Samuel - 213
MOORE, William - 96, 165
MOORE, Capt. - 279
MORAN, Thomas- 71
MORDOX, James - 63
MORE, James - 30, 235
MOREHEAD, Thomas - 150
MORFFEE, William - 48
MORGAN, Alexander - 64, 65, 83, 89, 209
MORGAN, Capt. James - 246
MORGAN, John - 190
MORGAN, Morris - 90
MORGAN, Richard - 95
MORRAH, Thomas - 105
MORRELL, Jacob - 262
MORRIS, Francis - 303
MORRIS, James - 58, 141, 200
MORRIS, John - 225
MORRIS, Joseph - 58
MORRIS, Patrick - 183
MORRIS, Samuel - 216
MORRIS, William - 144
MORRIS, (no first name given) 306
MORRISON, Archibald - 71
MORRISON, James - 141
MORRISON, John - 120
MORRISON, Matthew - 130
MORROW, James - 134
MORTON, Phebe - 190

MOSES - 30, 219, 220. 221 106
MOSS, Richard - 84
MOTT, Gershom - 311
MOTT, Capt.(first name unknown) - 311
MOUNCEKEEN, Jr. ,(first name unknown) - 215
MOUNTEER, William - 260
MOUSTON, Robert - 280
MOYLAN, Col. Stephen - 307
MUCKLEROY, Mary - 255
MULFORD, Benjamin - 220
MULFORD, Daniel - 173
MULFORD, Isaac - 177
MULFORD, Terence - 290
MULLAN, Patrick - 139
MULLAN, Thomas - 169
MULLHARRON [M'CARRON], Richard - 115
MULLOCK, Mr.(first name unknown) - 257
MULLUN, (first name unknown) - 234
MUMFORD, George - 98
MUNROW, George - 72, 272
MUNSEN, John Col. - 307
MURFEY, Daniel - 125
MURPHY, Bartholomew - 177
MURPH[E]Y, Edward - 128
MURPH[E]Y, James - 97
MURPHY, Garret - 156
MURPHY, Peter - 157, 189
MURPHY, Thomas - 144, 154. 192
MURRAY, Alexander - 83
MURRAY, Thomas - 184
MURRAY, William - 133
MURREY, Roger - 64
MYAH, Johan Jeremiah -

N

NALLON, James - 129
NALLS, William - 123
NAP, Daniel - 219
NAYLAND, James - 129
NEAL, Valentine - 76
NEALL, Daniel - 79
NEAN - 30, 245
NED - 30, 251
NEIL, John - 140
NELL - 26, 37, 256, 259
NELSON, Andrew - 307
NEMINS, Robert - 260
NEMINS, William - 260
NERO - 30, 225
NEVEL, Francis - 143
NEWBOLD, Caleb - 144
NEWBOLD, William - 110
NEWCOMB, John - 88
NEWELL, Hugh - 136
NEWELL, Robert – 80, 216
NEWLIN, Patrick - 285
NEWMAN, Thomas - 154
NEWTON, Jacob - 144
NICHOLAS - 208
NICHOLS, Joshua - 47
NICHOLS, William - 268
NICHOLSON, John - 125
NICHOLSON, Joseph - 169
NICKISON, Samuel - 133
NICKLE, William - 187
NIM - 27, 207
NIXSON; Patrick - 298
NOLAND, Richard - 61
NORMAN, John - 113
NORRIS, Daniel - 74
NORRIS, George - 101, 103
NORRIS, Thomas - 174, 286
NORTHRUP, Benjamin - 147

NORTON, James - 133
NORTON, Ralph - 125
NOWLAND, John - 109
NUGENT, Michael - 188

O

O'BRIAN, William - 195
O'BRYAN, John - 150
O'BRYAN, Mary Ann - 260
O'HANLON, Patrick - 103
O'NEIL, John - 194
O'NEILL, John - 198
OAKFORD, Charles - 62
OAKFORD, William - 79, 138
OGBURN, John - 112
OGDEN, Charles - 192
OGDEN, David - 216
OGDEN, John - 239
OGDEN, Moses - 200
OGDEN, Samuel - 117, 127
OGDEN (first name unknown) - 238
OGDEN family - 317
OGLE, Thomas - 154, 287
OKESON, Samuel - 241
OLDFORD, John - 189
OLIPHANT, Ephraim - 88
OLIVAR, John - 194
OLIVE, Edward - 83
OAKLEY (first name not given) - 226
ONELL, Daniel - 79
OPDIKE, John - 273
ORLIFF, Edward - 86
ORR, Ruth - 257
ORTMAN, Matthias - 131
OSBIN, Elisha - 205
OSBORN, John - 307
OSBORN - 30, 222
OSBORNE, Elisha - 308

OSBURN, Thomas - 123
OTTO, Frederick - 282
OTTWAY, John Harding - 276
OULDEN, John - 175
OVEM, Jacob - 87
OVERTHROW, William - 53
OVERTON, John Peter - 106
OWEN, Owen - 46, 235
OWINGS, Samuel Jr.- 182

P

PACK, Bartemius - 293
PAINTER, John - 57
PALMER, Anthony - 289
PALMER, Martin - 289
PALMER, Silas - 144
PANCOAST, Edward - 106
PANCOAST, Seth - 176, 177
PANCOOST, Samuel - 67
PANCOOST, William - 67
PARK, David - 275
PARKER, Adam - 121
PARKER, Alexander - 86
PARKER, Edward - 304
PARKER, Joseph - 261
PARKER, Nathaniel - 86
PARKER, Jr., Nathaniel - 119
PARKES, John - 159
PARLER, Sarah - 253
PARMYTER, Par - 270, 271
PARR, William - 281
PARRA, John - 78
PARROTT, William Lt. - 306
PARSCO, Simon - 219
PARSLOW, Stephen - 53
PARSONS, James - 193
PARSONS, William - 179
PARSTOW, Stephen - 65
PARVIN, Silas - 212
PASCAL, Benjamin - 49

PASS, John - 80
PATERSON, Joseph - 204
PATRICK, William - 61
PATTERSON, Enos - 30, 251
PATTERSON, John - 179
PATTISON, John - 108
PAUL, Samuel - 198
PAUL, Uriah - 165, 199, 243
PAULLIN, Jacob - 167, 196
PAULLIN, Joseph - 167
PAWLING, Henry - 100
PAXEN, Thomas - 189
PAYTON, William - 69
PEACE, Joseph - 47, 73, 74
PEARCE, John - 57
PEARSON, Crispi -199
PEARSON, Daniel -163, 164
PEARSON, Isaac -46, 54, 60, 150
PEARSON, Robert - 148
PECK, Nicholas - 204
PEET - 30, 209, 243
PEG - 229
PEIRSON, Robert - 208
PELTON, Benjamin - 94
PELTON, Samuel - 277
PEMBERTON, James - 30, 235
PEMBERTON, John - 193
PEN - 30, 235
PENNEL, (first name unknown) - 320
PERKINS, Abraham - 63
PERO - 30, 239
PERRY, Elizabeth - 254
PETER - 30, 213, 240, 248
PETERSON, Abraham - 310
PETERSON, Bates Williams - 242
PETERSON, Peter - 309
PETTERSON, John - 124
PHILIPS, Margaret - 255

PHILL - 247
PHILLIPS, Ephraim - 135, 138, 152. 227, 229, 233, 243
PHILLIPS, Jacob - 266
PHILLIPS, Jonathan Capt. - 307
PHILLIPS, (first name unknown) - 265
PHOEBE - 37, 262, 265
PIDGINETT, Francis Lawrence 201
PIERSON, Jonas - 234
PIKE, Zebulon Adjut. - 307
PINEYL -108
PINTER, John - 113
PITCHER, William - 156
PLASKETT, William - 254
PLUME, Isaac - 172
PLUMSTED, Thomas - 227
POIST, Adian - 298
POLSON, John - 291
POLSON, Capt. (first name unknown)- 291
POMPEE - 211
POMPEY - 27, 30, 207, 225, 239
POOL, John - 178, 263
POORE, Richard - 74
POPAW - 28, 207
PORTER, Patrick - 96
PORTER, Richard - 71
POSTGATE, Thomas - 55
POTTS, Daniel - 206
POTTS, Thomas - 187
POWELL, Benjamin - 176
POWELL, Howell - 121, 129, 221, 259
POWELL, Thomas - 64
POWELL, William - 160, 162
POWELSE, Jacob - 270
POWER, George - 301
POWER, Michael - 280
POWERS, George - 304

PRATT, James - 28, 30, 223
PRESTON, Abel - 55
PRESTON, Thomas -199
PREVOST, Mark - 242, 263
PRICE, Elizabeth - 254
PRICE, Ralph - 206
PRICE, Friend Robert - 111, 257
PRICE, William - 83
PRICKET, Jacob - 215
PRIEST, William - 96
PRIMUS- 30, 217
PRINCE - 30, 219, 227, 242, 244, 246, 249
PRINGLE, John - 129
PRITCHARD, John - 46
PRITTONS, Widow - 259
PROBASCO, Hendrick - 236
PROBASCO, Rynier - 167
PROBASCO, Stoffel - 236
PROSSER, William - 93
PRYM - 236
PURSLEY, John - 194
PURVIANCE, John - 184
PURVIANCE, Samuel - 184, 240
PUSEY, Thomas - 242, 263
PYWELL, William - 54

Q

QUASH - 30, 244
QUICK, Cornelius - 88
QUICK, Samuel - 242
QUIGLEY, Daniel - 56
QUIN, James - 147
QUIN, John - 133
QUITE, Charles - 30, 228

R

RACHAEL - 264
RAIN, Isaac - 187
RAINEY, Elizabeth - 259
RALSON, (first name not known) - 284
RAMBO, Benjamin - 170
RAMBO, John - 115, 130
RAMBO, Peter - 215
RAMBO Thomas - 93, 275
RAMPOON, John - 274
RAMSAY, Sarah - 247
RANDALL, Dr. Ananias - 280
RANDALL, Isaac - 211
RANE, William - 303
RANKIN, James - 149
RANKIN, William - 139
RATTOON, Thomas - 98
RAWLINS, William - 306
RAWSON, William - 183
RAY, James - 86
RAYMOND, John - 207
REA, Richard - 294
READ, Andrew - 73, 74
READ, Charles -111, 148, 149, 151, 168, 171, 214, 283
READ, John -129
READ, (first name not known) 281
READING, Sarah - 258
READING, Thomas - 138
READOR, Jacob - 87
REDFORD, John - 52, 275
REDIKEN, Edward - 73
REDMON, Thomas - 73
REED, Amos - 161
REED, Andrew - 212
REED, John - 53
REED, Joseph - 53, 255
REED, William - 47
REEKER, John - 124
REES, Jonas - 160

REES, Detrick - 177, 178
REID, Augustine - 226, 244
REID, John - 209
REID, Jr. John - 218
REIGN, Isaac - 187
REILEY, Jacob - 190
REILLY, James - 68
REINE, Joseph - 102
REMER, George - 276, 277
RESCARRICK, George - 45
RETTINGHOUSE, Isaac - 137
REYERSE [RYERSON], George - 217
REYNES, Daniel - 45
REYNOLDS, Broughton 154, 163
REYNOLDS, Patrick - 64, 94
RHEA, George - 224
RHINEDOLLOR, Jacob - 177
RICHARD, Edward - 132
RICHARD, Nathaniel - 289
RICHARD, Paul - 101
RICHARD - 30, 228
RICHARDS, John - 241
RICHARDS, Joseph - 175
RICHARDS, Nathaniel - 227, 232, 234
RICHARDSON, Anna - 253
RICHARDSON, William - 93, 185, 187, 298
RICHELSON, William - 185
RICHMAN, Abraham - 167, 196
RICHMAN, Andrew - 178
RICHMAN, Harmon - 66
RICHMAN, John -104, 119
RICKET, John - 198
RICKET, William - 198
RIDDLE, William - 112
RIDGWAY, David - 168
RIDGWAY, Henry - 168

RIDGWAY, Job - 142
RIDGWAY, Solomon - 143
RIGGS, Joseph - 179
RIGTON, Zachariah - 121
RINGAR, John - 294
RITCHIE, Robert -121, 122
RIVERS, Thomas - 182, 183
ROACH, John - 73
ROBARDS, Thomas - 56
ROBBINGS, Zachariah - 75
ROBBINS, Samuel - 264
ROBERTS, Bernard - 204
ROBERTS, Edward - 300
ROBERTS, Enoch - 96
ROBERTS, Ichabud - 172
ROBERTS, Jacob - 203
ROBERTS, James - 49
ROBERTS, John - 81, 138, 148
ROBERTS, Joshua -92
ROBERTSON, William - 293
ROBESON Benjamin - 303
ROBESON, Peter - 120
ROBESON, William - 303
ROBIN - 30, 210, 213, 215, 217, 235
ROBINS, Joseph - 268
ROBINS, Zachariah - 78
ROBINSON, Bryant - 205
ROBINSON, Henry - 224, 271
ROBINSON, Joseph - 224
ROBINSON, Thomas - 148, 172
ROCHESTER, Valentine - 303
ROCK, Henry - 75
RODDEN, John - 303
RODGERS, Samuel - 120
RODRIGO, Joseph - 202
RODRIGUES, Emanuel - 202
ROE, Michael - 311
ROFF, Michael - 183
ROGAN, Daniel - 181, 296
ROGERS, Daniel - 30, 222
ROGERS, Simon - 140, 260
ROOF, Michael - 186

ROSE, John - 175
ROSE, Peter - 51, 61, 203
ROSS, John - 58, 130, 131, 132
ROSS, Peter - 303
ROSS, William - 110
ROSSA, John - 162
ROUSE, James - 30, 212
ROWLAND, Elijah - 112
ROYALS, Samuel - 80
RUBB, Jacob - 95
RUBIE, Edward - 104
RUDDEROW, William - 258
RUFF, Peter - 108
RUMSEY, Daniel - 167
RUNYAN, Benjamin - 161
RUNYAN, John - 252
RUSCO, Capt Nathaniel - 290, 291
RUSSEL, James - 193
RUSSEL John - 176, 295
RUTH, James - 206
RUTHERFORD, Alexander -136
RUTHERFORD, Robert - 258
RUTHERFORD, Thomas - 104
RUTHERFORD, Walter - 248
RYAN, John - 146, 176
RYERSON, John - 217
RYERSON, Marten - 68
RYLEY, Timothy - 273
RYMER, Thomas - 289
RYNAN, William - 145

S

SALMON, John - 309
SALMON, Nathaniel - 236
SALMON family - 239

SALTER, Charles -304
SALTER, Lawrence - 128
SAM -30, 211, 212, 217, 233, 241
SAMBO -30, 221, 245, 246
SAMPSON -30, 212, 220
SAMSON -214
SAMUEL, Nevill -213
SANDERS, John W. -172
SANDERS, John Williams - 242
SANDY -30, 217
SANFORD, David -161
SARAH
SARGEANT, Jonathan -214
SARTIN, Richard -253
SAUNDERS, James -260
SAUNDERS, John -168
SAVAGE, John -271
SAVIN, Thomas -235
SAVINA - 37, 255
SAXTON, Jierard -118
SAYRE, Ananias
SAYRE, Samuel Maj.-307
SCANK, Garet
SCHAEFFER, Henry -132
SCHENK, Peter
SCHLAGEL, John Erhard -138
SCHLEYDORN, Henry -107
SCHOLEY, John-76
SCHOWTHRIP, Thomas-45
SCHUTTS, John Christopher - 112
SCHUYLER, Col. Peter -290, 291
SCIPIO -30, 248
SCOGGIN, Jonas -95
SCOTT, Andrew -309
SCOTT, John- 70, 97
SCOTT, Rachael- 162, 261
SCOTT, Robert -284
SCOUSS, Hannah Dorothy- 258
SCROGGS, Alexander -68

SCUDDER, Nathaniel - 265
SCULLEY, Thomas - 192
SEELY, Ephraim - 230
SEELY, Samuel - 312
SELTHRIDGE, William - 68, 69
SENNET, Arthur - 138
SERELS, William - 130
SERGEANT, Jonathan - 217
SETON, Andrew - 138
SETON, Robert - 138
SEVERNS, John - 244
SEVERNS, Thomas - 234
SEXTON, James - 258
SHAMBOUGH, Joseph - 299
SHANKLAND, John - 62
SHARP, Jack - 230
SHARP, Henry - 167
SHARP, Hugh - 263
SHARP, Joseph - 32
SHARP, Samuel - 135, 139
SHAW, John - 249
SHAW, Thomas - 292
SHEHAN, Dennis - 153
SHEPERD, Joseph - 89
SHEPHERD, Ephraim - 173
SHEPHERD, John - 217
SHEPPARD, Job - 77
SHEPPERD, Nathaniel - 193
SHEPPERD, Thomas - 79
SHERWOOD, Robert - 104
SHFRONE, Matthew - 201
SHIELDS, John - 264
SHIELDS, Thomas - 239, 240
SHINN, Caleb - 274
SHINN, Thomas - 276
SHIVERS, Samuel - 107, 221
SHOARS, Jonathan - 204
SHOCKMAPLE (first name not given) - 263
SHRACK, John - 299
SHREAVE, Joshua - 136

SHREVE, Abraham - 175
SHREVE, Joshua - 186
SHREVE, Thomas - 101
SHREVE, William - 129
SHREVES, Col. Israel - 300, 301, 303, 304, 305, 307
SHRIEVE, Joshua - 183
SHULL, Tobias - 247
SHURTS, John - 110
SHUTE, Lieut.(first name unknown) - 294
SICKELS, Hendrick - 289
SIDENHAM, John - 225
SILAS - 30, 235
SIM - 30, 224
SIMMONDS, John - 92
SIMMONDS, Joseph - 112
SIMMS, Henry - 142
SIMON - 30, 210
SIMONS, John - 143
SIMPSON, John - 189
SIMPSON, Lt. Michael - 300
SIMPSON, William - 295
SIMPSON, William Harrison - 170
SIMS, James - 101
SIMSON, William - 72
SINGLETON, Richard - 75
SINNICKSON, Andrew - 103, 188, 190
SINNICKSON, Thomas - 174
SITES, John - 231
SKEEN, Abraham - 299
SKEY, Capt. (first name not known) - 293
SKILLMAN, Thomas - 240
SKILTON and EMBLY - 286
SKINNER, Jonathan - 179
SKINNER, John - 105
SKINNER, Stephen - 149
SKIRM, Abraham - 204
SLADES, Christopher - 59
SMALLWOOD, John - 193
SMART, James - 28, 30, 223

SMAULES, Timothy - 179
SMITH, Benjamin - 61, 176, 179
SMITH, Christian - 178
SMITH, Christopher - 280
SMITH, Conrad - 121
SMITH, David - 173, 281
SMITH, Edward - 291
SMITH, Ezekiel - 59
SMITH, Francis - 56, 66
SMITH, Gilbert - 223
SMITH, George - 55
SMITH, Hugh - 198
SMITH, James - 30, 54, 118, 208, 224, 302
SMITH, Jecamiah - 236, 239
SMITH, John - 51, 92, 126, 166, 189, 203, 220, 270, 275, 283, 286, 308
SMITH, Jonathan - 96
SMITH, Joseph - 118
SMITH, Mary - 255
SMITH, Capt. Matthew - 300
SMITH, Nicholas - 234, 299
SMITH, Paulus - 101
SMITH, Perro - 36, 227
SMITH, Jr. Richard - 182
SMITH, Robert - 161, 163
SMITH, Samuel - 45, 106, 168, 286
SMITH, Solomon - 115
SMITH, Stephen - 190
SMITH, Talman - 241-42
SMITH, Thomas - 69, 102, 215
SMITH, William - 149, 161, 175, 195
SMITH, William P. - 234
SMITH, William Peartree - 219
SMOCK, John - 234
SMYTH, Lawrence - 47
SNELL, Richard - 203

SNOWDEN, William - 59, 258
SOLEM, Cornelius - 270
SOLOMON, John - 30, 242
SOOY, Joseph - 214
SOUBRIAN, William - 137
SPACKHOLTZ, Baltus - 99
SPARKS, Henry - 63, 199, 243
SPARLING, John - 83
SPARLING, William - 130
SPARROW, John - 50
SPEDDY, James - 182
SPENCE, George - 136
SPENCER, Col. Oliver - 305, 306
SPICER, Thomas - 46
STACK, Henry - 50
STACY, Mahlon - 59, 64
STAKEPOLE, Lawrence - 57
STANIARD, Joseph - 223
STARN, Jacob - 117, 137, 141, 144, 145, 154, 166, 283, 284
STEDHAM, John - 115
STEELMAN, John - 155
STEENHAAGEN, Henry - 204
STELLE, Gabriel - 52
STELLE, Isaac - 52
STEPHENSON, John - 305
STERN, Jacob - 114
STERRET, James - 264
STEUART, Andrew - 259
STEVENS, Dennis - 153
STEVENS, Lieut. Col. Ebenezer - 311, 313, 314, 315
STEVENS, Richard - 75
STEVENS, Thomas - 166
STEVENSON and PLOWMAN - 149
STEVENSON, Thomas - 62
STEWARD, Steven - 305
STEWARD, (first name not given)
STEWART, Archibald - 159
STEWART, John - 290

STEWART, Robert - 93, 303
STEWART, William - 109
STEWART, Col. (first name not given) - 250, 265
STILES, Thomas - 286
STILLE, Jacob - 201
STILLWELL, John - 113
STILLWELL, Richard - 102, 218
STITES, Michael - 140
STOCKDALE, Mary - 49
STOCKTON, Job - 144, 280
STOCKTON, Robert - 286
STOCKTON, William - 217
STOFFELS - 208
STOITS, Christopher Frederick - 197
STOKES, John - 86, 113
STONE, Daniel - 88
STONE, Samuel - 151
STORY, Thomas - 121
STOUT, Jr. Benjamin -239, 240
STOUT, Jonathan - 105, 107
STOUT, Sr. Samuel - 239, 240
STOUT, Jr,. Samuel - 239, 240, 259
STOUT, Thomas - 198
STOUT, Zebulon - 209
STRAHAN, David - 253
STRINGER, William - 102
STYMETS, John - 147
SUE - 259
SULLIVAN, Cornelius - 81, 84
SULIVAN, Daniel - 202
SULLIVAN, Mary - 255
SULLIVAN, Michael - 276
SUMMERL, John - 176- 179
SUSAN - 254
SUTHARD; Abraham - 294
SUTLIFF, William - 245
SWACARNOCKUM - 30, 228
SWAN, John - 79
SWEYZE, Caleb - 175
SWINDLE, Thomas - 298
SWINK, Capt. Martin - 300
SY - 235
SYKES, Samuel - 143
SYRON - 235

T

TAILER, Isaac - 65
TALLMAN, Peter - 238
TALLMAN, Jr. Stephen - 150, 154, 155, 240
TALMAN, James - 243
TALMAN, John - 223
TALMAN, Dr. Stephen - 105
TALMAN, Thomas - 99
TANEY, Daniel - 299
TANEY, Jacob - 299
TAPPEN, Isaac - 241
TATE, George - 98
TATEHAM, William - 63
TATUM, John - 175
TATUM, William - 271
TAYLOR, Abraham - 275
TAYLOR, Daniel - 147
TAYLOR, Jacob - 109, 140, 260
TAYLOR, James - 157
TAYLOR, John - 278
TAYLOR, Col. John - 310, 311
TAYLOR, Joseph - 210
TAYLOR, Robert -121, 154
TAYLOR, William - 53, 62, 91
TAYLOUR, Robert - 145
TEACLE, Richard - 165
TEN EICK, Peter - 100
TEN EYCK, Anthony - 238
TENBROOK, Wessel - 211
TENNANT, Richard - 236

TENSLE, Lawrence - 107
TEST, Edward - 150, 278
TETEHAM, William - 66
THACKERY, John - 254
THARE, John - 303
THATCHER, Elizabeth - 14
THATCHER, Samuel - 152
THETFORD, Richard - 125
THOMAS, John - 292
THOMAS, Joseph -24, 39, 140, 284, 285
THOMAS, William - 233
THOMPSOM, J. - 90
THOMPSON, Abraham - 298
THOMPSON, James - 209
THOMPSON, John - 308
THOMPSON, Samuel - 137, 201, 202
THOMPSON, Thomas - 311
THOMPSON, William - 85, 100
THOMPSON, Col (first name unknown) - 250, 265
THOMSON, Benjamin - 74
THOMSON, (first name not given) - 68
THRAGMORTON, Samuel 51
THROCKMORTON, Job - 224
THROCKMORTON, John - 46
TIBB, Henry - 85
TICE, Gilbert -183
TILLDINE, Jeory - 69
TINDALL, Thomas - 211
TINSTON, Duke - 52
TITUS - 30, 213
TITUS, Philip - 95
TOBIN, Thomas - 188
TOBY - 30, 218, 222
TOBY, Isaac - 298
TOLEN, Michael -195

TOLLMAN, Stephen - 110
TOM - 209, 213, 217, 220, 224, 225, 230, 236, 246, 247
TOMLIN, William - 180
TOMPSON, George - 52
TONE - 248
TONEY - 224, 234, 280
TONKIN, Charles - 272
TONKIN, Edward- 145
TONY - 214, 223, 280
TOOKER, Charles - 238
TOOL, John -72, 272
TOWN, John - 196
TOWNSEND, Jacob - 136
TOWNSEND, Sylvanus - 279
TOWNSHEND, Edward - 67
TOWNSHEND, Richard - 127
TOY, Daniel - 87
TRASO - 30, 222
TRENCHARD, Curtis- 164, 170, 171
TRENCHARD, George - 116
TUCKER, Samuel - 121, 133, 6 278
TUCKER, William - 153, 155
TUDER, Henry - 123
TUFFT, William - 271
TURNER, John - 141
TURNER, Joseph - 154
TURNER, Samuel - 303
TURRY, Daniel - 196
TUTTLE, William - 274
TWELVES, Godfrey - 204

U

ULRICK, Widow (first name unknown) - 291
USTICK, HENRY - 38, 262
USTICK, THOMAS - 57

V

VAHAN, James - 81
VAN ARSDALL, Parson - 265
VAN BLRCUM, Isaac - 243
VAN BUSHKIRK, Abraham -216
VAN BUSCURK, Peter - 291
VAN BUSHERK, James - 217
VAN CAMPIN, Cornelius - 100
VAN CLEAVE, Benjamin - 264
VAN CORTLANDT, Stephen -107
VAN COURT, Elias - 116
VAN DERSLICE, Thomas- 299
VANDERVERE, Cornelius- 214
VAN DERVEER, Jacobus - 233
VANDERVEER, James - 198
VAN DORN, John - 225
VANDYKE, Lambert - 259
VANHART, Adam - 265
VAN HARLIGEN, Ernest - 232, 233
VAN HORNE, Cornelius - 63, 254
VAN HORNE, Mathias - 101
VAN HORN, Cornelius - 248
VAN KIRK, Arthur - 107
VAN LEER, Benjamin - 198
VAN MATER, Cyrenius- 230
VAN METER, Daniel - 233
VAN NORDEN, John - 255
VAN RIPER, (first name unknown) - 249
VAN SICKLE, James - 198
VAN SICKLE, John - 198
VAN WAGGENON, Jacobus - 109
VAN ZILE, Evant - 152
VANCE, John - 197
VANOTE, Joseph - 148
VANURDER, Peter - 273
VEIGHT, Nicholas - 229
VENUS - 258
VERNON, John - 278
VILLANY, Charles - 133
VINCENT, Judith - 208, 209
VINIGAR, Hendrick -166
VINING, Benjamin - 55
VIOLET - 240
VOGLUM, Benjamin - 364
VON BEVERHOUDT, Lucas - 249
VOORHEES, John - 119
VORHEES, Garret - 180

W

WADE, Francis - 170
WAHUP, William - 70
WAKE, Baldwin - 242
WALDREN, Peter - 30, 209
WALDRON, Daniel - 209
WALDRON, Leffert 232
WALKER, John - 156
WALKER, Matthias - 135
WALKER , William - 92
WALLACE, James -115
WALLACE, John - 103, 112
WALSH, William - 141
WALTON, John- 69
WALTON, William- 101
WAN - 27, 79, 209, 218
WANNER, Jacob - 205
WANNER, John George - 204

WARD Jr., George - 72
WARD, James - 53
WARD, Moses - 63
WARD, Nathaniel - 86
WARD, Owen - 57, 304
WARDELL, John - 217
WARE, Joseph - 62, 63
WARE, Michael - 297
WARE, Thomas - 260
WARNE, Samuel - 48
WARNER, Simon - 50
WARRELL (first name unknown) - 62
WARREN, John - 168, 172
WARREN, Richard - 281
WARRICK, Jacob - 76
WARRINGTON, Jacob - 173
WATKINS, Henry - 65
WATSON, Isaac - 47
WATSON, James - 306, 312
WATSON, Thomas - 177, 245
WATSON (first name not given) - 249
WATT, Adam - 174
WATTS, William - 294
WEAVER, Capt.(first name unknown) - 203
WEBB Capt. John - 295
WEIBEL, John - 136
WEIGKEL, John - 177
WEIGNER, Christopher - 122
WEISDORF, Peter - 168
WELCH, John - 88
WELCH, Michael - 76
WELCH, Morris - 306
WELCH, Philip - 53
WELCH, Thomas - 84
WELDON, Patrick - 106
WELLS, John - 175
WELLS, Capt. Richard - 292
WELLS, Thomas - 161

WELSH, Anthony - 30, 238
WELSH, Hugh - 306
WELSH, James - 77
WELSH, Philip - 96
WESCOT, Richard - 222
WEST, John - 132
WEST, Samuel - 294
WESTOVER, Oliver - 295
WESTBURN, William - 195
WHARTON, Charles - 229
WHEALON, Michael - 170, 173
WHEATON, Daniel - 170
WHEELER, David - 72
WHEELER, John - 177
WHEELER, Mary Ann - 177
WHEELER, Maurice - 75
WHITACRE, Richard - 147
WHITAKAR, Elias - 193
WHITAKER, Richard - 147
WHITALL, James - 259
WHITE, Anthony - 307
WHITE Christopher - 195
WHITE, Eleanor - 40, 253
WHITE, James - 106
WHITE, John - 118, 309
WHITE, Richard - 70
WHITE, Thomas - 210, 301
WHITE, Capt.(first name not known) - 295
WHITE, (first name not known) - 273
WHITEHEAD, James - 237
WHITEHEAD, Robert - 94
WIGGINS, James - 201, 202
WILCOX (first name unknown) - 234
WILEY, Joseph - 170
WILKINS, Isaac - 238
WILKINS, William - 89
WILKINSON, James - 148
WILKINSON, Thomas - 137
WILL - 30, 207, 230, 235, 236, 249

WILLIAMS, Abraham - 123
WILLIAMS, Benjamin - 219
WILLIAMS, Ennion- 46
WILLIAMS, George - 161
WILLIAMS, Jack - 251
WILLIAMS, Jesse - 247
WILLIAMS, John - 60, 121, 158, 210, 253, 270, 302
WILLIAMS, Moses - 211
WILLIAMS, Nicholas - 282
WILLIAMS, Owen - 194, 309
WILLIAMS, Renselear - 109
WILLIAMS, Richard - 314
WILLIAMS, William -137
WILLIAMSON, David - 127, 130
WILLIAMSON, Jacob - 252
WILLIAMSON, Matthias - 114
WILLINGS, David - 550
WILLIS, Joel - 243
WILLIS, Samuel - 110
WILLIS, William- 52
WILLS, Daniel - 70
WILLSON, James - 50
WILLSON, Thomas, - 49
WILLSON, William - 49
WILSON, Albert -185, 186
WILSON, Elizabeth Louisa - 260
WILSON, Hugh - 142, 283
WILSON, James -30, 231, 274, 275
WILSON, John - 199
WILSON, Joseph - 275
WILSON, William - 160, 176, 291
WILSON, Mrs. (first name unknown) - 250, 265
WINANTS, Josiah - 125
WINGATE, Henry - 65
WINTER, Garret - 136
WISTAR, Richard - 139, 141, 158
WITHERILL, Jr., Thomas - 93
WITTEN, Moses - 88
WOLFF, John - 136
WOOD, Jonathan - 199
WOOD, John - 66, 101, 231
WOOD, Joseph - 91
WOOD, Robert - 280
WOOD, Thomas - 92
WOOD, Sacheverall - 117
WOOD, Wiley - 285
WOOD, William - 55, 172, 301, 303
WOODCOCK, Anthony - 135
WOODFORD, Peter - 165
WOODRUFF, Isaac - 234
WOODRUFF, Uzal - 117
WOODSEN, Samuel - 62
WOODWARD, Thomas - 60
WOODWARD, William - 90, 256
WOOLMAN, Jonah - 199
WOOLSTON, Jabez - 203
WOOTON, John - 292
WORSTILL, William - 206
WORT, John - 192
WREN, Peter - 51
WRIGHT, Fretwell - 78
WRIGHT, Israel - 160, 234
WRIGHT, Mahlon - 178
WRIGHT, Nathan - 195
WRIGHT, Richard - 46
WRIGHT, Samuel - 30, 47, 231
WRIGHT, Thomas - 268
WRIGHT, William - 71, 169
WYCKOFF, Jacob - 249
WYCKOFF, Martin - 249
WYNKOOP, Henry - 60

Y

YAMANS, Moses - 175

YARD, Joseph - 57, 123
YARD, William - 207
YARDLEY, Samuel - 265
YARIALL, Widow - 192
YARNOD, Matthias - 110
YATES, James - 63

YATES, Mary - 259
YOUNG, John - 303
YOUNG, Susanna - 263
YOUNG, William - 287

www.ingramcontent.com/pod-product-compliance
Lightning Source LLC
Chambersburg PA
CBHW071226230426
43668CB00011B/1322